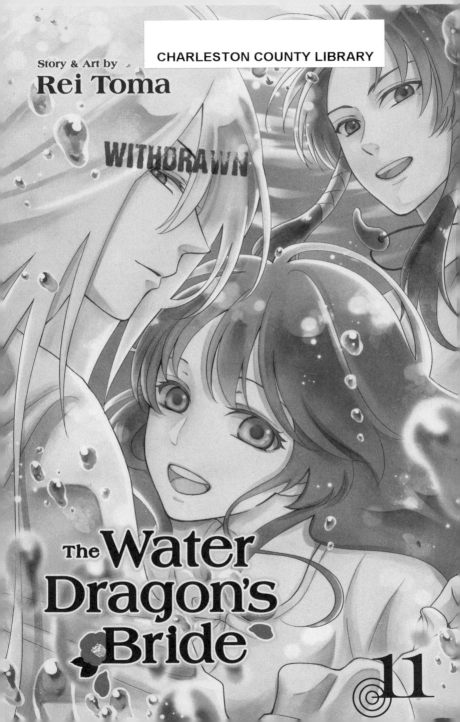

Story & Art by
Rei Toma

The **Water Dragon's Bride**

11

The Water Dragon's Bride

CHARACTER INTRODUCTIONS

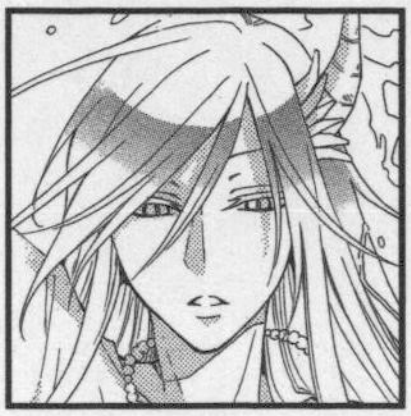

The Water Dragon God

The god who rules over the waters. Though he hates humans, he is intrigued by Asahi and feels compassion for her.

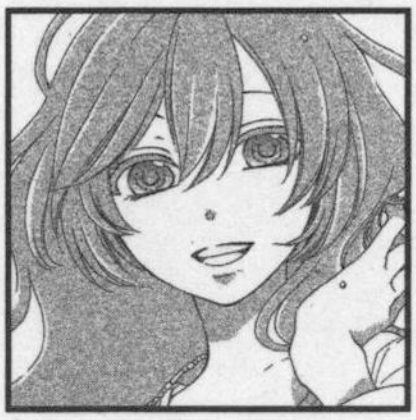

Asahi

She was transported to another world when she was young. Subaru's mother sacrificed her to the water dragon god.

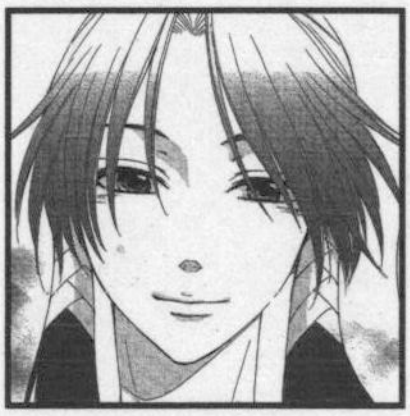

Subaru

He is drawn to Asahi and has resolved to protect her.

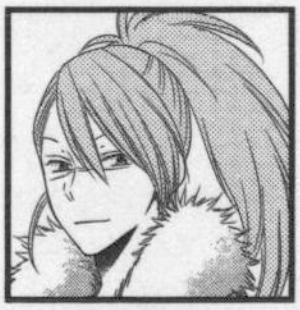

Kogahiko

He's seeking the water dragon god's power by targeting Asahi.

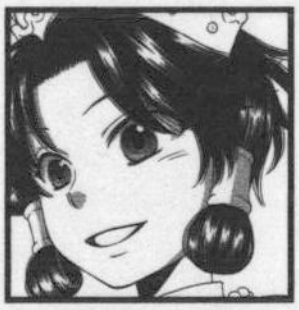

The Emperor

A young boy, the emperor of the country of Naga.

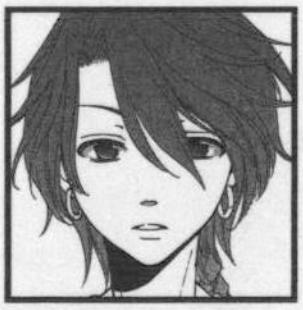

Tsukihiko

Asahi's caretaker. He has the ability to sense people's thoughts and emotions.

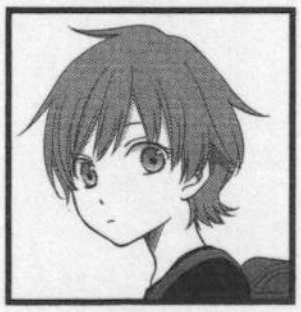

Haruki

Asahi's younger brother. He didn't know he even had a slster.

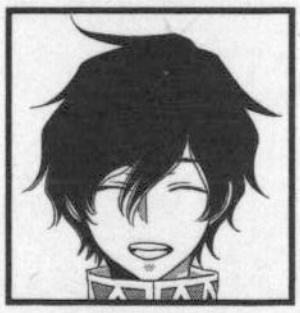

Kurose

His heart was plunged into darkness, and there he dlscovered Tokoyaml.

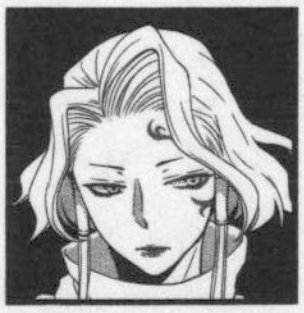

Tokoyami

The god of darkness. He summons Kurose from the modern-day world.

STORY THUS FAR

◎ Asahi is living a normal, sheltered life when she suddenly gets pulled into a pond and is transported to a strange new world. She gets sacrificed to a water dragon god, and he takes her voice from her. Because of her connection to the water dragon god's mysterious powers, Asahi is elevated to the position of priestess in her village. She is unable to find a way to return home, and time passes. As Asahi and the water dragon god spend time together, their relationship begins to change.

◎ A priestess of Naga informs the emperor of Asahi's and the water dragon god's existence, so he orders Asahi to lend him her power. When Kogahiko tries to kidnap Asahi a second time, the water dragon god and Asahi's friends rescue her. Tsukihiko, whose mother was in the same situation as Asahi before, attempts to trade his life for Asahi's freedom.

◎ The emperor of Naga asks for Asahi's hand in marriage. In order to protect Asahi, the water dragon god sends her back to her own world. Asahi is finally reunited with her family, but she can't forget the water dragon god and the friends she's left behind. She's so troubled that she returns to the other world during a ceremony to call rain.

◎ Meanwhile, a young man named Kurose in the modern-day world is plunged into darkness. The god of darkness, Tokoyami, places Kurose in this other world where Kurose gets a measure of peace. Unfortunately, war with a neighboring country causes Kurose to lose Hino, the person he cares most about, so he joins Tokoyami in his schemes. Asahi sees that they are using Tokoyami's powers to trick the villagers into war, so she borrows the water dragon's power to stop the fighting. However, by letting his godly powers flow into Asahi, the water dragon god becomes weak and risks being completely destroyed!

The Water Dragon's Bride

11

CONTENTS

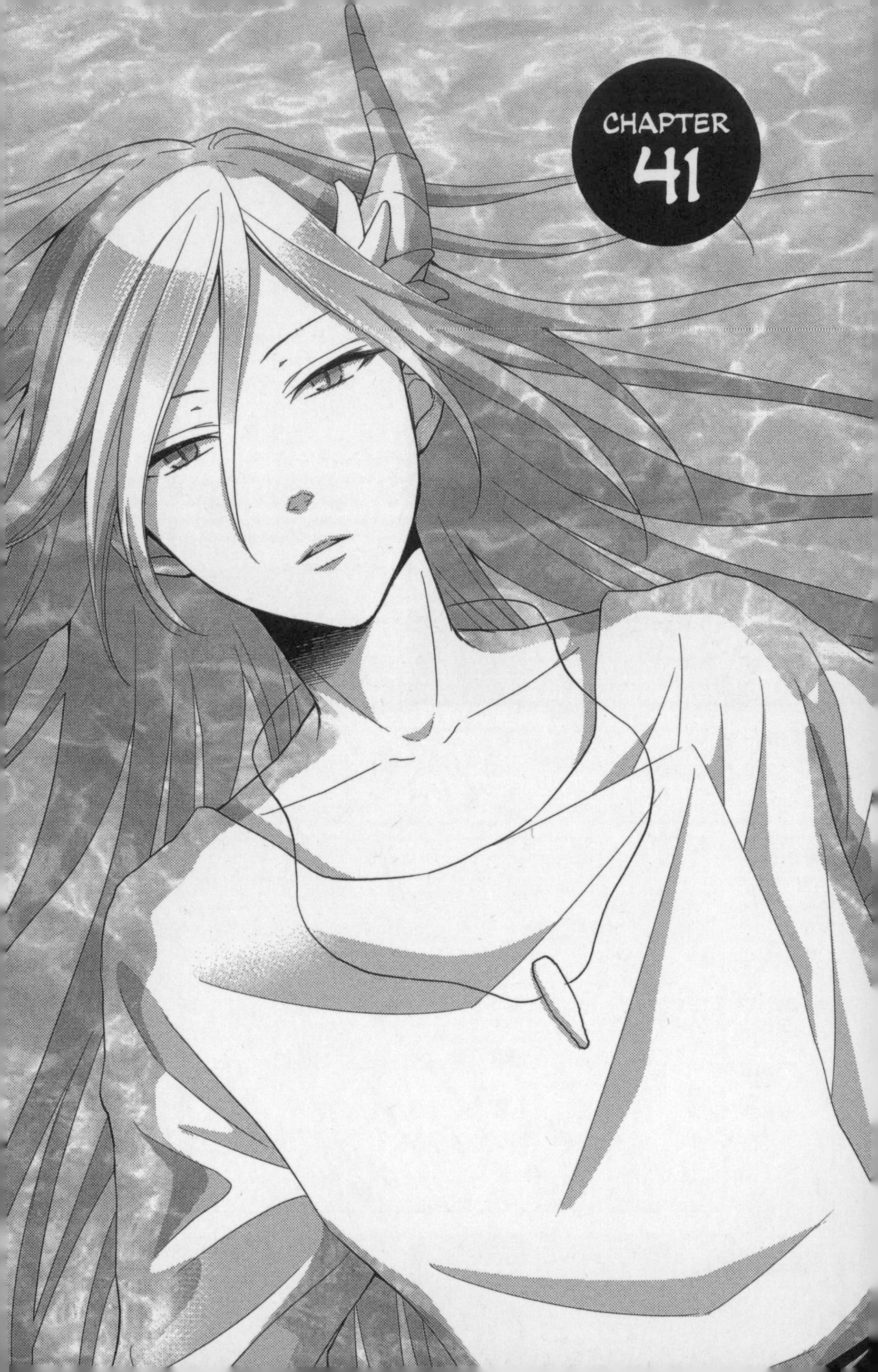
CHAPTER
41

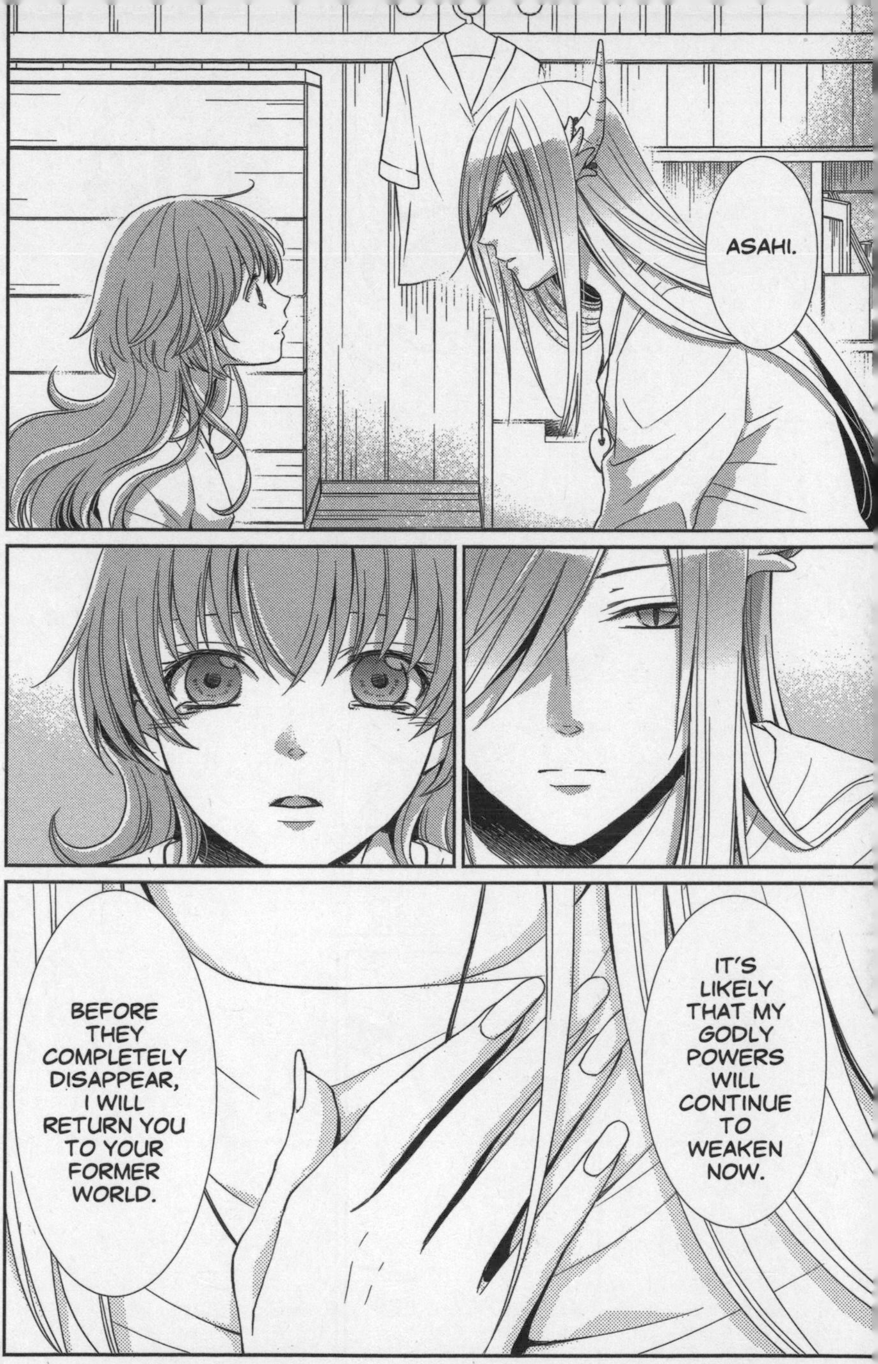
ASAHI.
IT'S LIKELY THAT MY GODLY POWERS WILL CONTINUE TO WEAKEN NOW.
BEFORE THEY COMPLETELY DISAPPEAR, I WILL RETURN YOU TO YOUR FORMER WORLD.

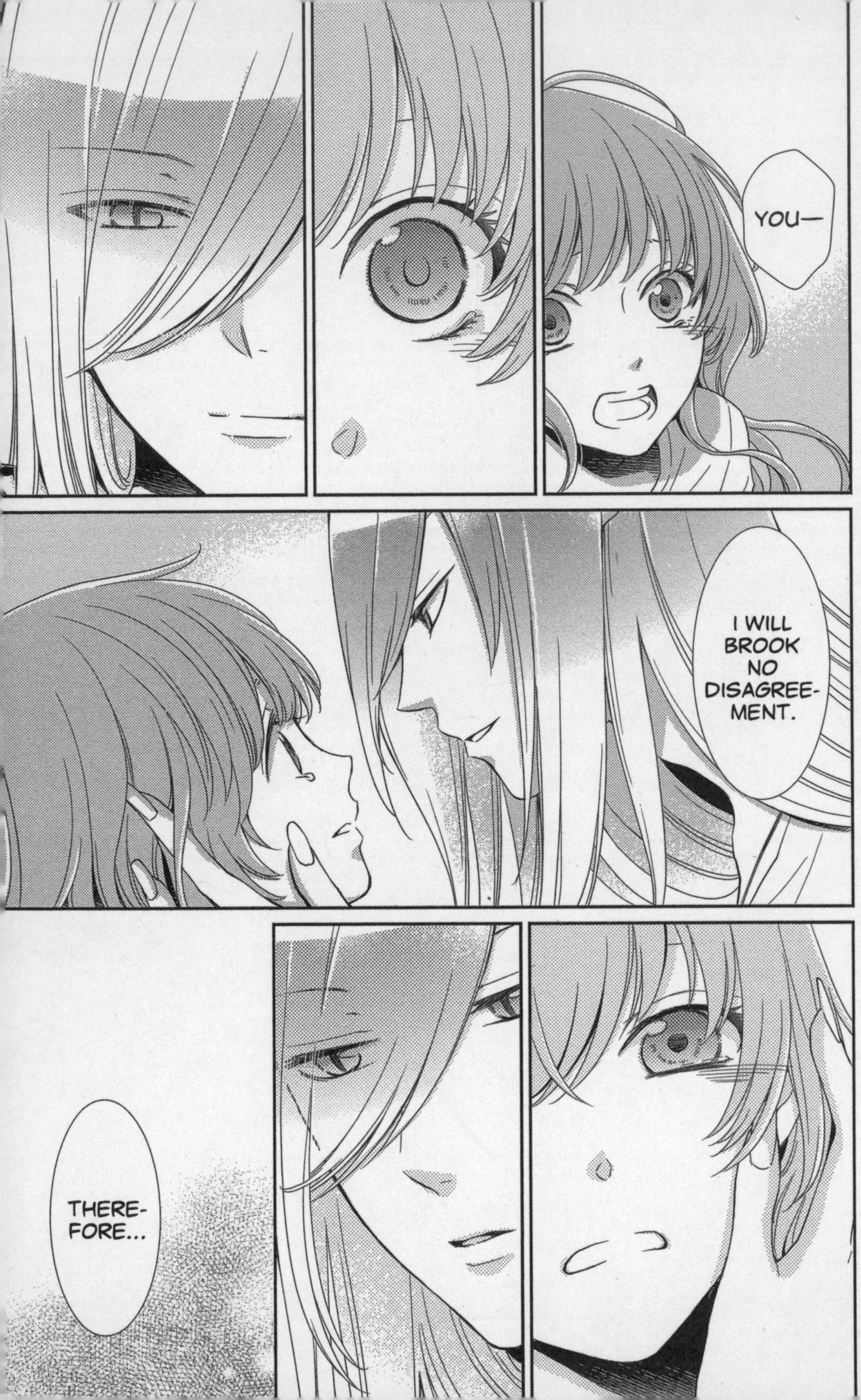
YOU—
I WILL BROOK NO DISAGREE-MENT.
THERE-FORE...

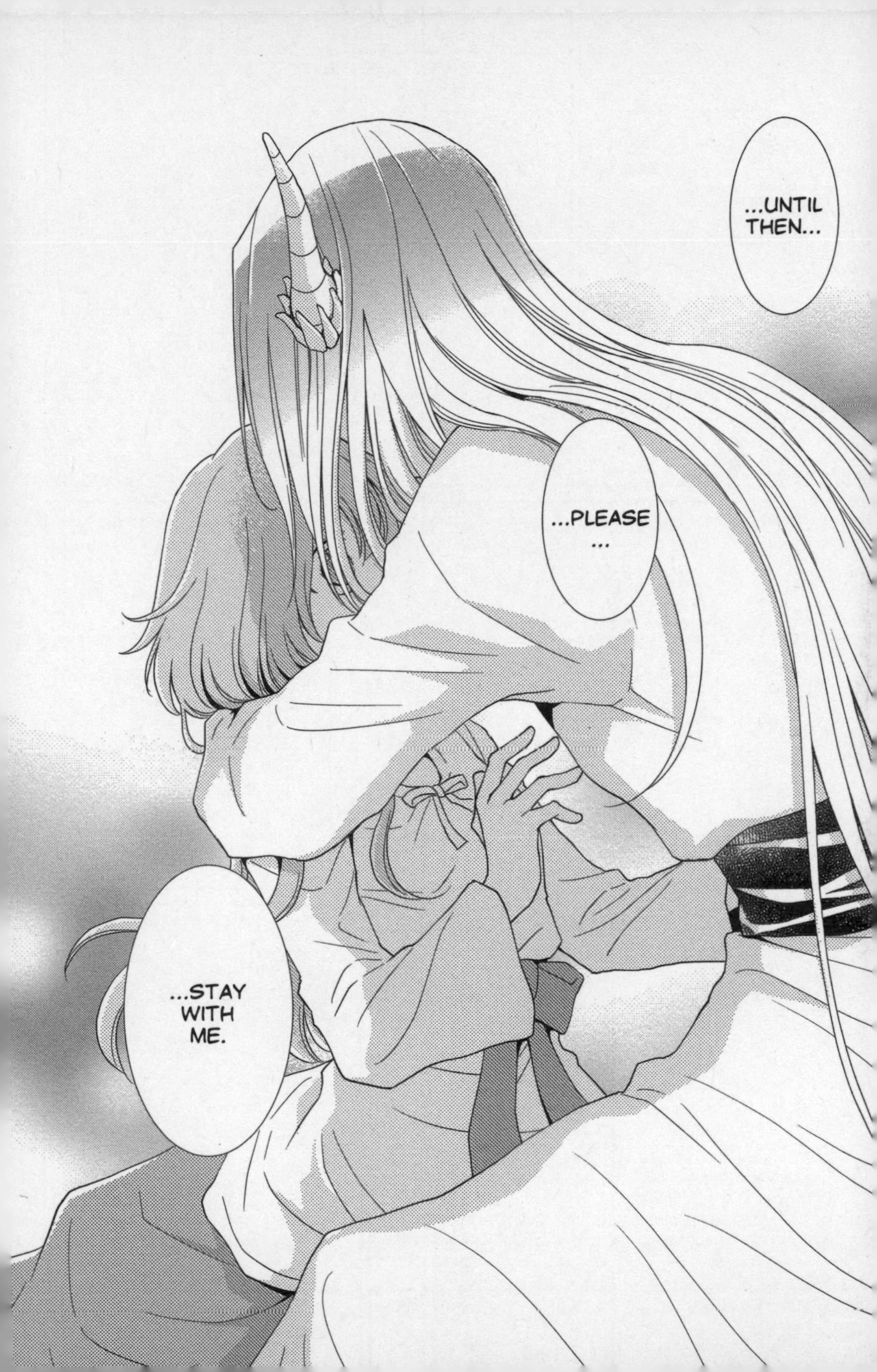
...UNTIL THEN...
...PLEASE ...
...STAY WITH ME.

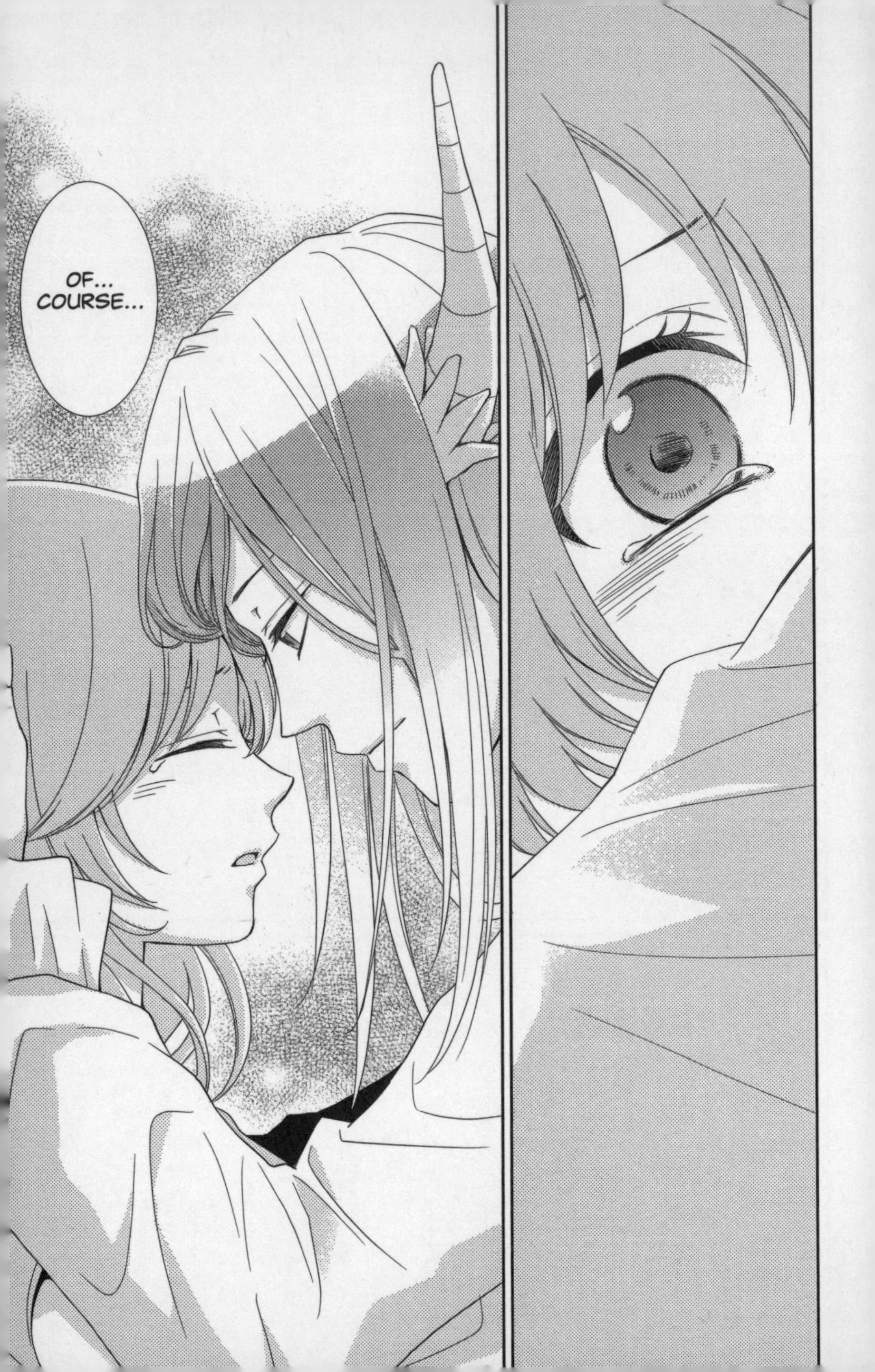
OF... COURSE...

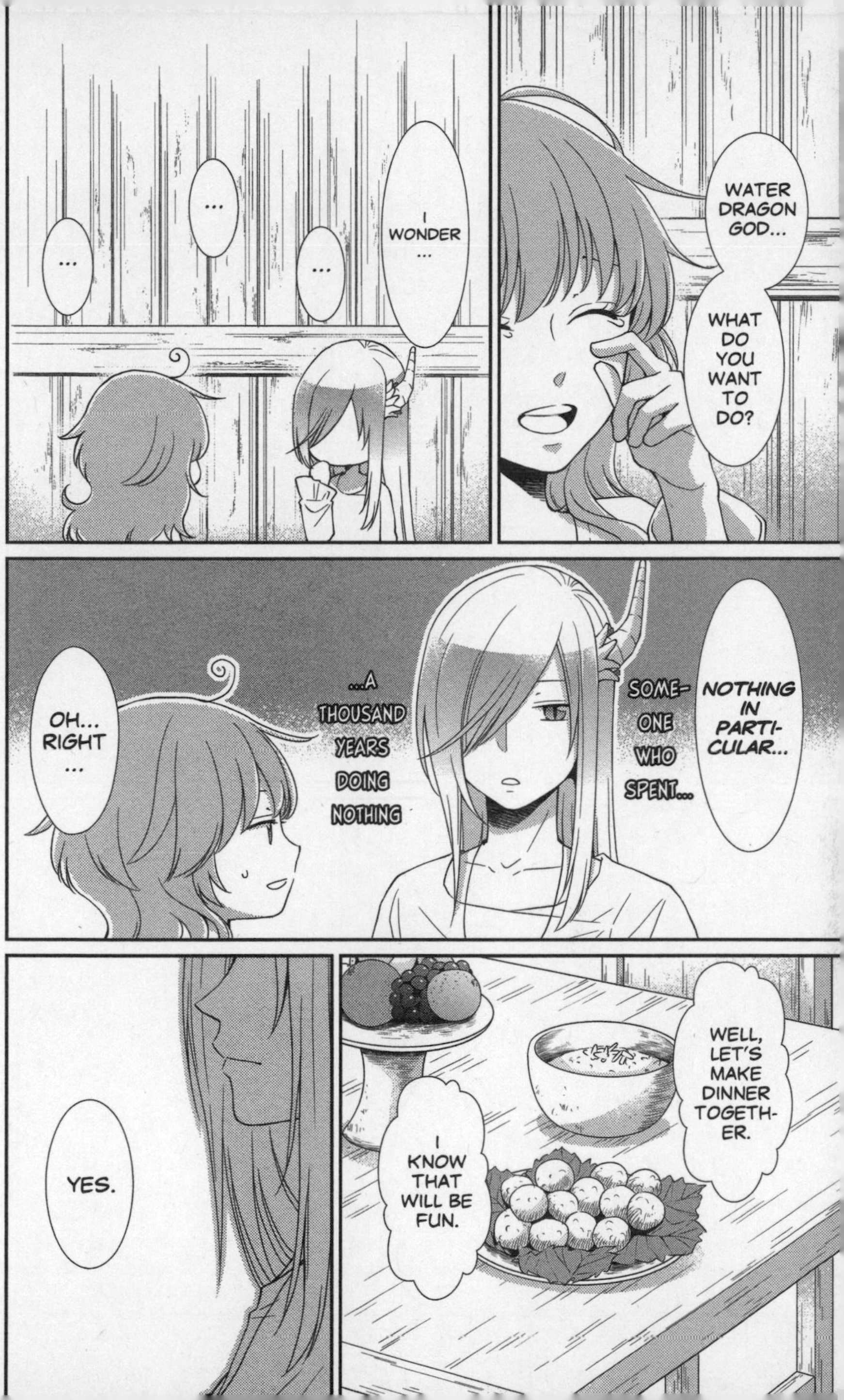
WATER DRAGON GOD...
WHAT DO YOU WANT TO DO?
I WONDER...
...
...
...
NOTHING IN PARTICULAR...
SOME-ONE WHO SPENT...
...A THOUSAND YEARS DOING NOTHING
OH... RIGHT...
WELL, LET'S MAKE DINNER TOGETH-ER.
I KNOW THAT WILL BE FUN.
YES.

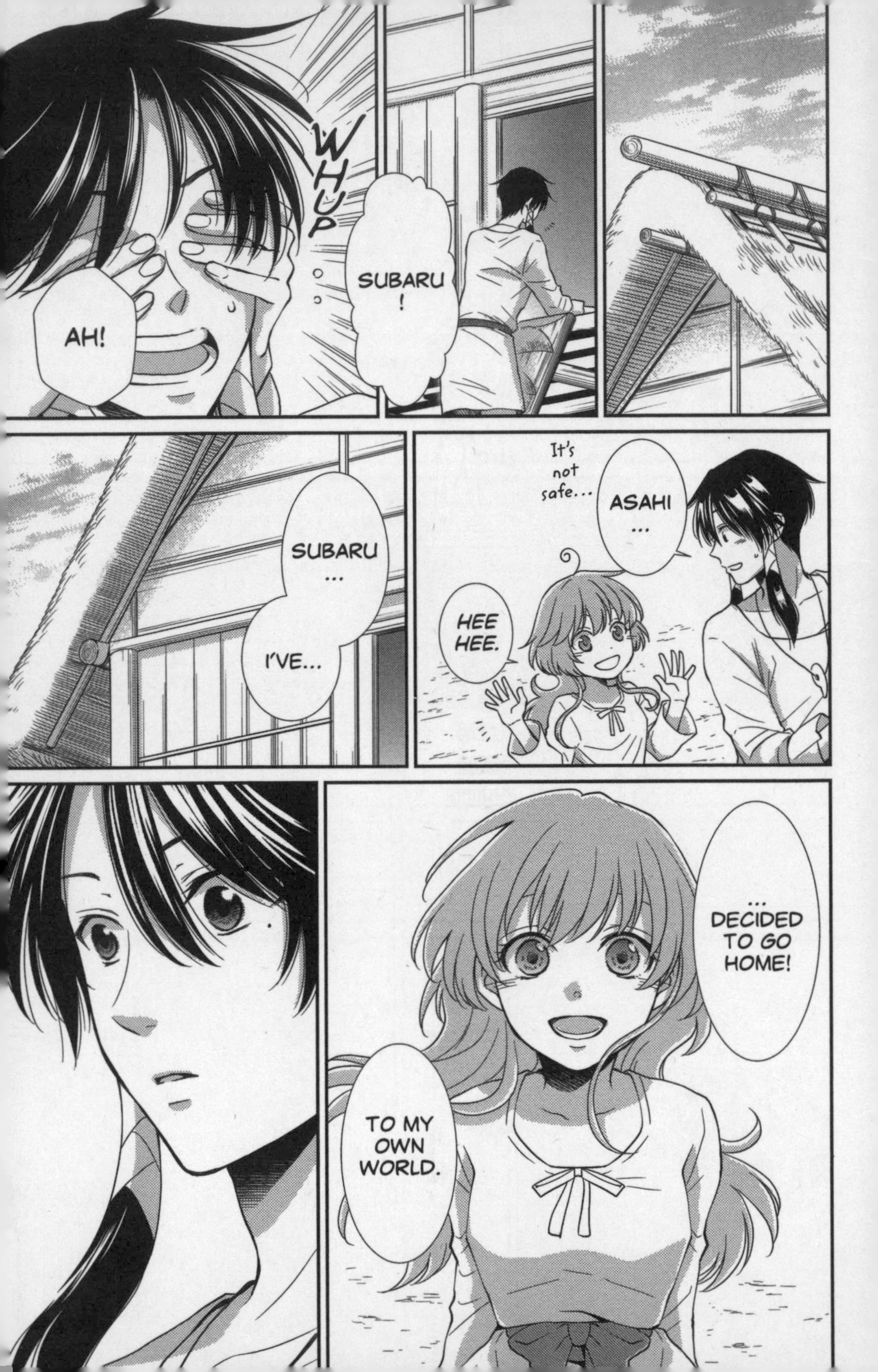
SUBARU!
WHUP
AH!
ASAHI...
It's not safe...
HEE HEE.
SUBARU...
I'VE...
...DECIDED TO GO HOME!
TO MY OWN WORLD.

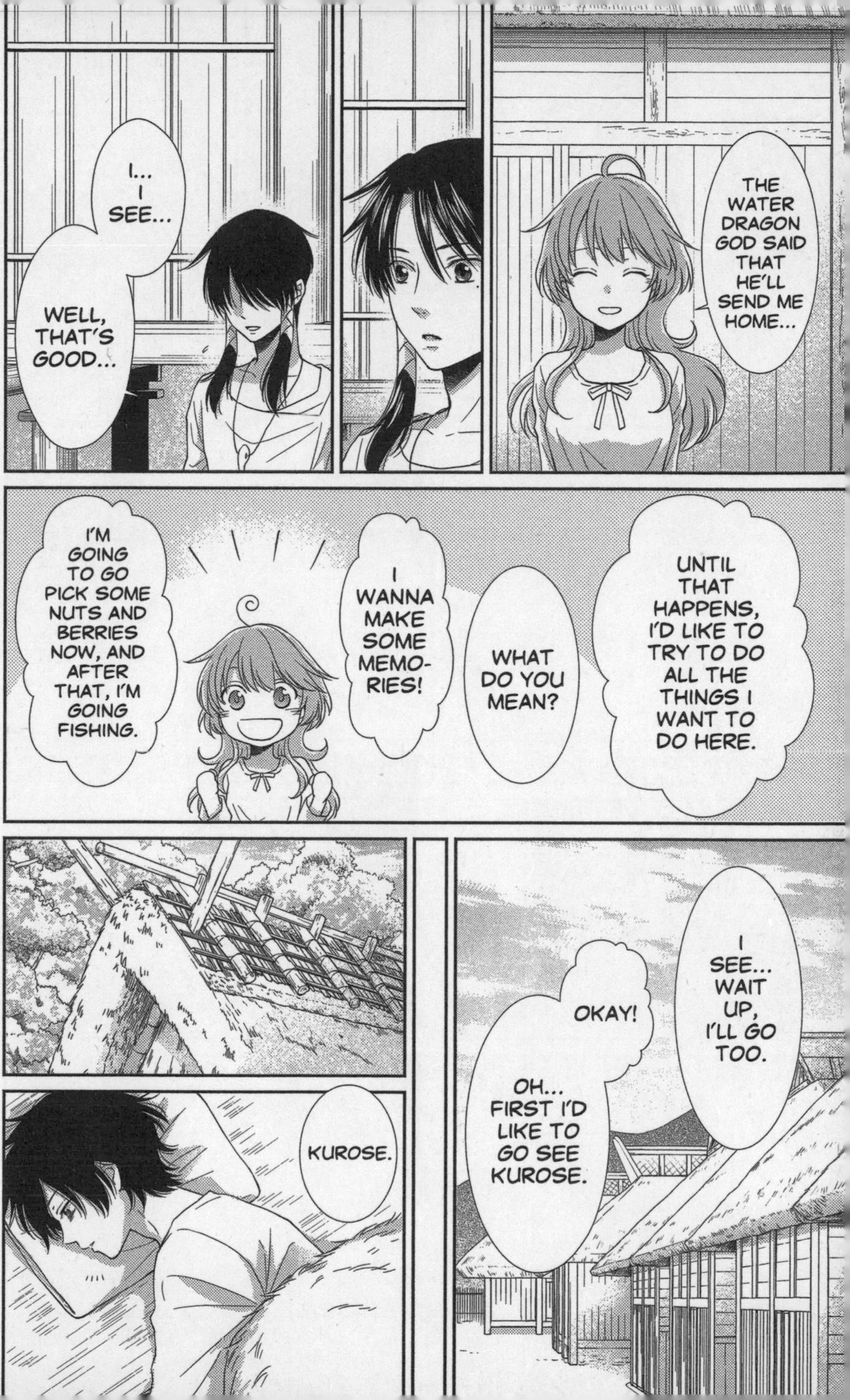
THE WATER DRAGON GOD SAID THAT HE'LL SEND ME HOME...
I... I SEE...
WELL, THAT'S GOOD...
UNTIL THAT HAPPENS, I'D LIKE TO TRY TO DO ALL THE THINGS I WANT TO DO HERE.
WHAT DO YOU MEAN?
I WANNA MAKE SOME MEMO-RIES!
I'M GOING TO GO PICK SOME NUTS AND BERRIES NOW, AND AFTER THAT, I'M GOING FISHING.
I SEE... WAIT UP, I'LL GO TOO.
OKAY!
OH... FIRST I'D LIKE TO GO SEE KUROSE.
KUROSE.

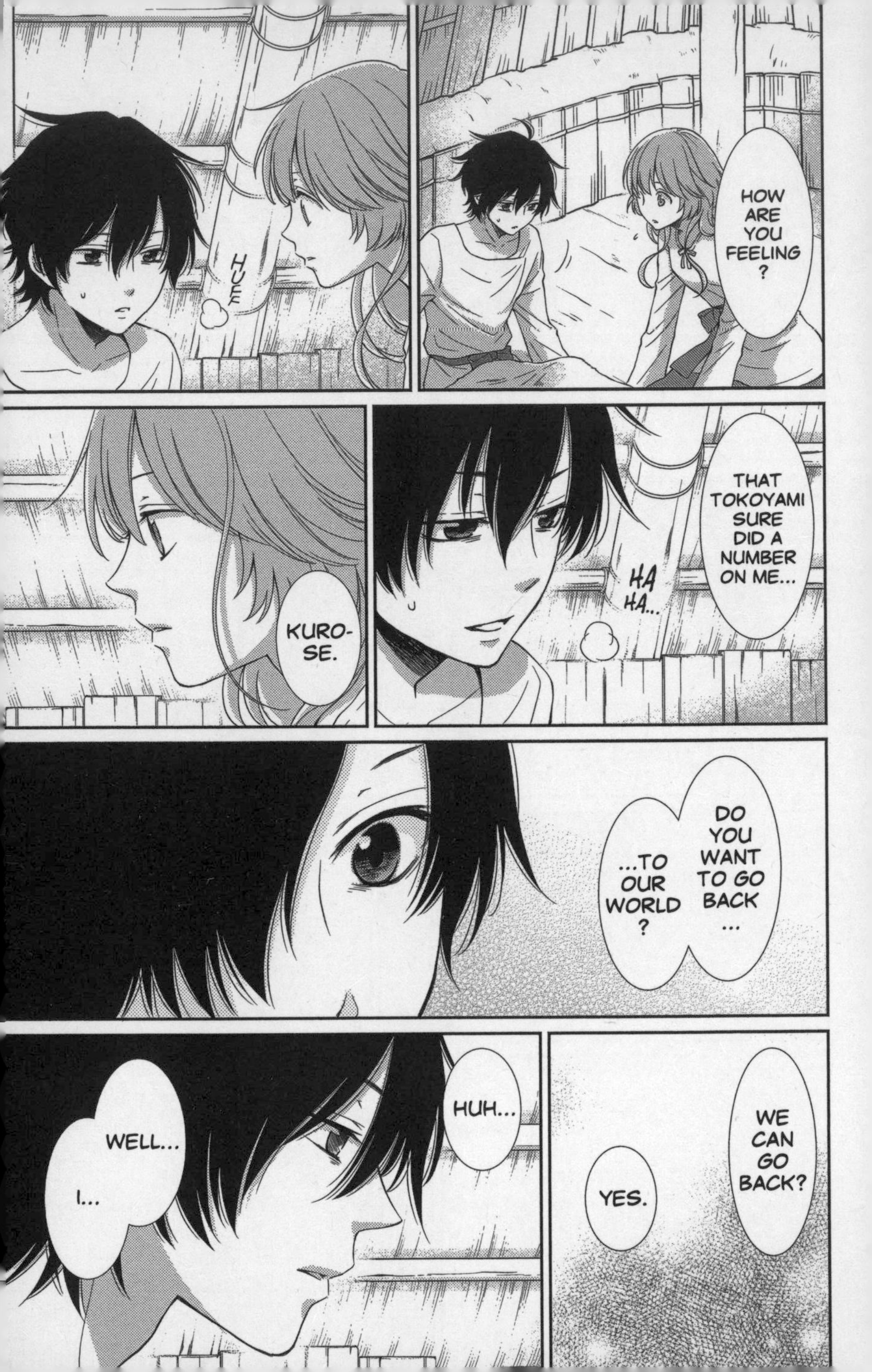
HOW ARE YOU FEELING?
HUFF
THAT TOKOYAMI SURE DID A NUMBER ON ME...
HA HA...
KURO-SE.
DO YOU WANT TO GO BACK...
...TO OUR WORLD?
WE CAN GO BACK?
YES.
HUH...
WELL... I...

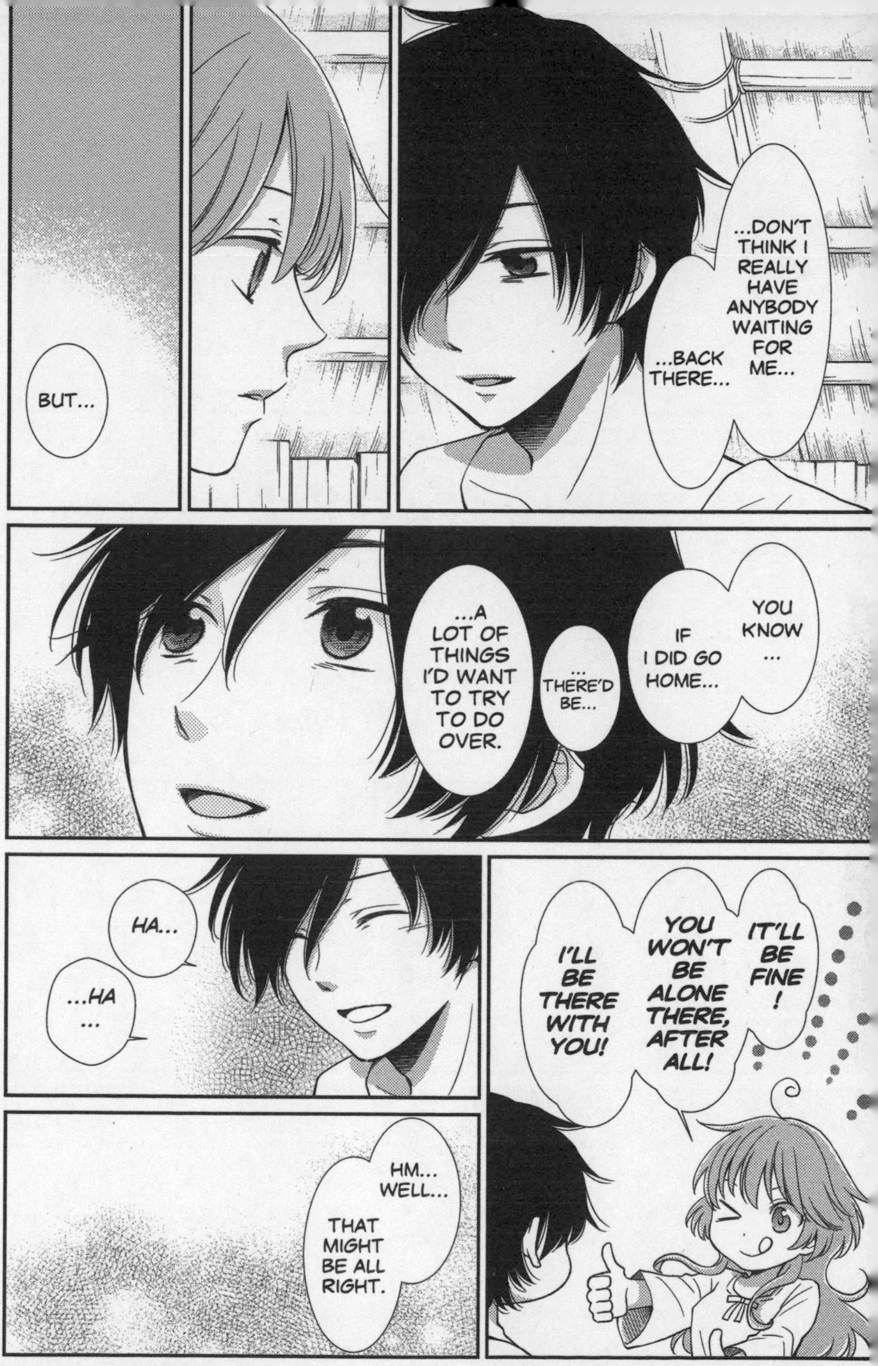
...DON'T THINK I REALLY HAVE ANYBODY WAITING FOR ME...
...BACK THERE...
BUT...
YOU KNOW ...
IF I DID GO HOME...
... THERE'D BE...
...A LOT OF THINGS I'D WANT TO TRY TO DO OVER.
IT'LL BE FINE!
YOU WON'T BE ALONE THERE, AFTER ALL!
I'LL BE THERE WITH YOU!
HA...
...HA ...
HM... WELL...
THAT MIGHT BE ALL RIGHT.

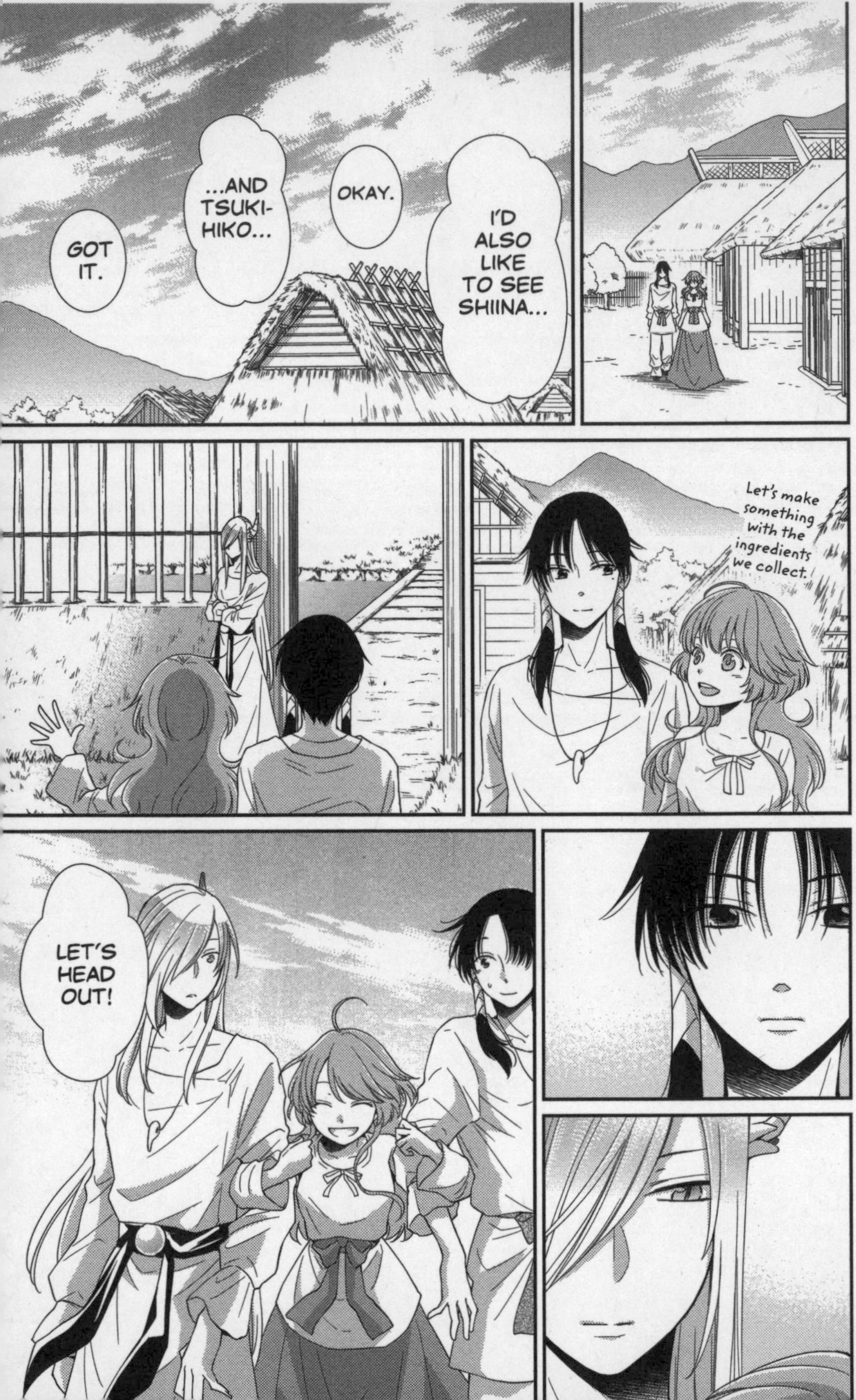
I'D ALSO LIKE TO SEE SHIINA...
OKAY.
...AND TSUKI-HIKO...
GOT IT.
Let's make something with the ingredients we collect.
LET'S HEAD OUT!

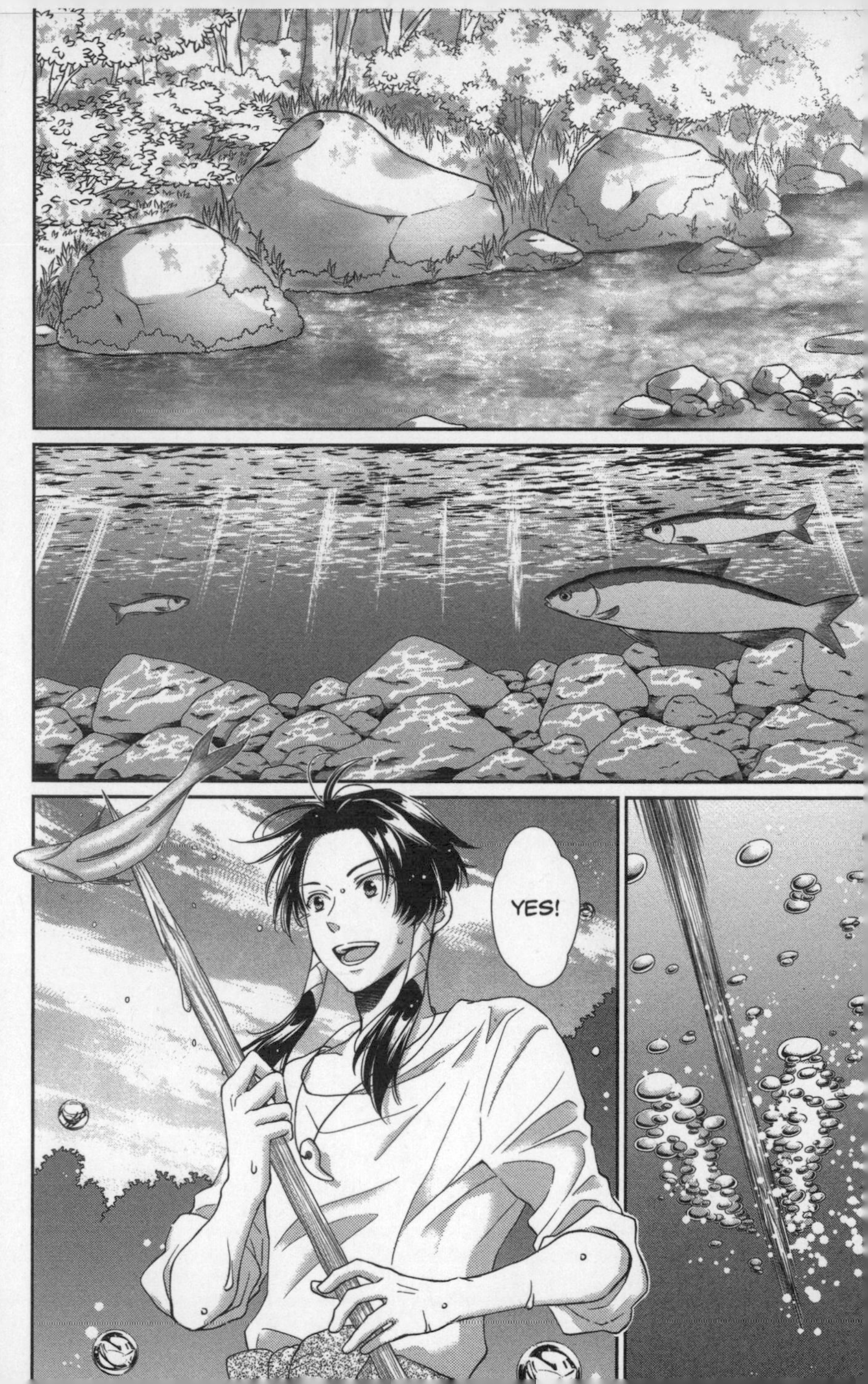
YES!

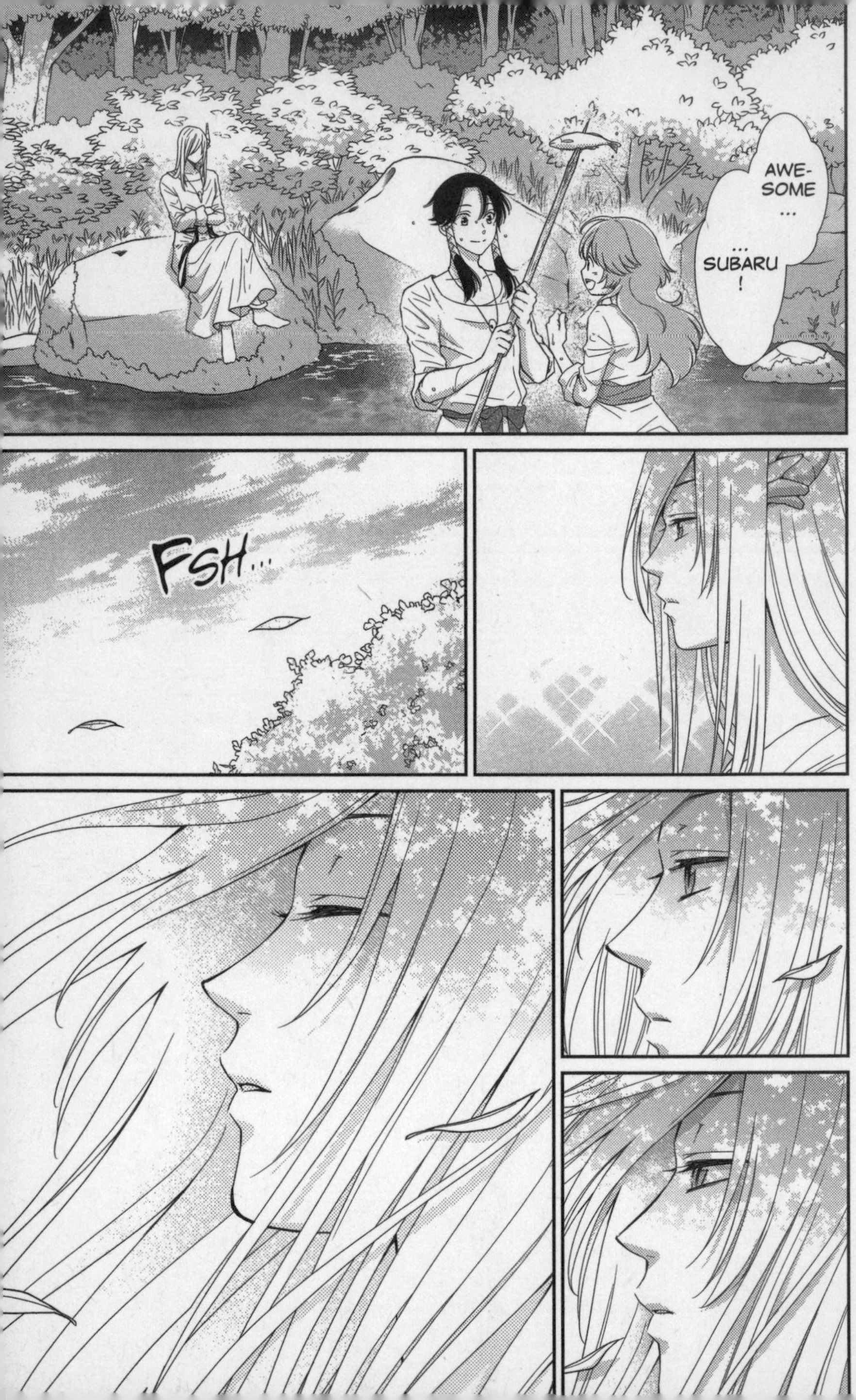
AWE-SOME... ...SUBARU!
FSH...

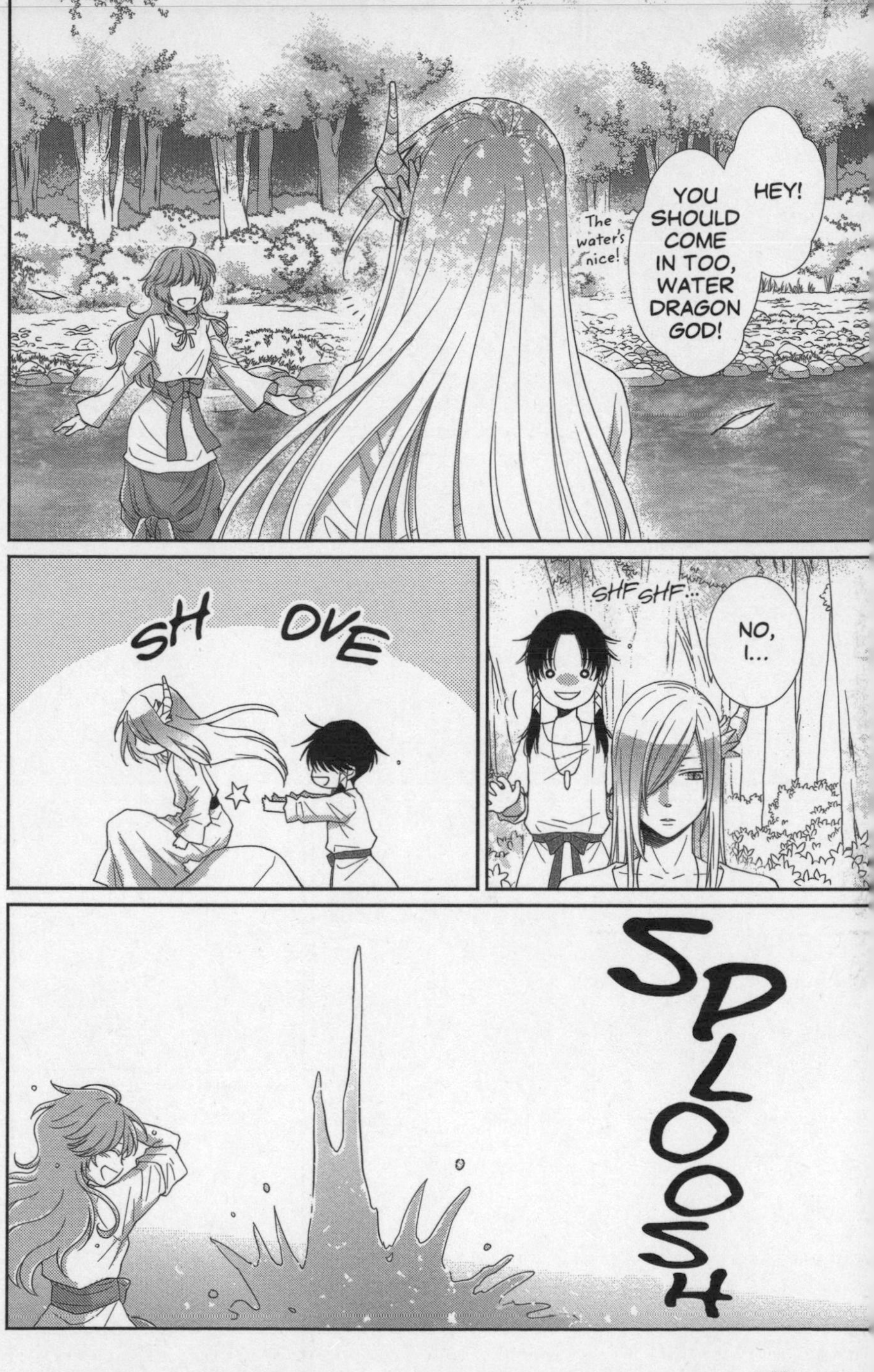
HEY!
YOU SHOULD COME IN TOO, WATER DRAGON GOD!
The water's nice!
SHF SHF...
NO, I...
SH OVE
SPLOOSH

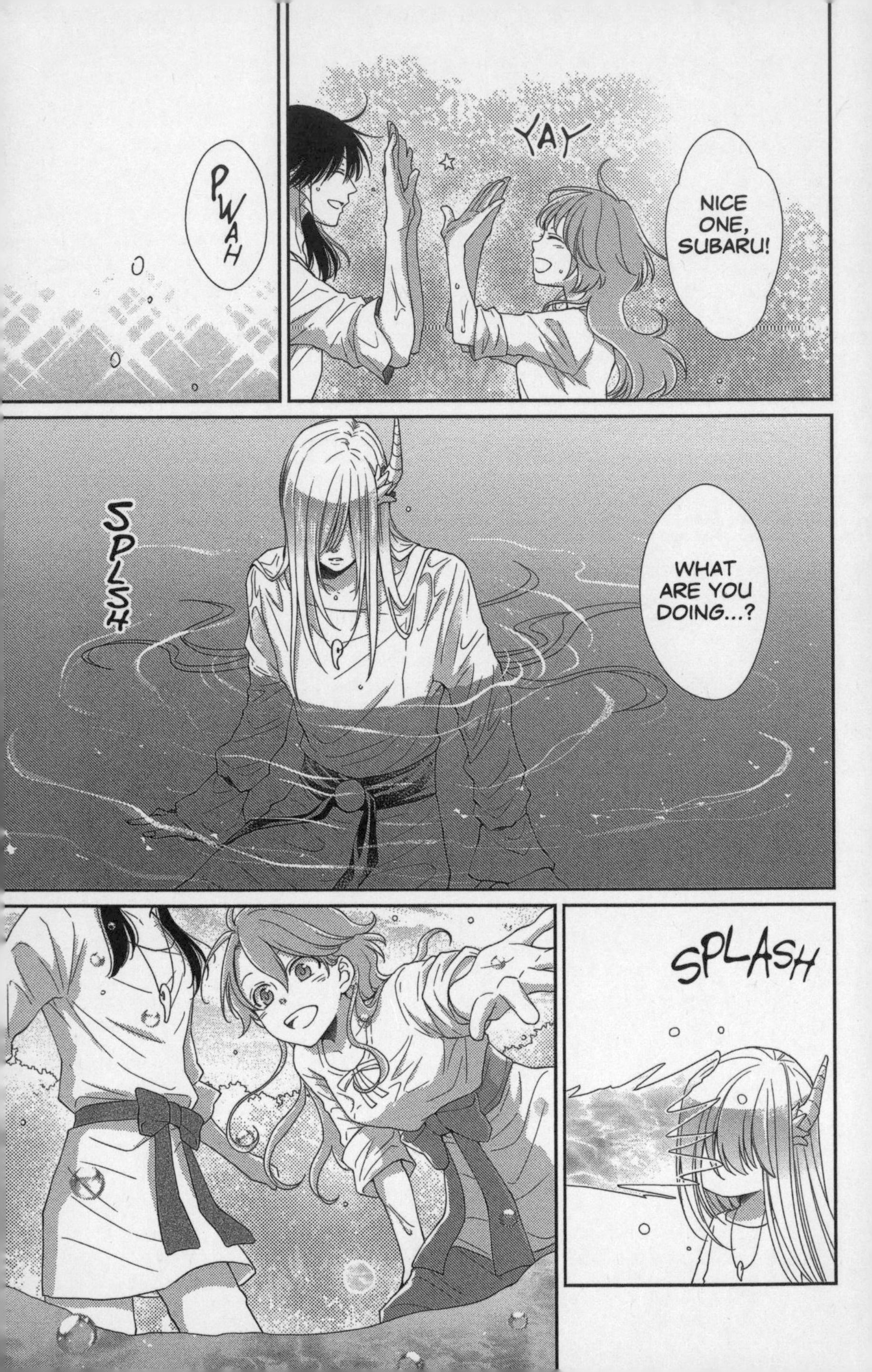
NICE ONE, SUBARU!
YAY
PWAH
WHAT ARE YOU DOING...?
SPLSH
SPLASH

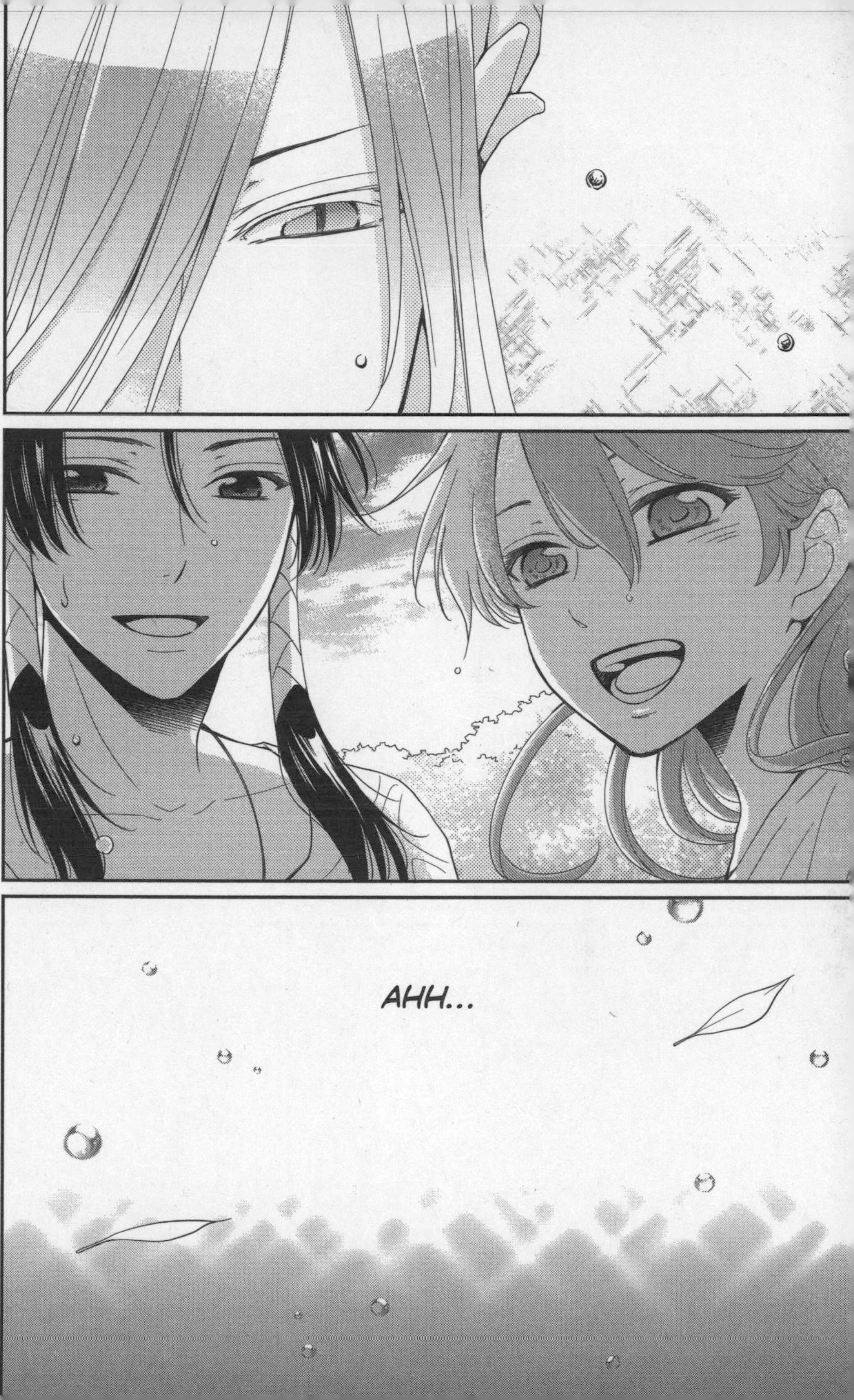
AHH...

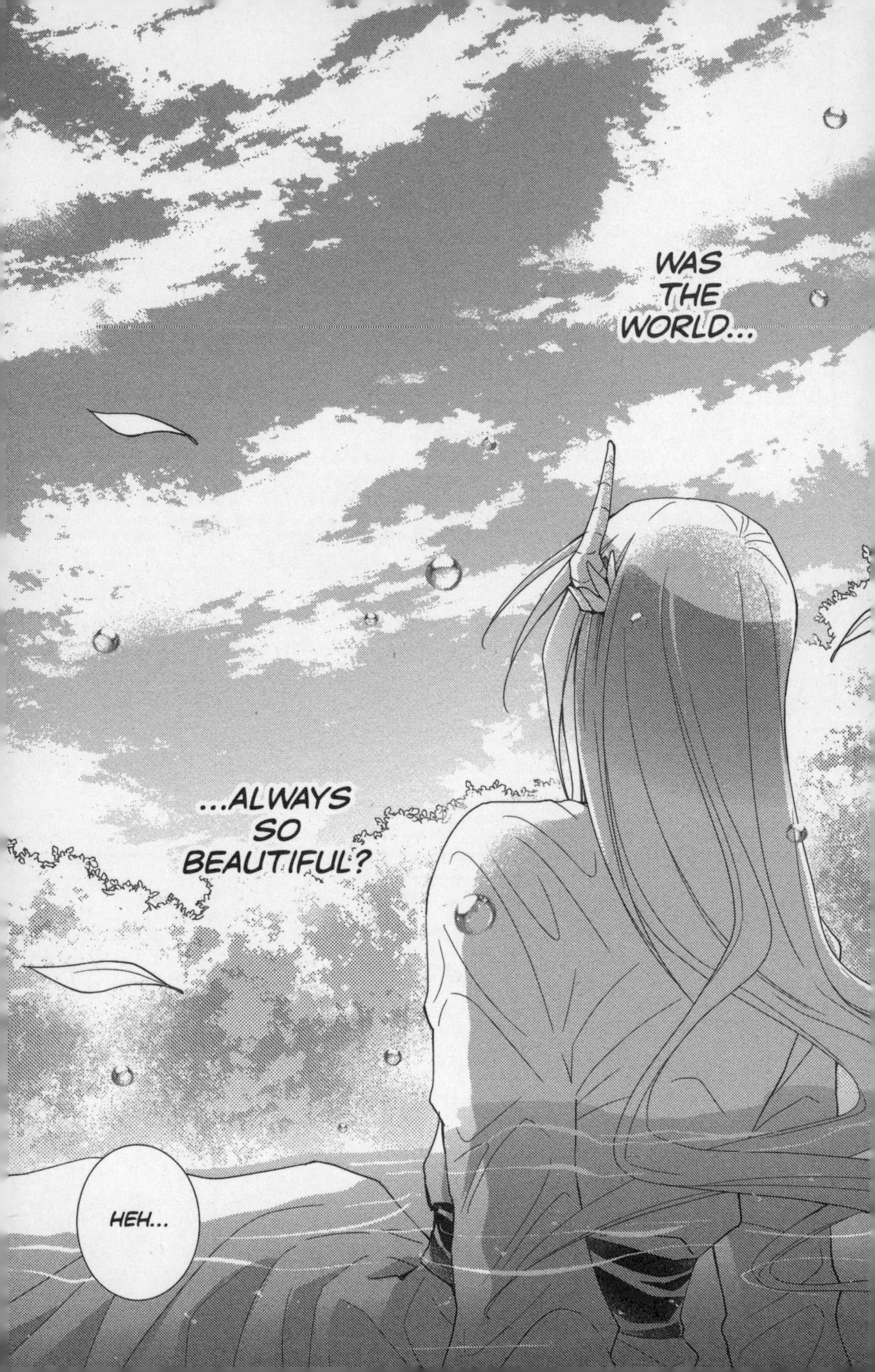
WAS THE WORLD...
...ALWAYS SO BEAUTIFUL?
HEH...

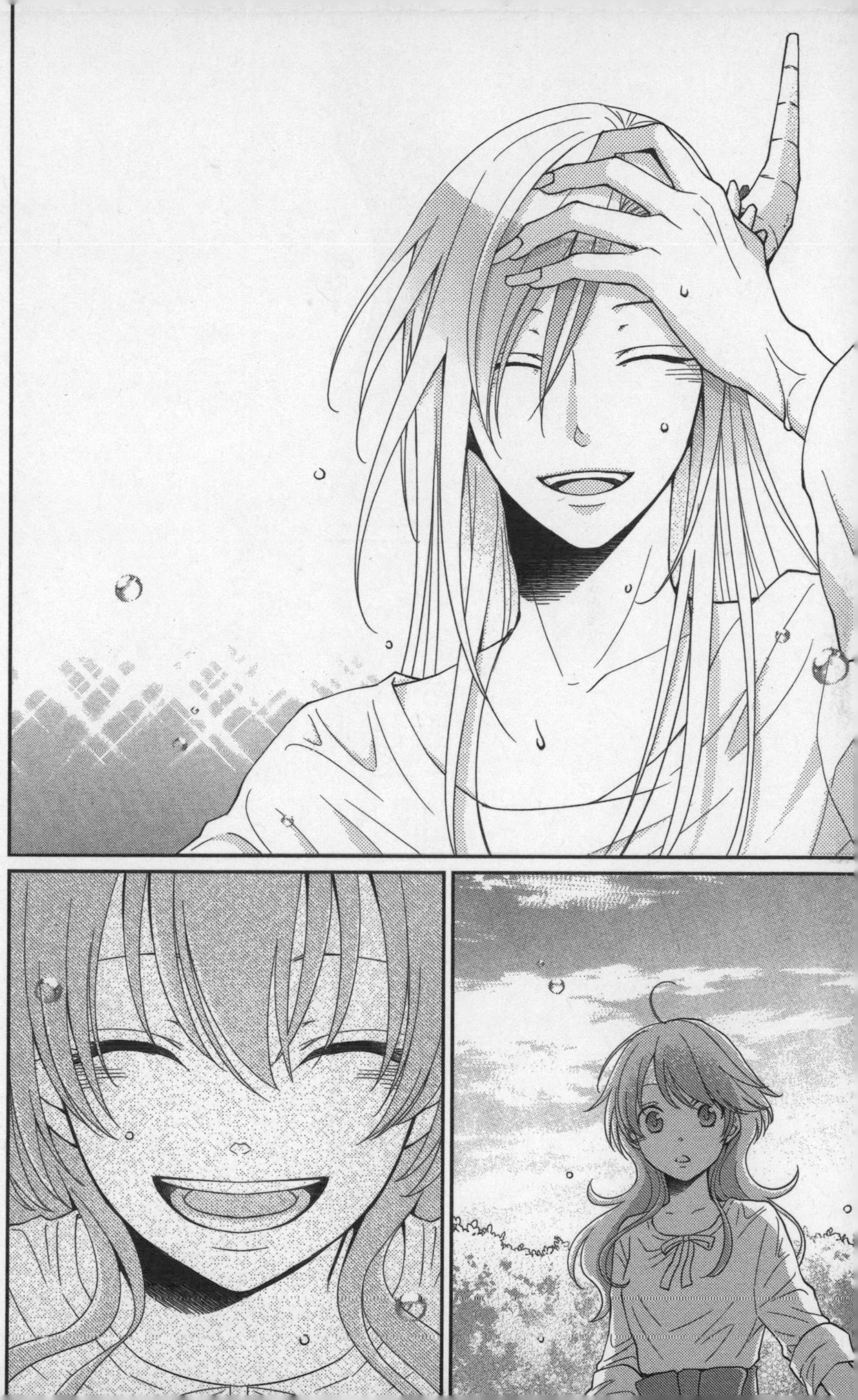

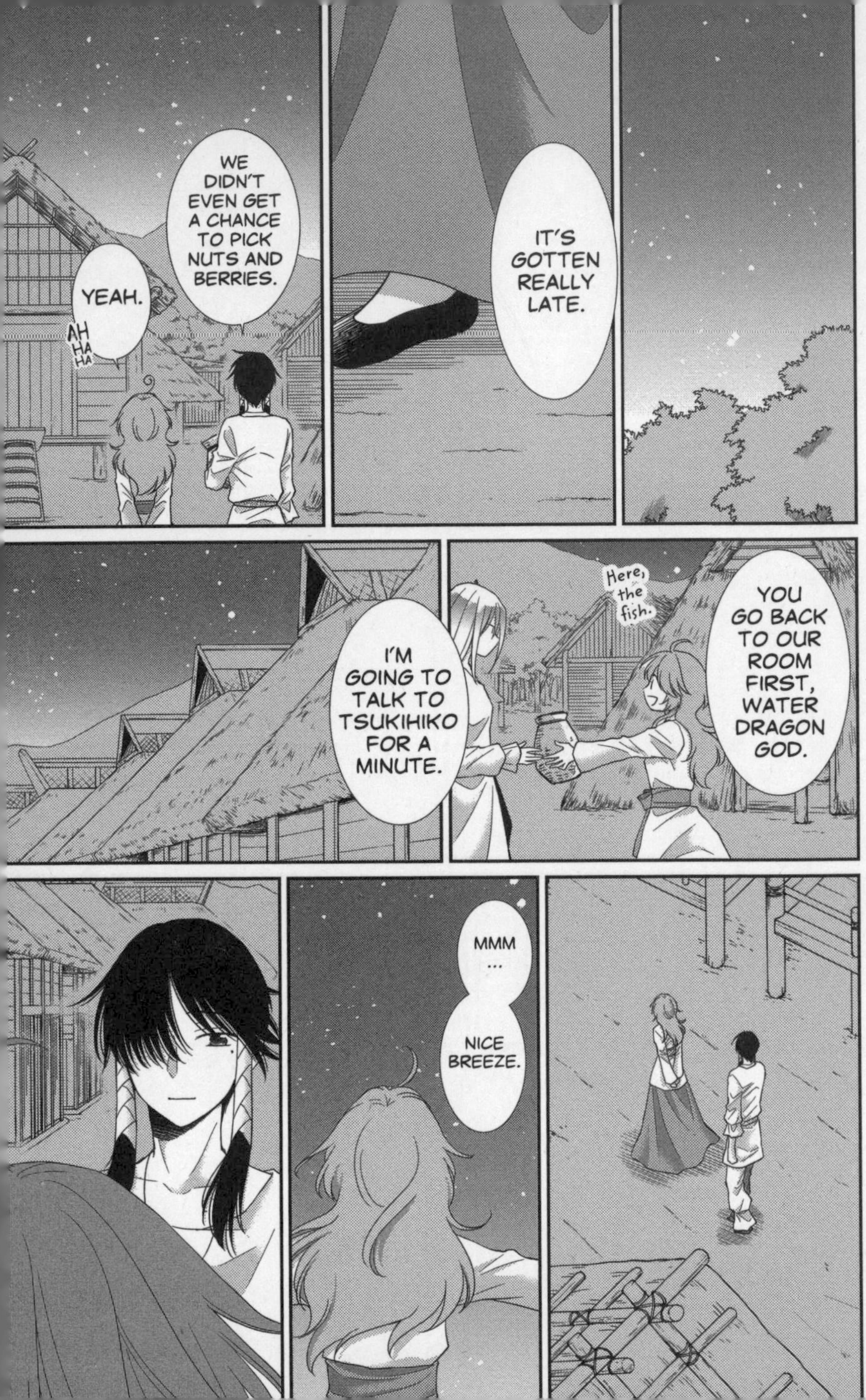
IT'S GOTTEN REALLY LATE.
WE DIDN'T EVEN GET A CHANCE TO PICK NUTS AND BERRIES.
YEAH.
AH HA HA
YOU GO BACK TO OUR ROOM FIRST, WATER DRAGON GOD.
Here, the fish.
I'M GOING TO TALK TO TSUKIHIKO FOR A MINUTE.
MMM...
NICE BREEZE.

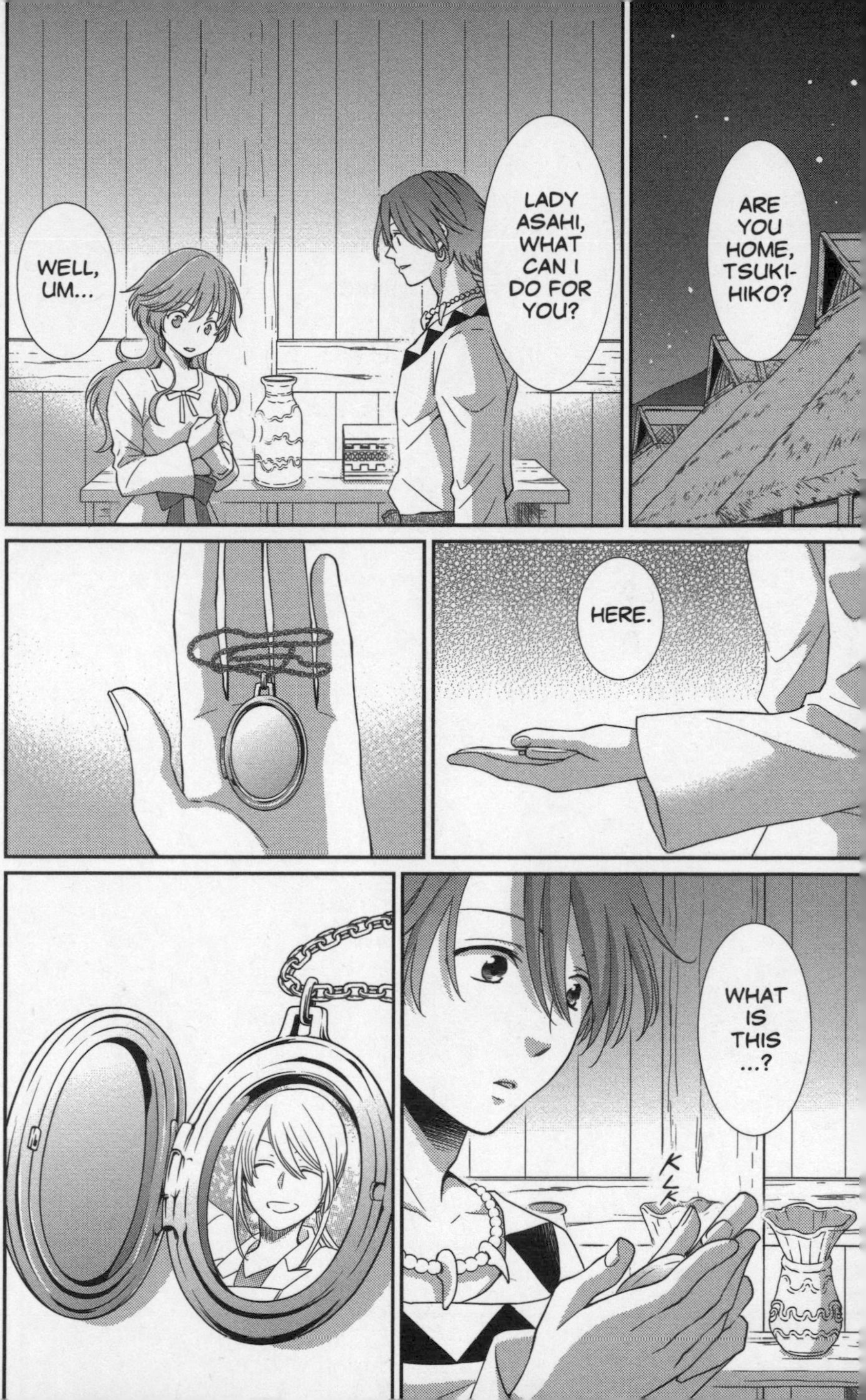
ARE YOU HOME, TSUKI-HIKO?
LADY ASAHI, WHAT CAN I DO FOR YOU?
WELL, UM...
HERE.
WHAT IS THIS ...?
KLIK

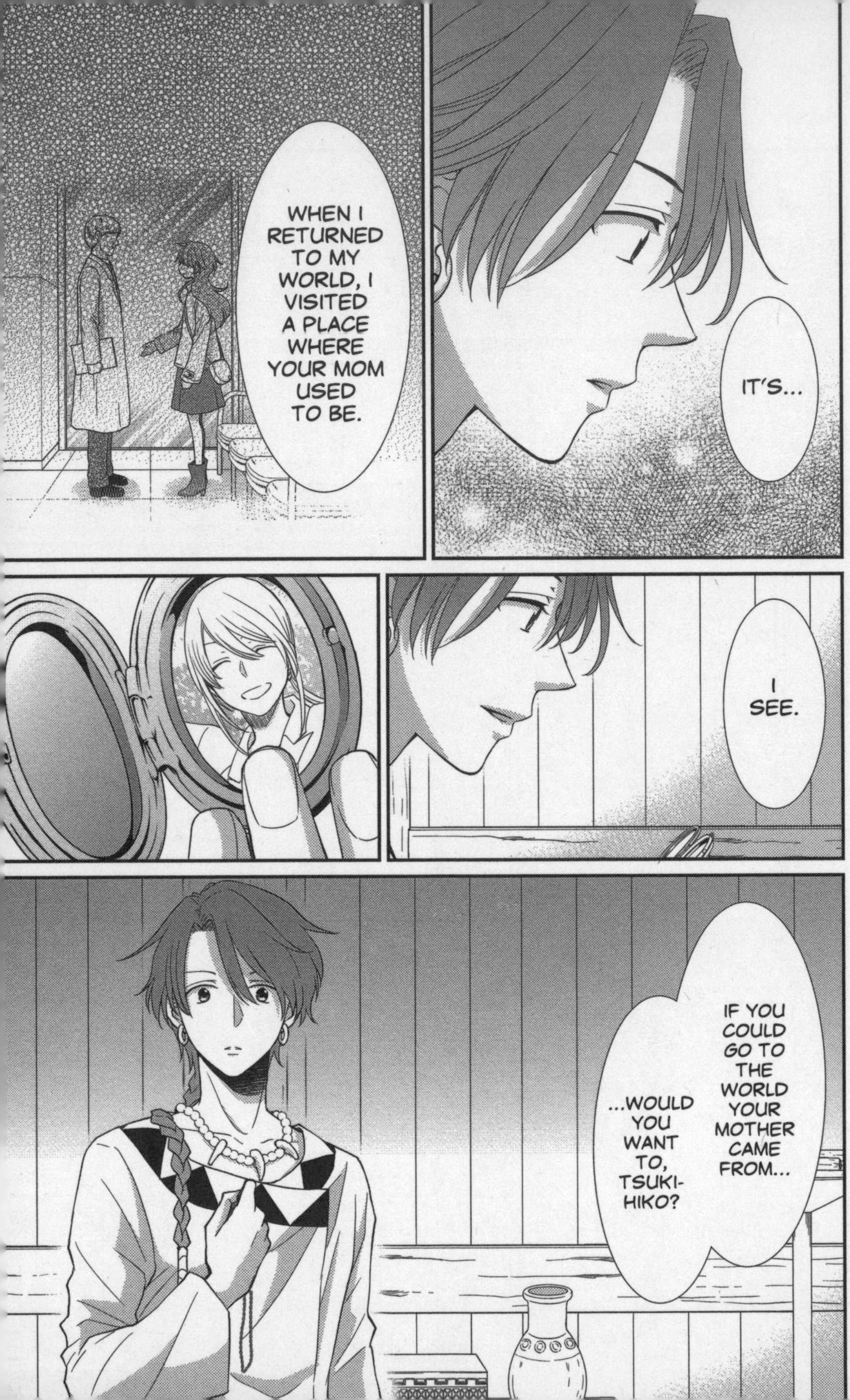
IT'S...
WHEN I RETURNED TO MY WORLD, I VISITED A PLACE WHERE YOUR MOM USED TO BE.
I SEE.
IF YOU COULD GO TO THE WORLD YOUR MOTHER CAME FROM...
...WOULD YOU WANT TO, TSUKI-HIKO?

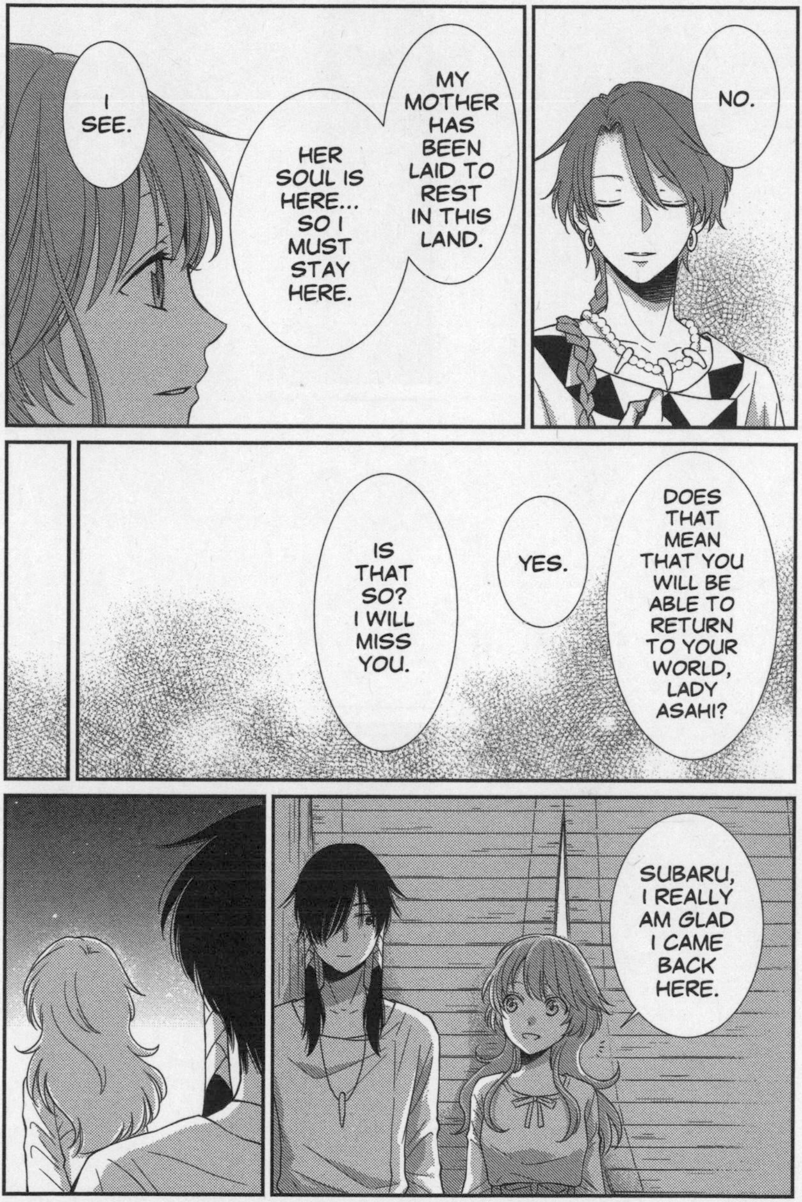
NO.
MY MOTHER HAS BEEN LAID TO REST IN THIS LAND.
HER SOUL IS HERE... SO I MUST STAY HERE.
I SEE.
DOES THAT MEAN THAT YOU WILL BE ABLE TO RETURN TO YOUR WORLD, LADY ASAHI?
YES.
IS THAT SO? I WILL MISS YOU.
SUBARU, I REALLY AM GLAD I CAME BACK HERE.

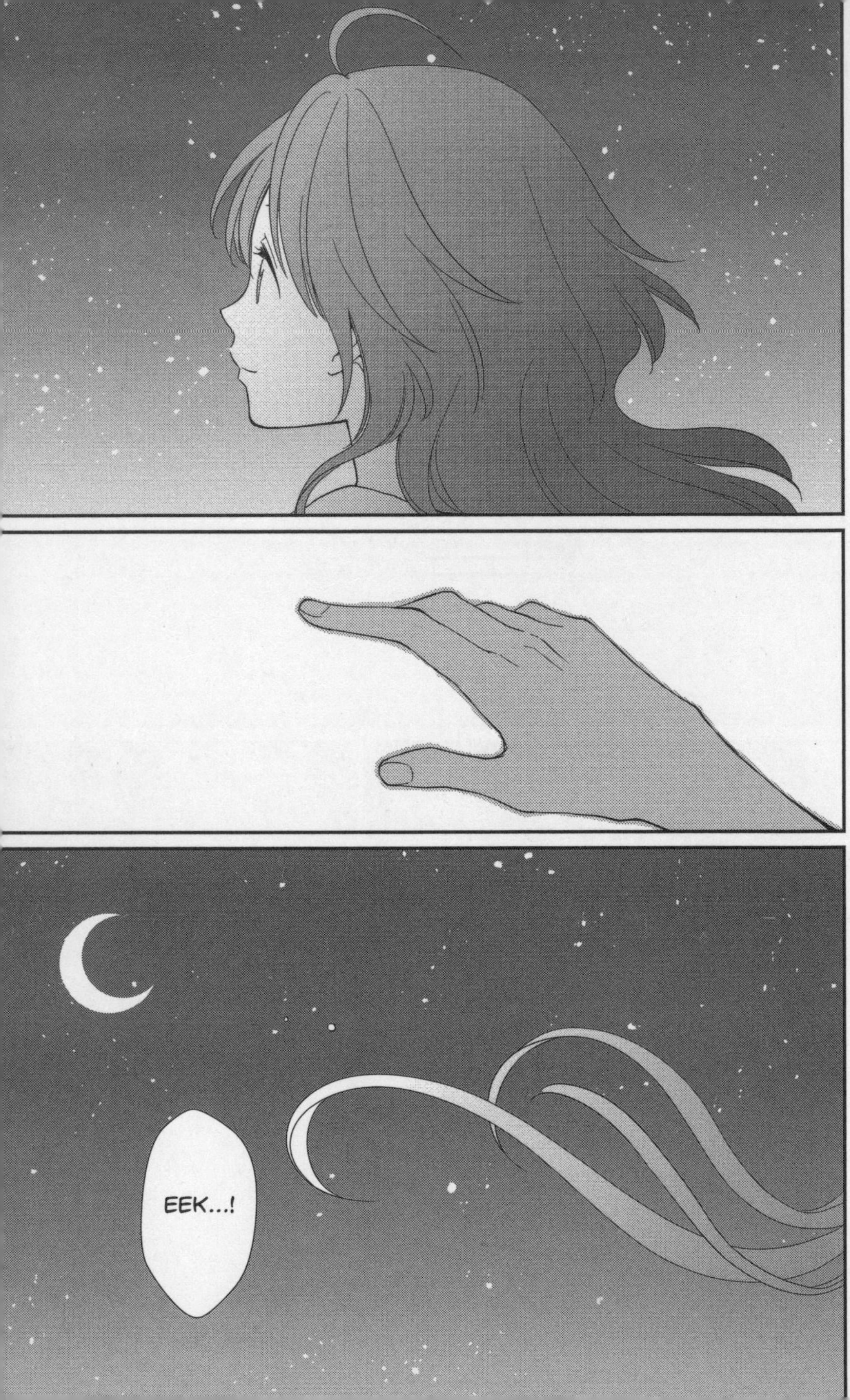
EEK...!

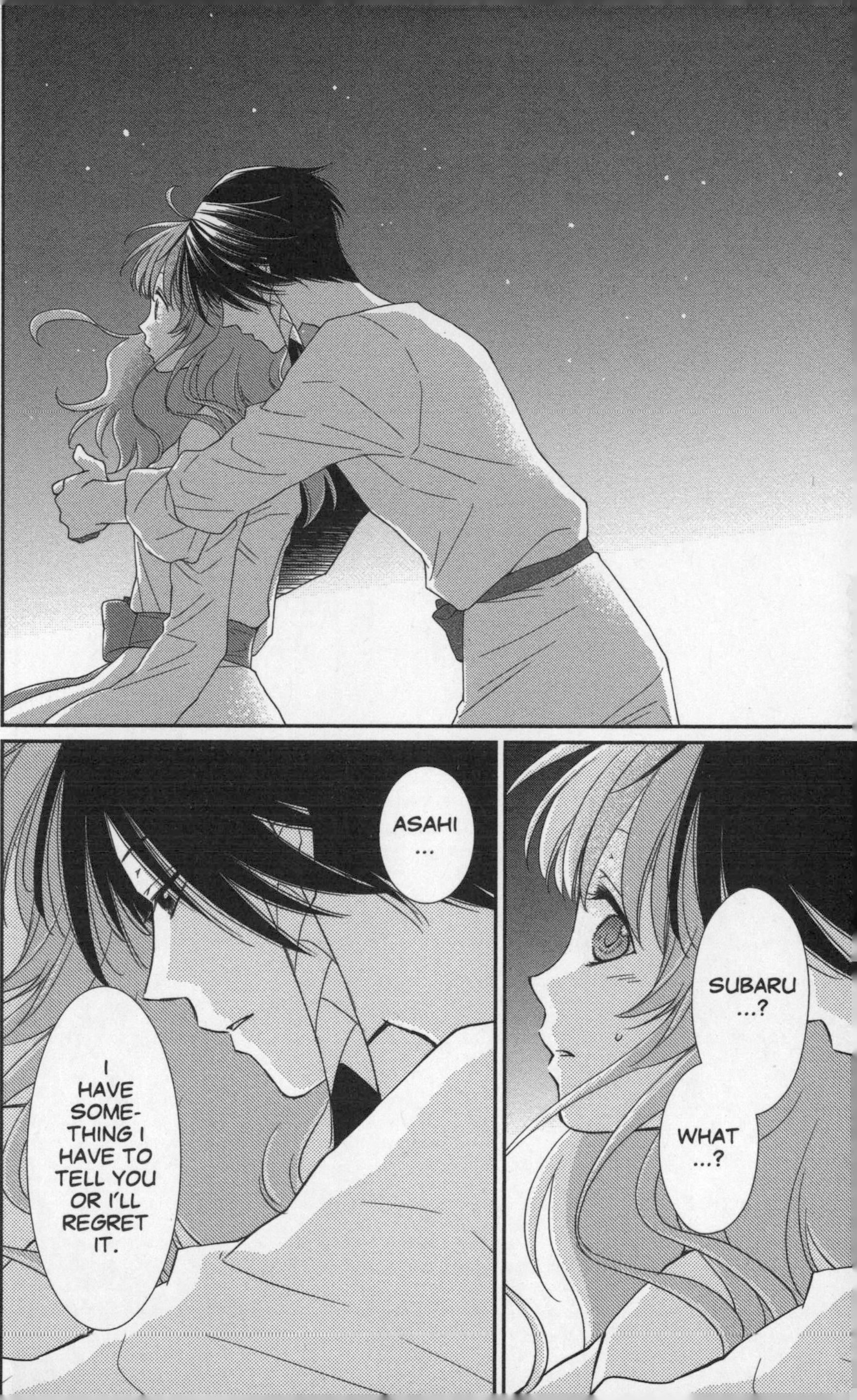
SUBARU ...?
WHAT ...?
ASAHI ...
I HAVE SOME-THING I HAVE TO TELL YOU OR I'LL REGRET IT.

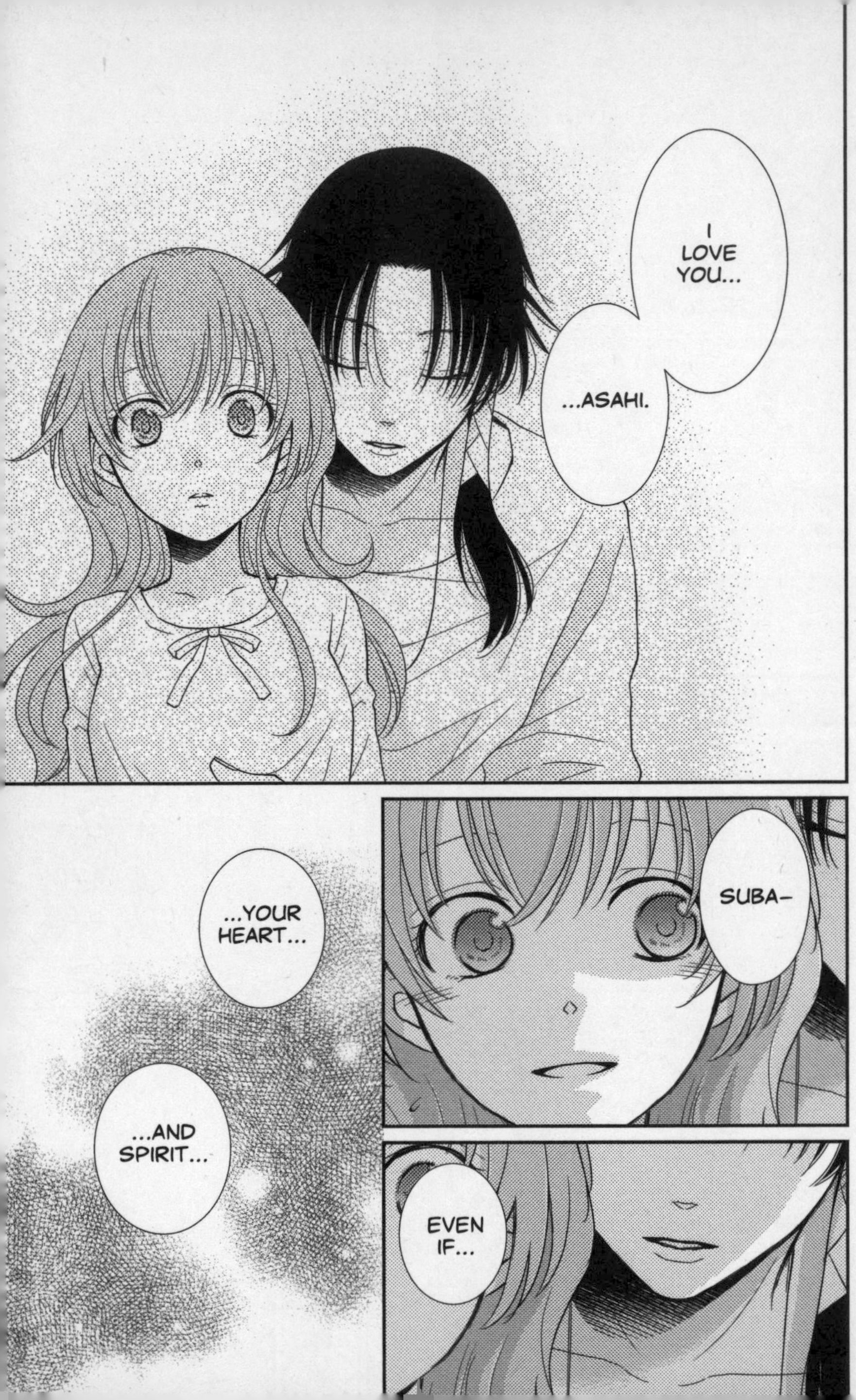
I LOVE YOU...
...ASAHI.
SUBA-
EVEN IF...
...YOUR HEART...
...AND SPIRIT...

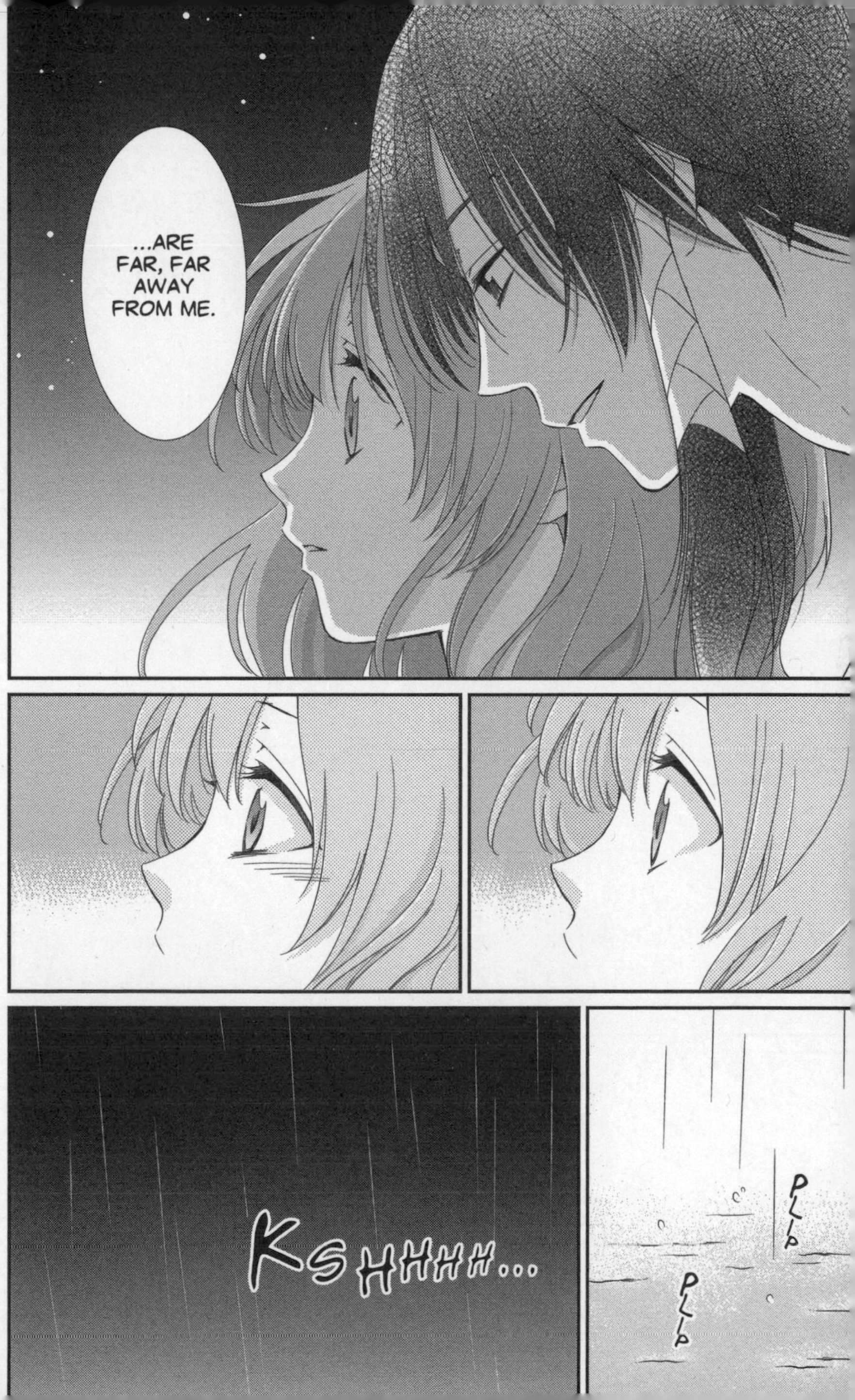
...ARE FAR, FAR AWAY FROM ME.
PLIP
PLIP
KSHHHH...

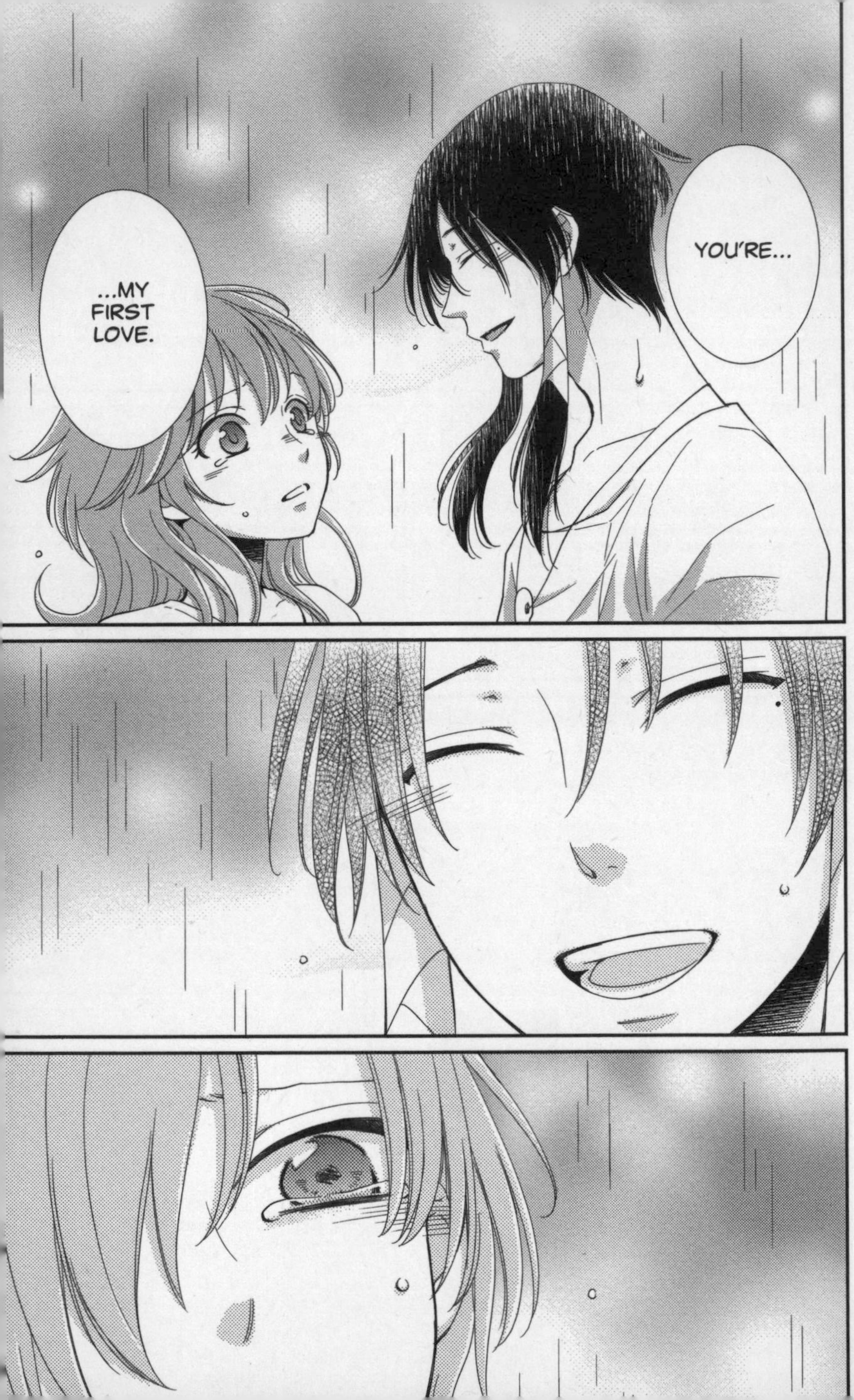
YOU'RE...
...MY FIRST LOVE.

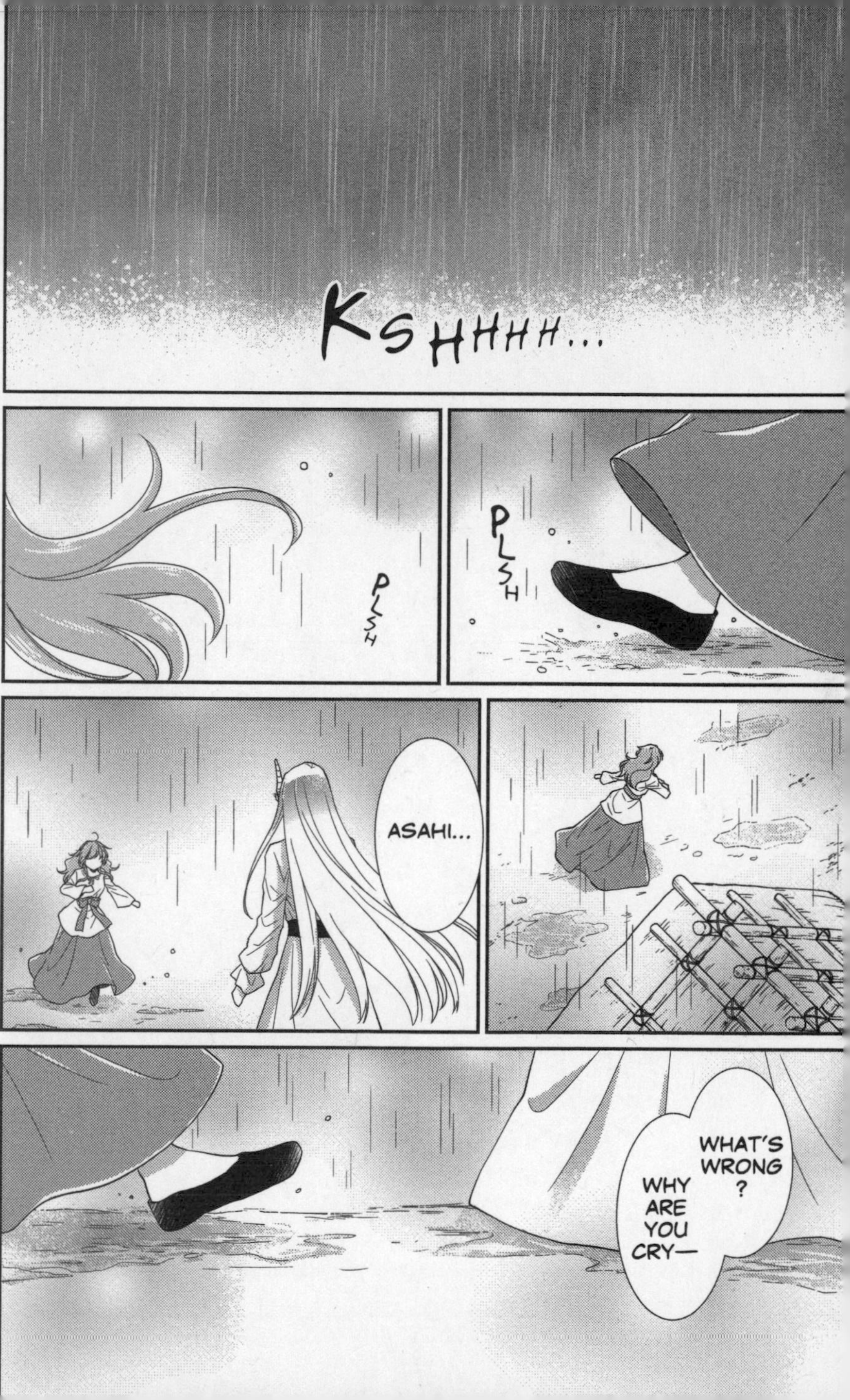
KSHHHH...
PLSH
PLSH
ASAHI...
WHAT'S WRONG?
WHY ARE YOU CRY—

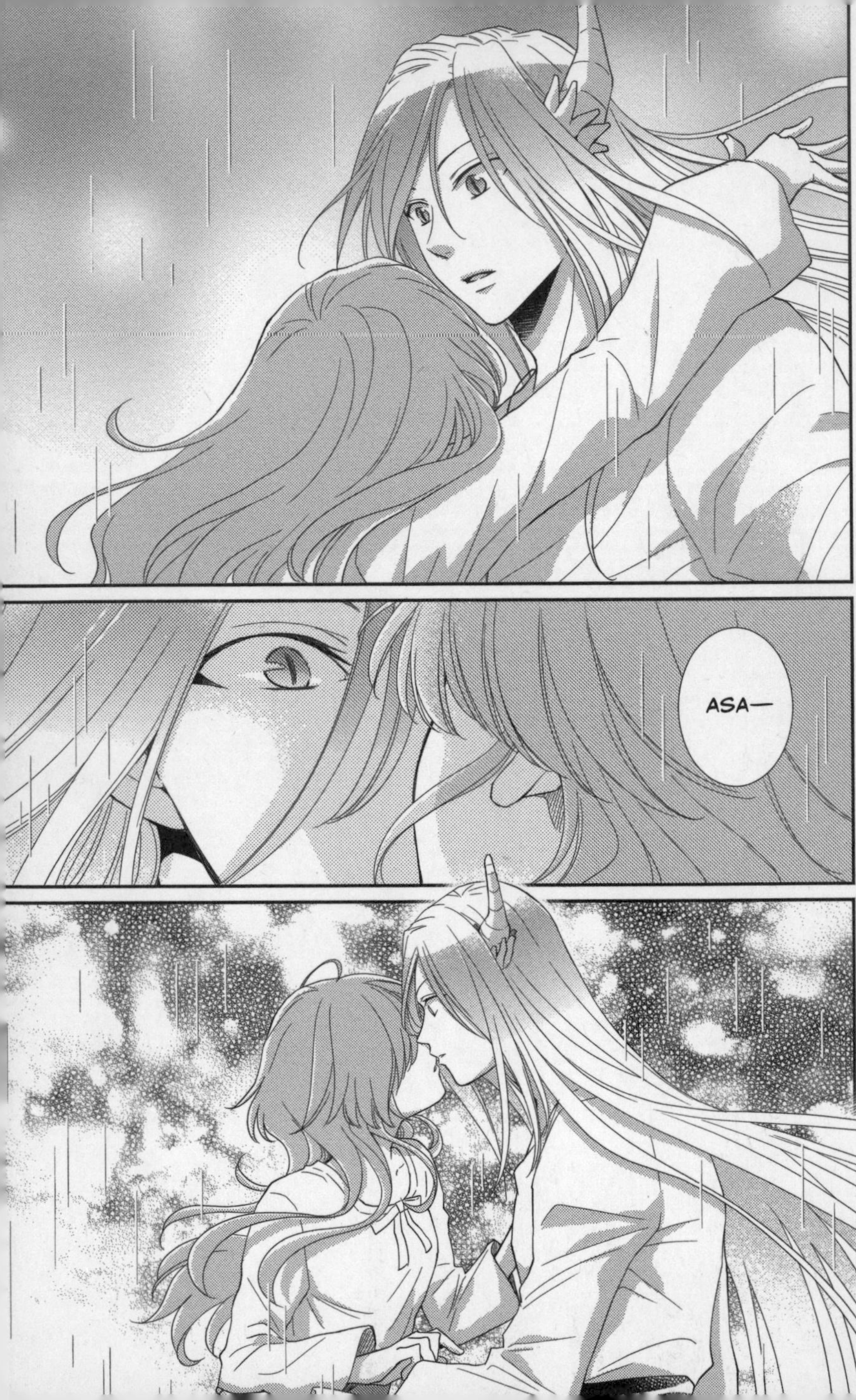
ASA—

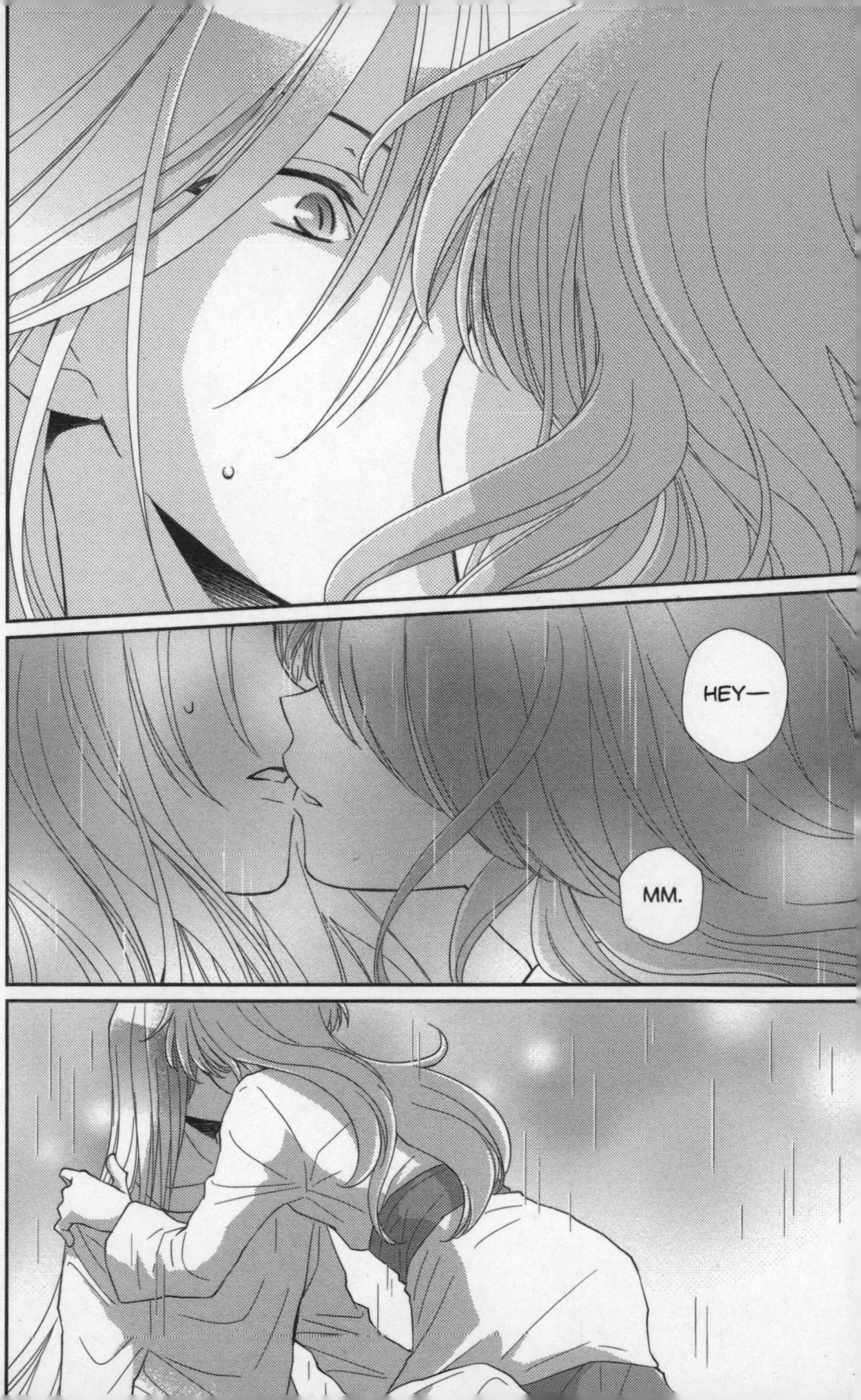
HEY—
MM.

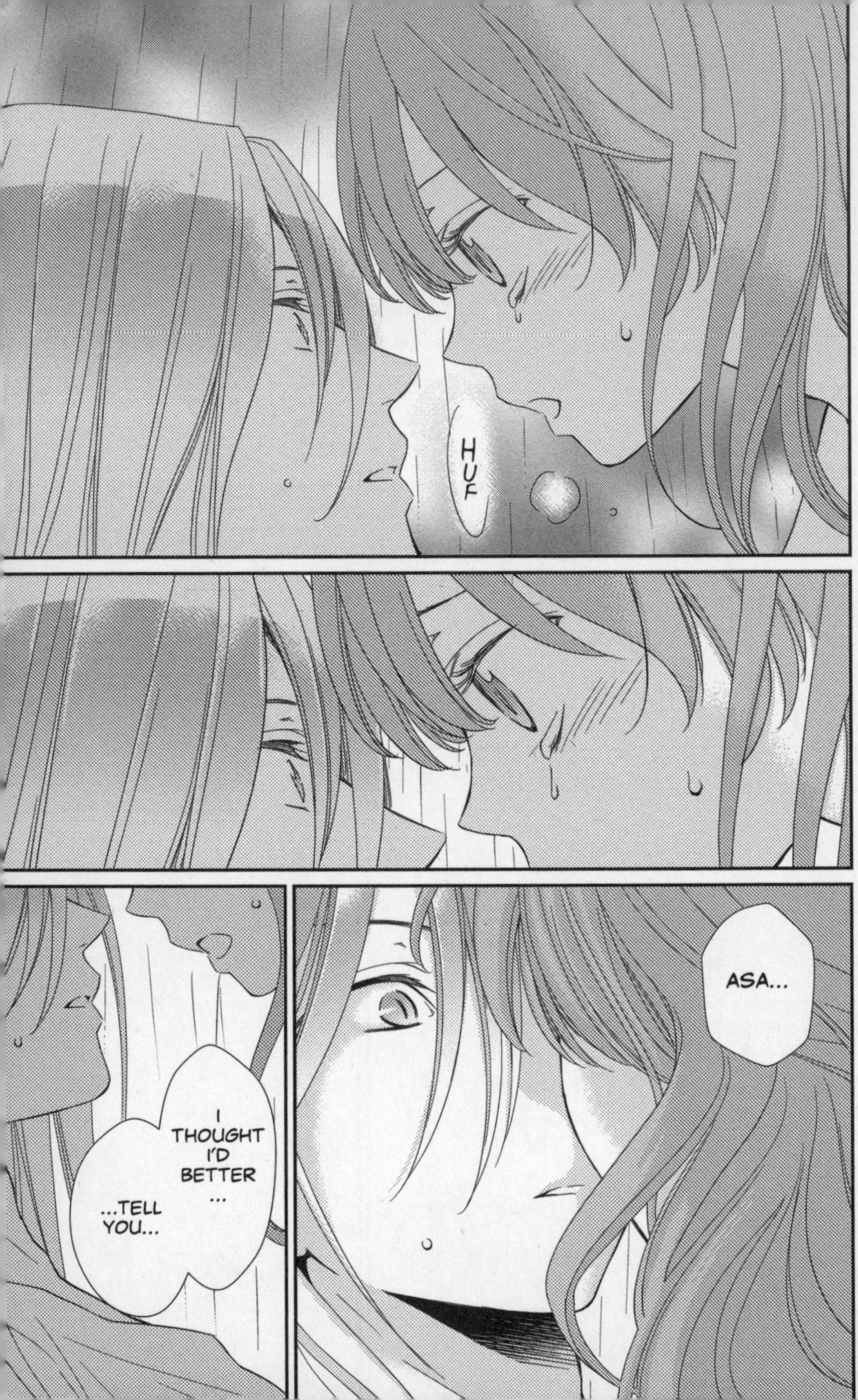
HUF
ASA...
I THOUGHT I'D BETTER ...
...TELL YOU...

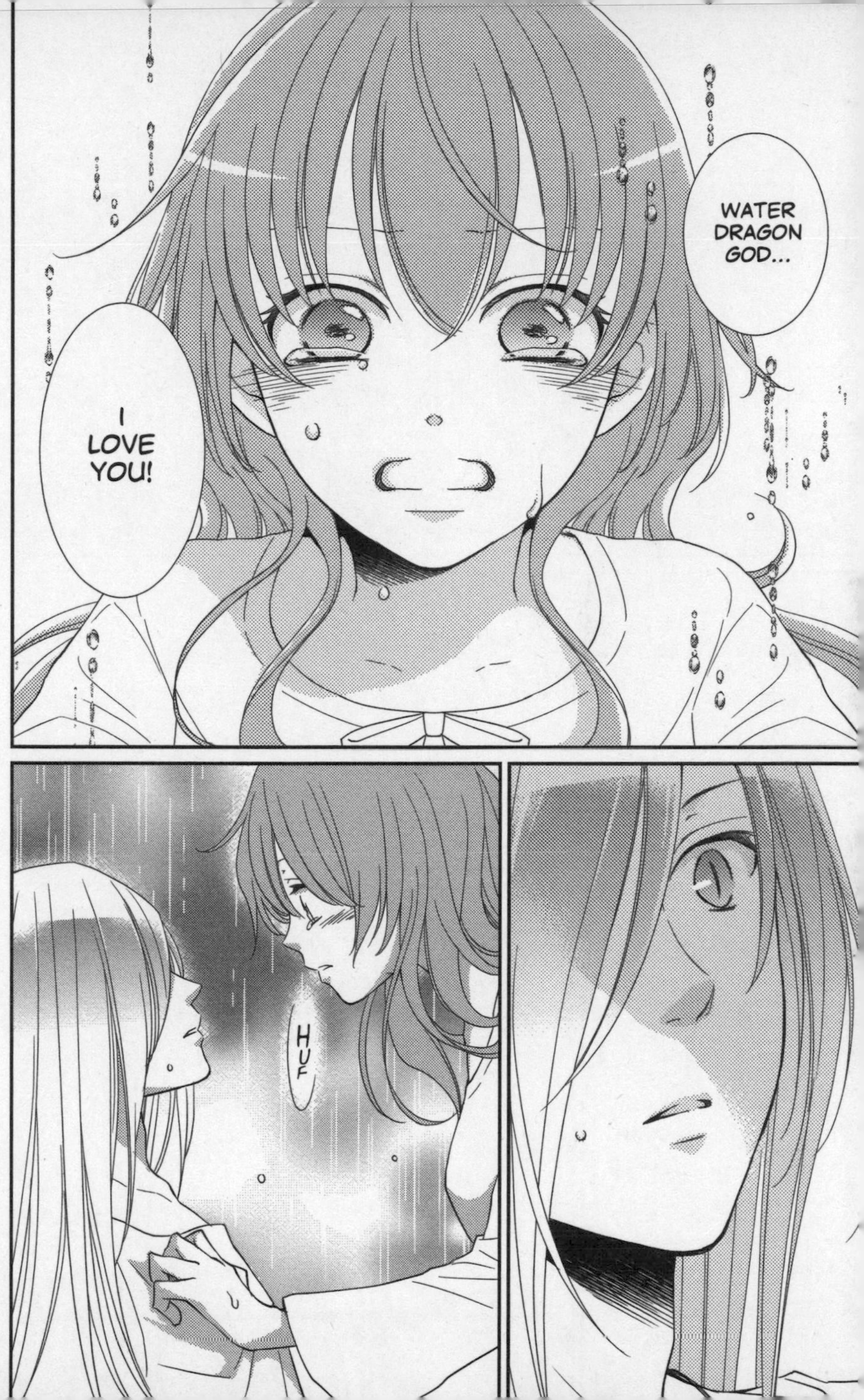
WATER DRAGON GOD...
I LOVE YOU!
HUF

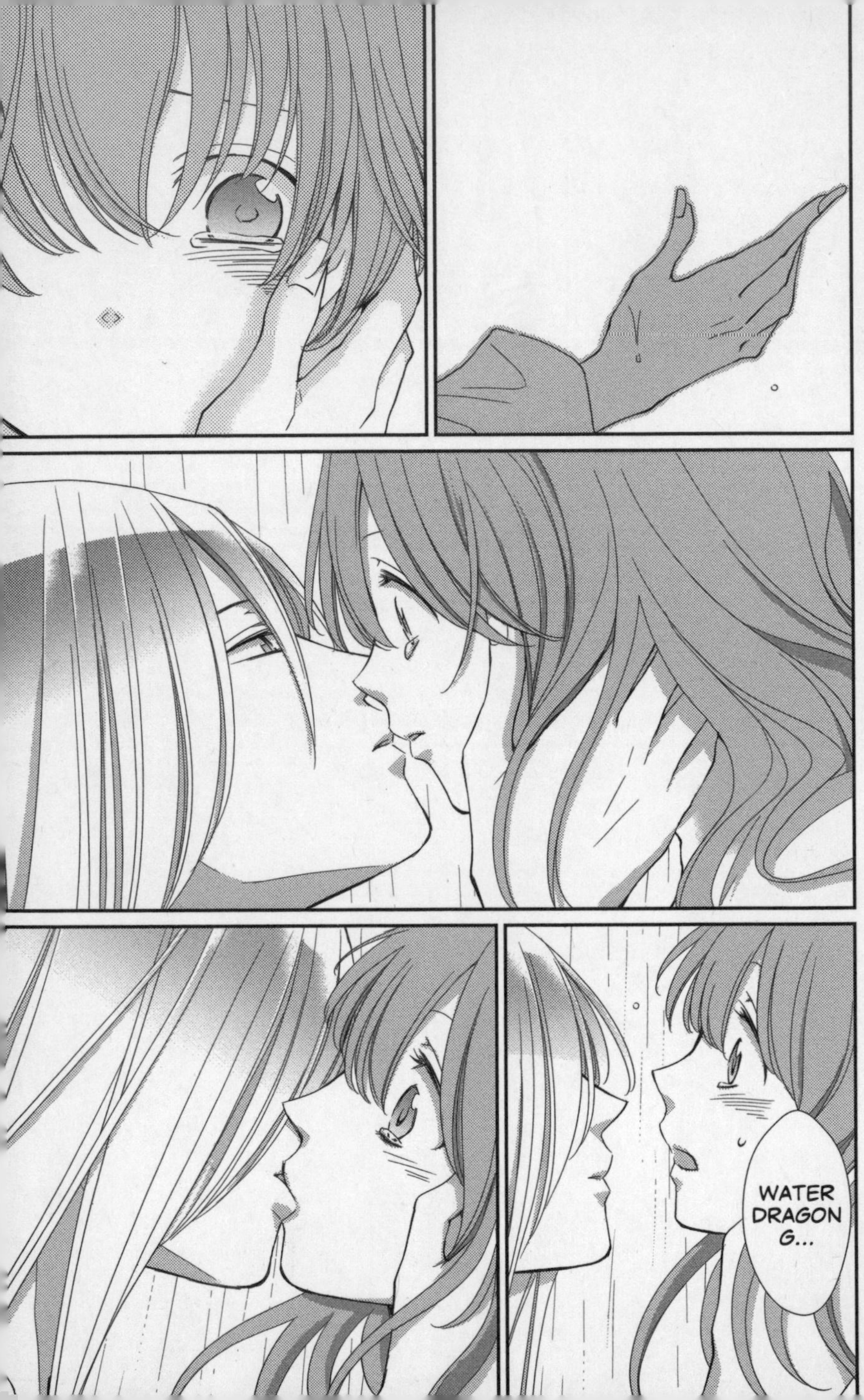
WATER DRAGON G...

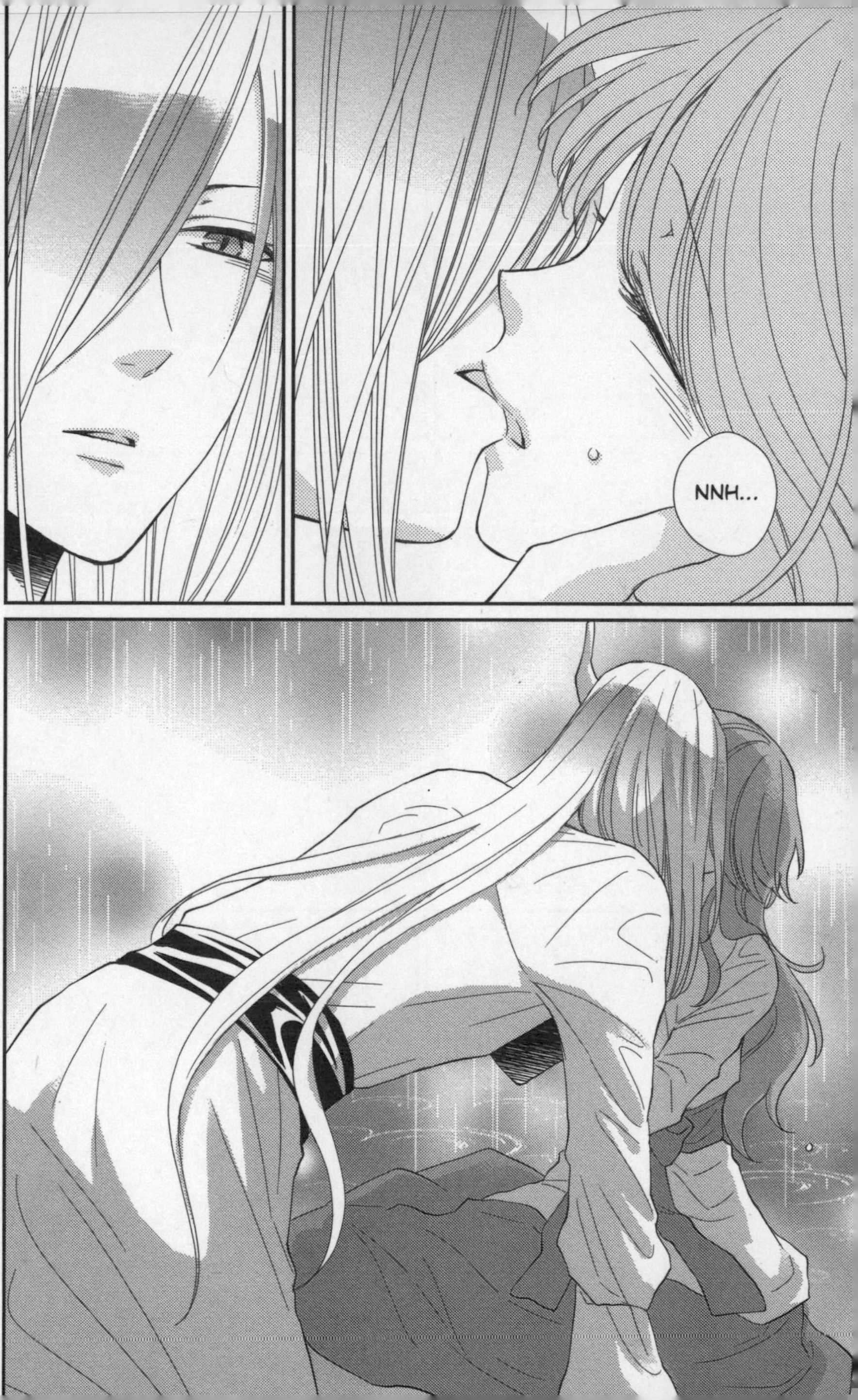
NNH...

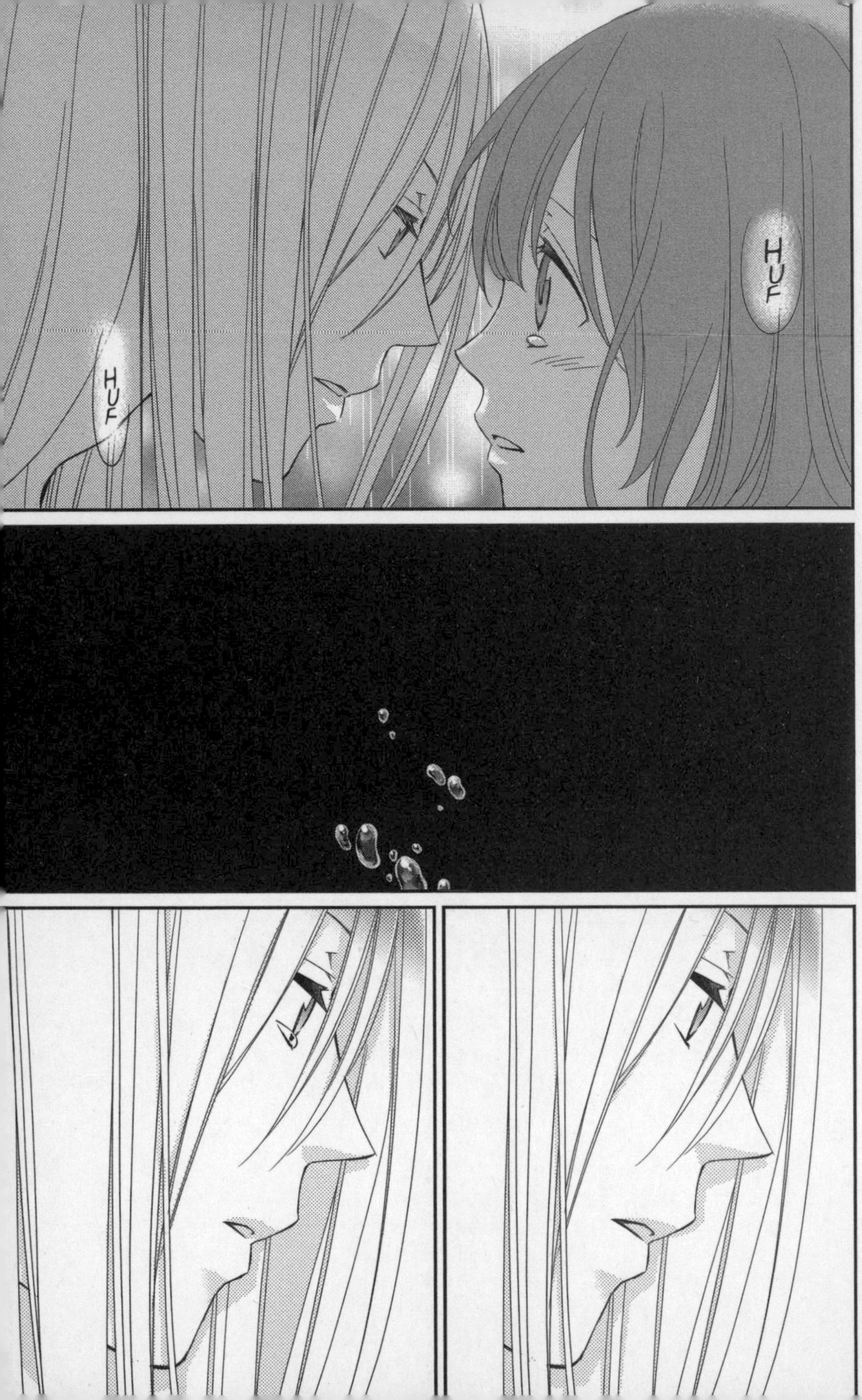
HUF
HUF

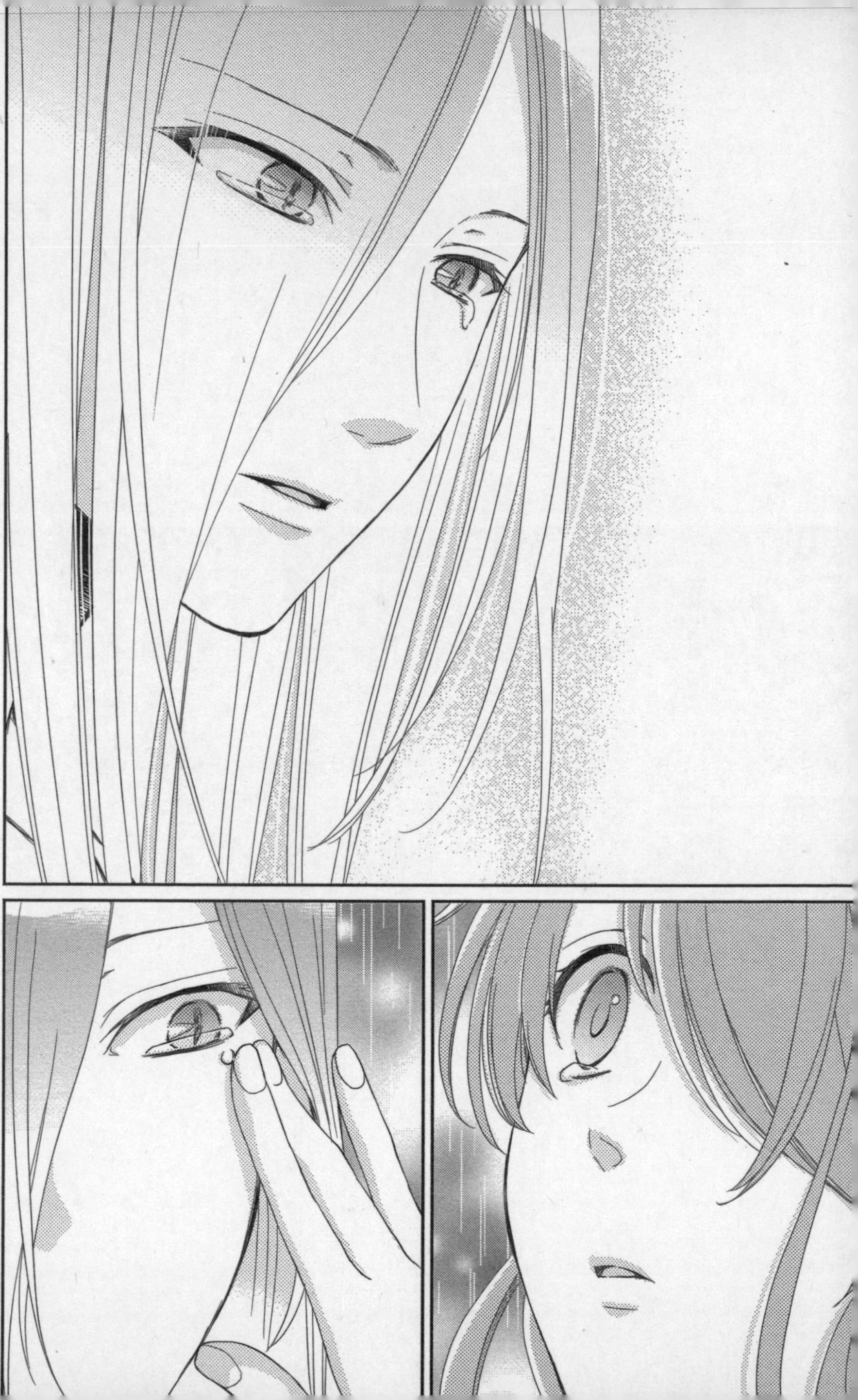

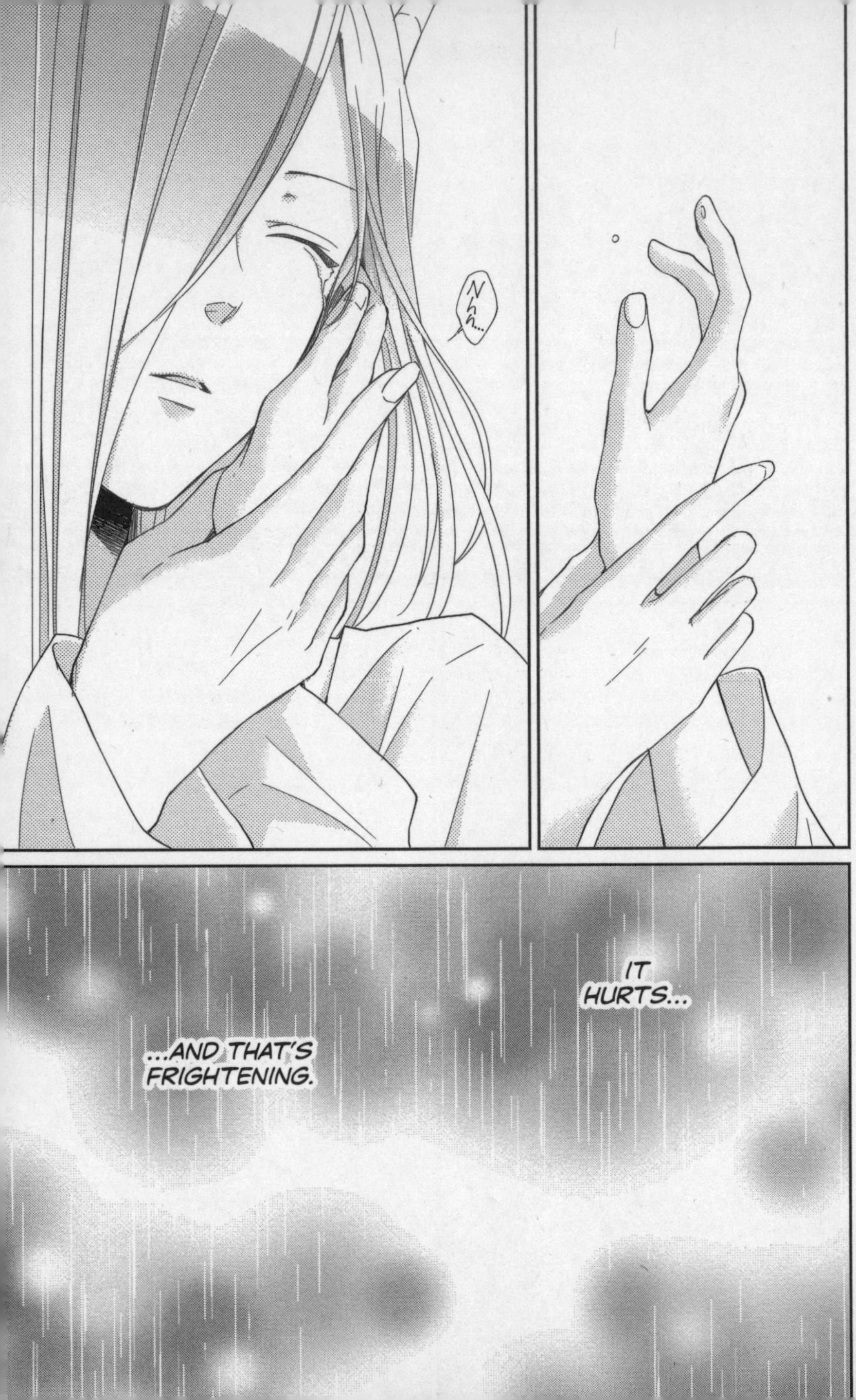
Nhh...
IT HURTS...
...AND THAT'S FRIGHTENING.

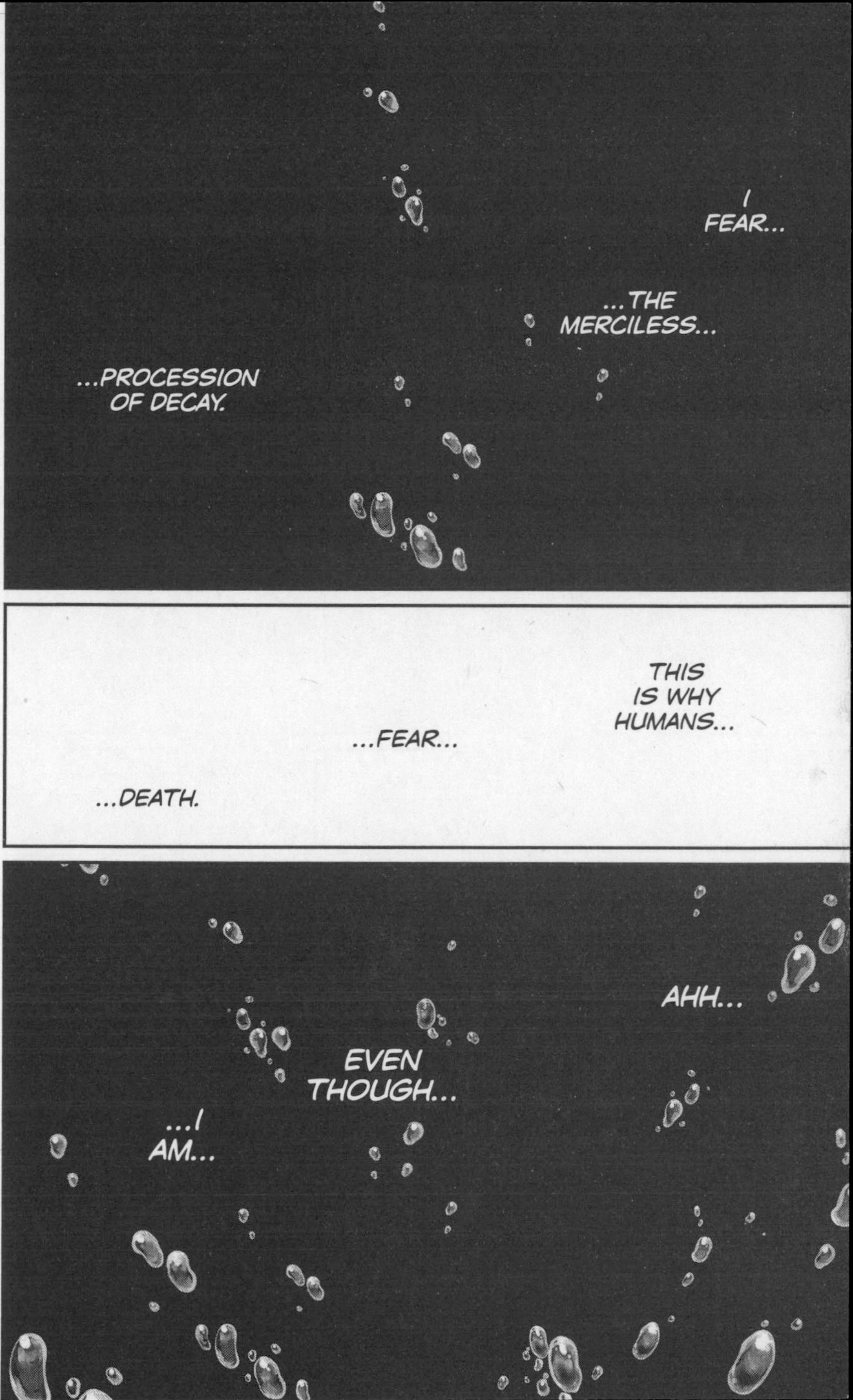
I FEAR...
...THE MERCILESS...
...PROCESSION OF DECAY.
THIS IS WHY HUMANS...
...FEAR...
...DEATH.
AHH...
EVEN THOUGH...
...I AM...

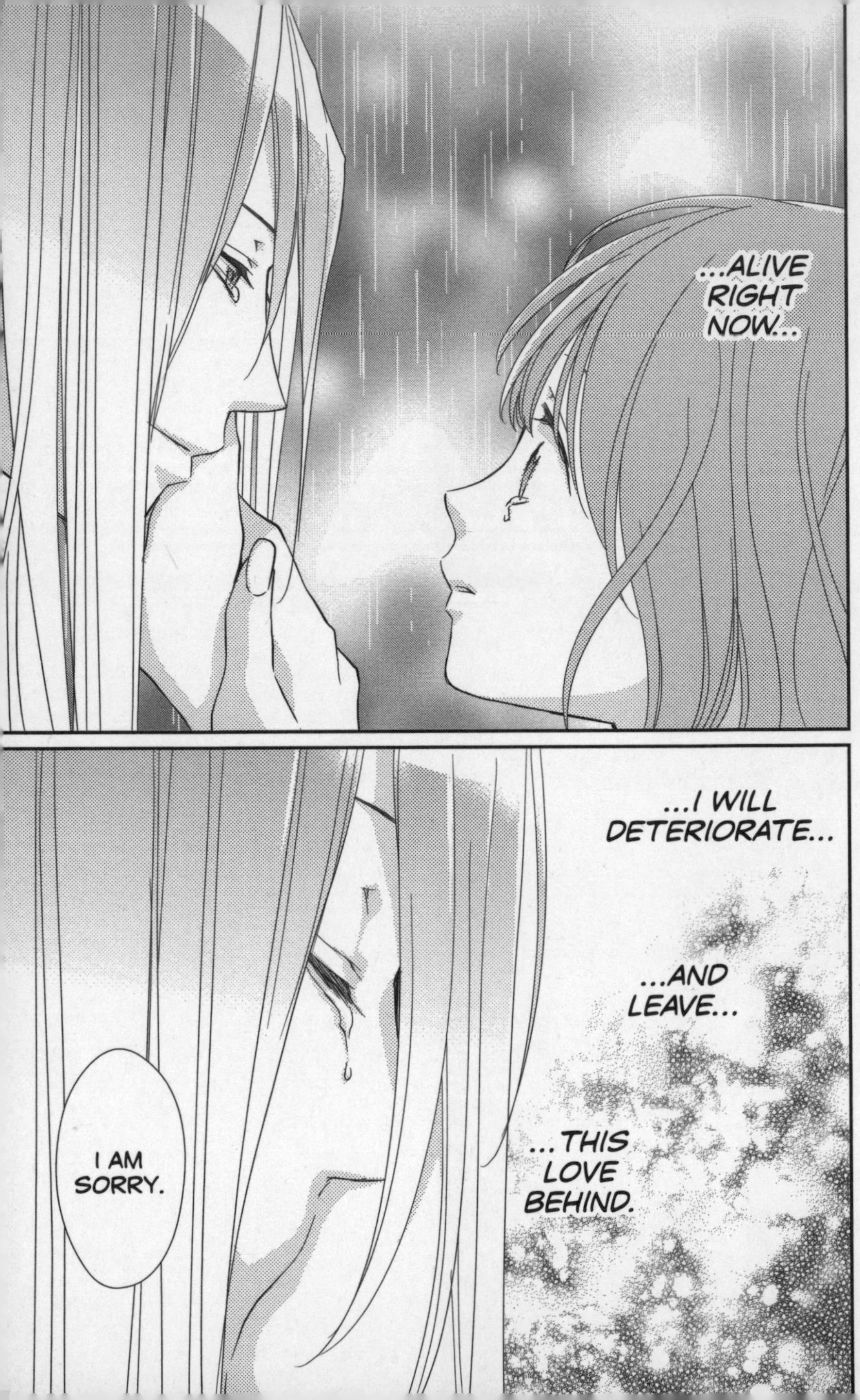
...ALIVE RIGHT NOW...
...I WILL DETERIORATE...
...AND LEAVE...
...THIS LOVE BEHIND.
I AM SORRY.

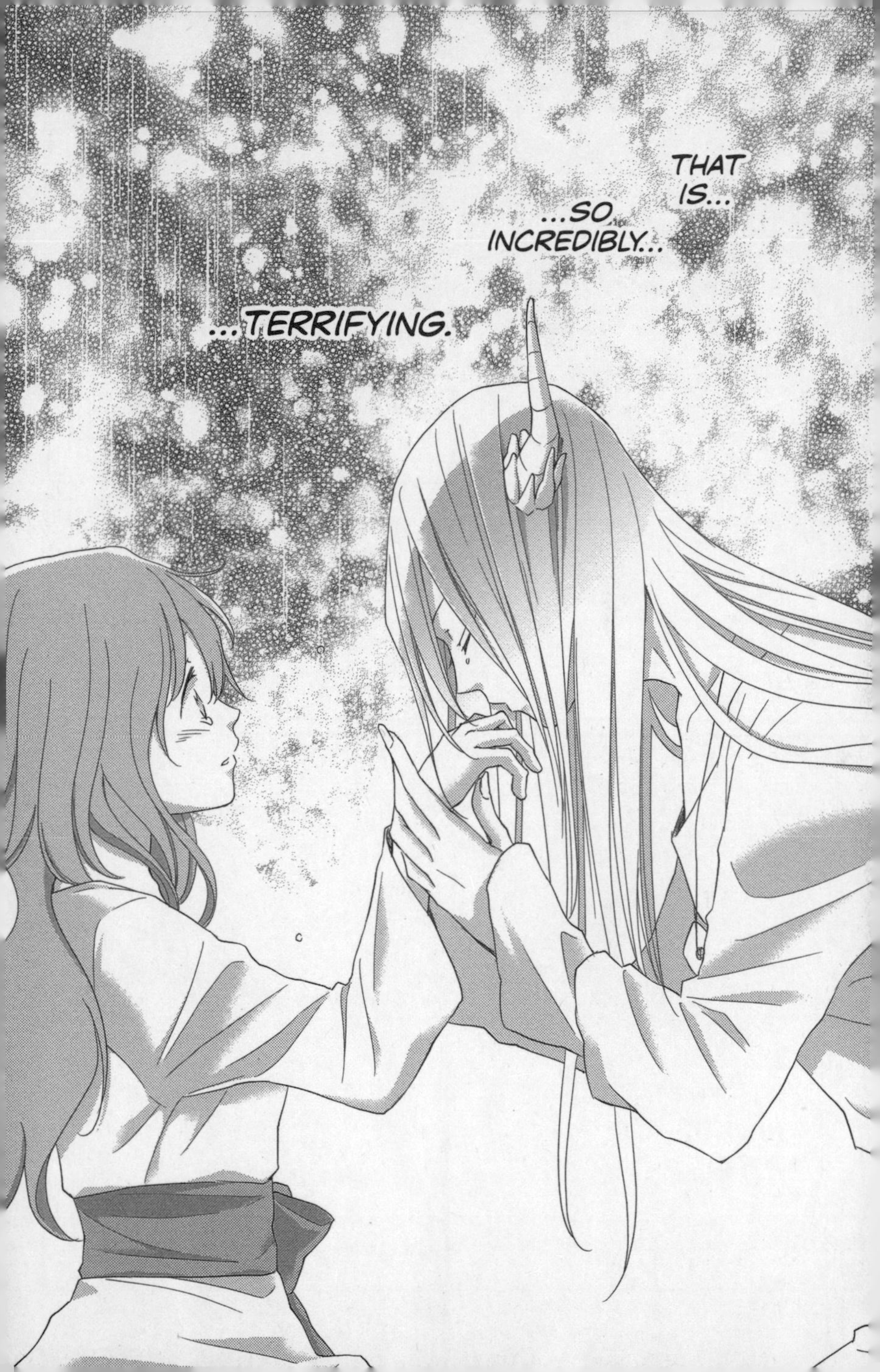
THAT IS...
...SO INCREDIBLY...
...TERRIFYING.

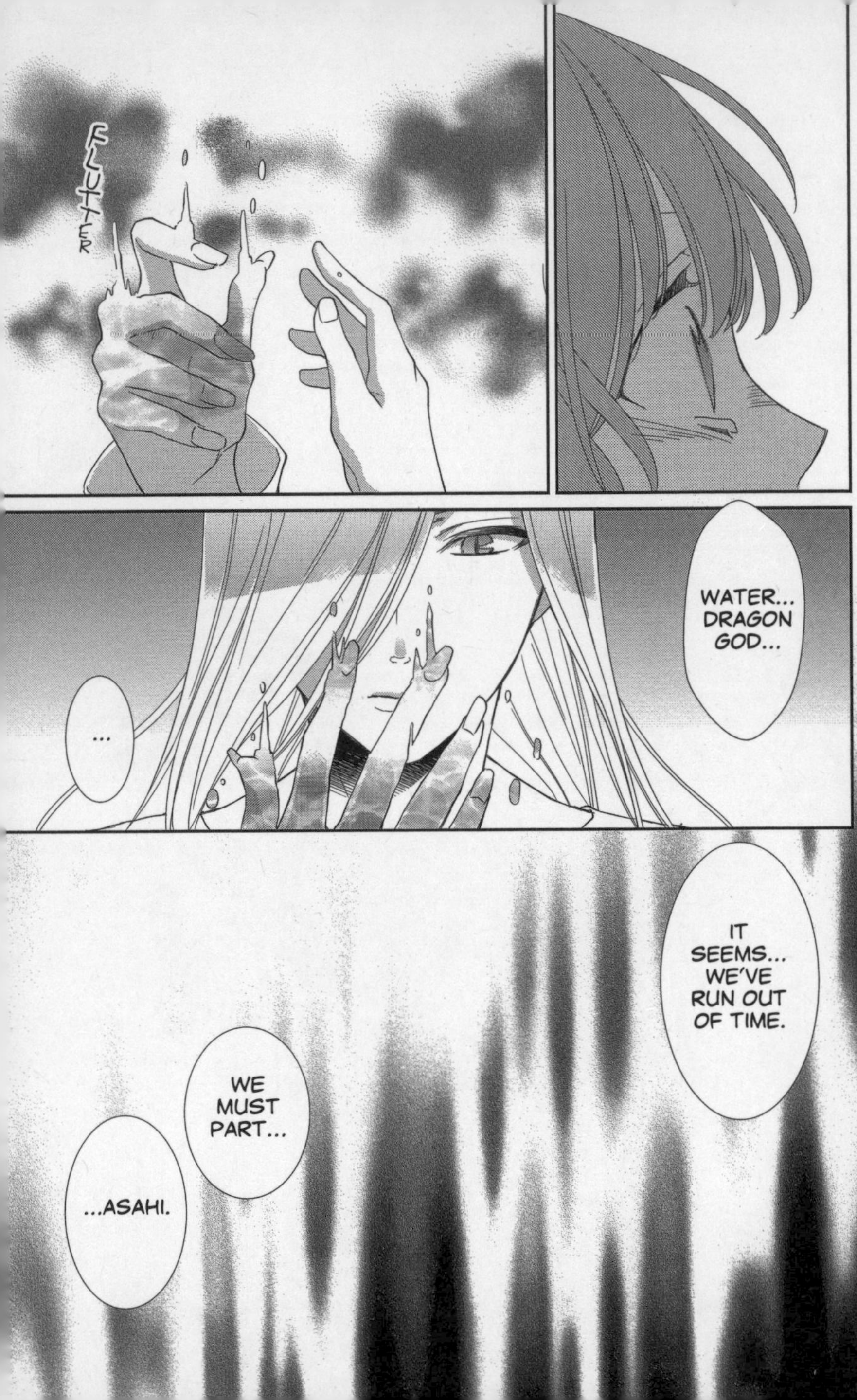
FLUTTER
WATER... DRAGON GOD...
...
IT SEEMS... WE'VE RUN OUT OF TIME.
WE MUST PART...
...ASAHI.

The Water Dragon's Bride: Conclusion

This series ended up being 11 volumes. I feel like it went by in the blink of an eye. The last chapter has some flashbacks to some scenes I wrote earlier, and there are some reimaginings as well, so please go ahead and read the series over from the beginning. That way you can draw out the reverberation of the finale a little bit longer.

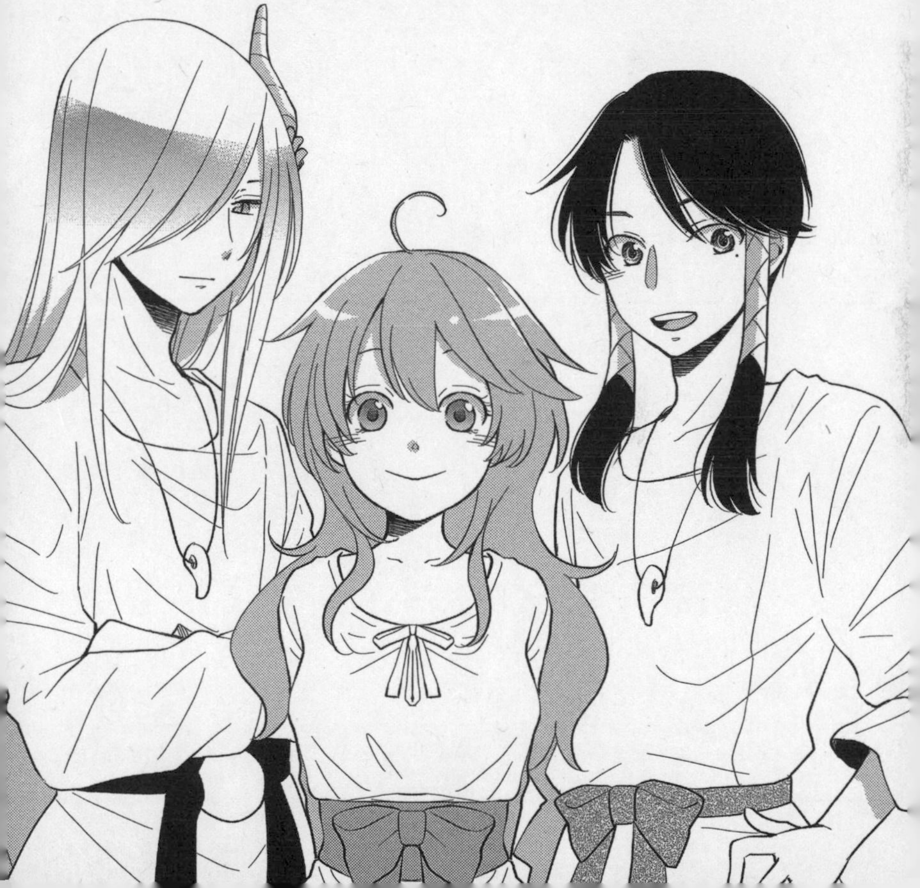

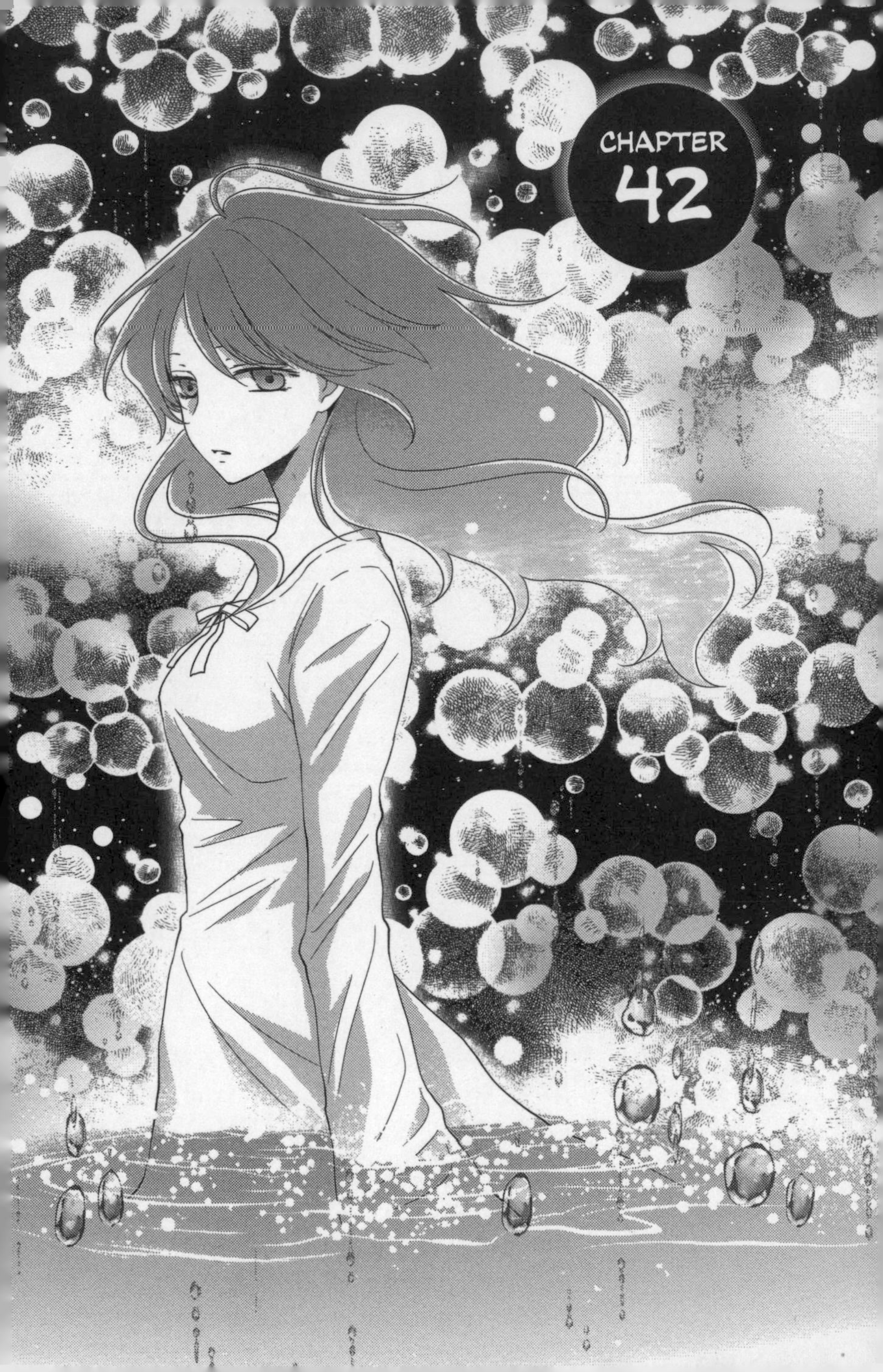
CHAPTER
42

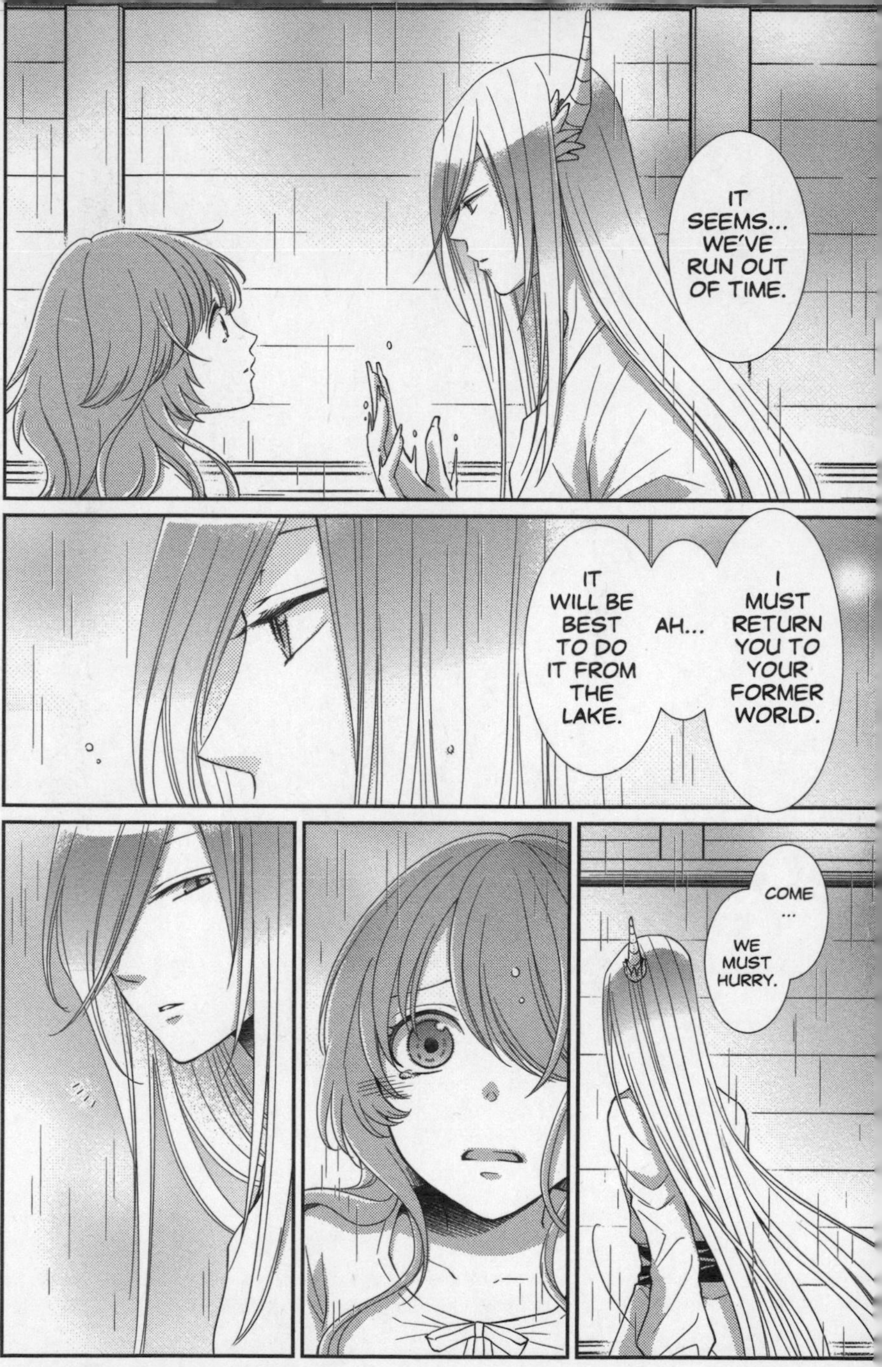
IT SEEMS... WE'VE RUN OUT OF TIME.
I MUST RETURN YOU TO YOUR FORMER WORLD.
AH...
IT WILL BE BEST TO DO IT FROM THE LAKE.
COME ... WE MUST HURRY.

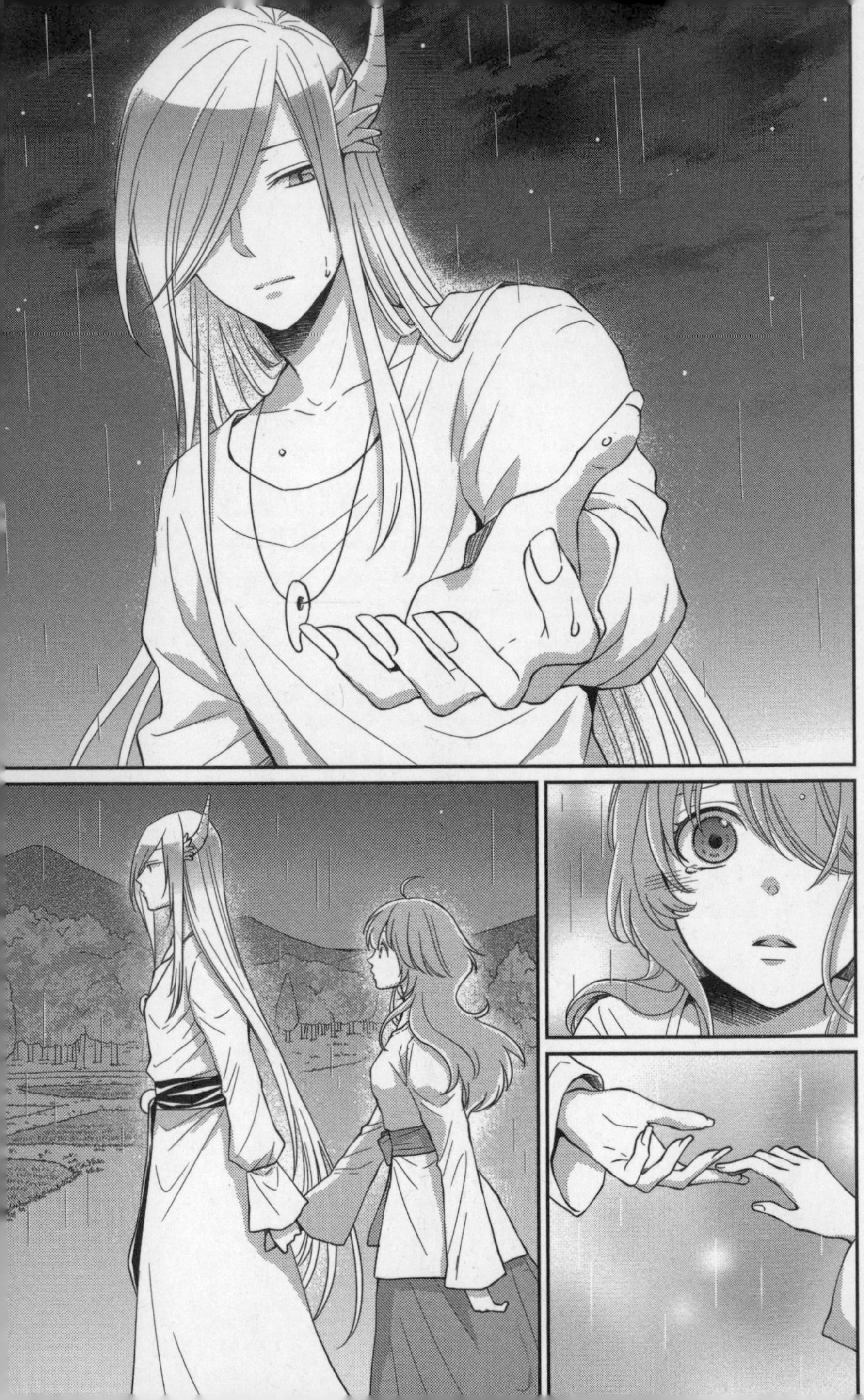

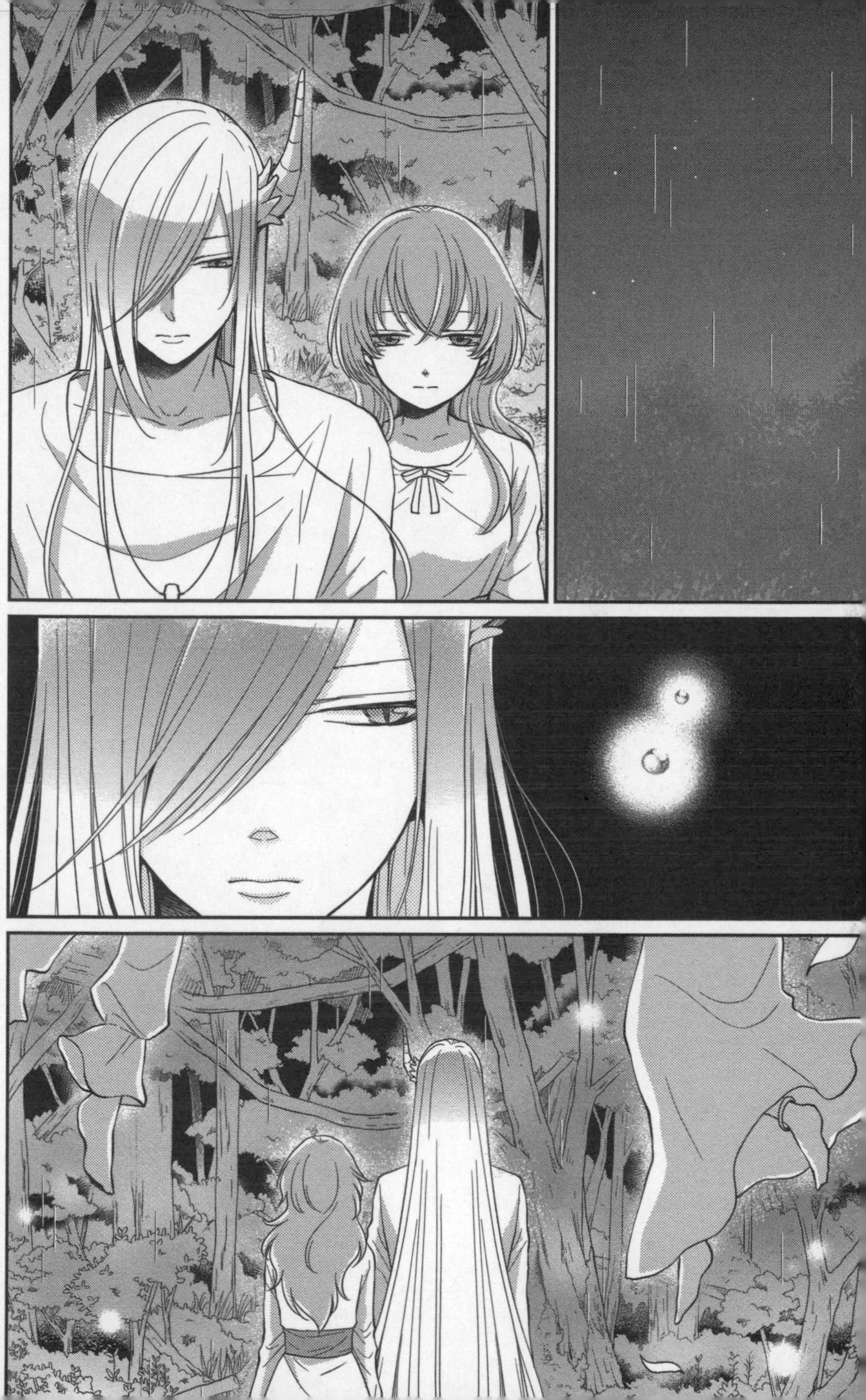

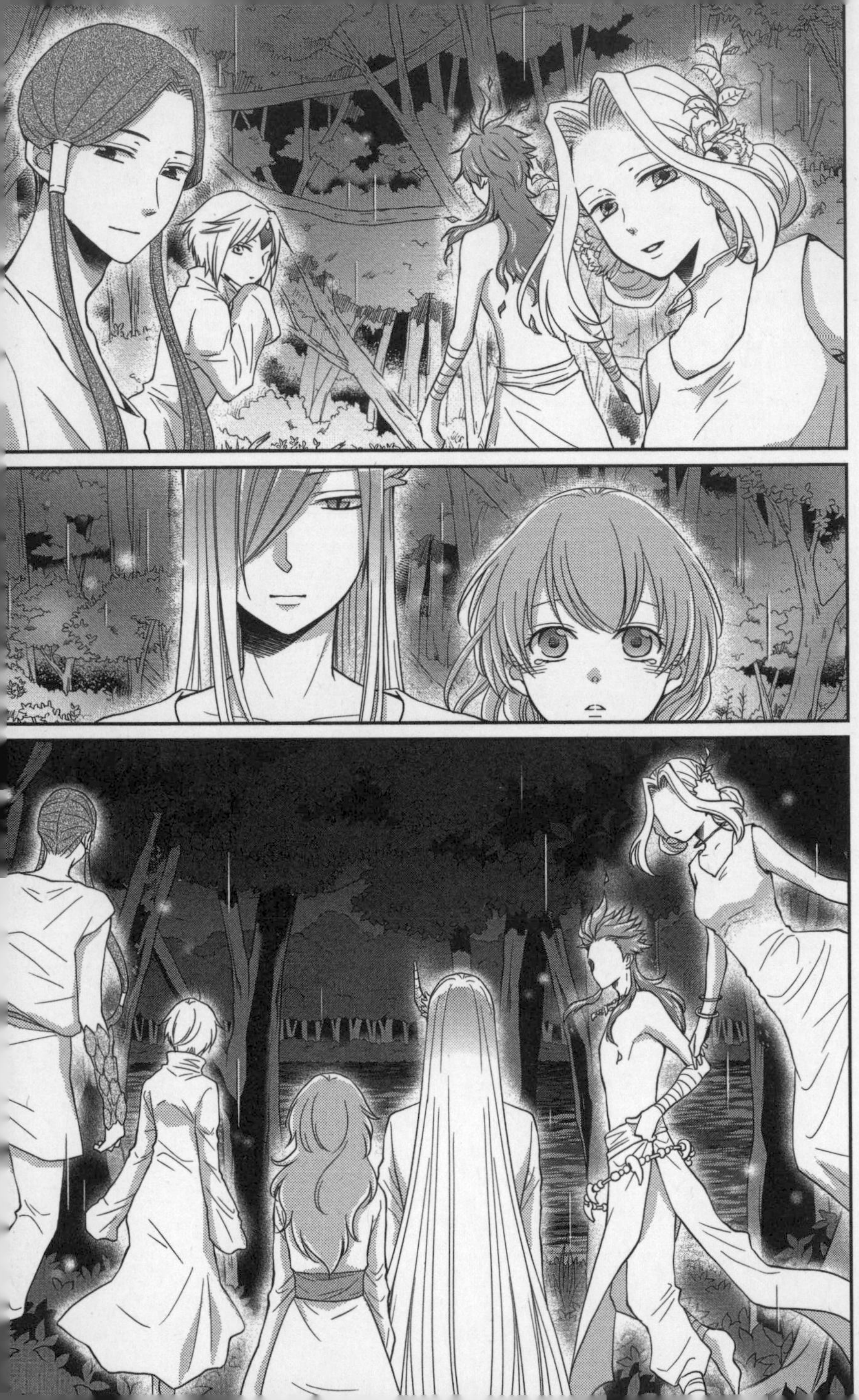

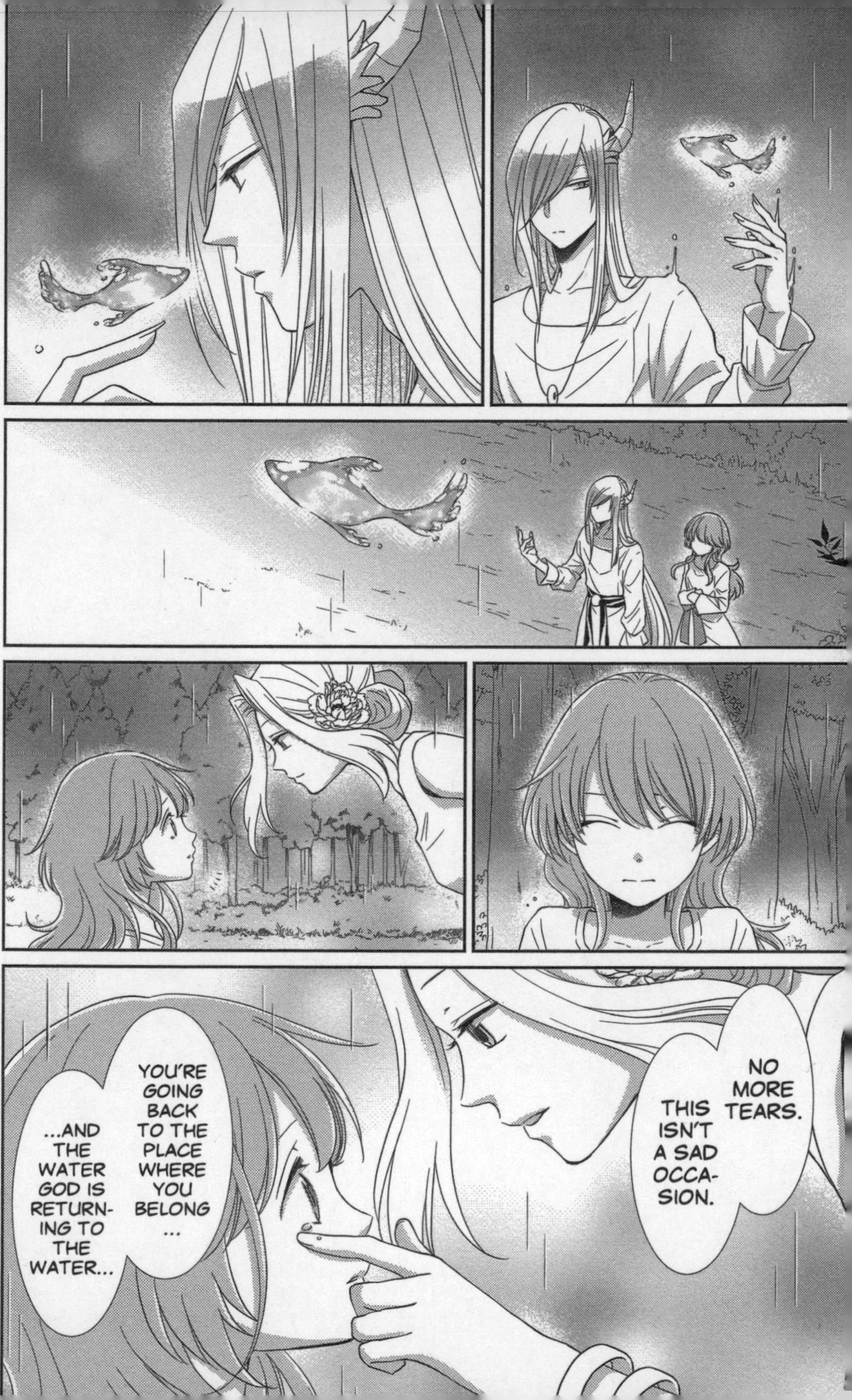
NO MORE TEARS.
THIS ISN'T A SAD OCCASION.
YOU'RE GOING BACK TO THE PLACE WHERE YOU BELONG ...
...AND THE WATER GOD IS RETURNING TO THE WATER...

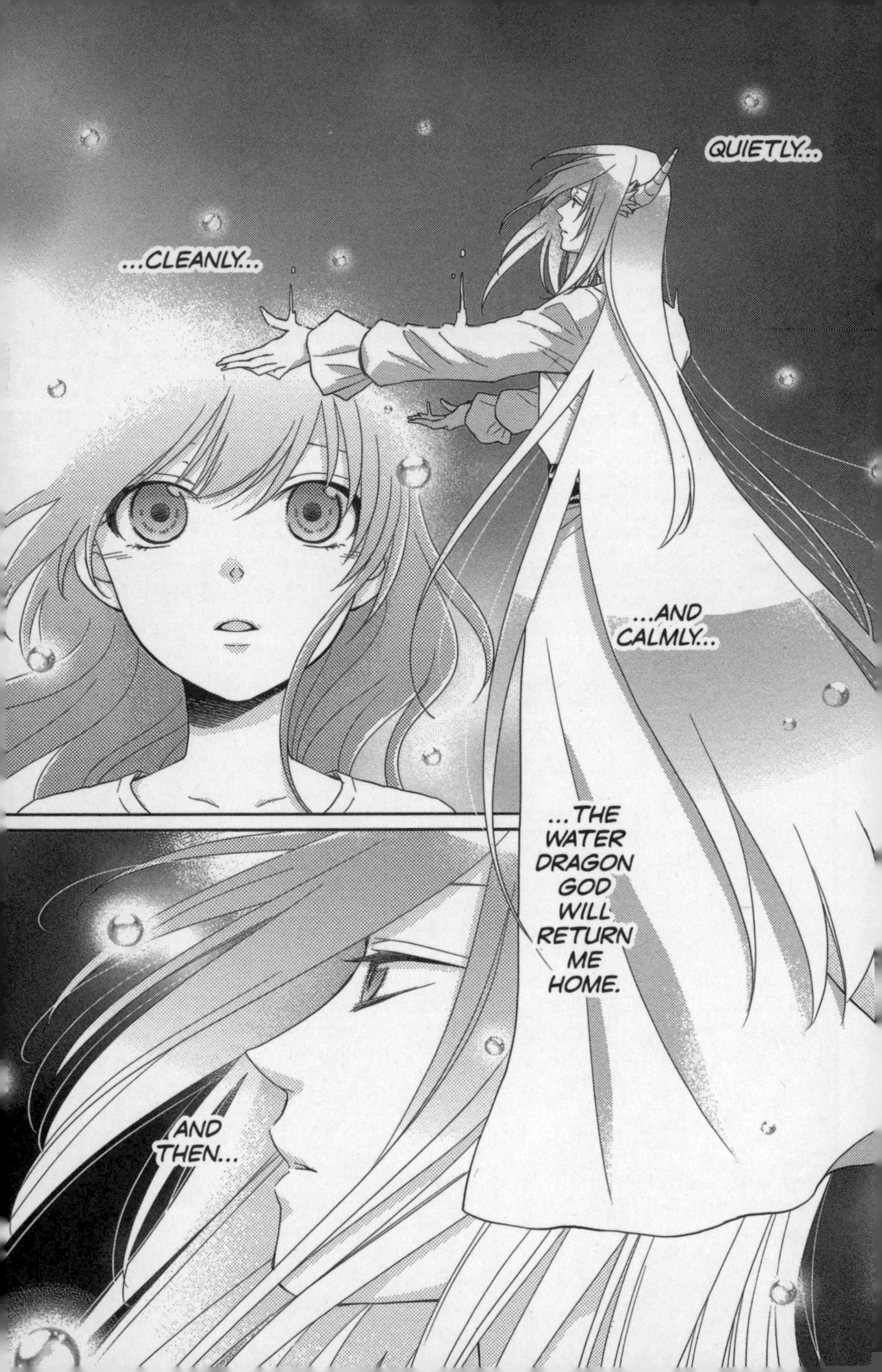
QUIETLY...
...CLEANLY...
...AND CALMLY...
...THE WATER DRAGON GOD WILL RETURN ME HOME.
AND THEN...

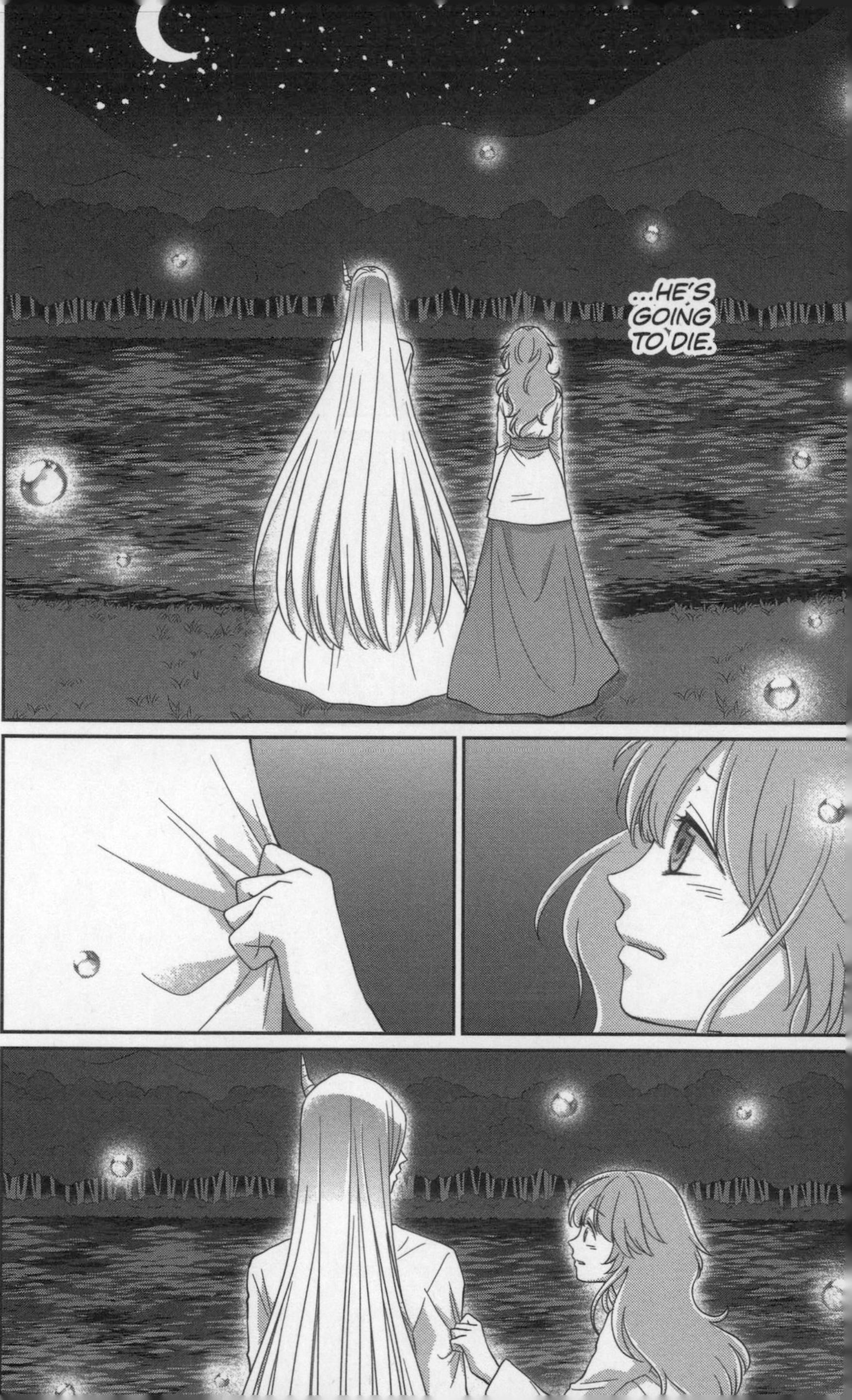
...HE'S GOING TO DIE.

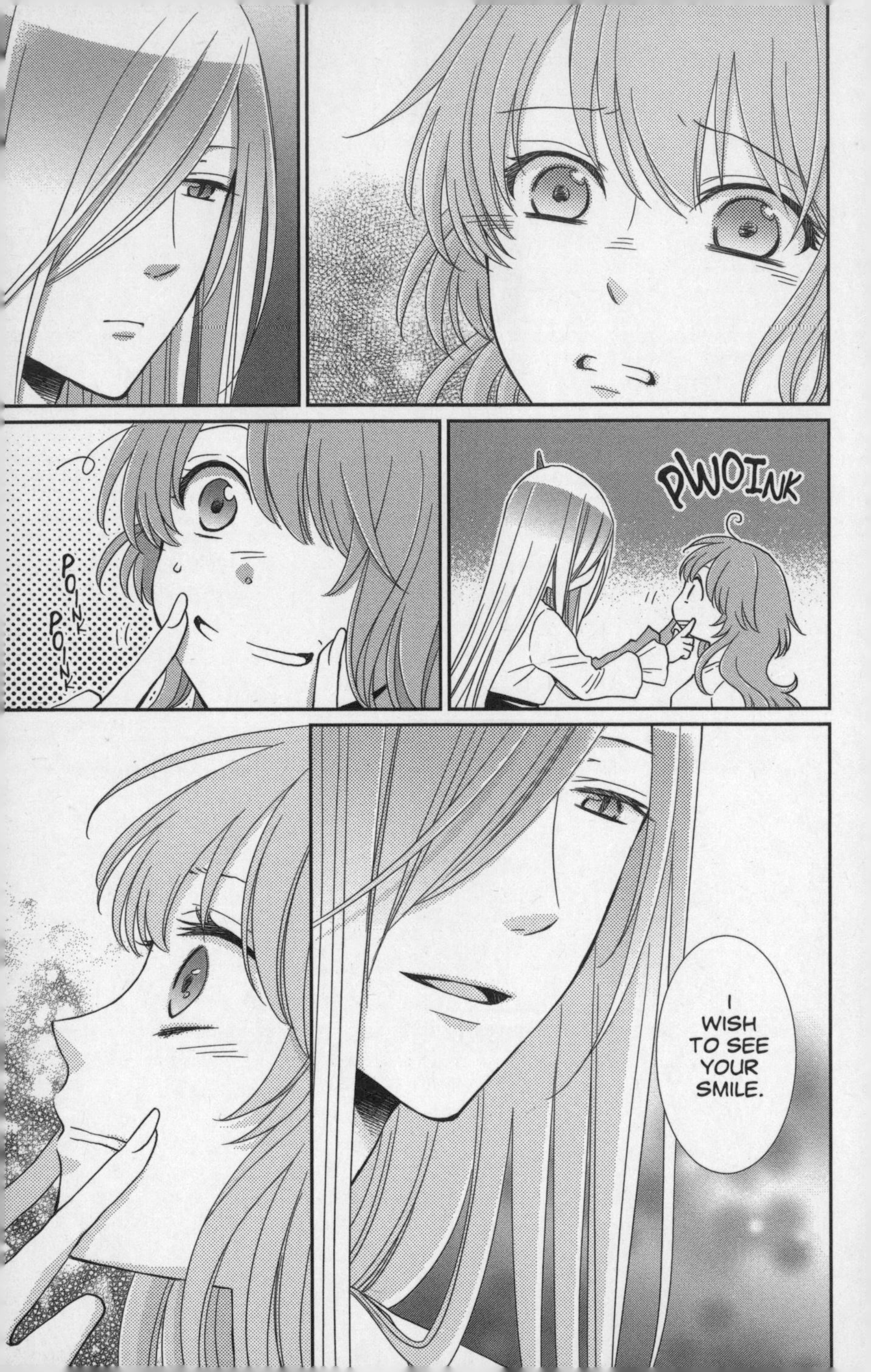
PWOINK
POINK POINK
I WISH TO SEE YOUR SMILE.

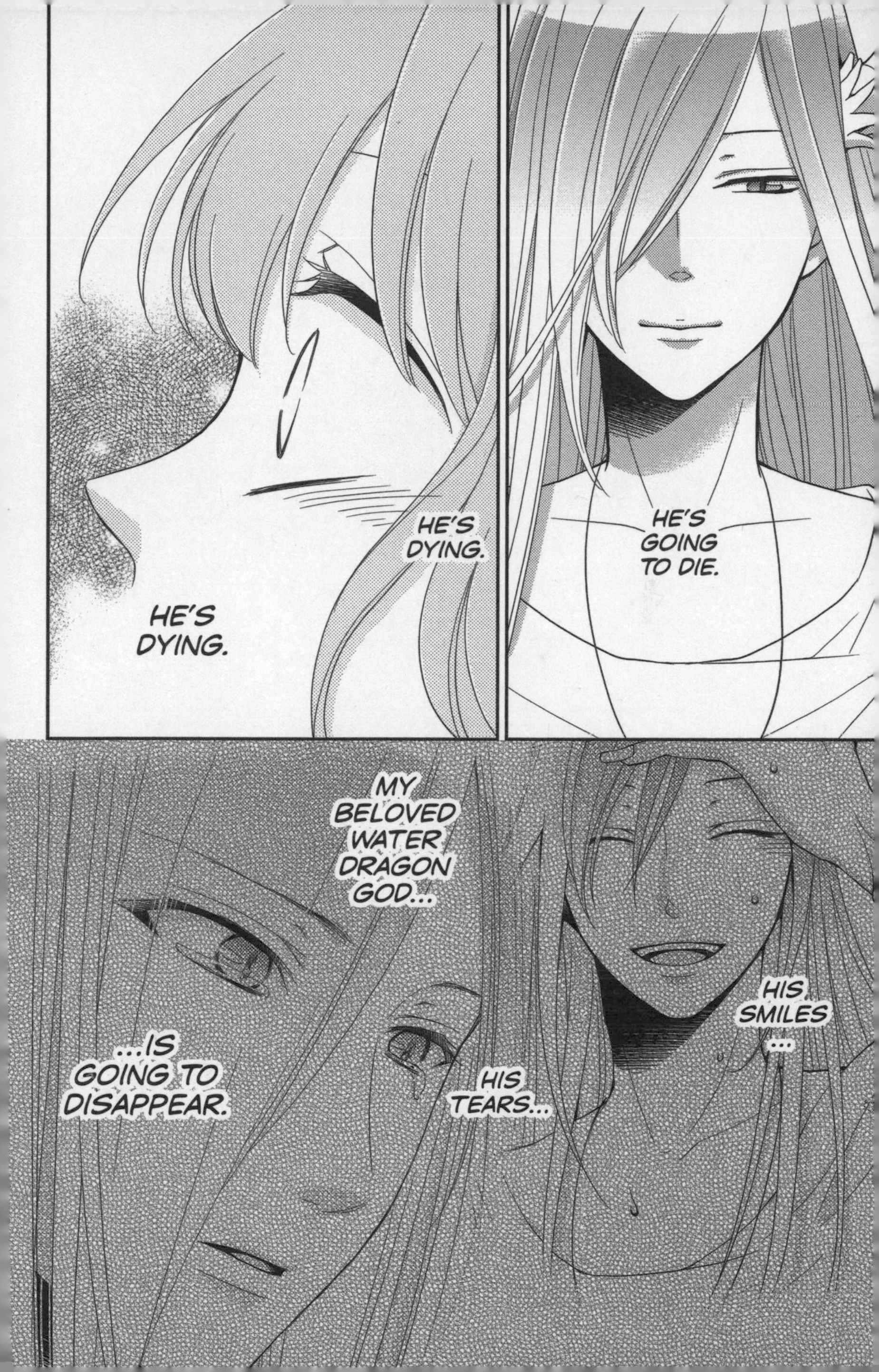
HE'S GOING TO DIE.
HE'S DYING.
HE'S DYING.
MY BELOVED WATER DRAGON GOD...
HIS SMILES...
HIS TEARS...
...IS GOING TO DISAPPEAR.

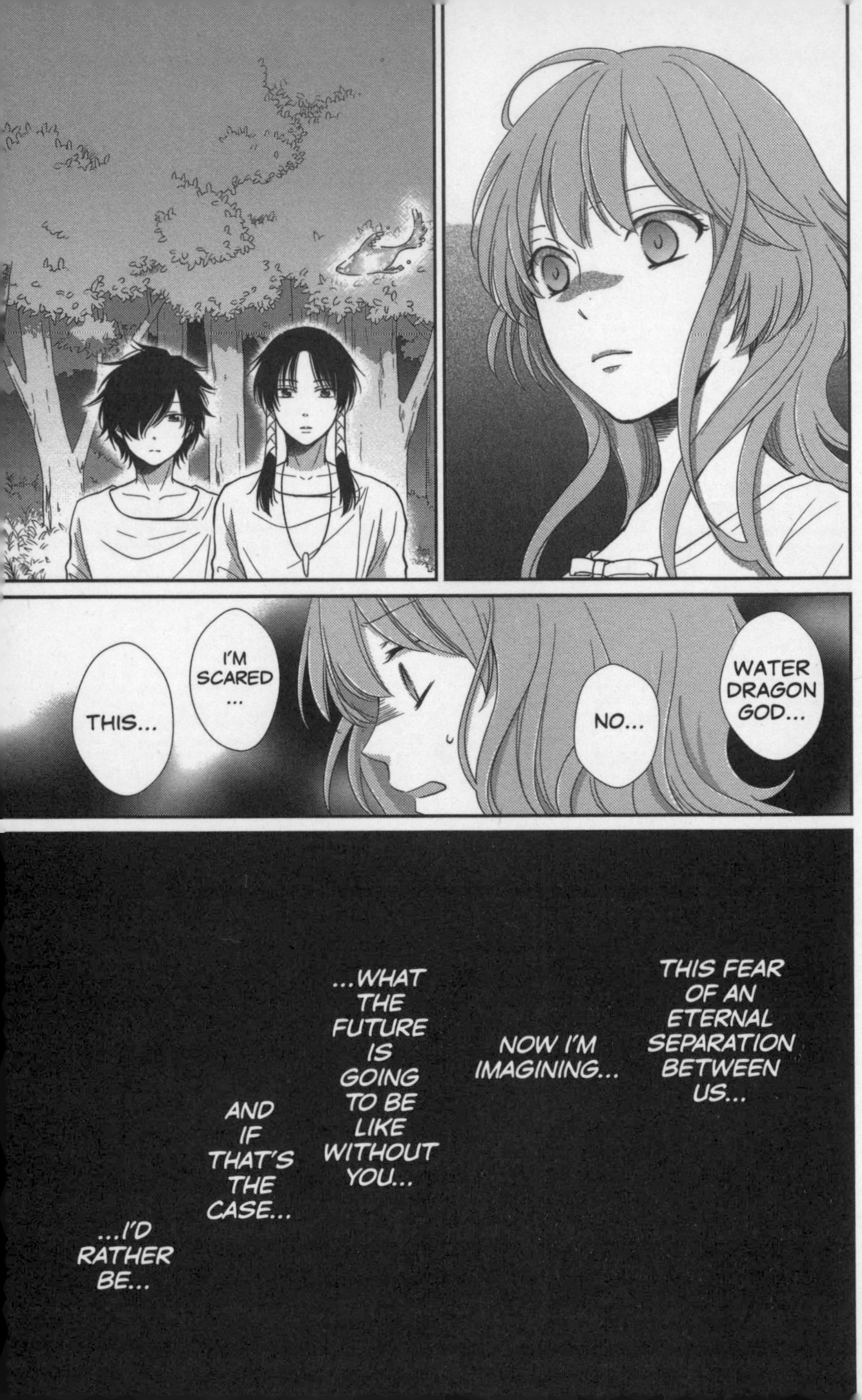
WATER DRAGON GOD...
NO...
I'M SCARED...
THIS...
THIS FEAR OF AN ETERNAL SEPARATION BETWEEN US...
NOW I'M IMAGINING...
...WHAT THE FUTURE IS GOING TO BE LIKE WITHOUT YOU...
AND IF THAT'S THE CASE...
...I'D RATHER BE...

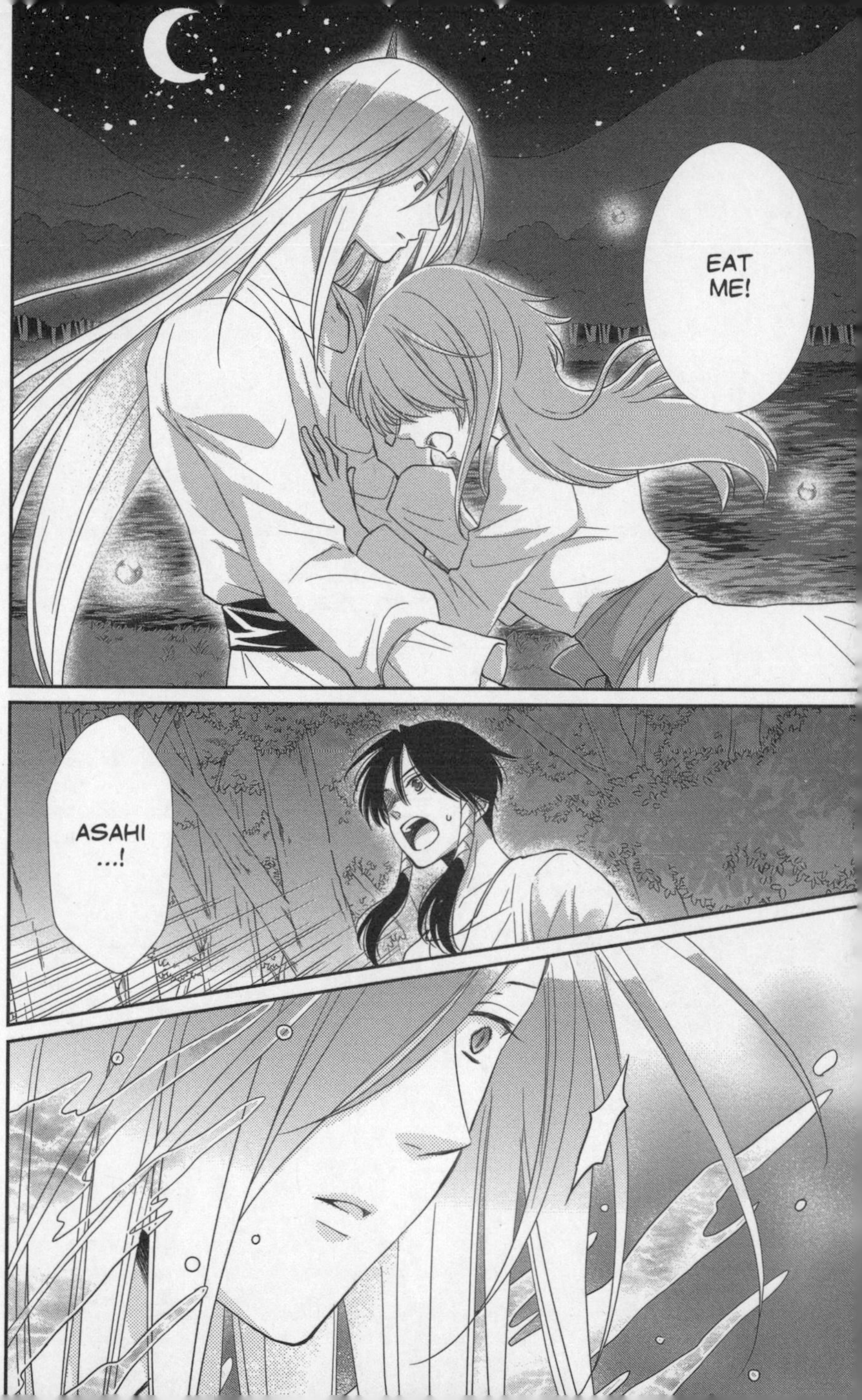
EAT ME!
ASAHI ...!

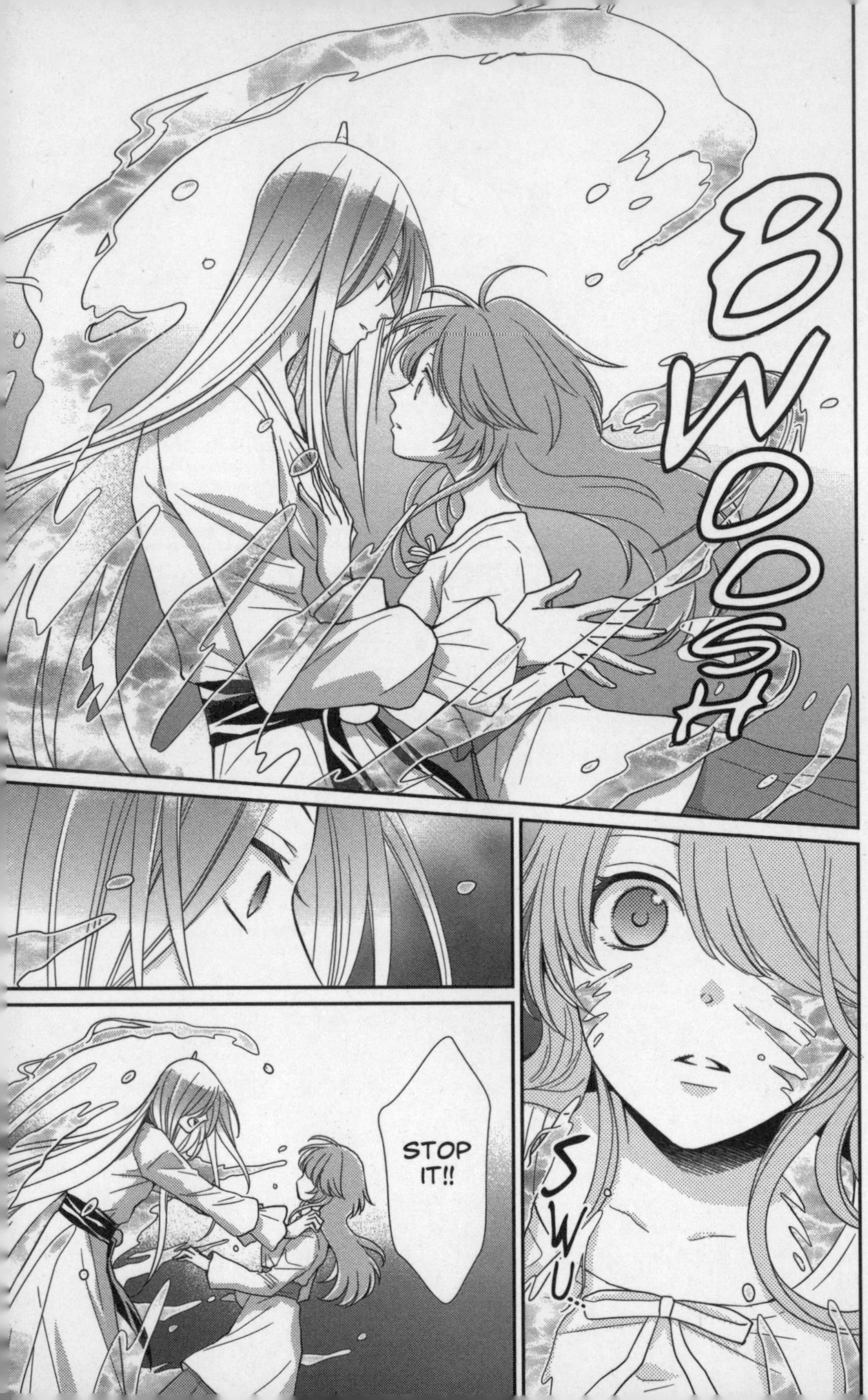
BWOOSH
SWU...
STOP IT!!

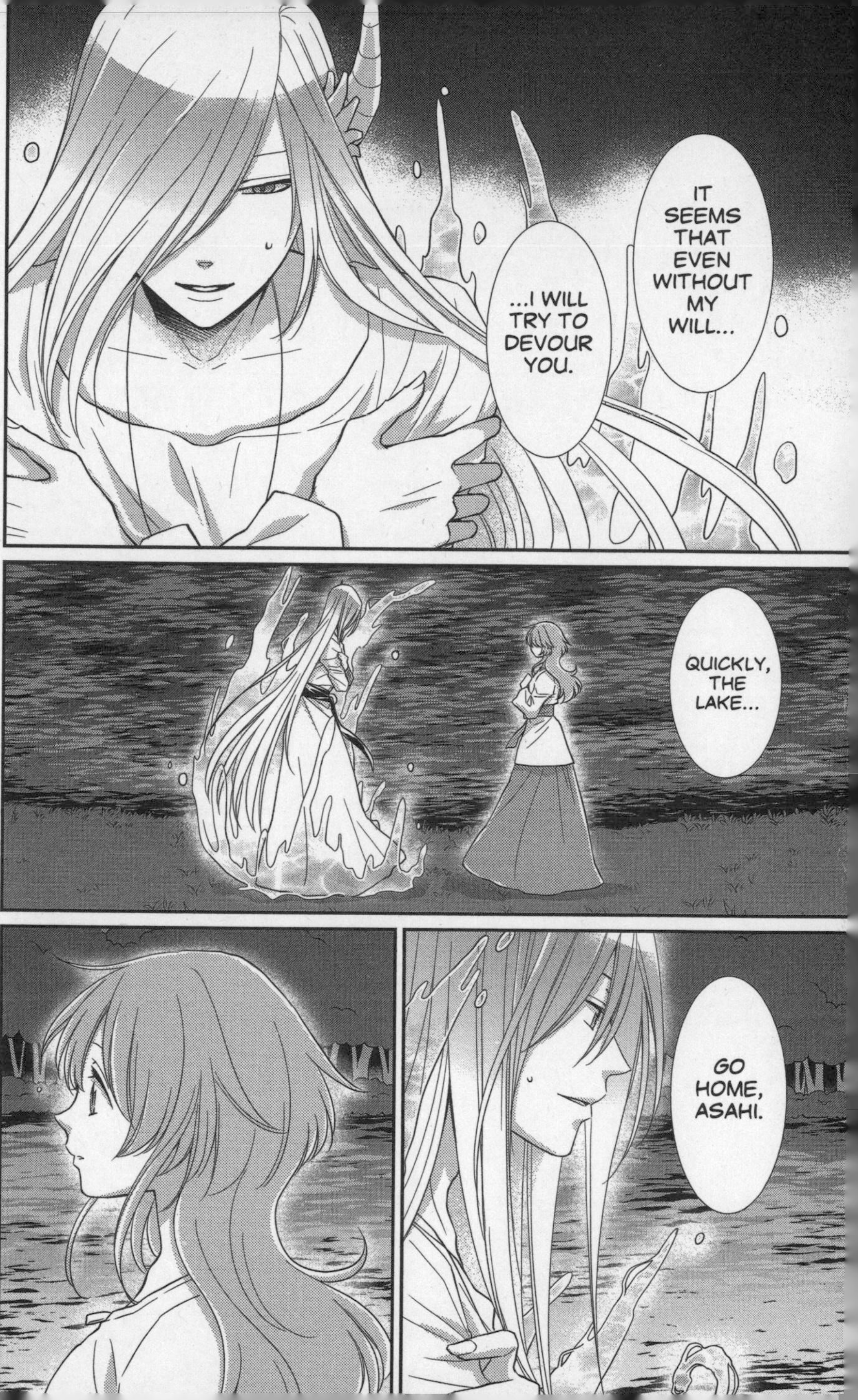
IT SEEMS THAT EVEN WITHOUT MY WILL...
...I WILL TRY TO DEVOUR YOU.
QUICKLY, THE LAKE...
GO HOME, ASAHI.

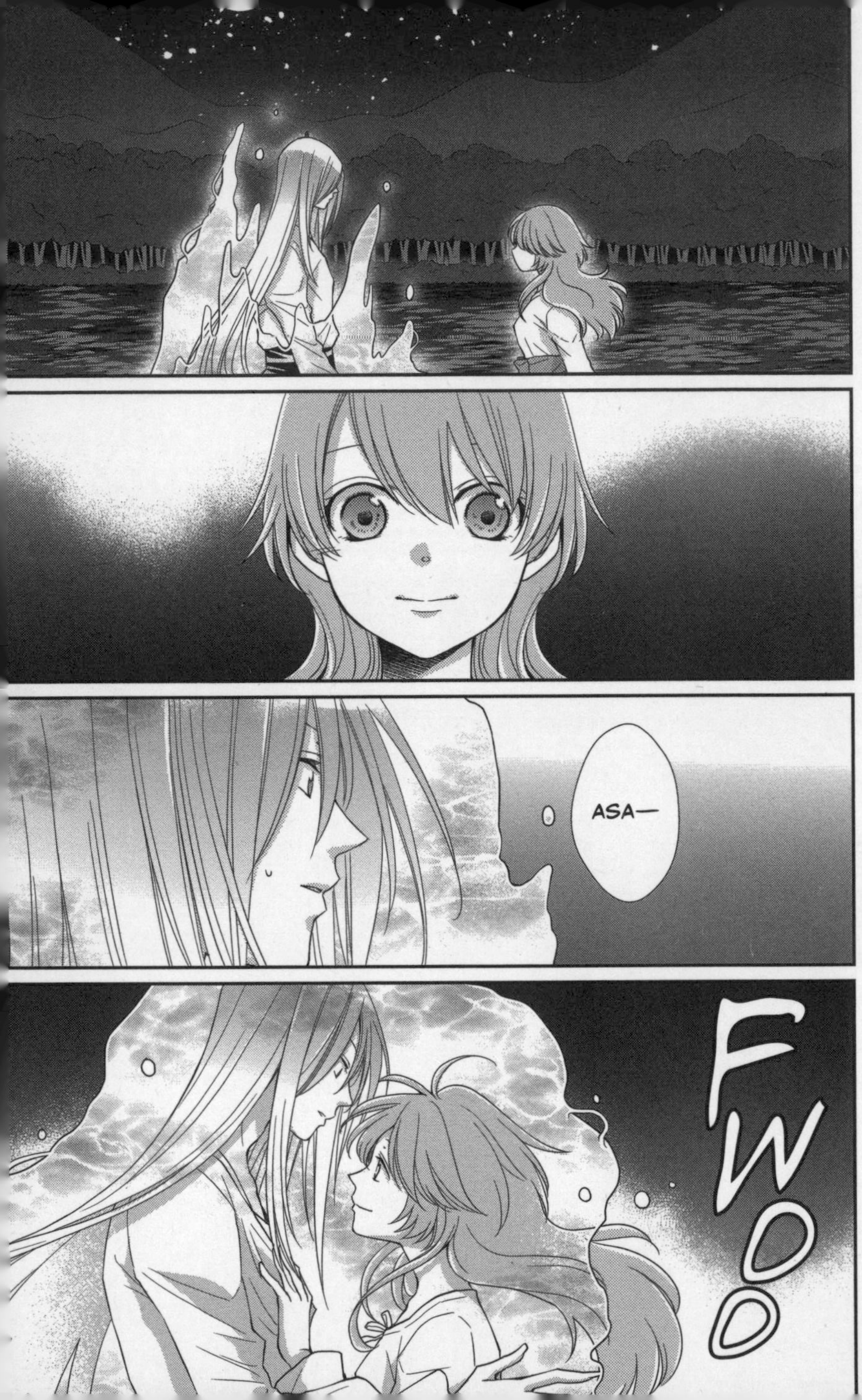
ASA—
FWOO

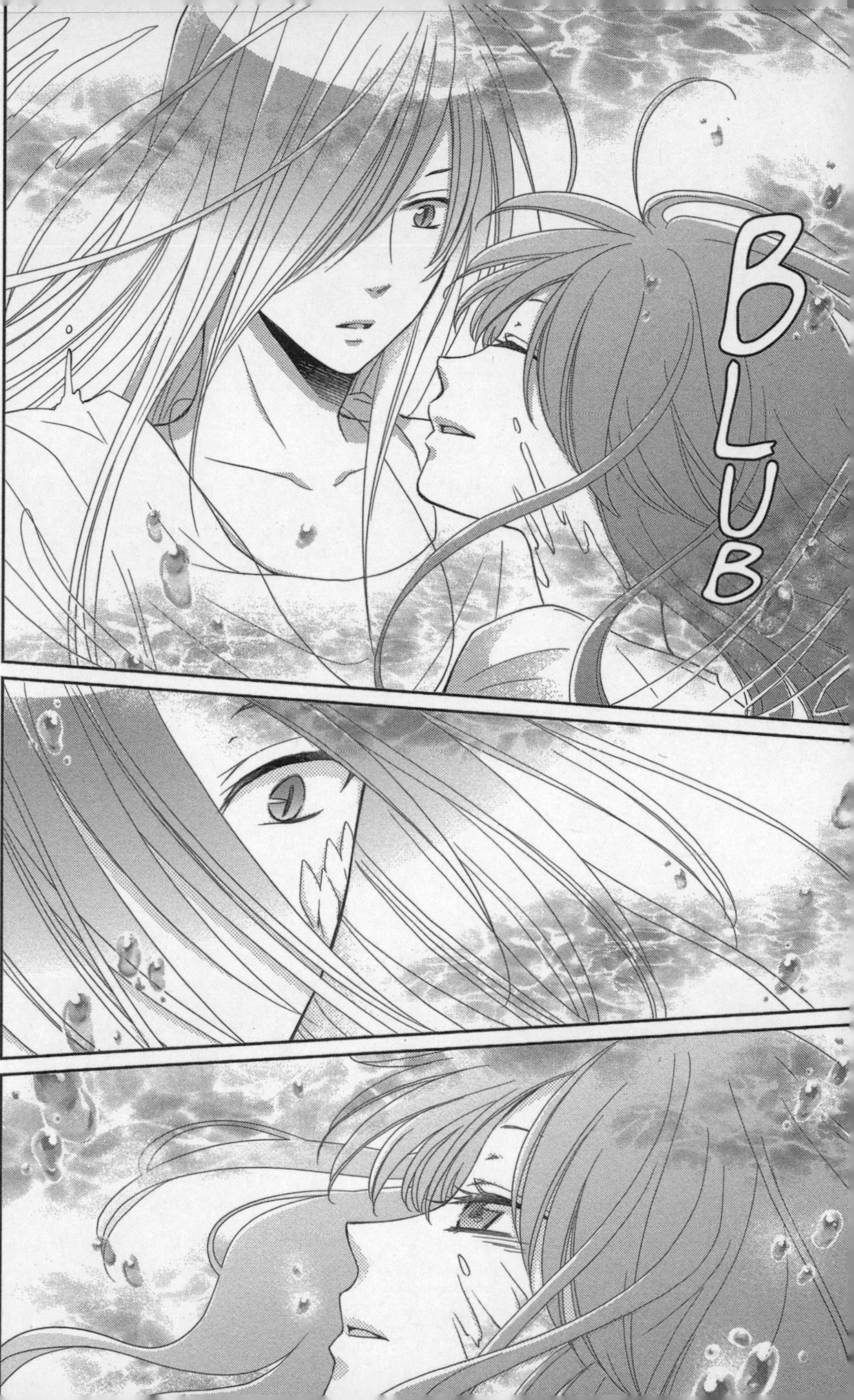
BLUB

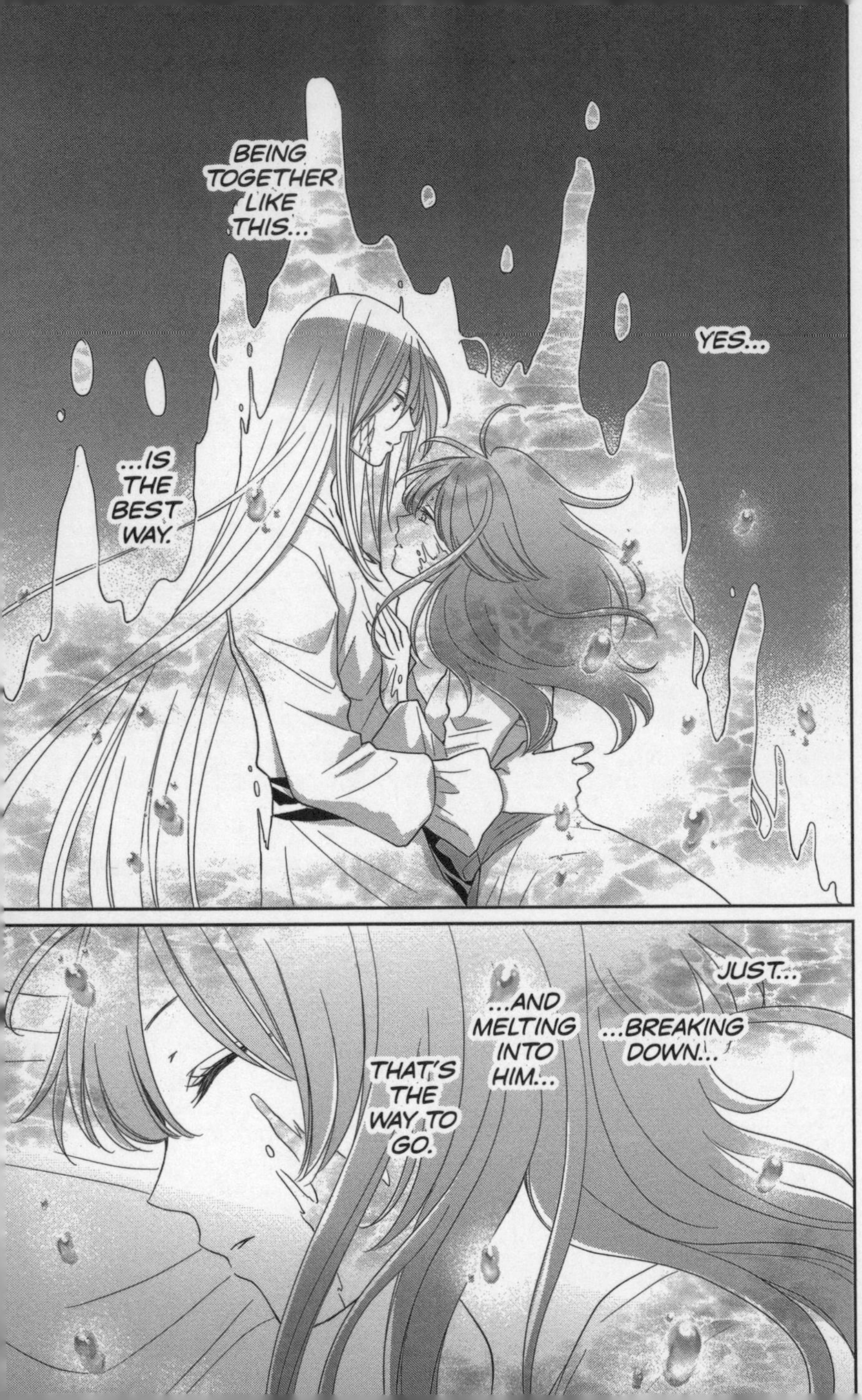
BEING TOGETHER LIKE THIS...
...IS THE BEST WAY.
YES...
JUST...
...BREAKING DOWN...
...AND MELTING INTO HIM...
THAT'S THE WAY TO GO.

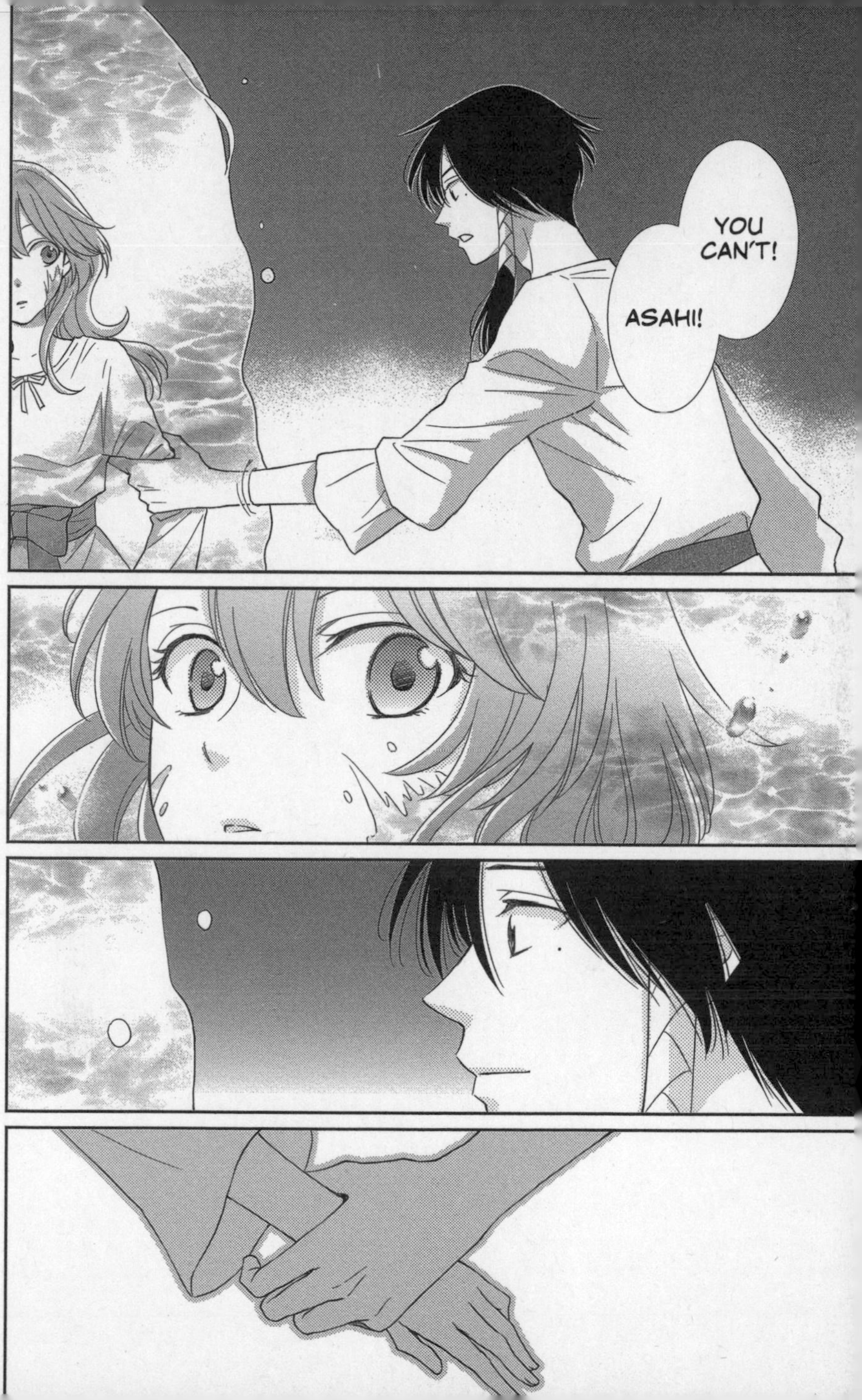
YOU CAN'T!
ASAHI!

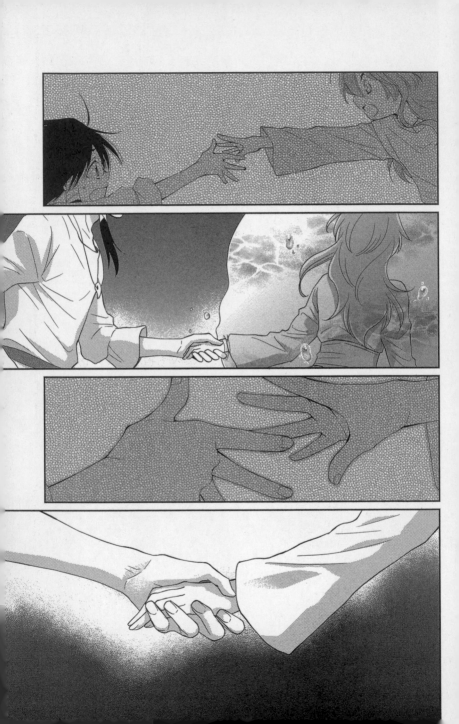

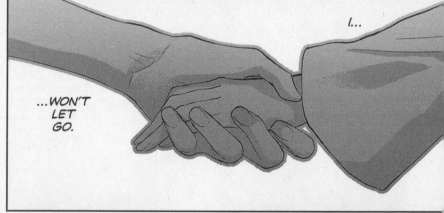

I...

...WON'T
LET
GO.

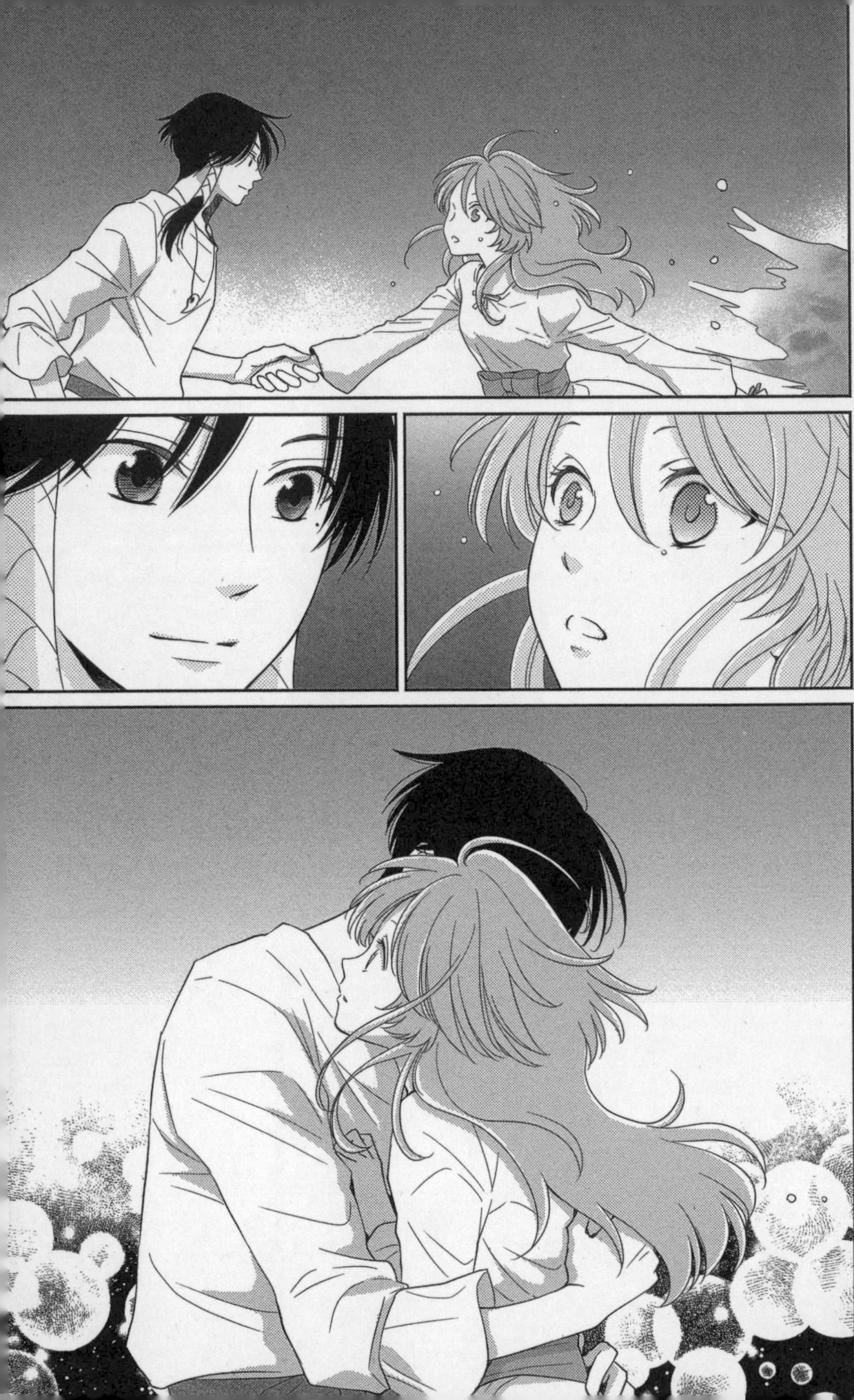

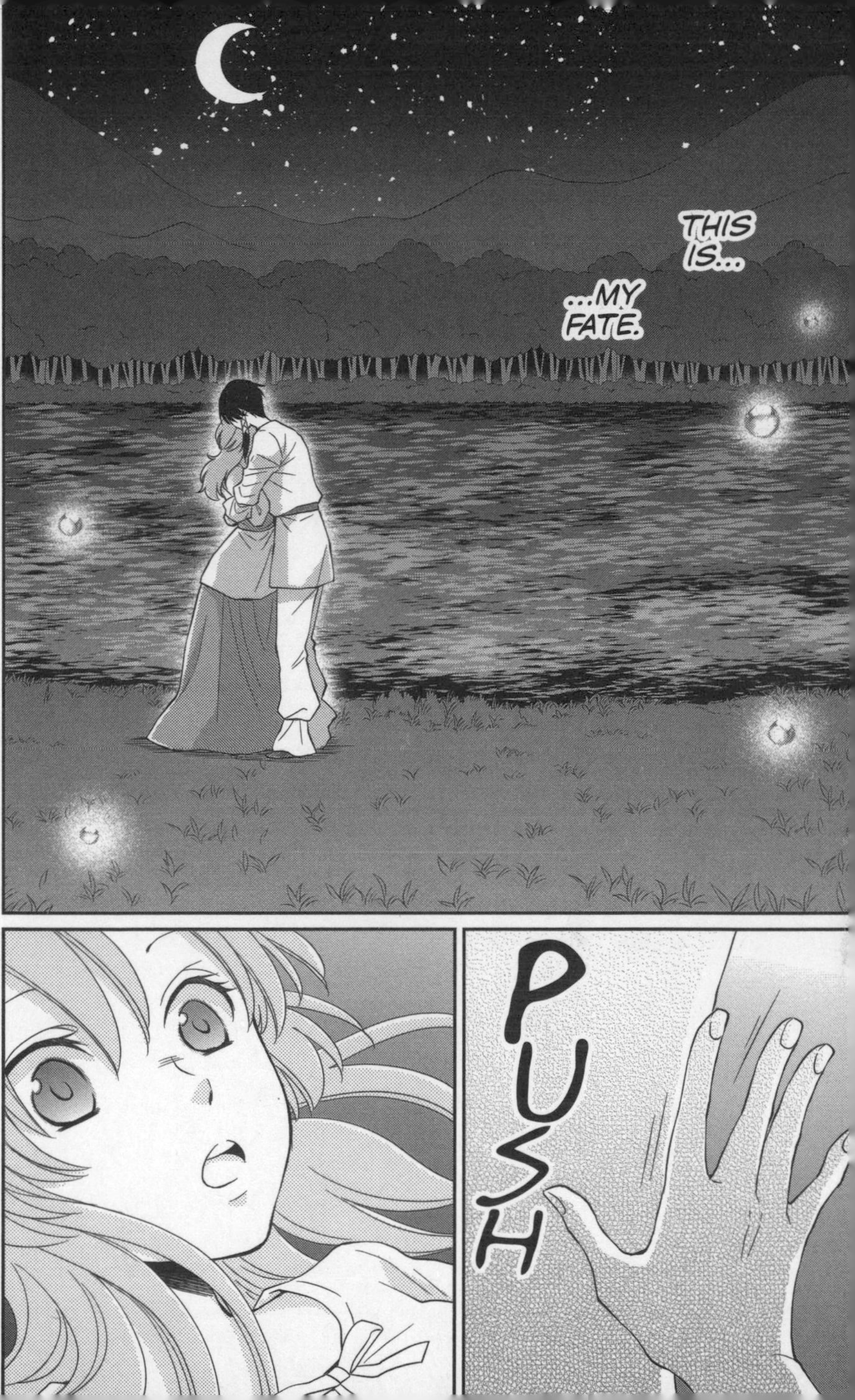
THIS IS...
...MY FATE.
PUSH

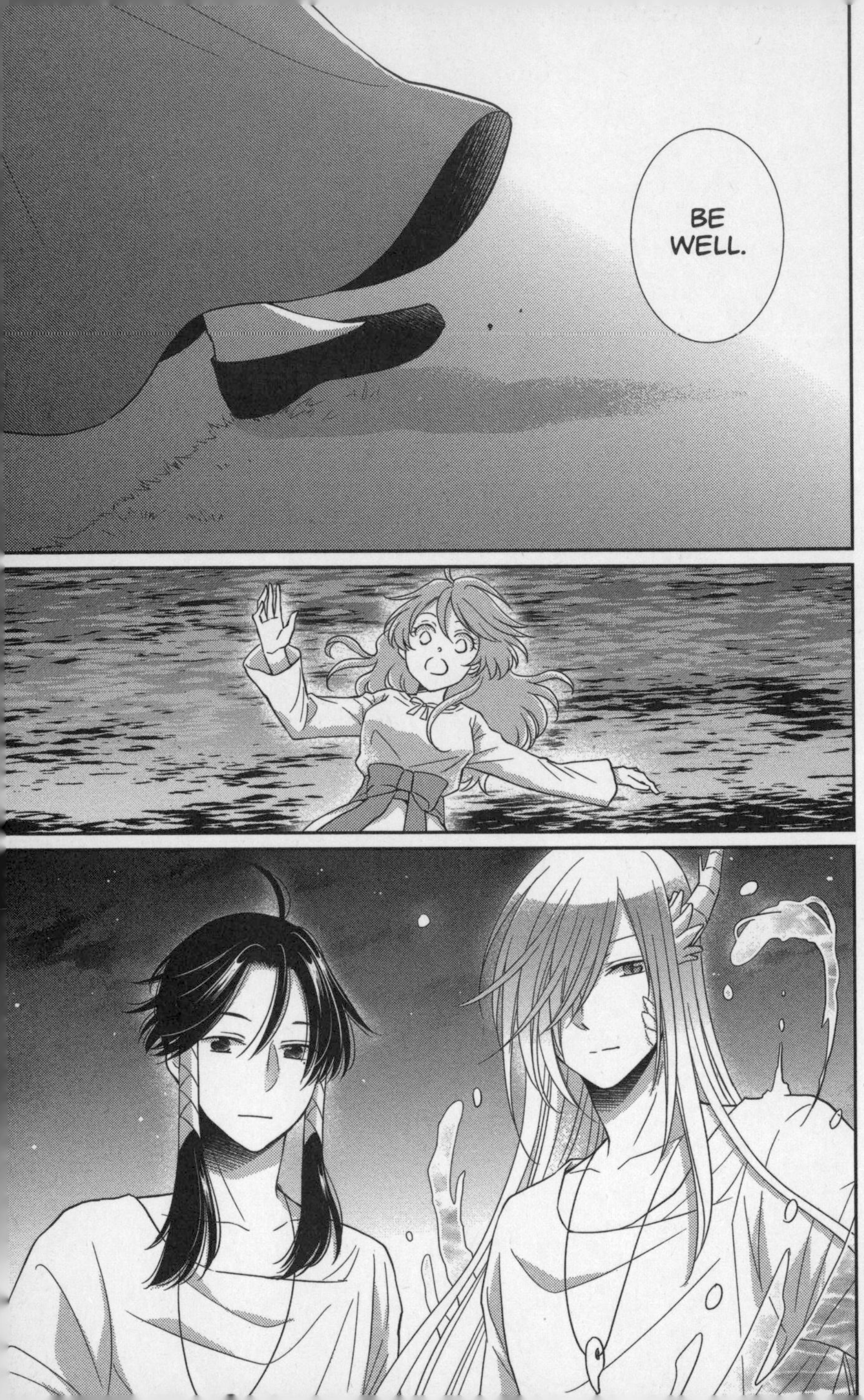
BE WELL.

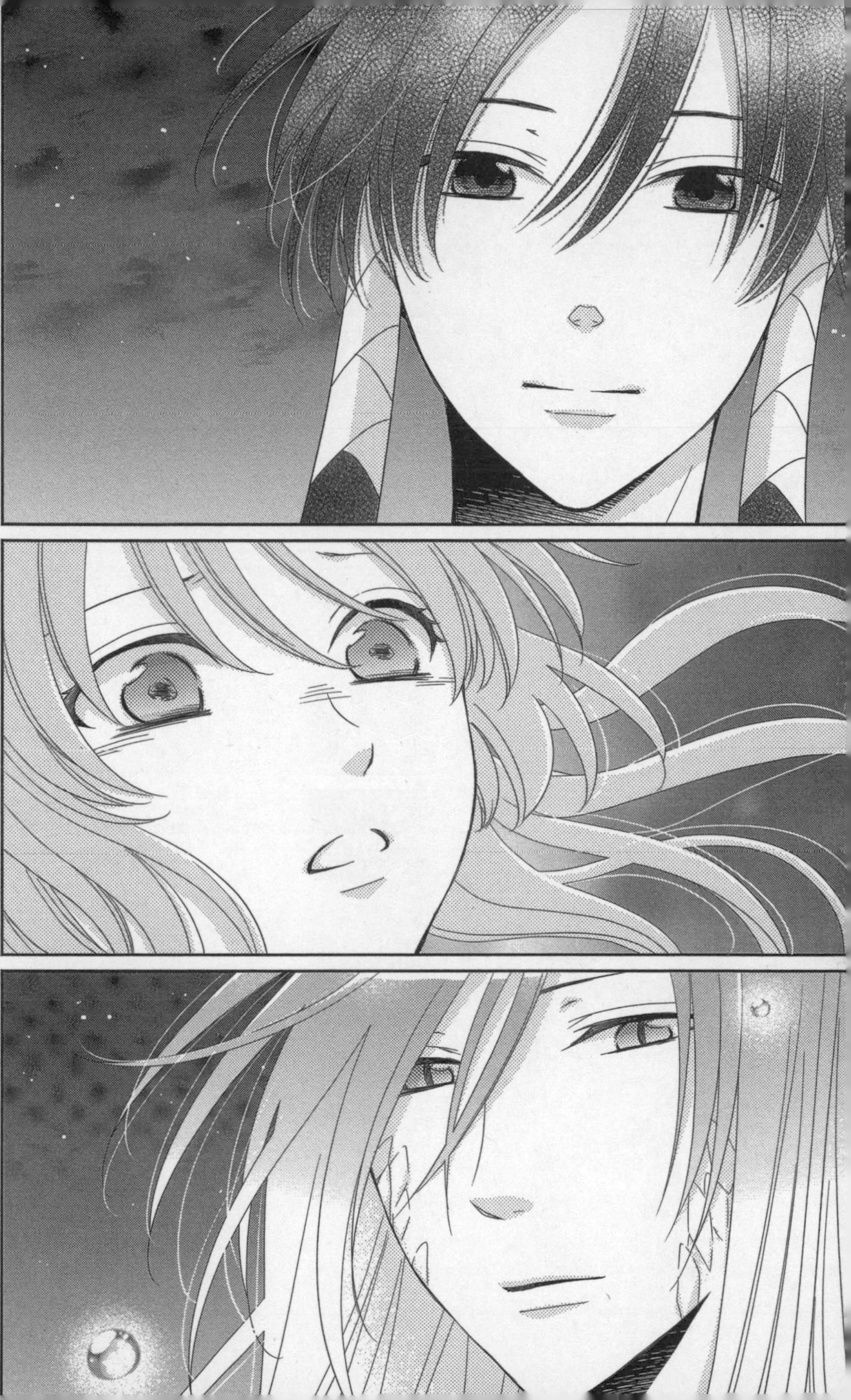

SPLOOSH

YOU
HAVE
MY
THANKS
...

...
SUBARU.

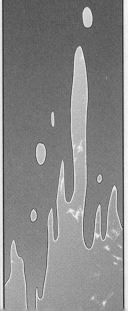

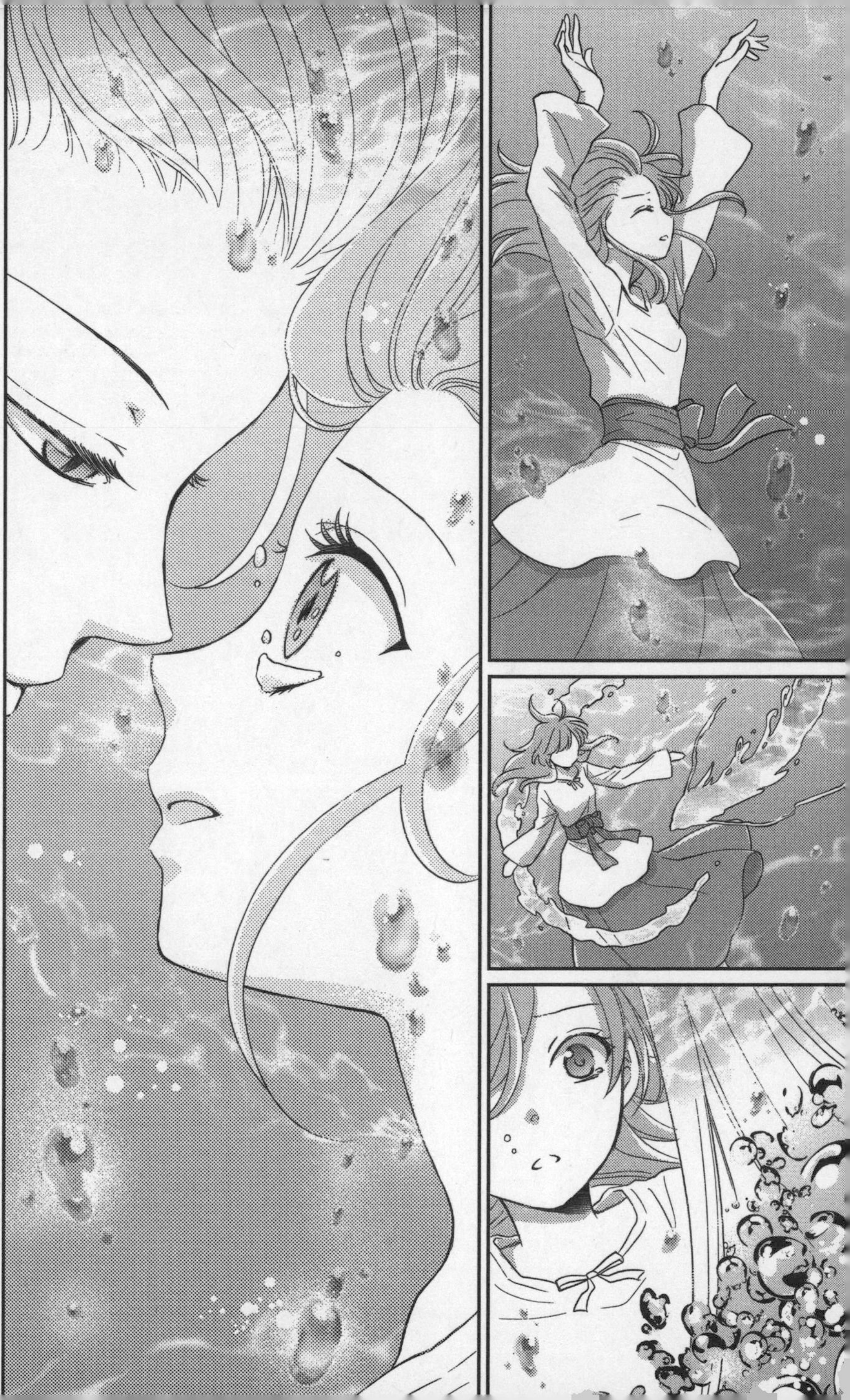

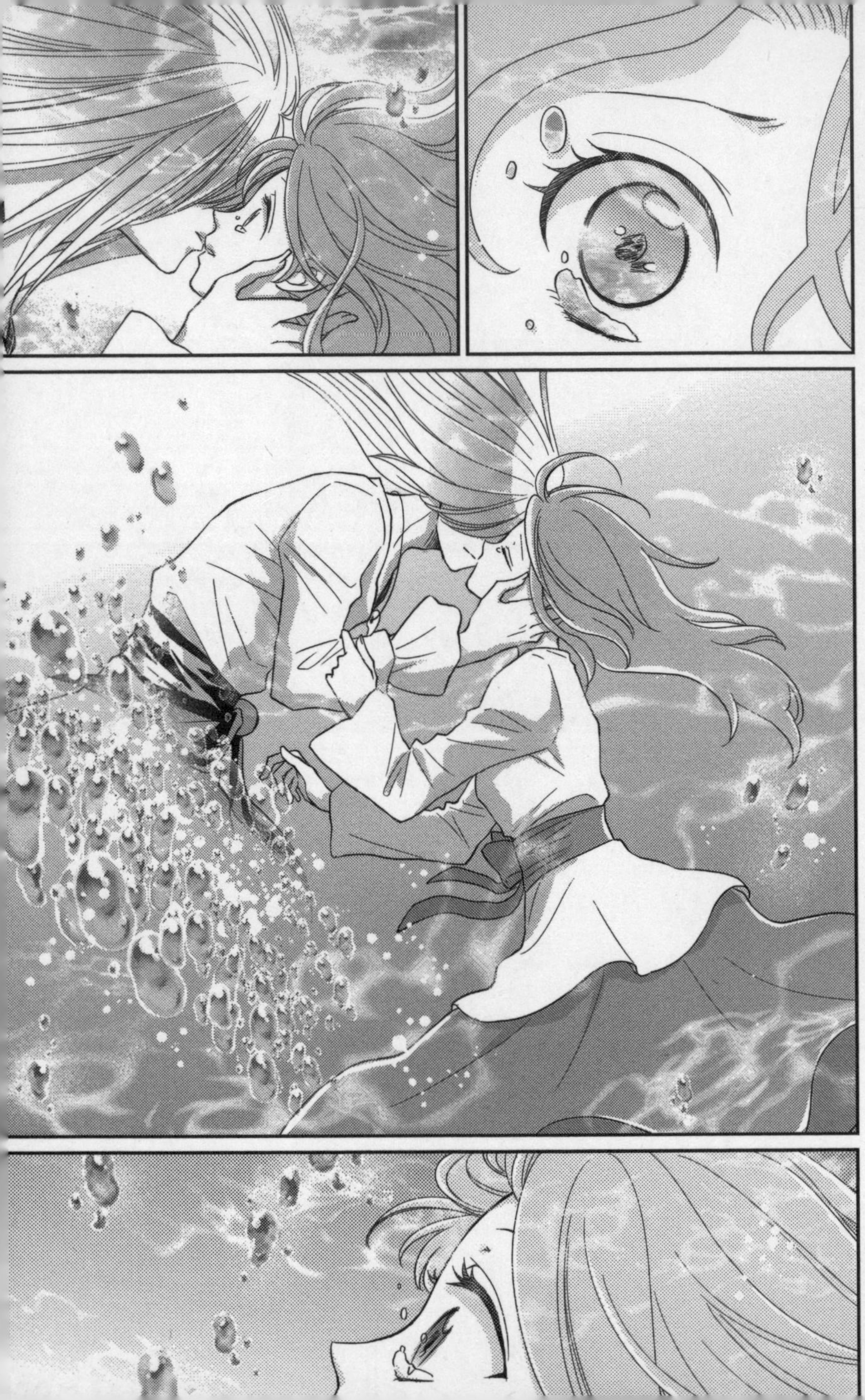

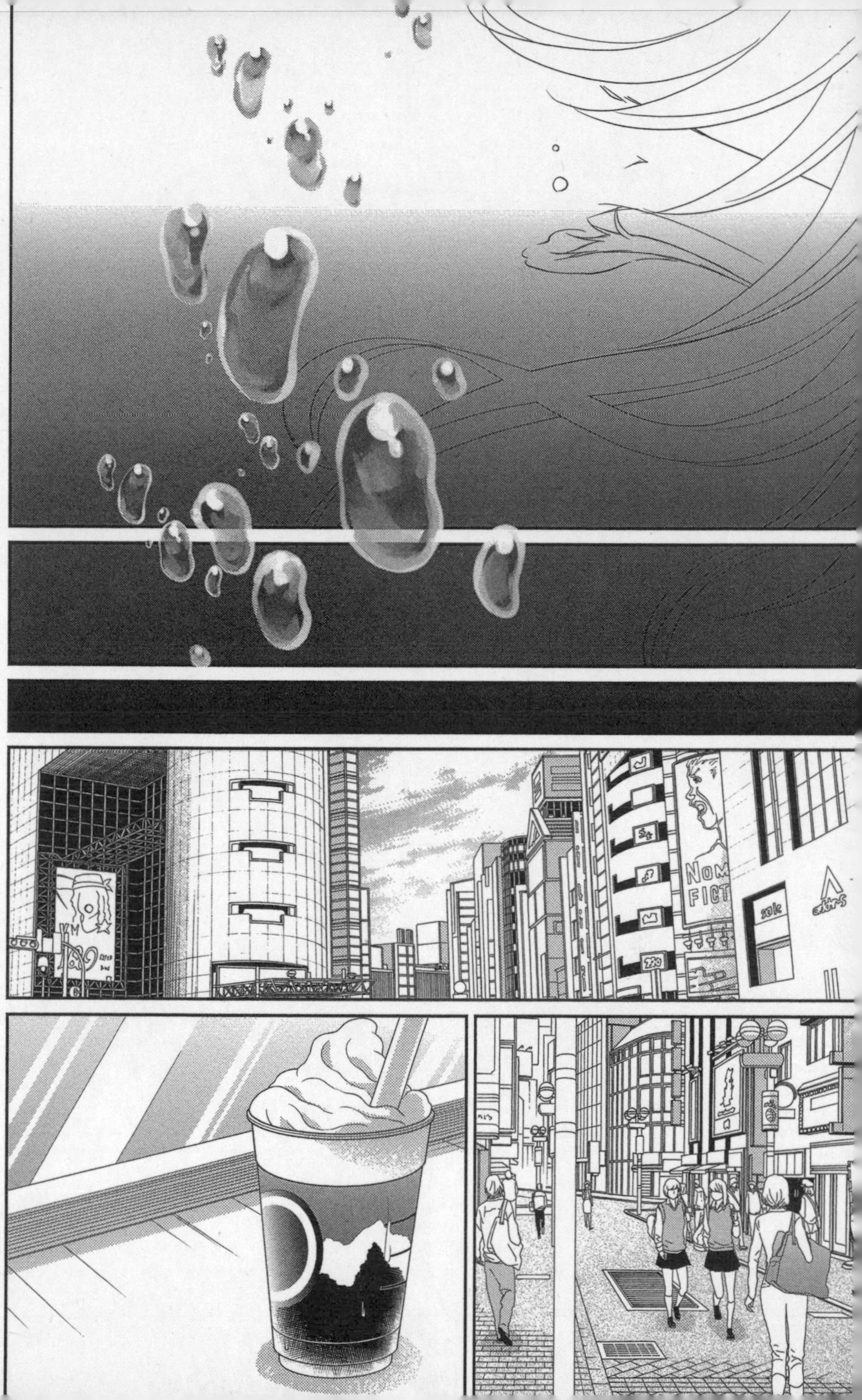
NOM
FICT

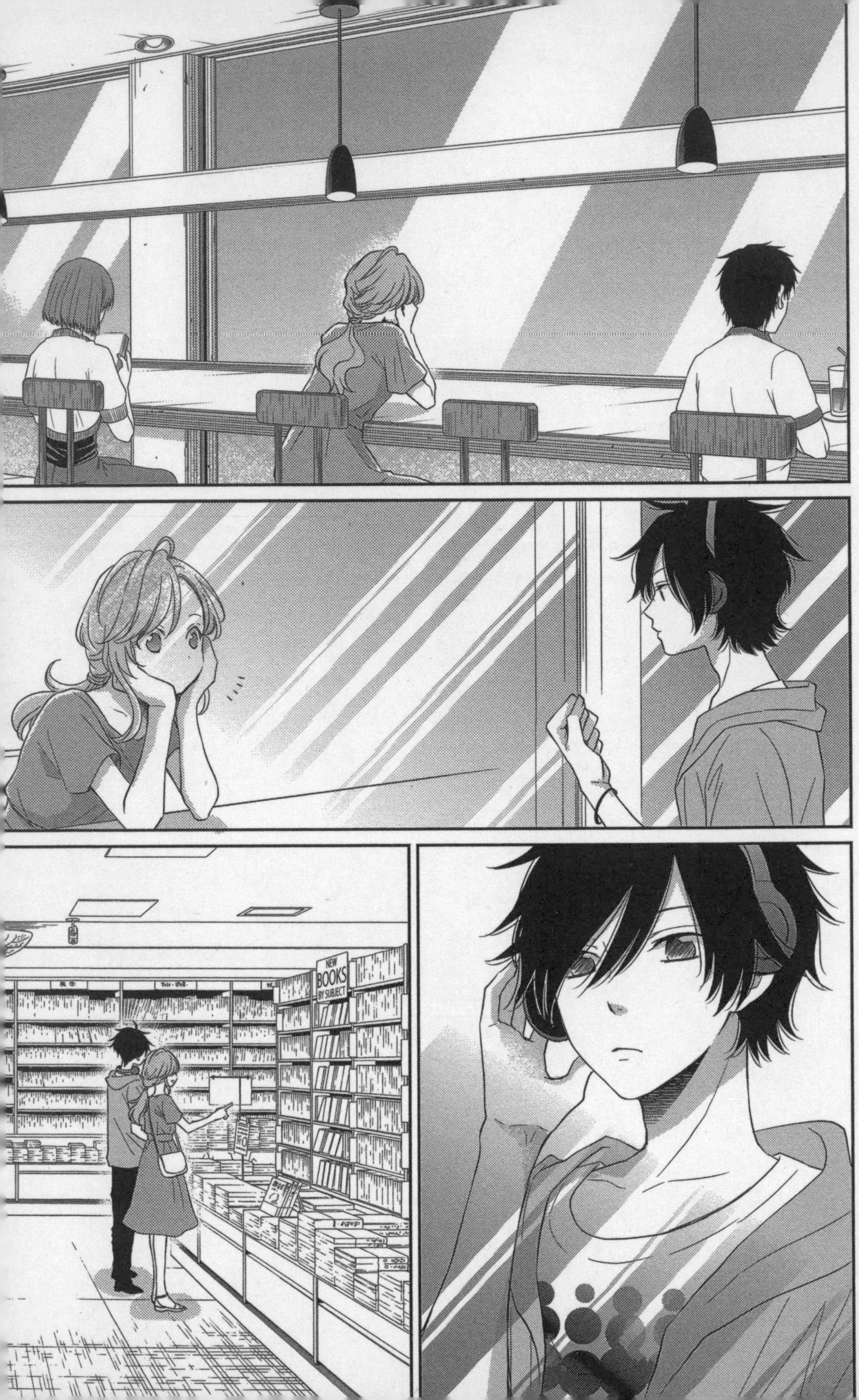
NEW BOOKS BY SUBJECT

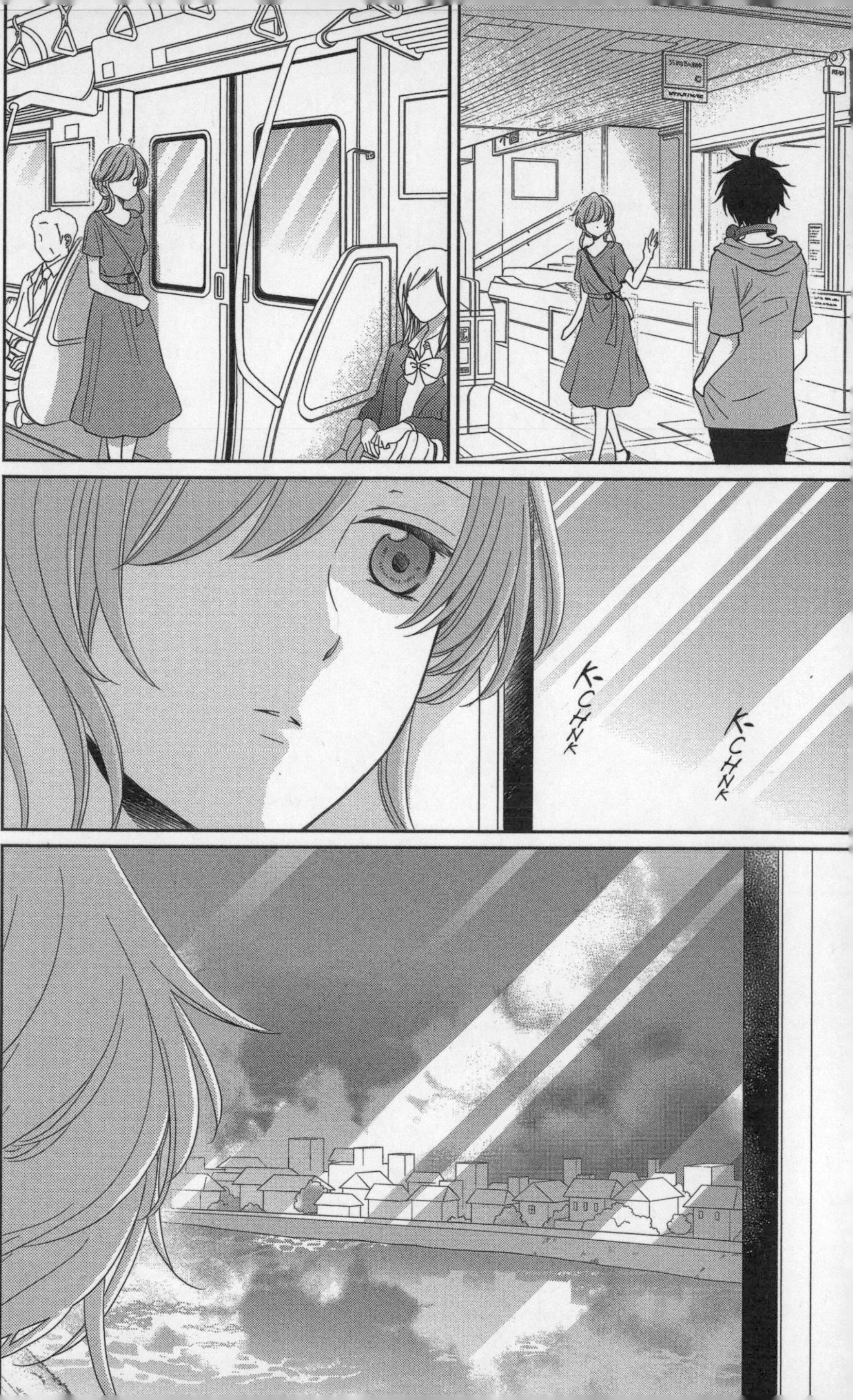
K-CHNK
K-CHNK

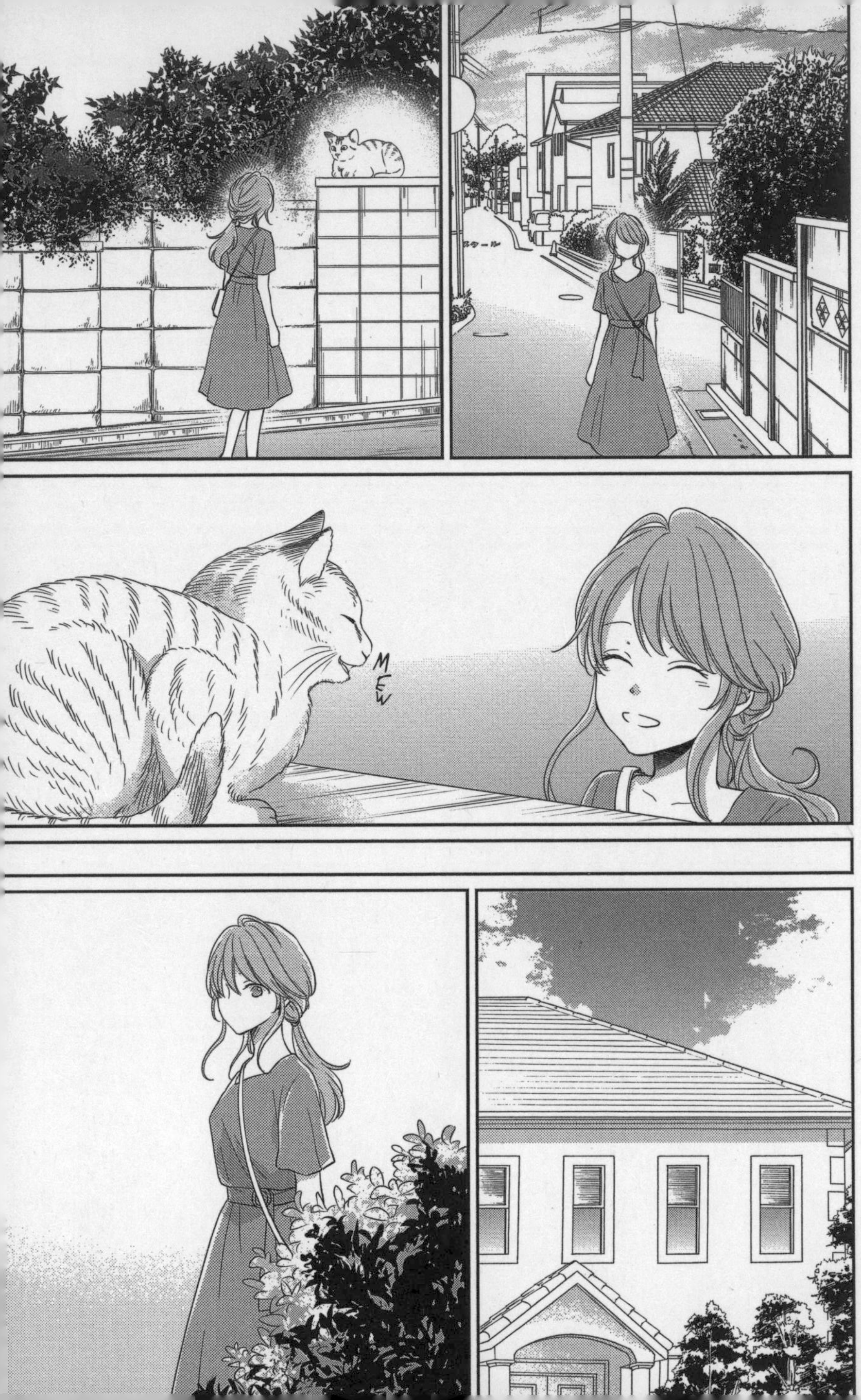
MEW

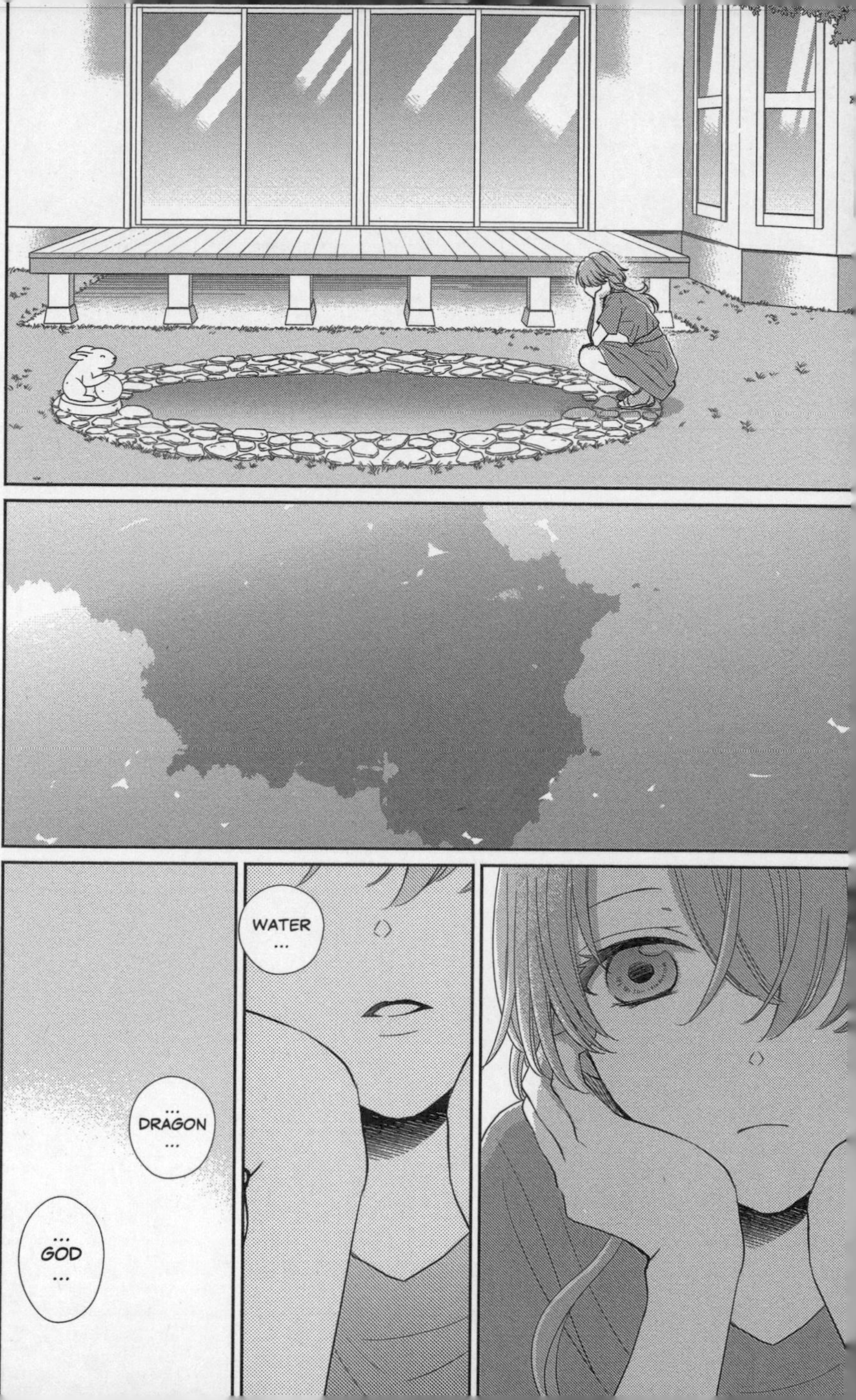
WATER ...
... DRAGON ...
... GOD ...

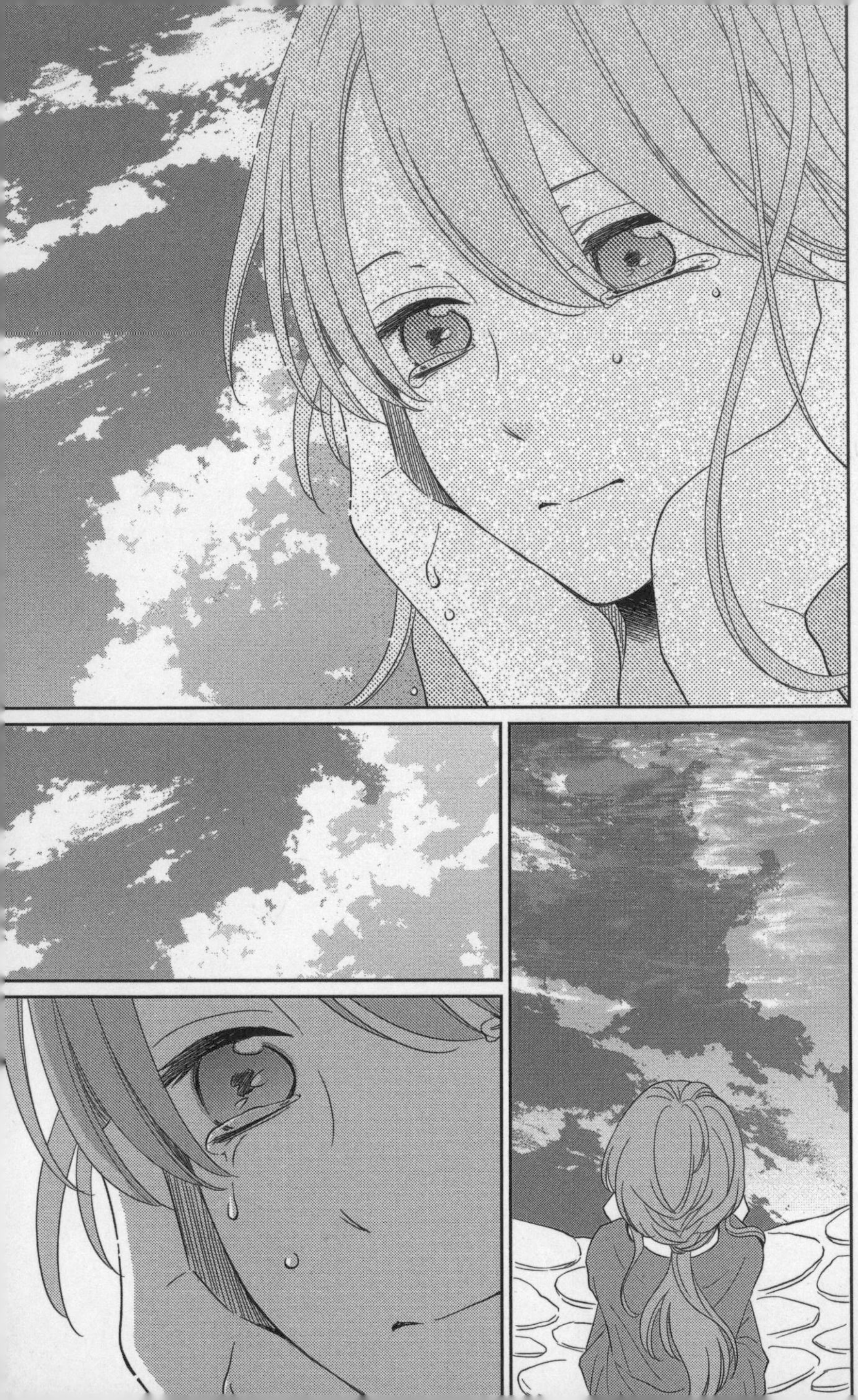

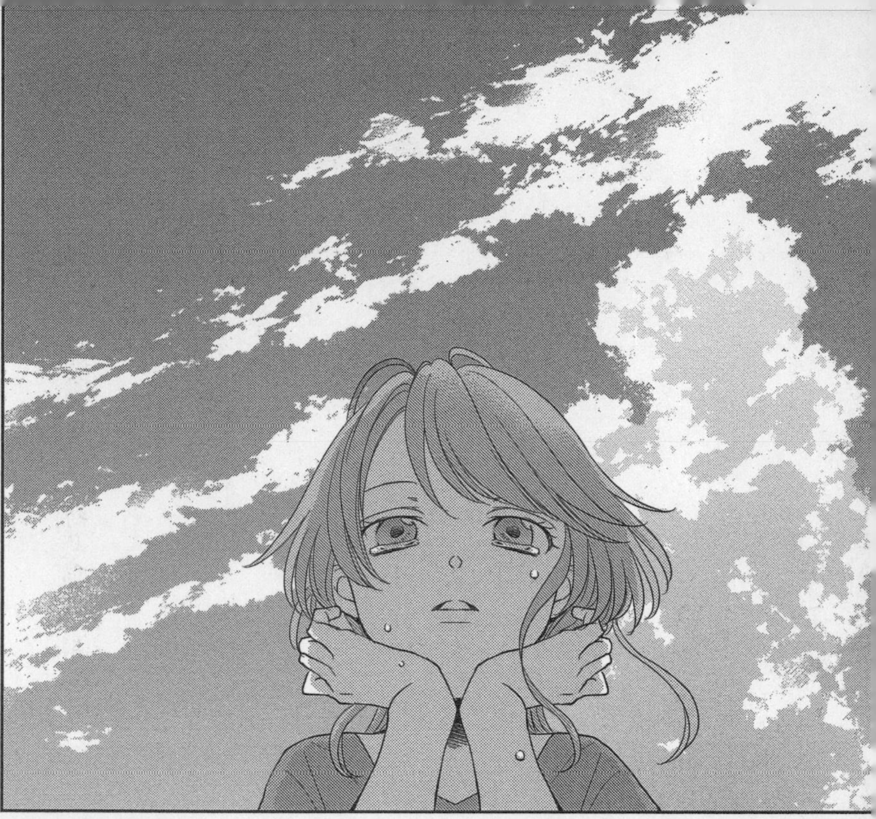
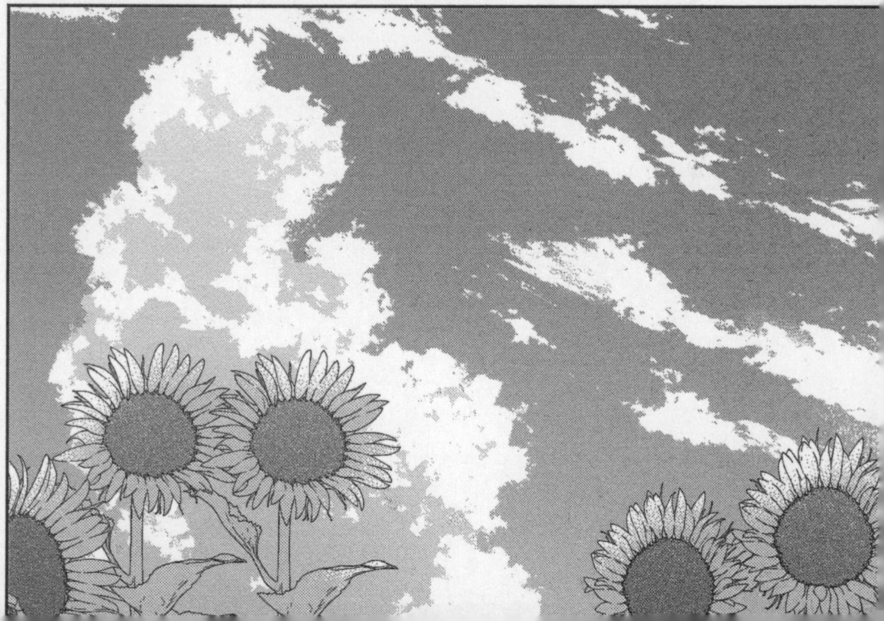

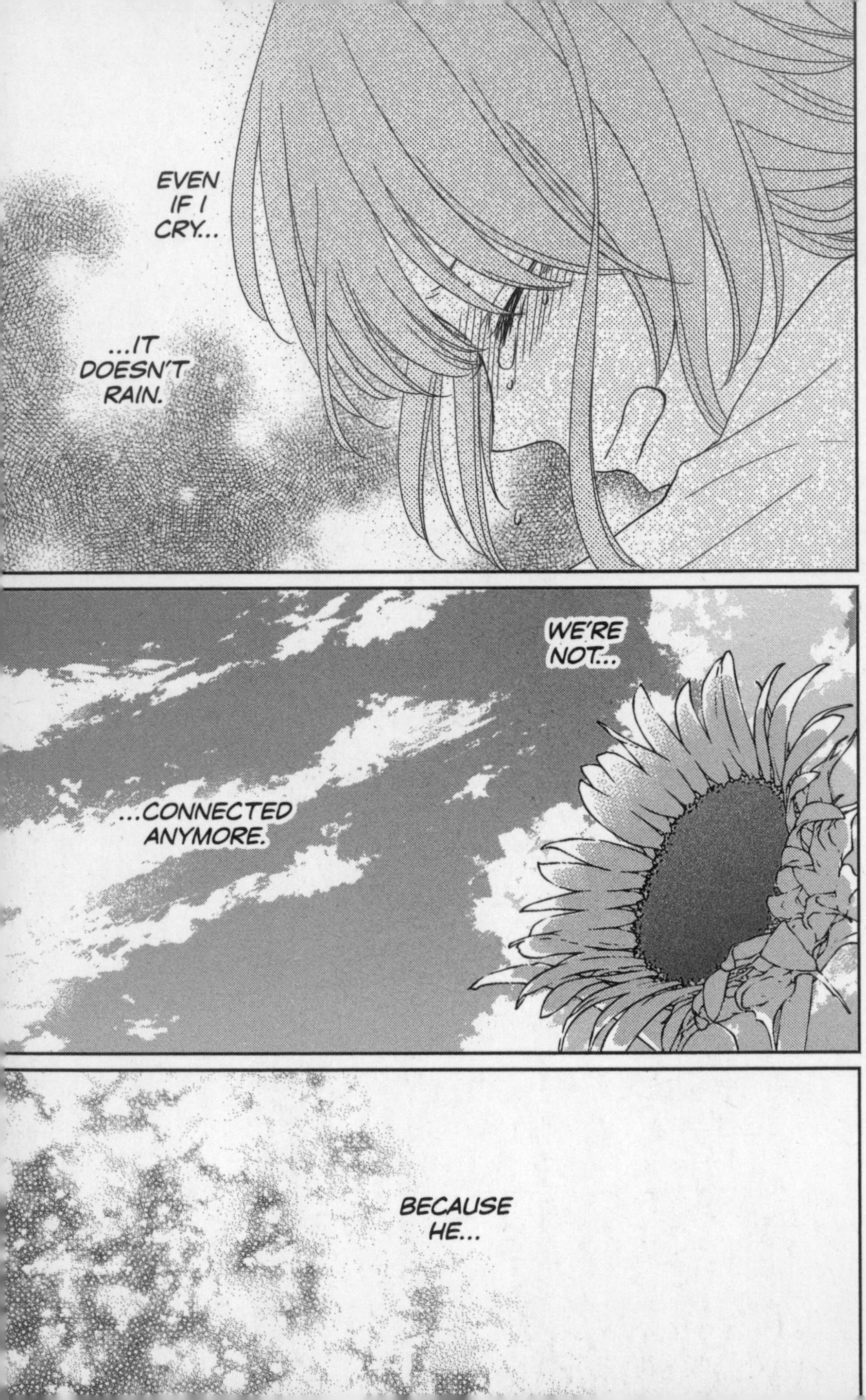
EVEN IF I CRY...
...IT DOESN'T RAIN.
WE'RE NOT...
...CONNECTED ANYMORE.
BECAUSE HE...

...DOESN'T
EXIST...

...ANYMORE.

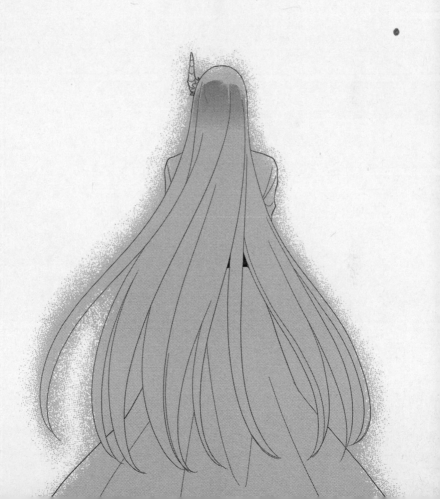

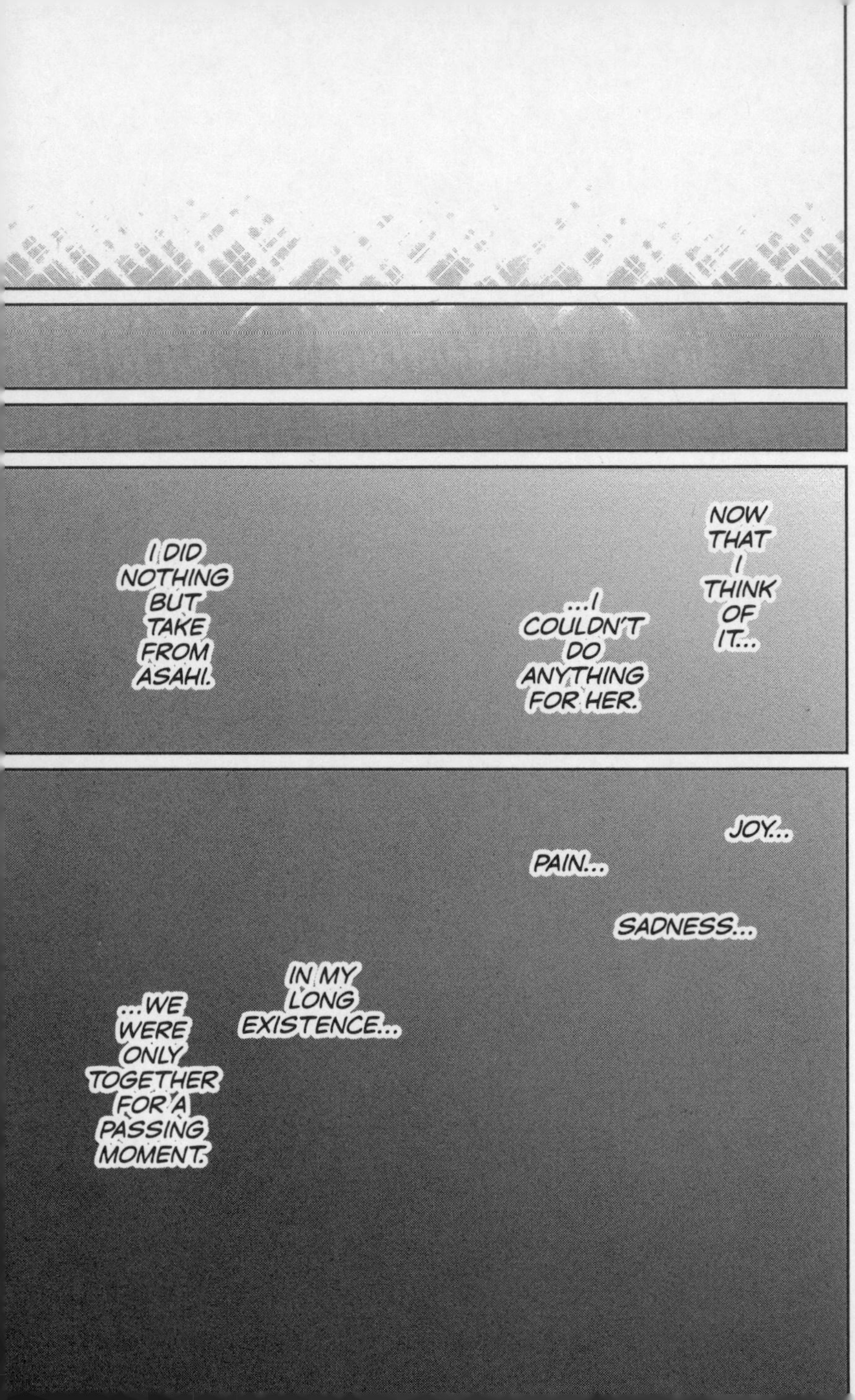
NOW THAT I THINK OF IT...
...I COULDN'T DO ANYTHING FOR HER.
I DID NOTHING BUT TAKE FROM ASAHI.
JOY...
PAIN...
SADNESS...
IN MY LONG EXISTENCE...
...WE WERE ONLY TOGETHER FOR A PASSING MOMENT.

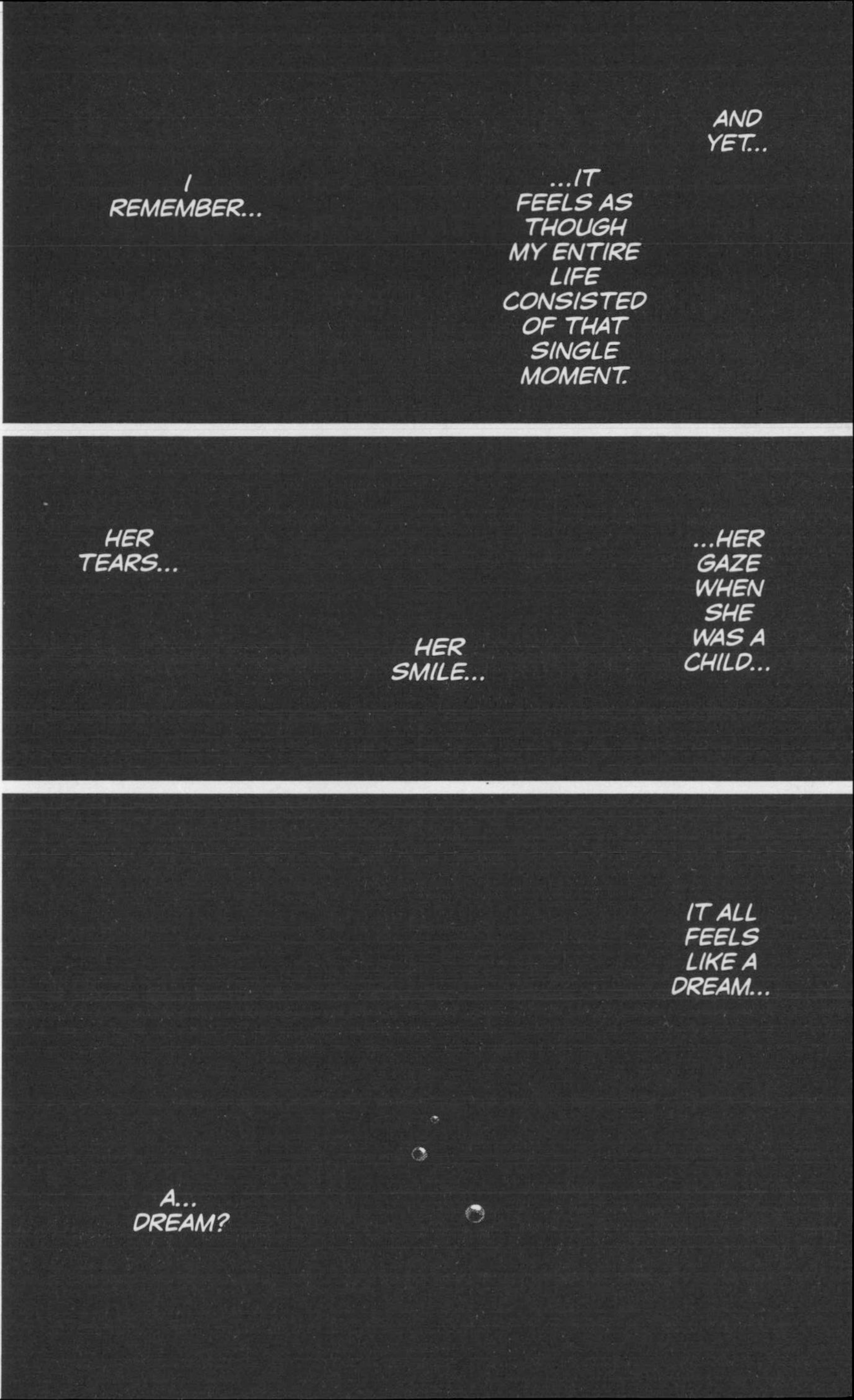
AND YET...
...IT FEELS AS THOUGH MY ENTIRE LIFE CONSISTED OF THAT SINGLE MOMENT.
I REMEMBER...
...HER GAZE WHEN SHE WAS A CHILD...
HER SMILE...
HER TEARS...
IT ALL FEELS LIKE A DREAM...
A... DREAM?

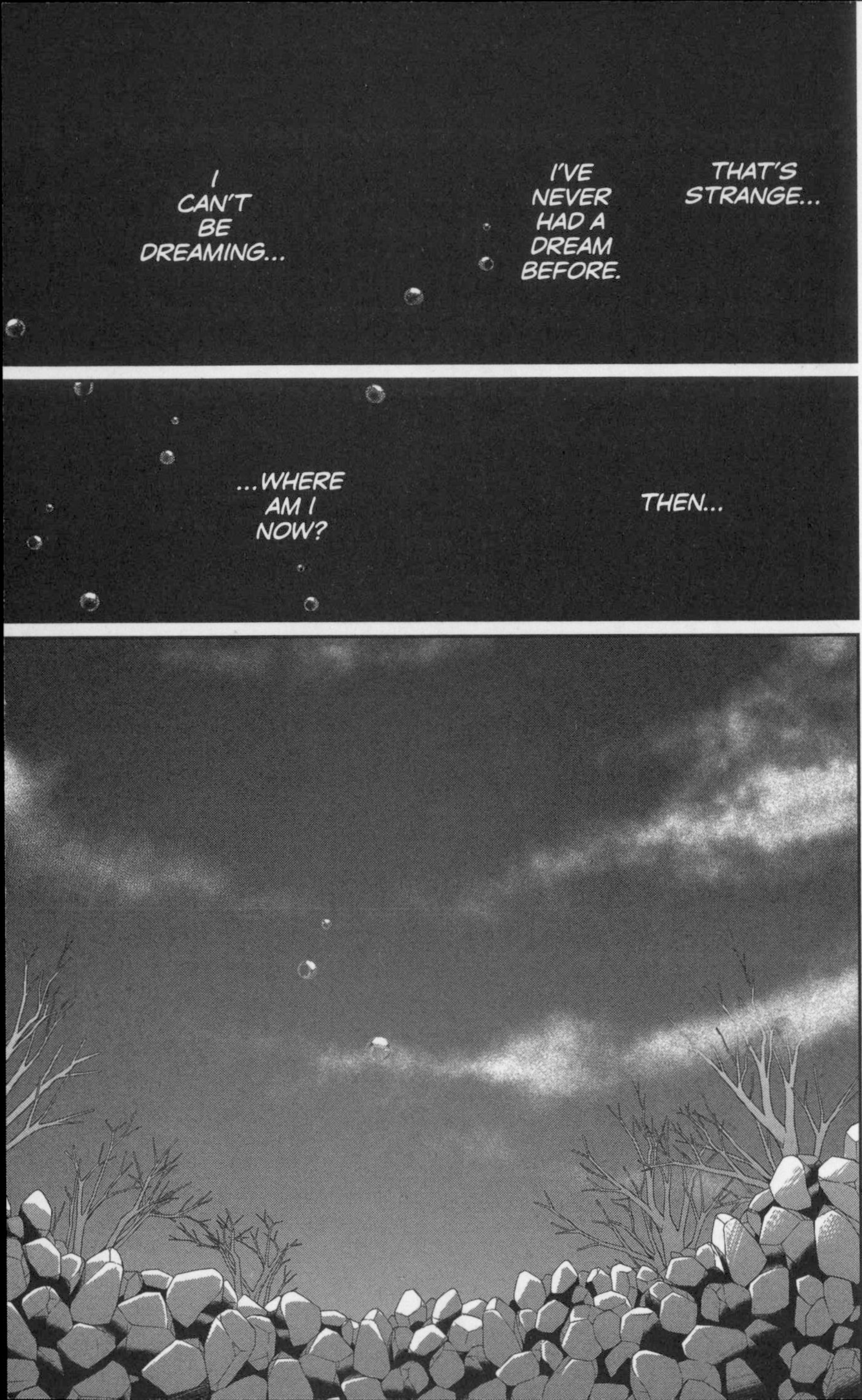
THAT'S STRANGE...
I'VE NEVER HAD A DREAM BEFORE.
I CAN'T BE DREAMING...
THEN...
...WHERE AM I NOW?

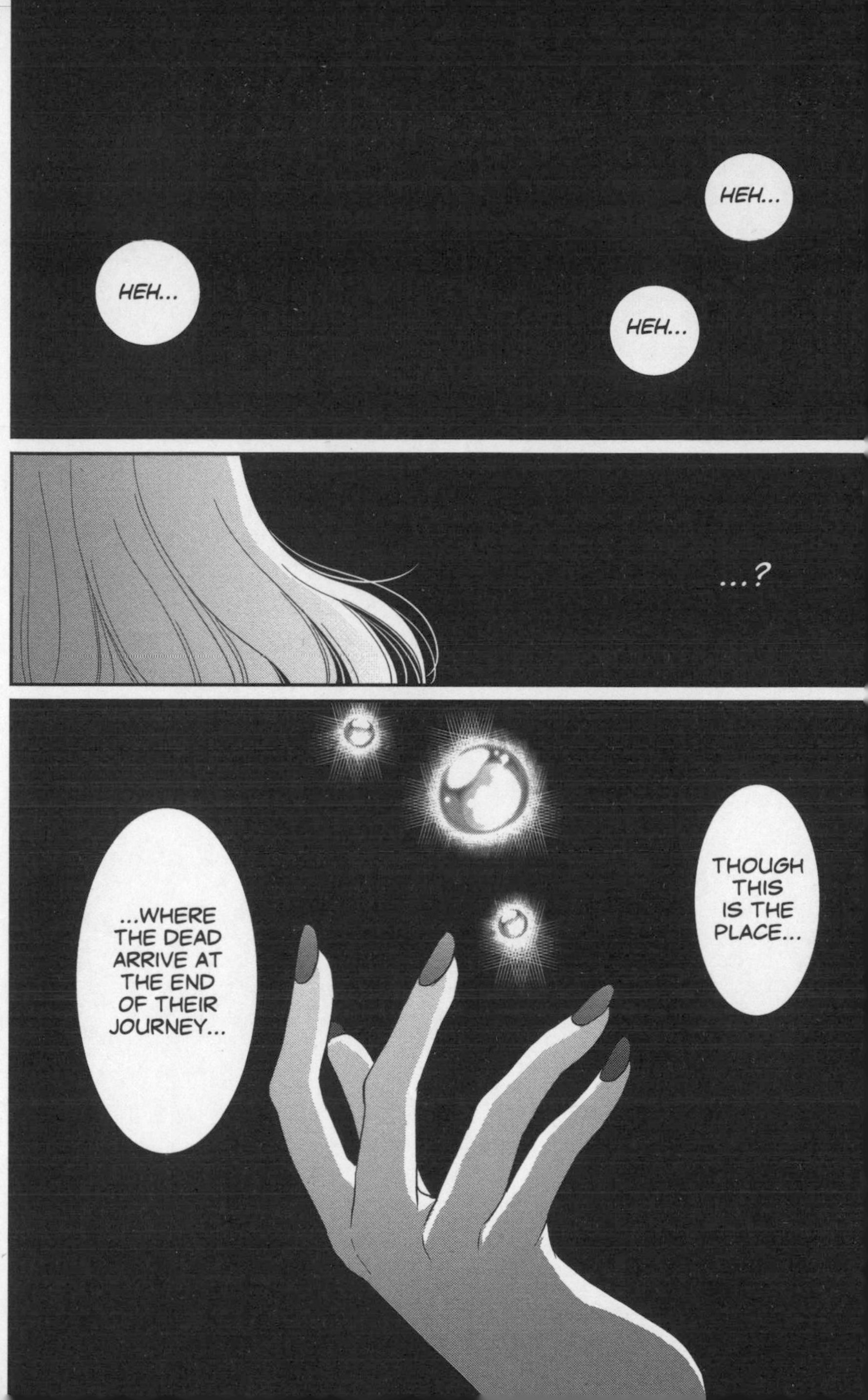
HEH...
HEH...
HEH...
...?
THOUGH THIS IS THE PLACE...
...WHERE THE DEAD ARRIVE AT THE END OF THEIR JOURNEY...

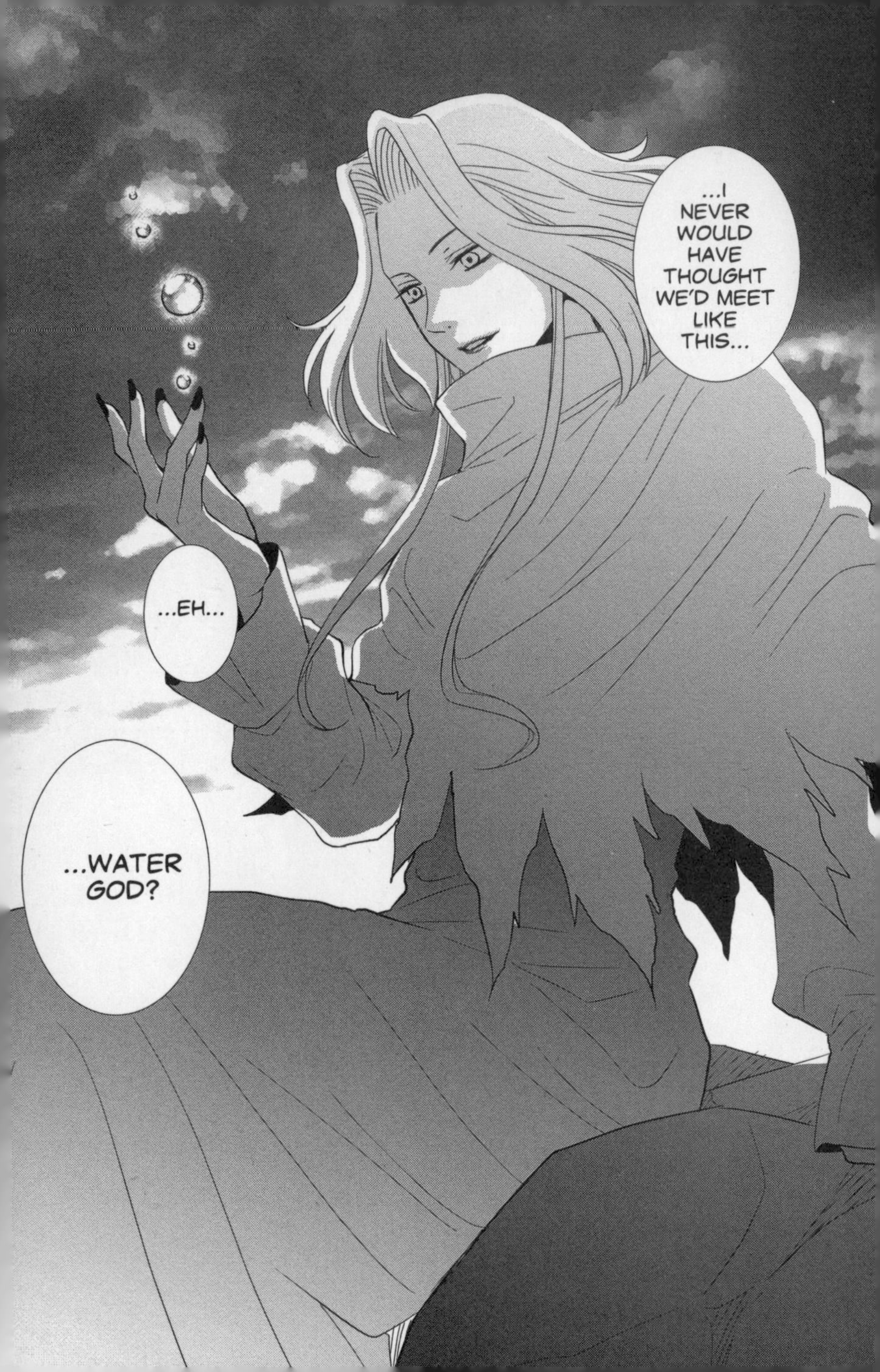
...I NEVER WOULD HAVE THOUGHT WE'D MEET LIKE THIS...
...EH...
...WATER GOD?

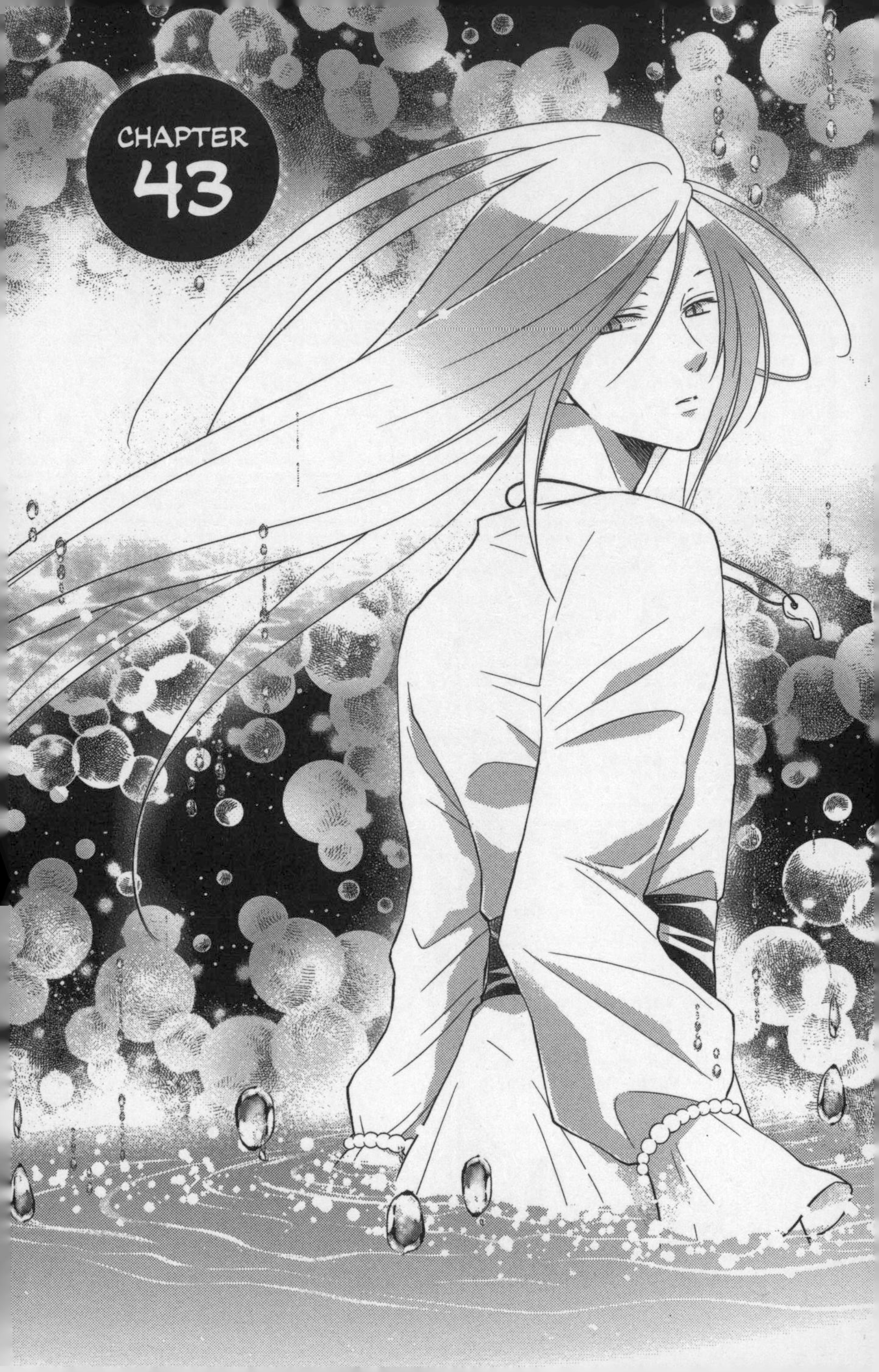
CHAPTER 43

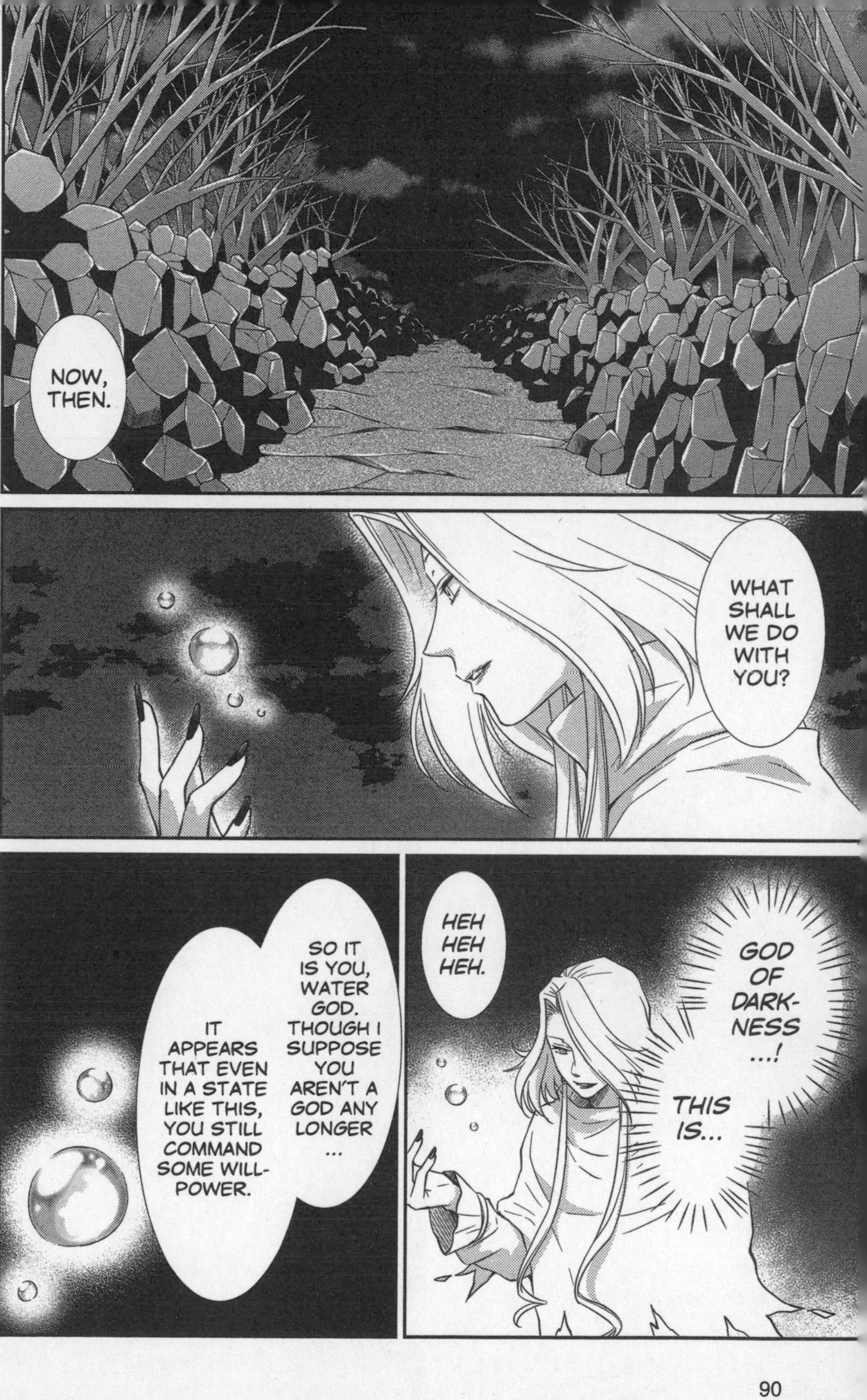
NOW, THEN.
WHAT SHALL WE DO WITH YOU?
THIS IS...
GOD OF DARKNESS...!
HEH HEH HEH.
SO IT IS YOU, WATER GOD. THOUGH I SUPPOSE YOU AREN'T A GOD ANY LONGER...
IT APPEARS THAT EVEN IN A STATE LIKE THIS, YOU STILL COMMAND SOME WILL-POWER.

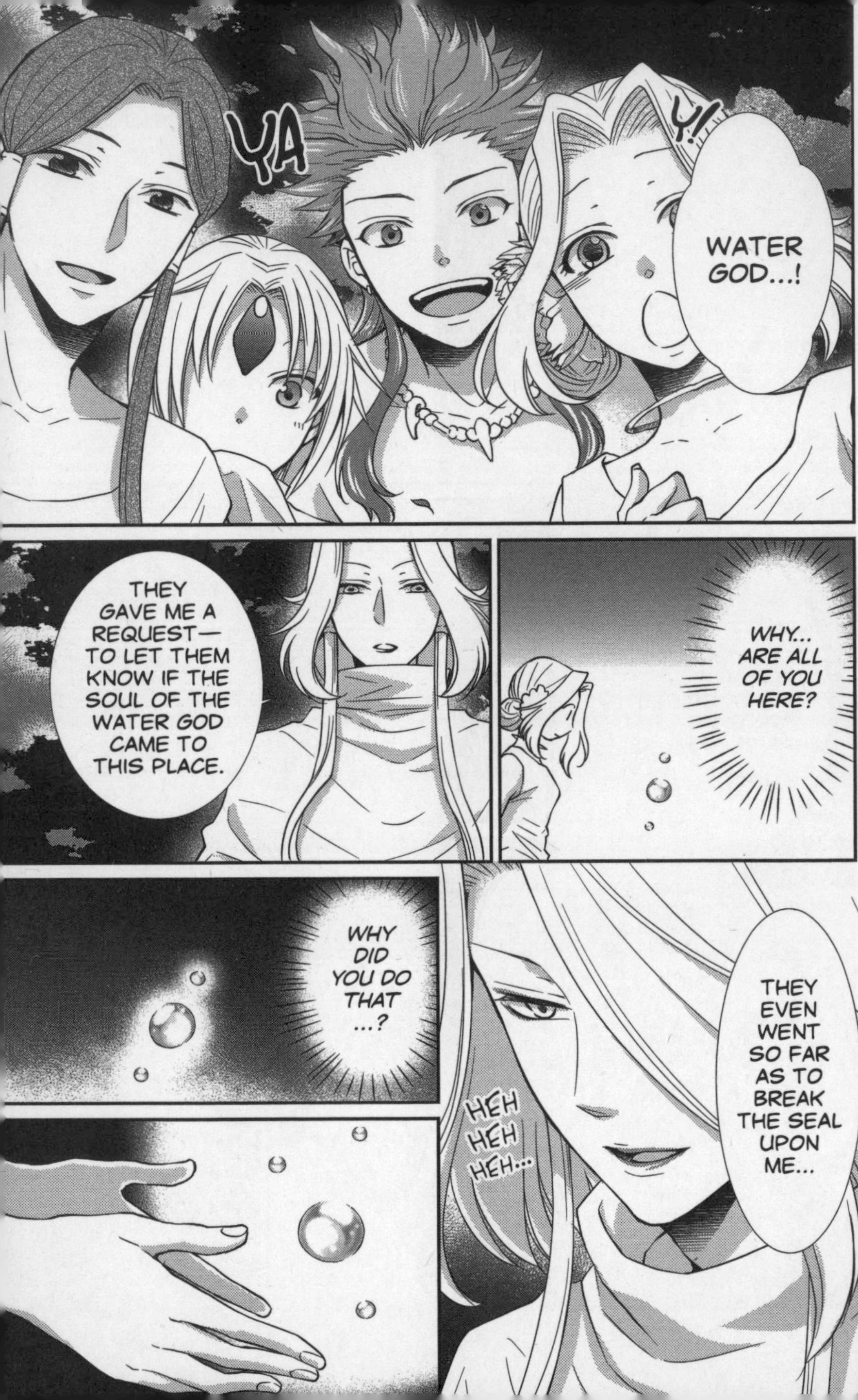
YA
Y!
WATER GOD...!
WHY... ARE ALL OF YOU HERE?
THEY GAVE ME A REQUEST— TO LET THEM KNOW IF THE SOUL OF THE WATER GOD CAME TO THIS PLACE.
THEY EVEN WENT SO FAR AS TO BREAK THE SEAL UPON ME...
HEH HEH HEH...
WHY DID YOU DO THAT ...?

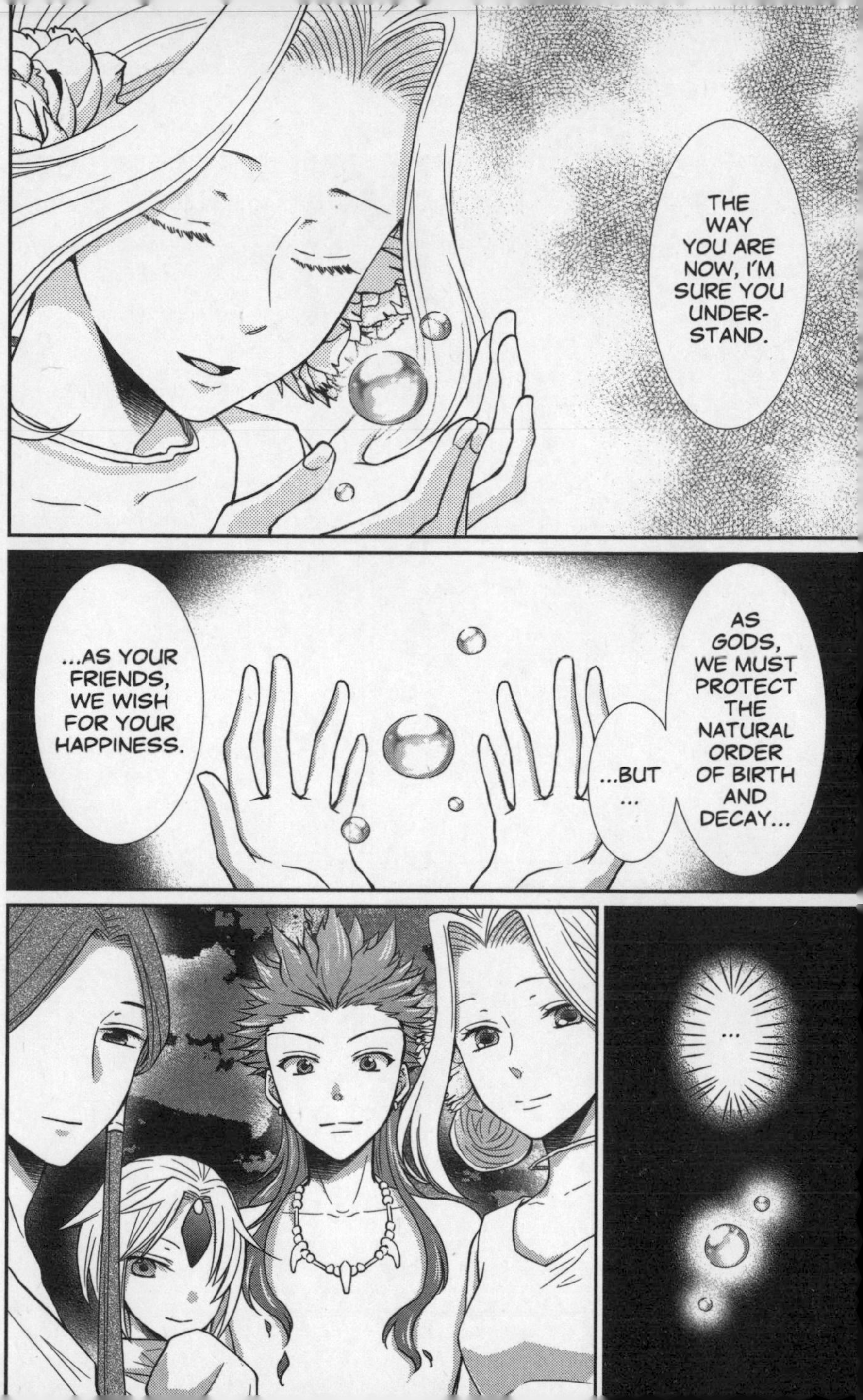
THE WAY YOU ARE NOW, I'M SURE YOU UNDER-STAND.
AS GODS, WE MUST PROTECT THE NATURAL ORDER OF BIRTH AND DECAY...
...BUT ...
...AS YOUR FRIENDS, WE WISH FOR YOUR HAPPINESS.
...

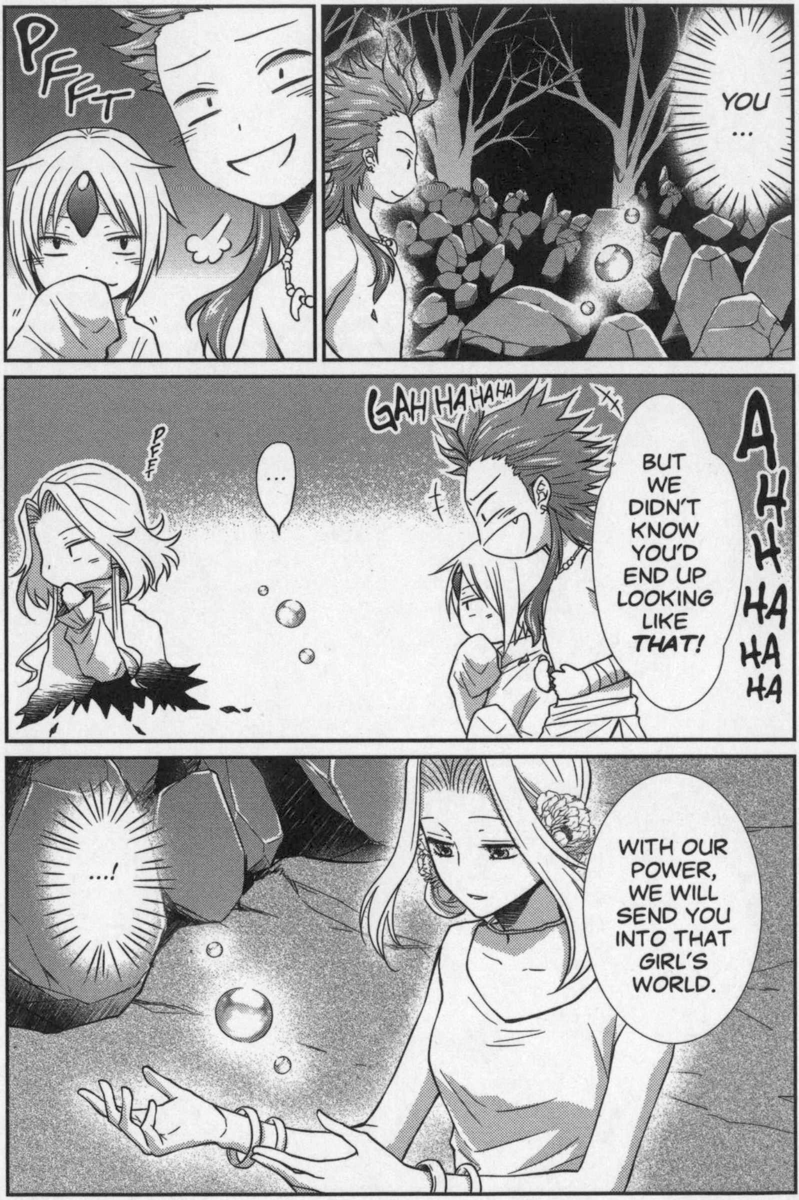
YOU ...
PFFFT
AHHHAHAHAHA
BUT WE DIDN'T KNOW YOU'D END UP LOOKING LIKE *THAT!*
GAH HAHAHA
...
PFFT
WITH OUR POWER, WE WILL SEND YOU INTO THAT GIRL'S WORLD.
...!

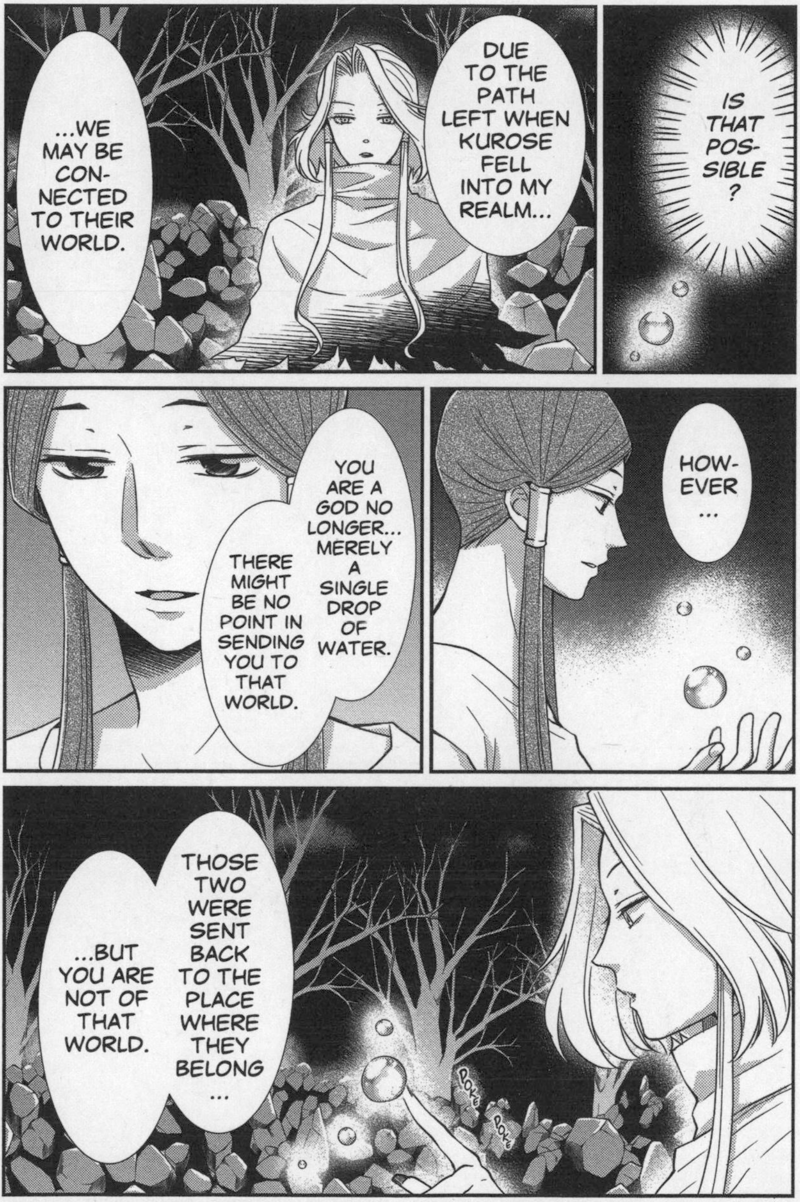
IS THAT POS-SIBLE?
DUE TO THE PATH LEFT WHEN KUROSE FELL INTO MY REALM...
...WE MAY BE CON-NECTED TO THEIR WORLD.
HOW-EVER...
YOU ARE A GOD NO LONGER... MERELY A SINGLE DROP OF WATER.
THERE MIGHT BE NO POINT IN SENDING YOU TO THAT WORLD.
THOSE TWO WERE SENT BACK TO THE PLACE WHERE THEY BELONG...
...BUT YOU ARE NOT OF THAT WORLD.
POKE
POKE

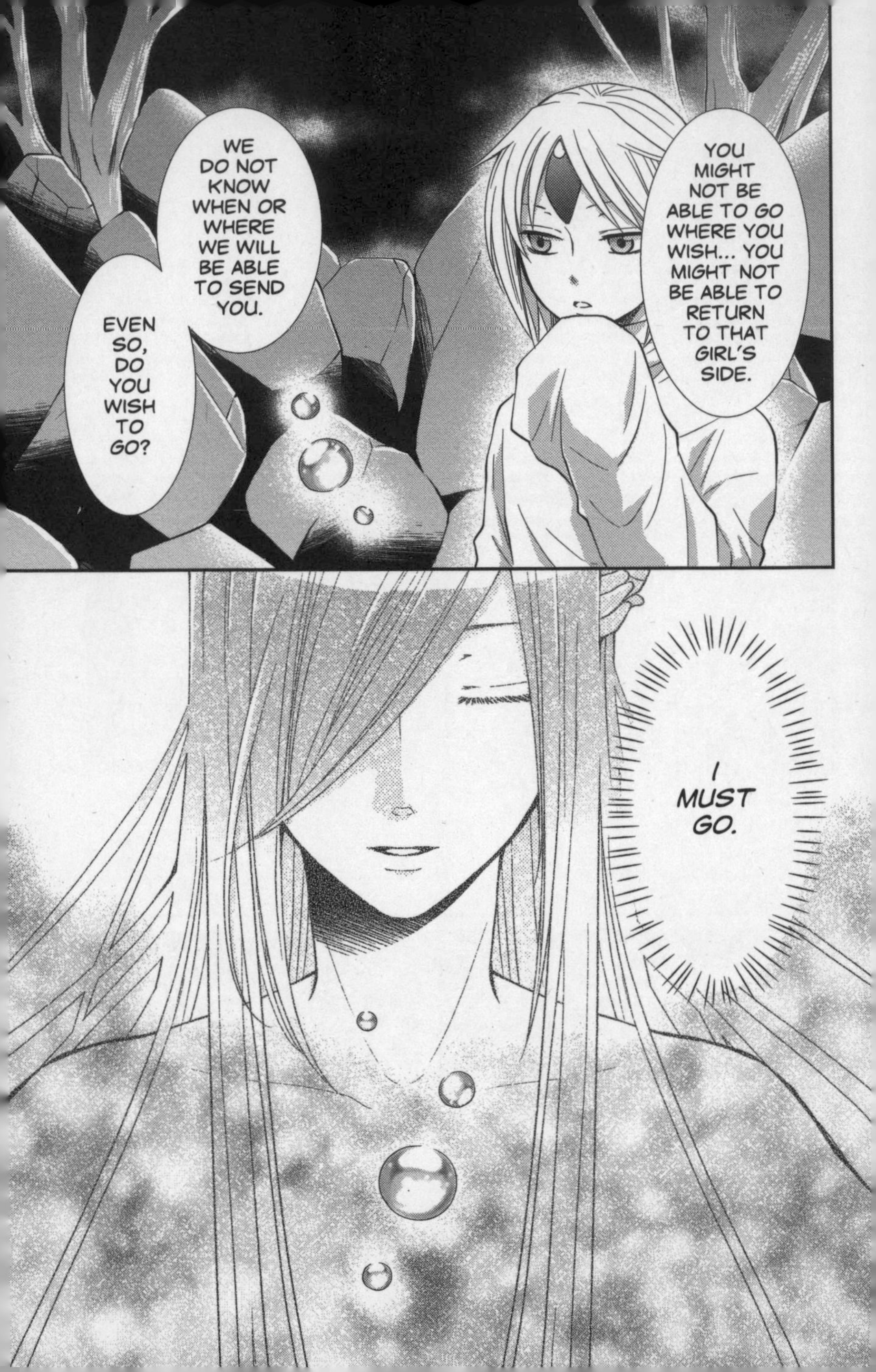
YOU MIGHT NOT BE ABLE TO GO WHERE YOU WISH... YOU MIGHT NOT BE ABLE TO RETURN TO THAT GIRL'S SIDE.
WE DO NOT KNOW WHEN OR WHERE WE WILL BE ABLE TO SEND YOU.
EVEN SO, DO YOU WISH TO GO?
I MUST GO.

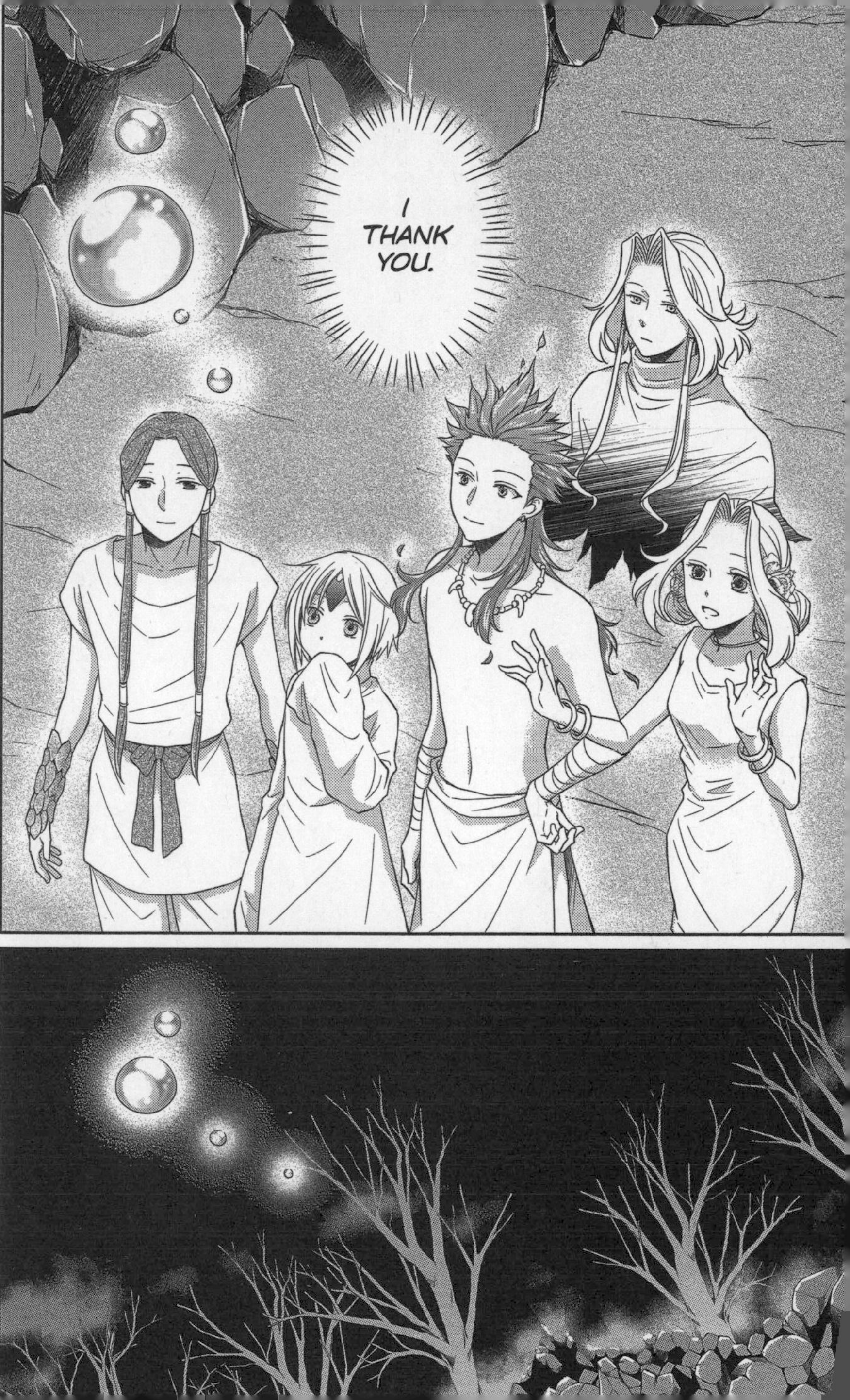
I THANK YOU.

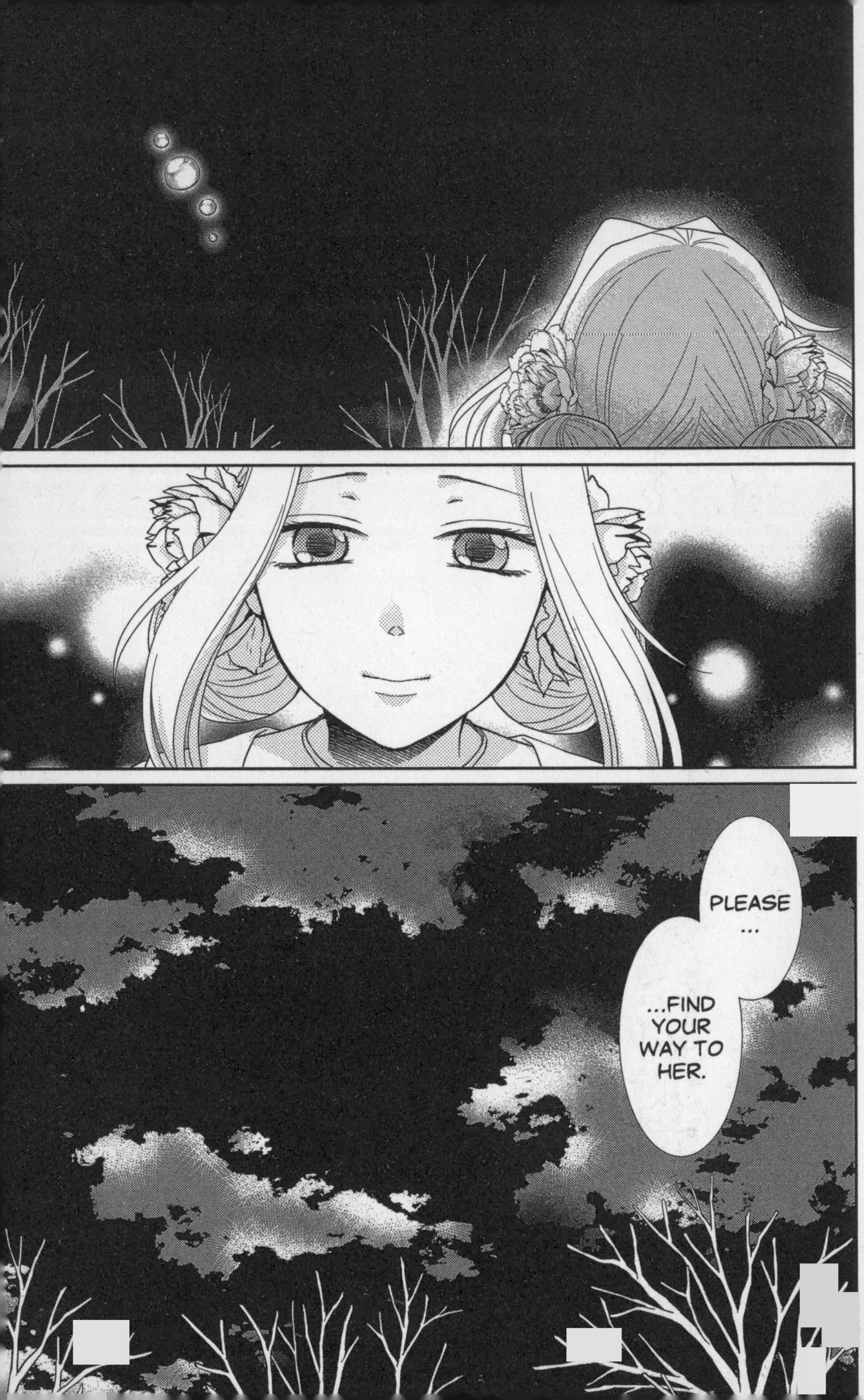
PLEASE ...
...FIND YOUR WAY TO HER.

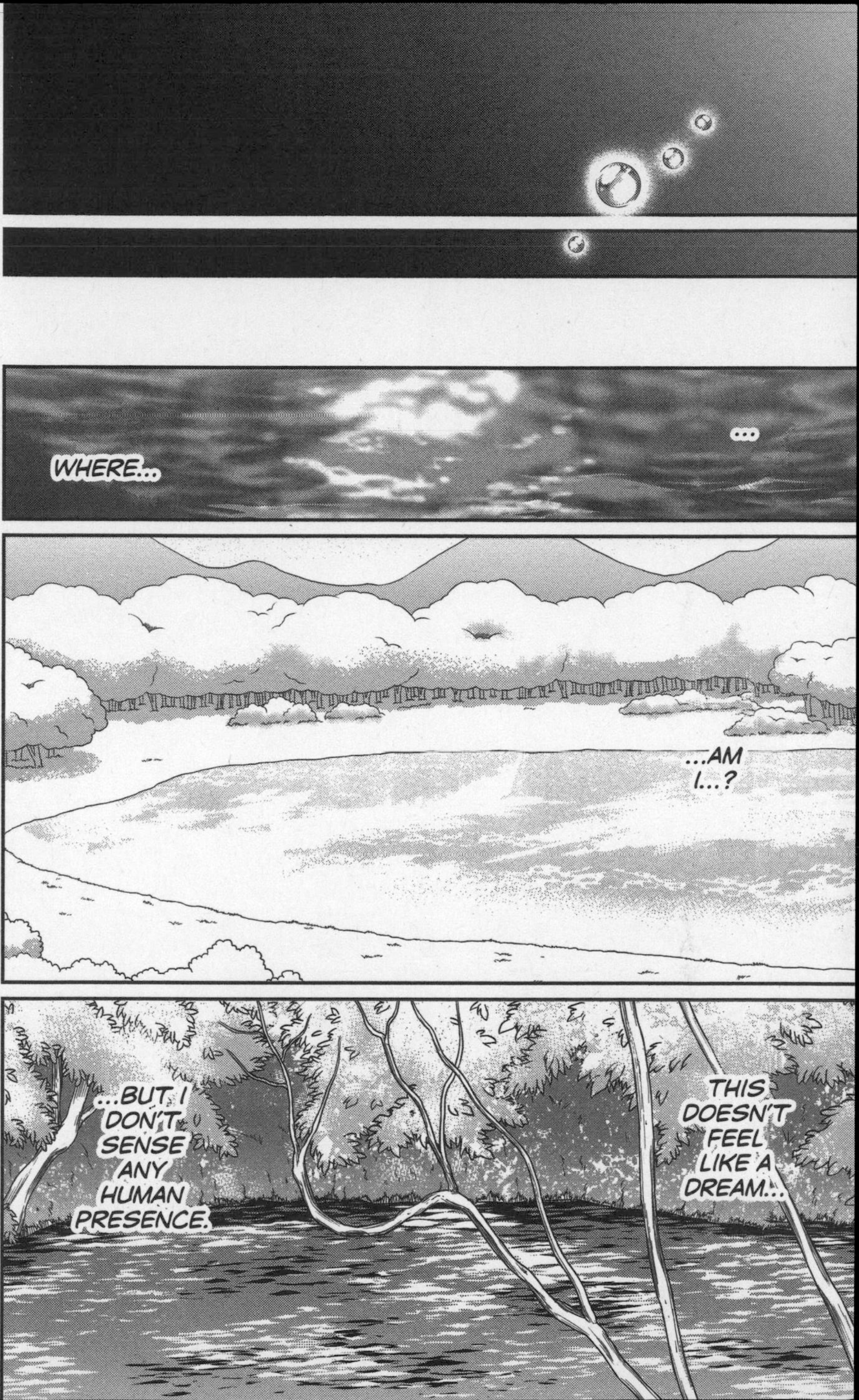
...
WHERE...
...AM I...?
THIS DOESN'T FEEL LIKE A DREAM...
...BUT I DON'T SENSE ANY HUMAN PRESENCE.

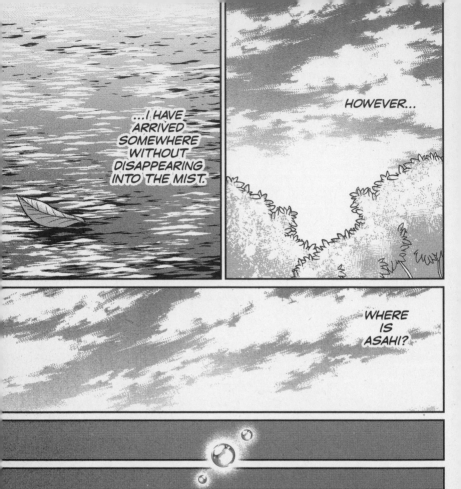

...I HAVE ARRIVED SOMEWHERE WITHOUT DISAPPEARING INTO THE MIST.

HOWEVER...

WHERE IS ASAHI?

I FEEL AS IF I'M WAITING QUITE A LONG TIME...

MUCH LIKE I DID WHEN I WAS A GOD...

...IN ETERNAL SOLITUDE.

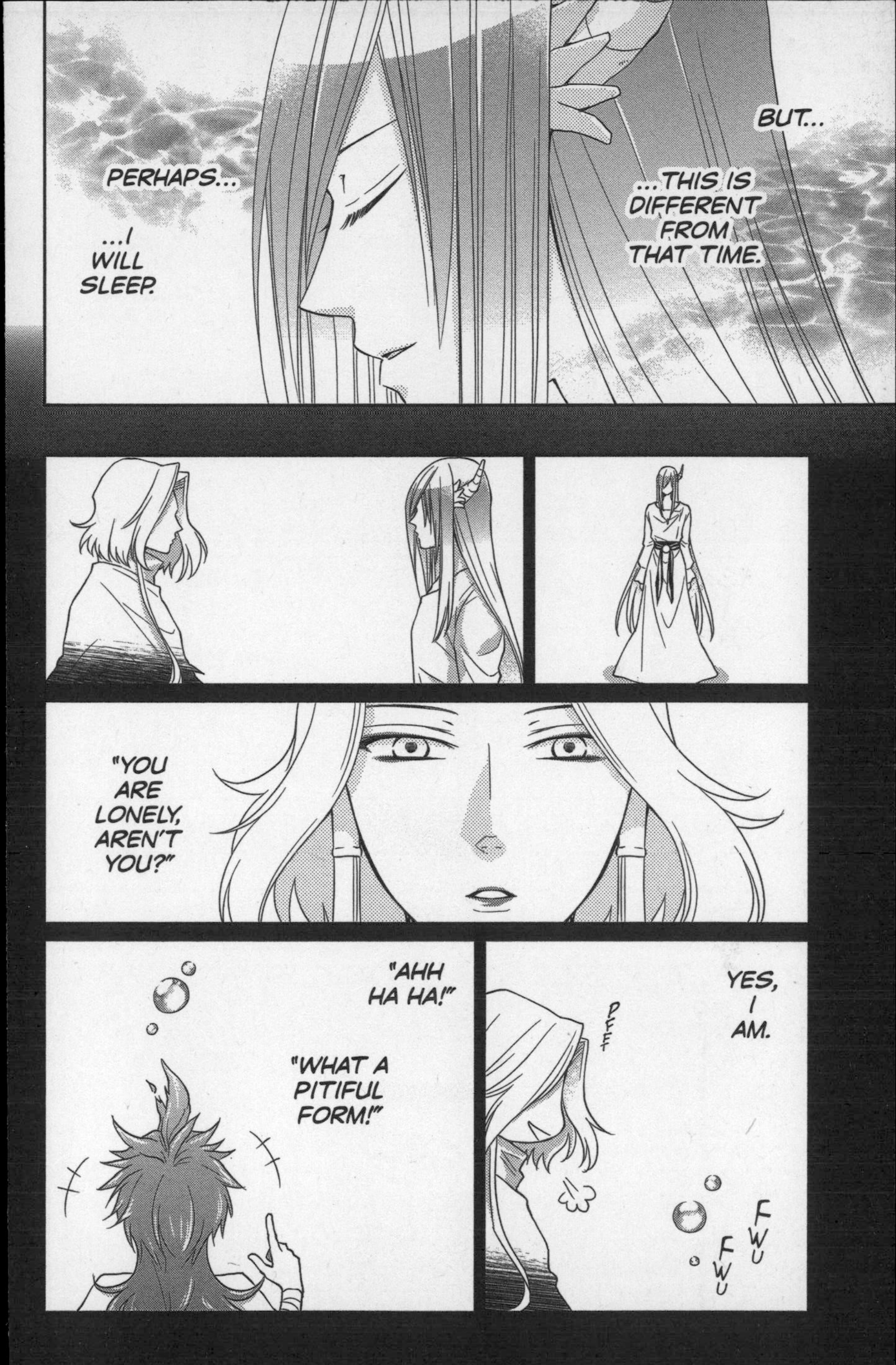
BUT...
...THIS IS DIFFERENT FROM THAT TIME.
PERHAPS...
...I WILL SLEEP.
"YOU ARE LONELY, AREN'T YOU?"
YES, I AM.
FWU
FWU
"AHH HA HA!"
"WHAT A PITIFUL FORM!"

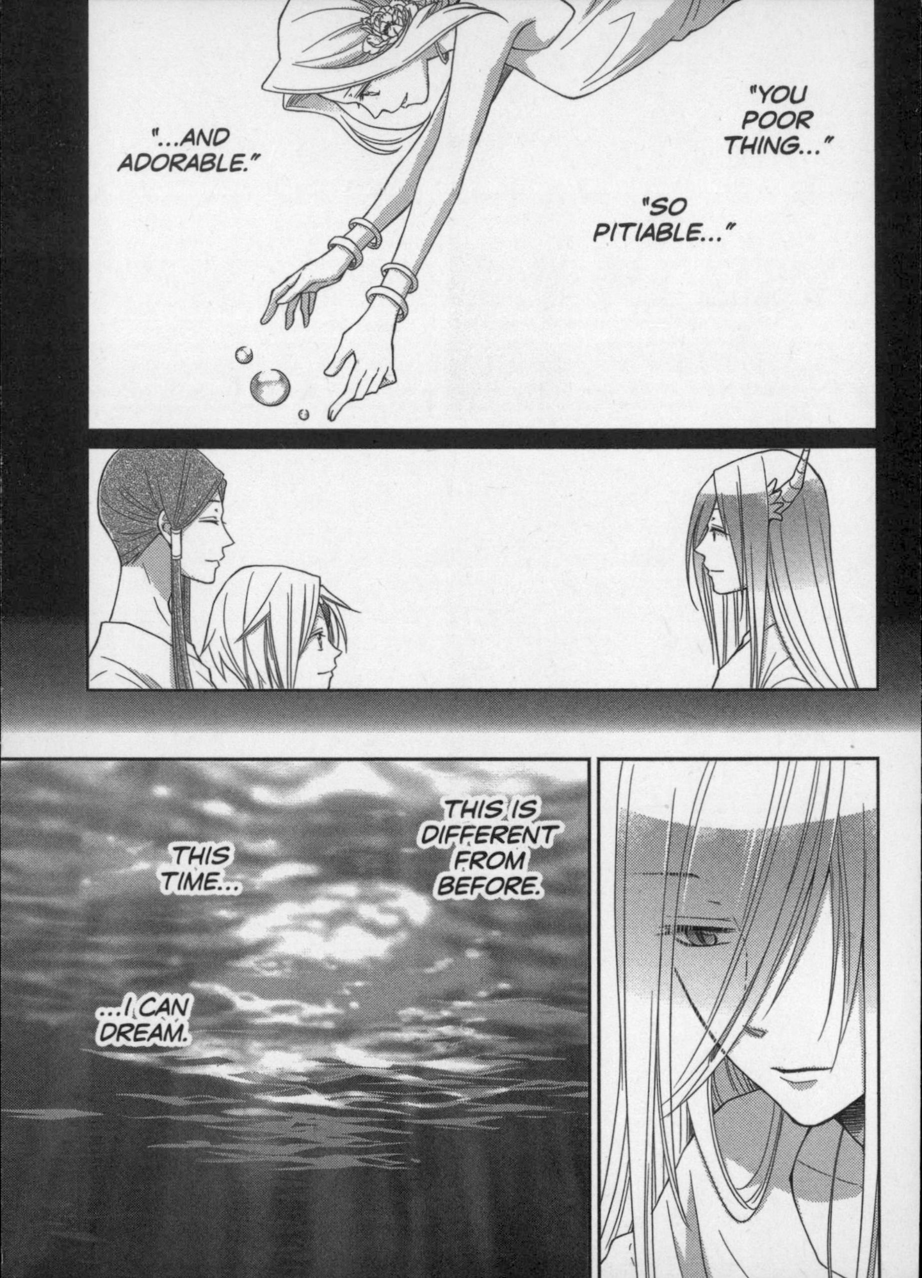
"YOU POOR THING..."
"SO PITIABLE..."
"...AND ADORABLE."
THIS IS DIFFERENT FROM BEFORE.
THIS TIME...
...I CAN DREAM.

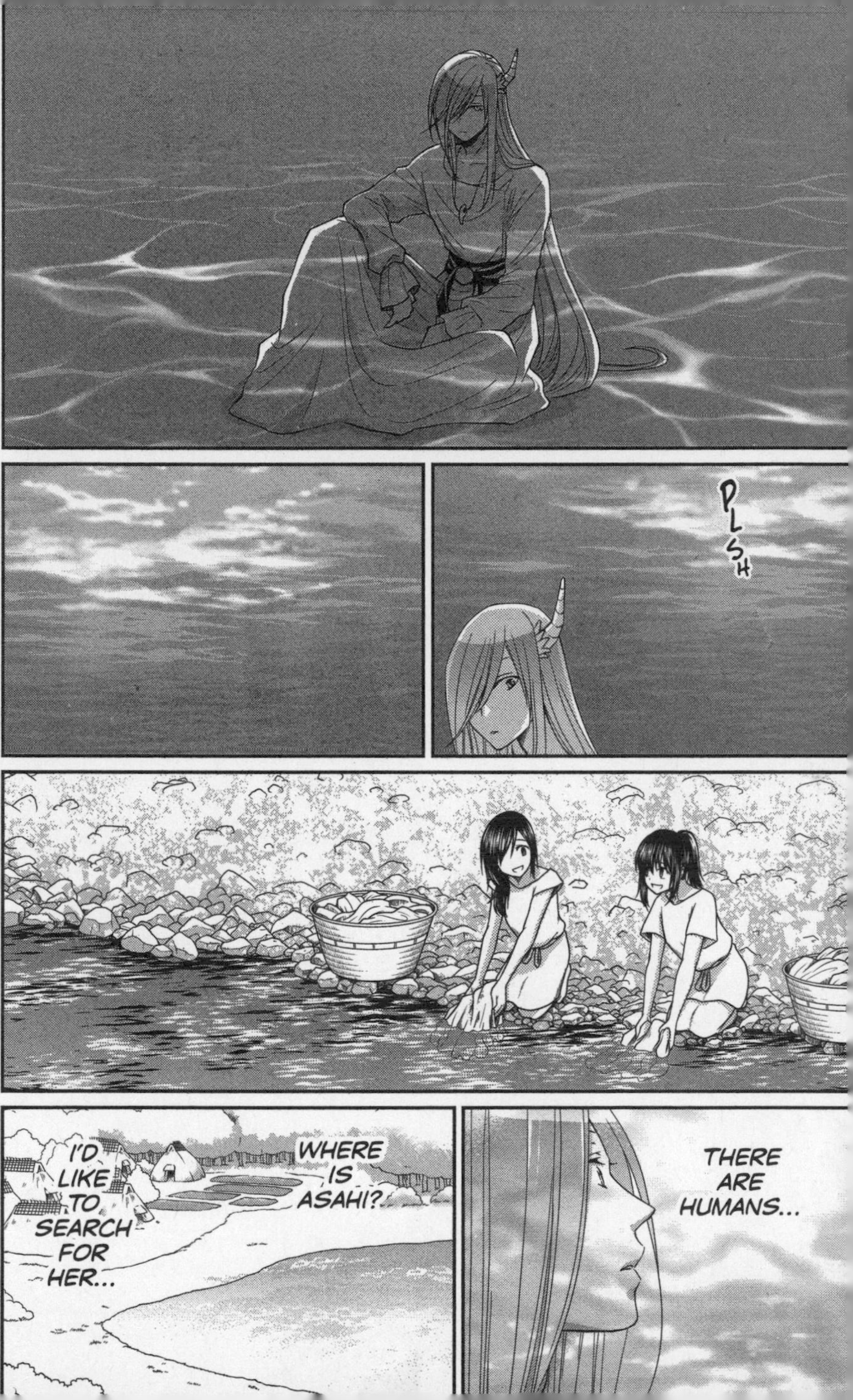
PLSH
THERE ARE HUMANS...
WHERE IS ASAHI?
I'D LIKE TO SEARCH FOR HER...

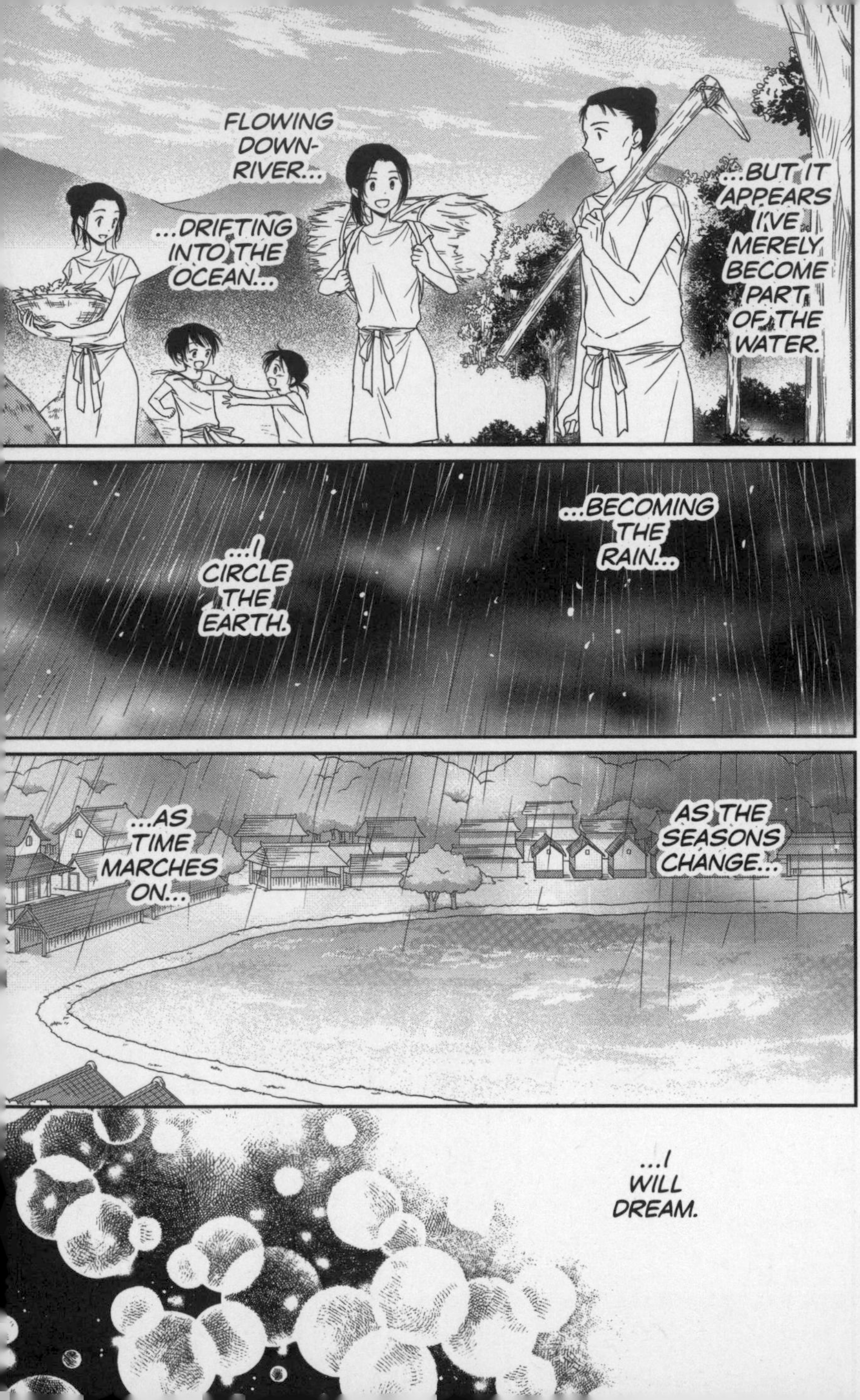
...BUT IT APPEARS I'VE MERELY BECOME PART OF THE WATER.
FLOWING DOWN-RIVER...
...DRIFTING INTO THE OCEAN...
...BECOMING THE RAIN...
...I CIRCLE THE EARTH.
AS THE SEASONS CHANGE...
...AS TIME MARCHES ON...
...I WILL DREAM.

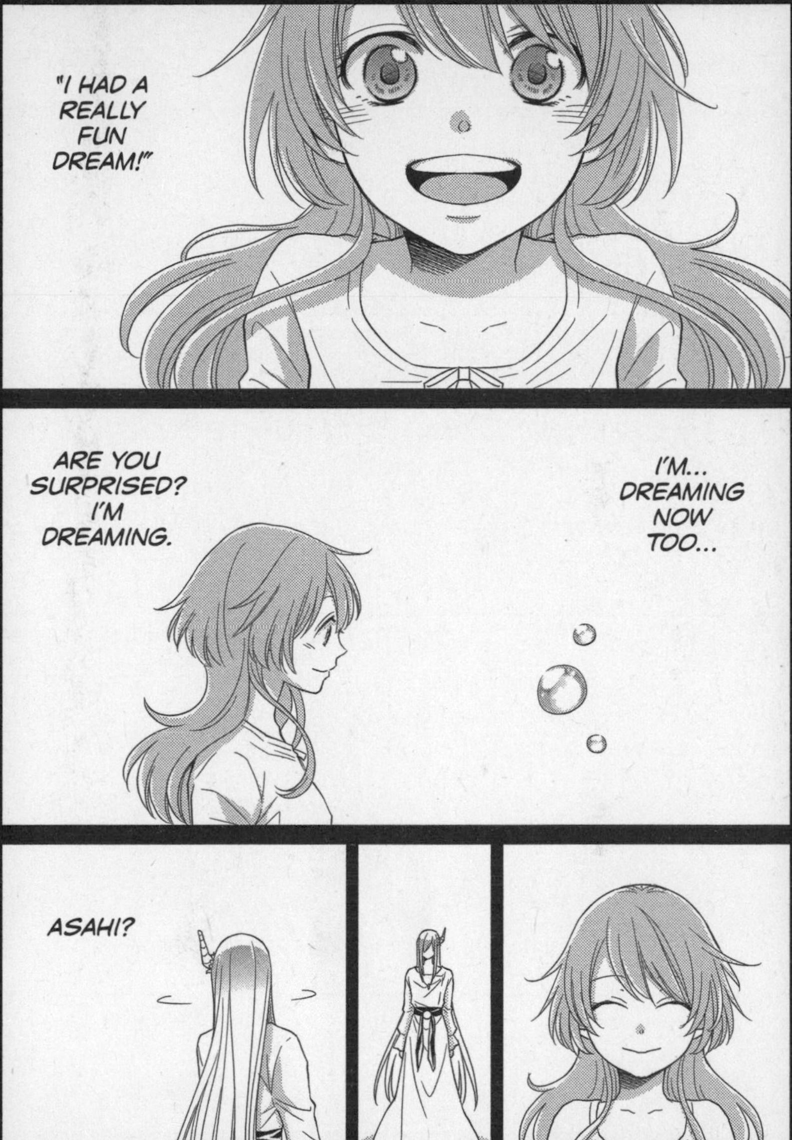
"I HAD A REALLY FUN DREAM!"
I'M... DREAMING NOW TOO...
ARE YOU SURPRISED? I'M DREAMING.
ASAHI?

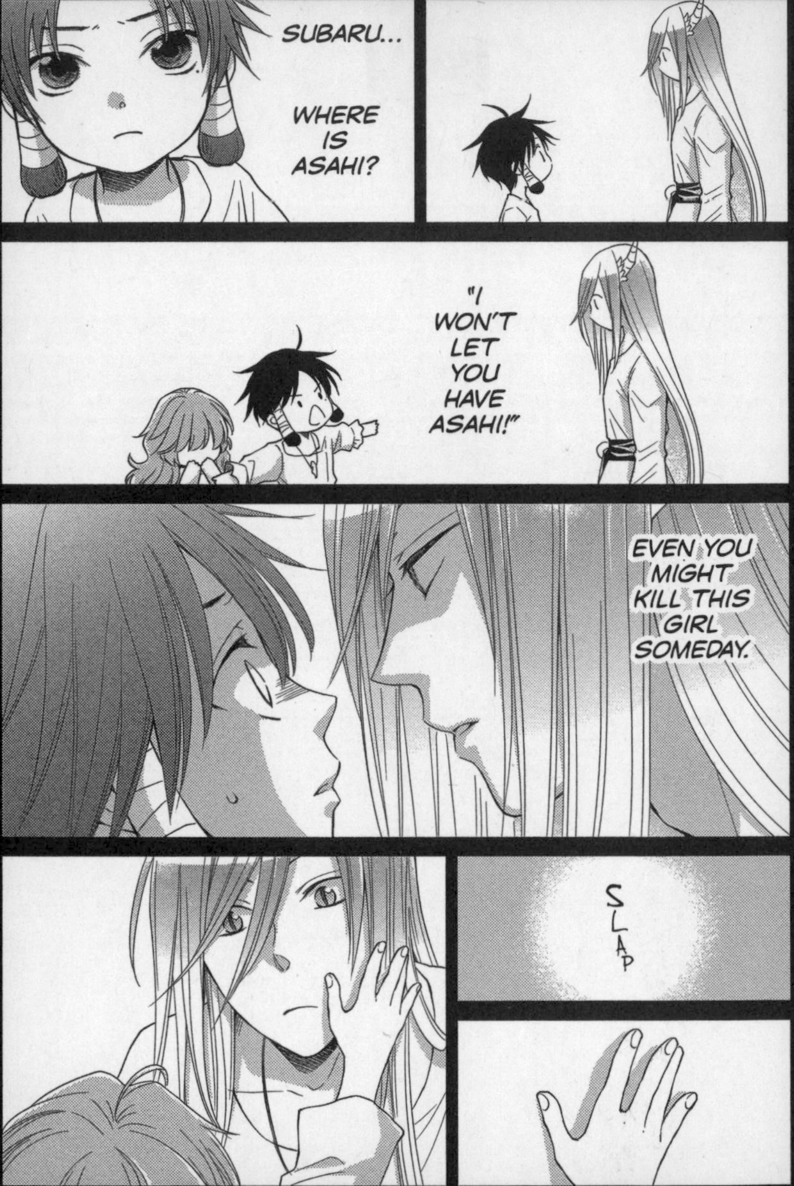
SUBARU...
WHERE IS ASAHI?
"I WON'T LET YOU HAVE ASAHI!"
EVEN YOU MIGHT KILL THIS GIRL SOMEDAY.
SLAP

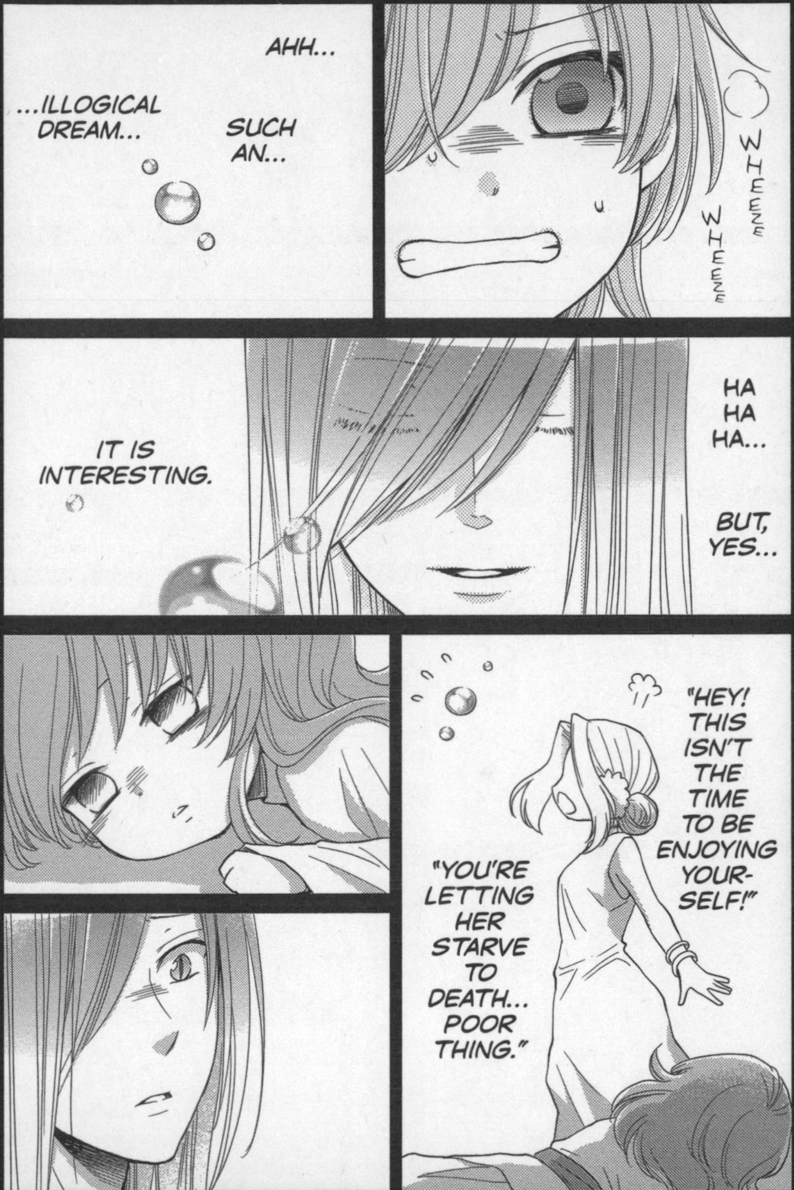
WHEEZE
WHEEZE
AHH...
SUCH AN...
...ILLOGICAL DREAM...
HA HA HA...
BUT, YES...
IT IS INTERESTING.
"HEY! THIS ISN'T THE TIME TO BE ENJOYING YOURSELF!"
"YOU'RE LETTING HER STARVE TO DEATH... POOR THING."

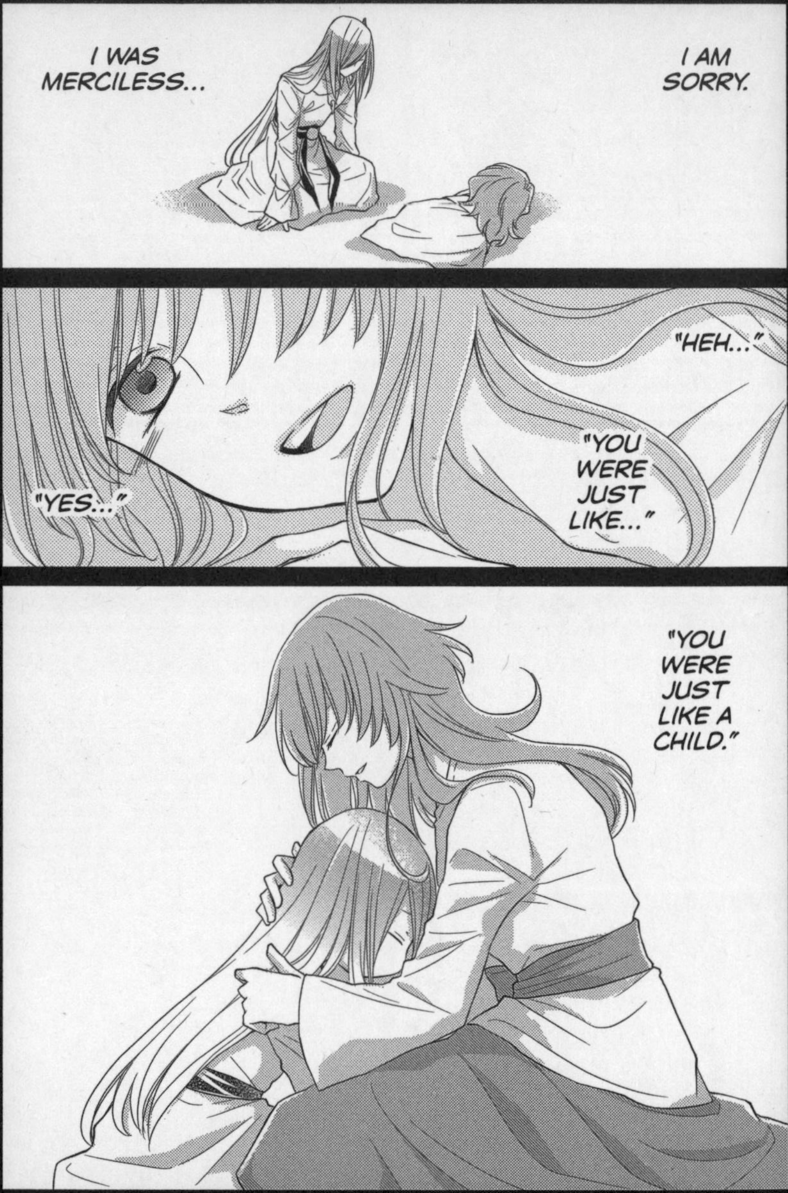
I AM SORRY.
I WAS MERCILESS...
"HEH..."
"YOU WERE JUST LIKE..."
"YES..."
"YOU WERE JUST LIKE A CHILD."

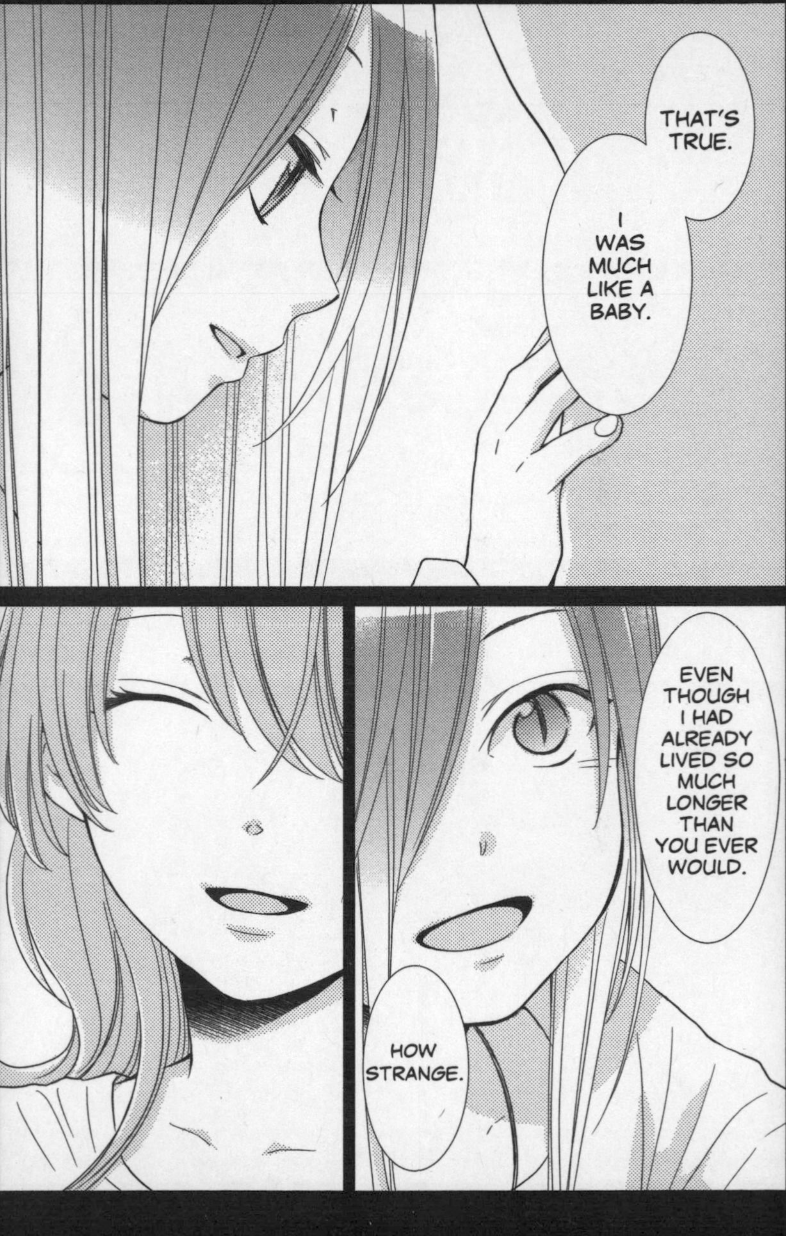
THAT'S TRUE.
I WAS MUCH LIKE A BABY.
EVEN THOUGH I HAD ALREADY LIVED SO MUCH LONGER THAN YOU EVER WOULD.
HOW STRANGE.

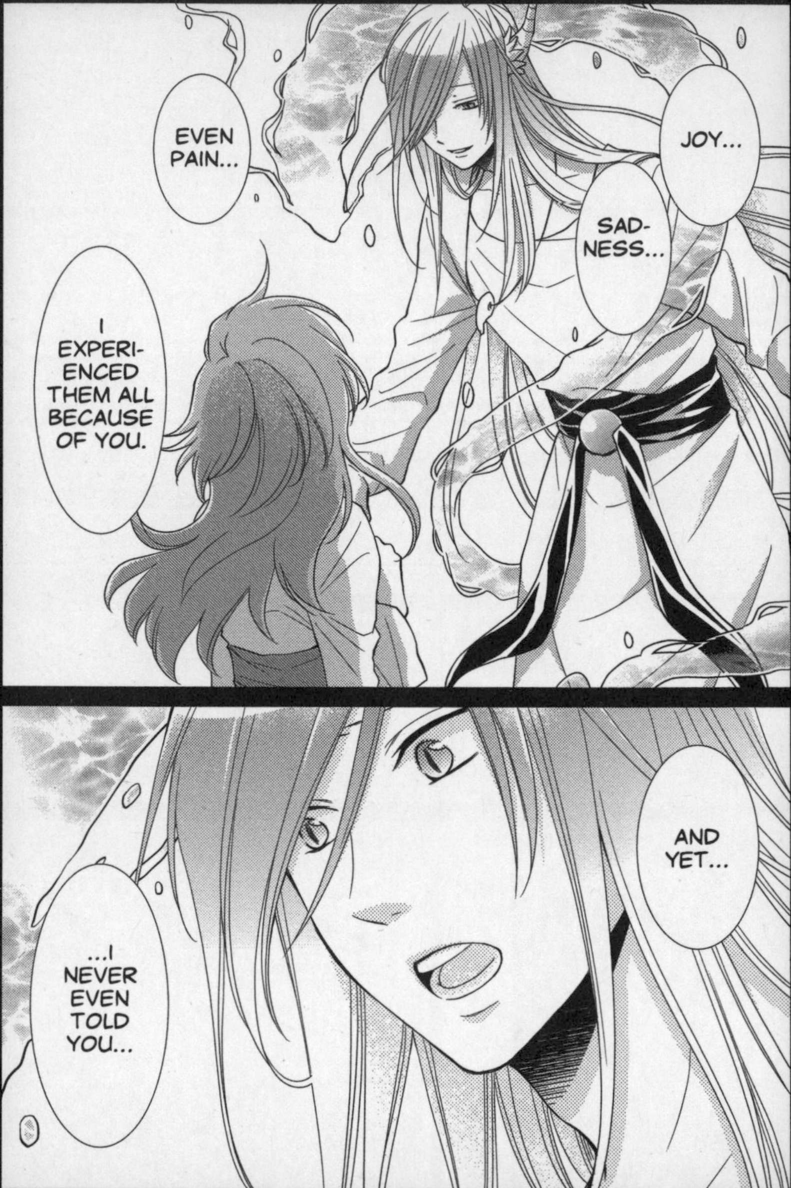
JOY...
SAD-NESS...
EVEN PAIN...
I EXPERI-ENCED THEM ALL BECAUSE OF YOU.
AND YET...
...I NEVER EVEN TOLD YOU...

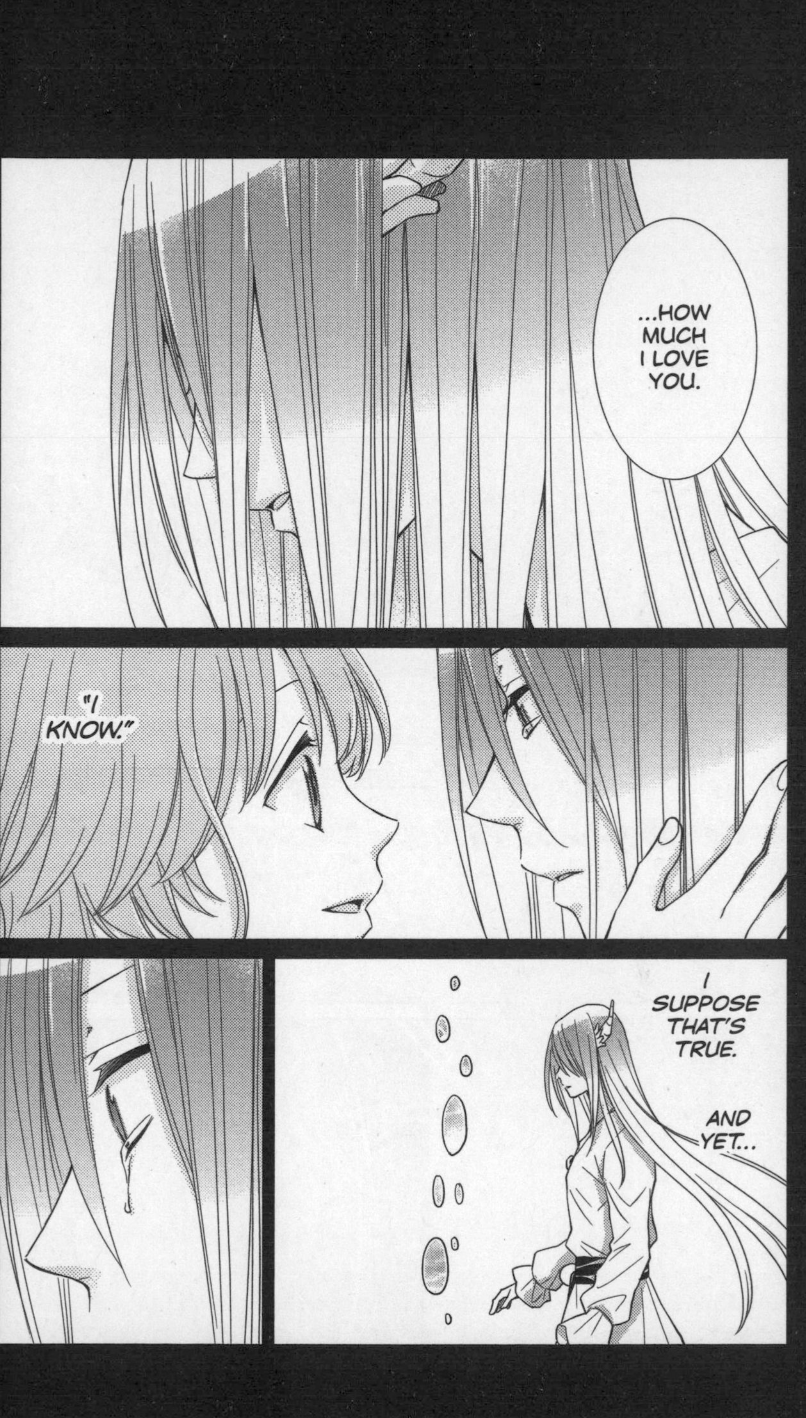
...HOW MUCH I LOVE YOU.
"I KNOW."
I SUPPOSE THAT'S TRUE.
AND YET...

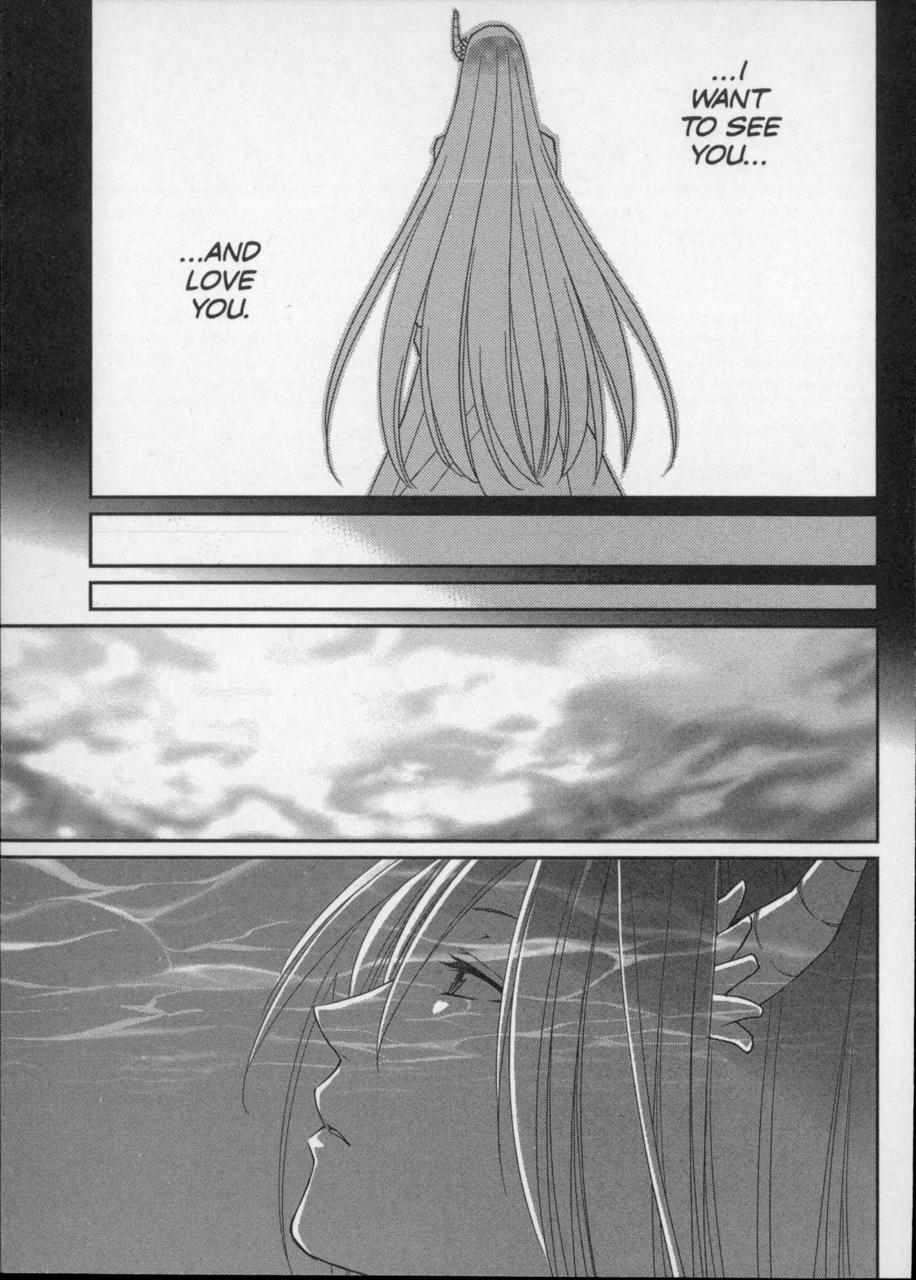
...I WANT TO SEE YOU...
...AND LOVE YOU.

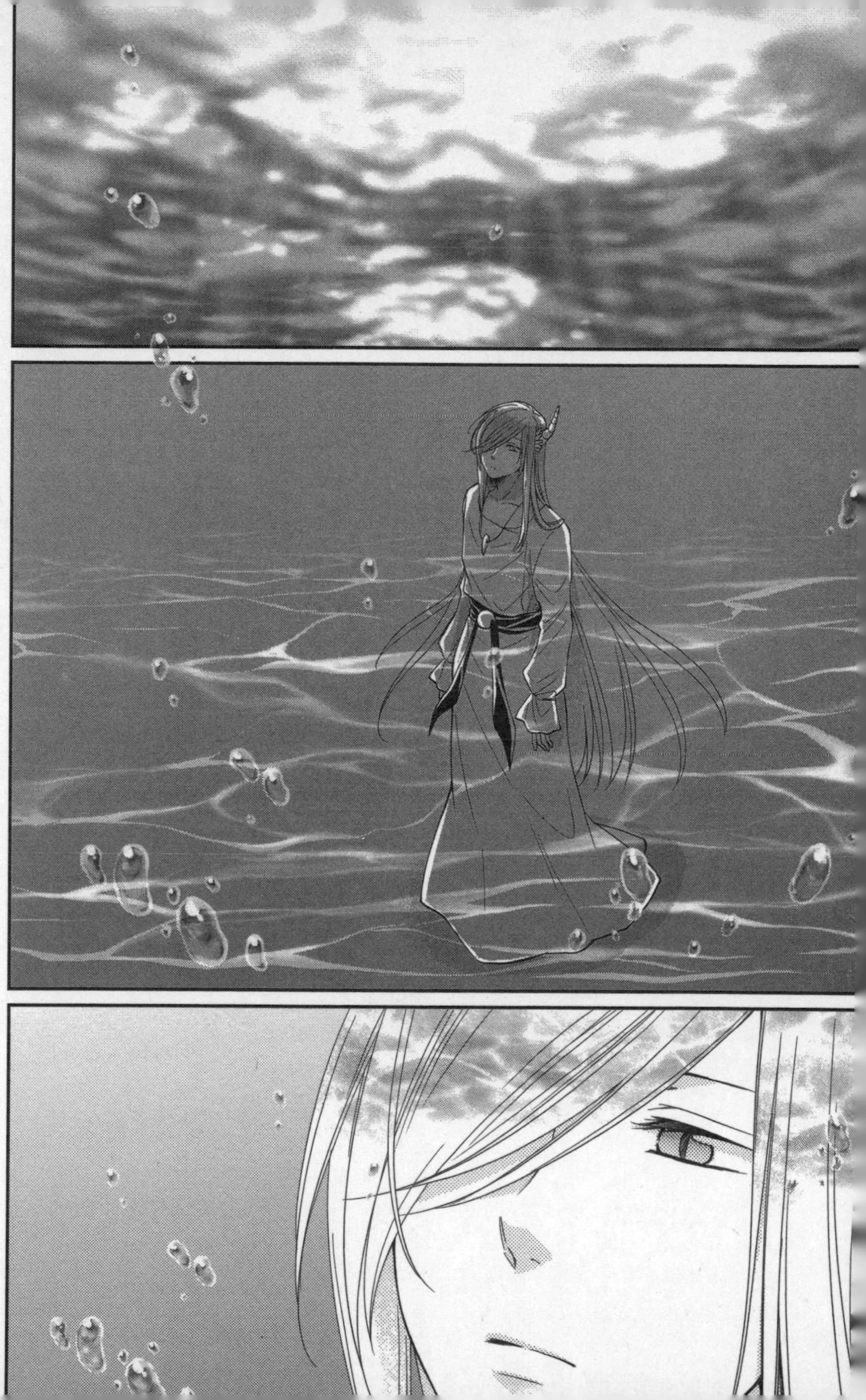

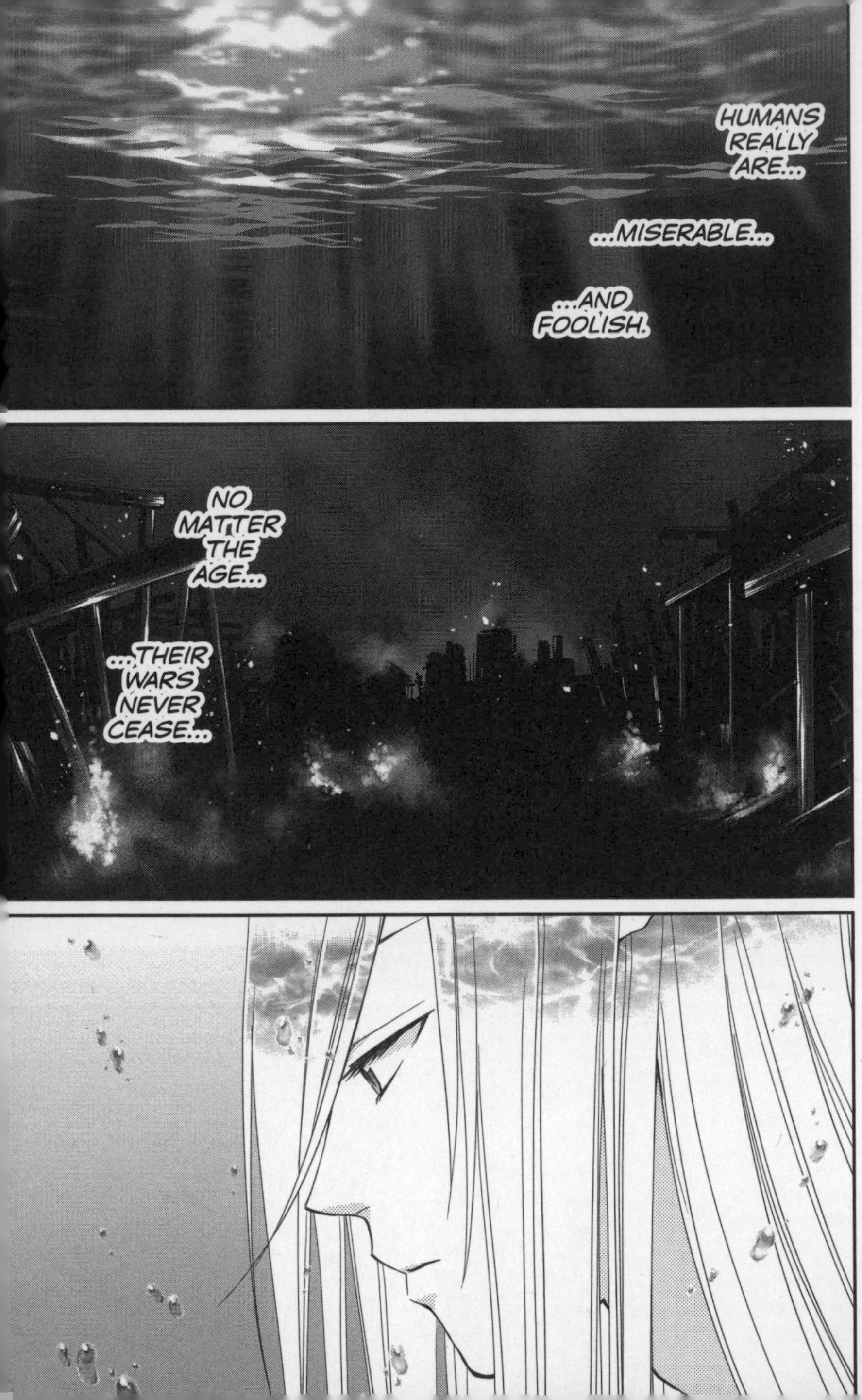
HUMANS REALLY ARE...
...MISERABLE...
...AND FOOLISH.
NO MATTER THE AGE...
...THEIR WARS NEVER CEASE...

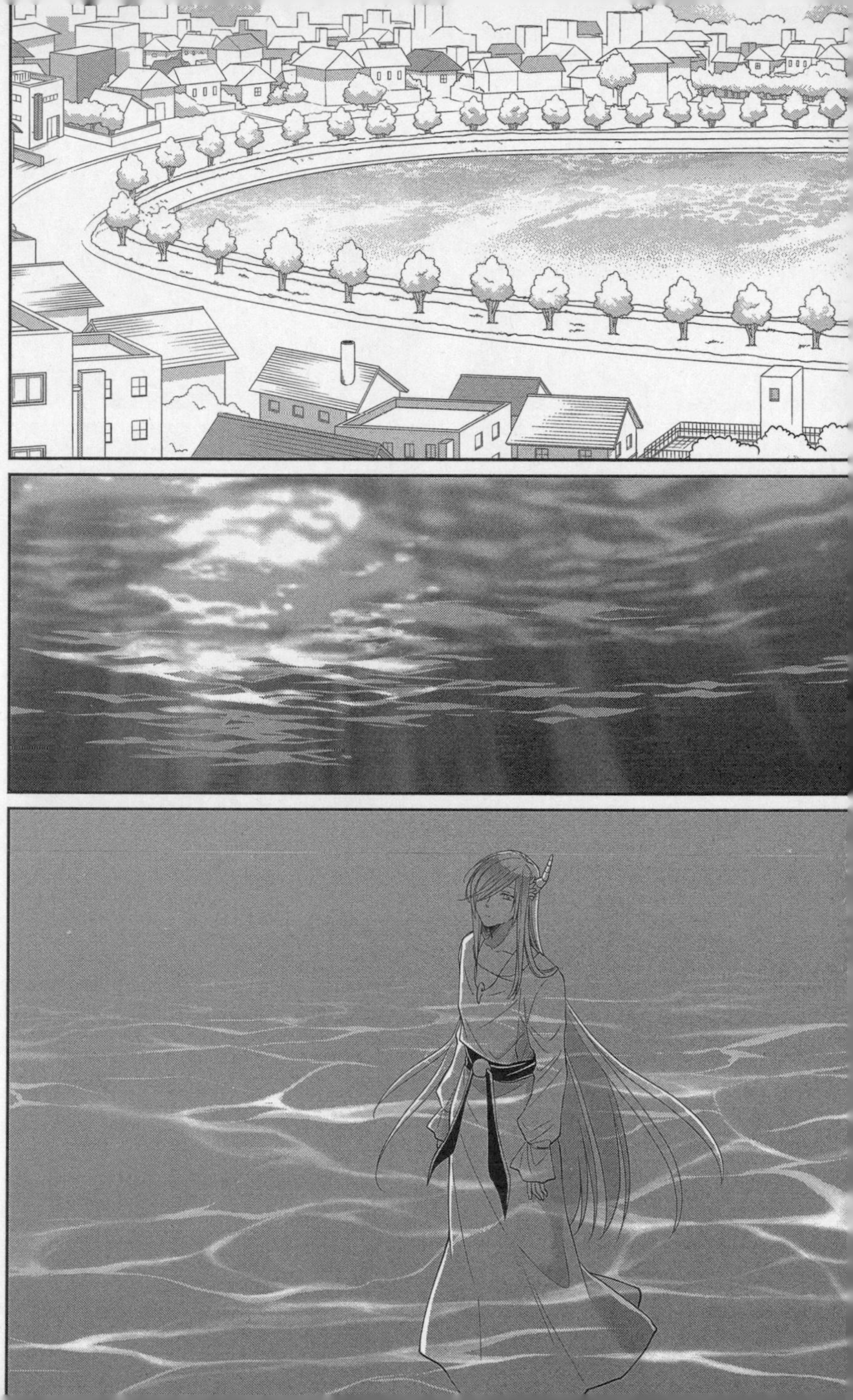

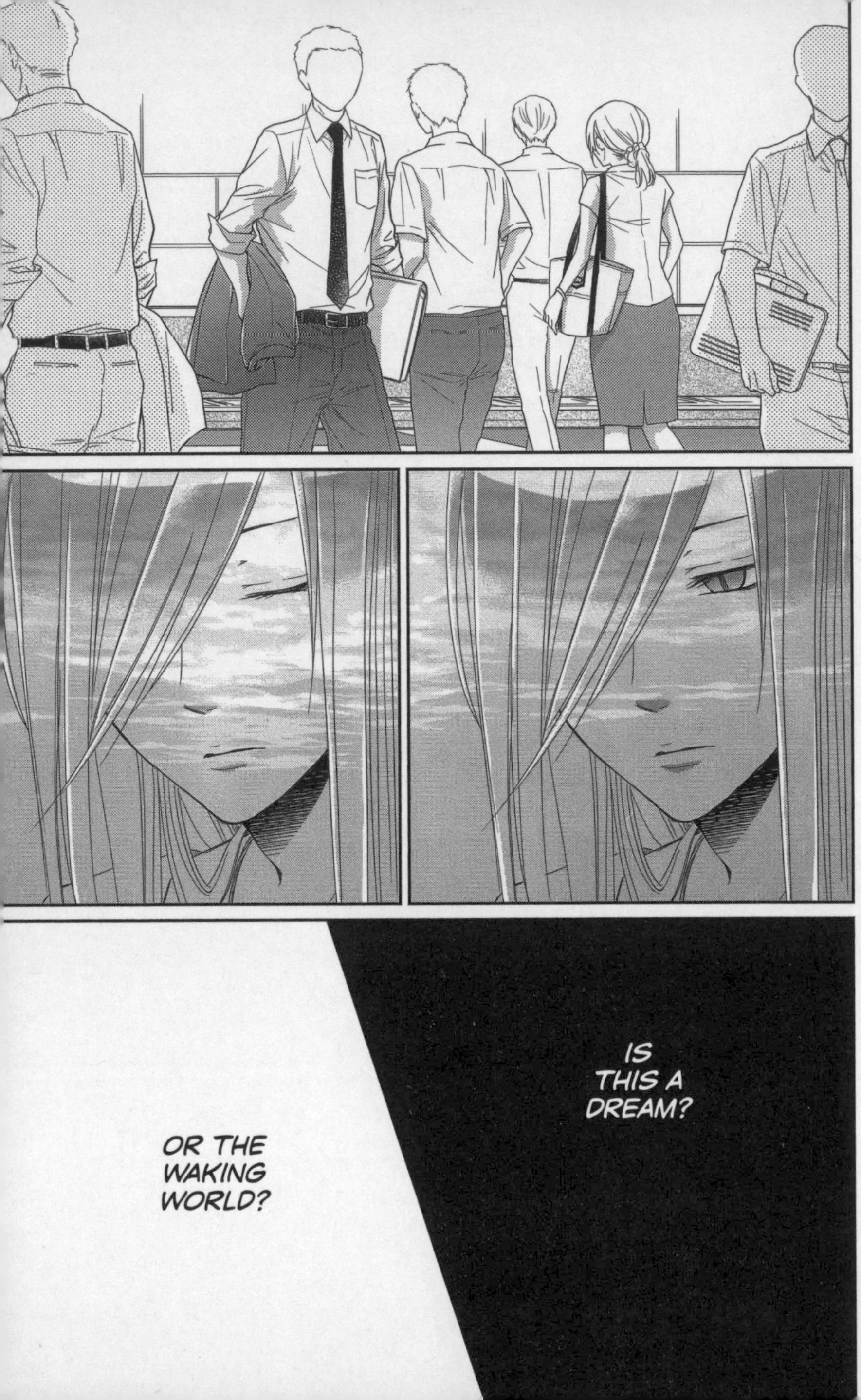
IS THIS A DREAM?
OR THE WAKING WORLD?

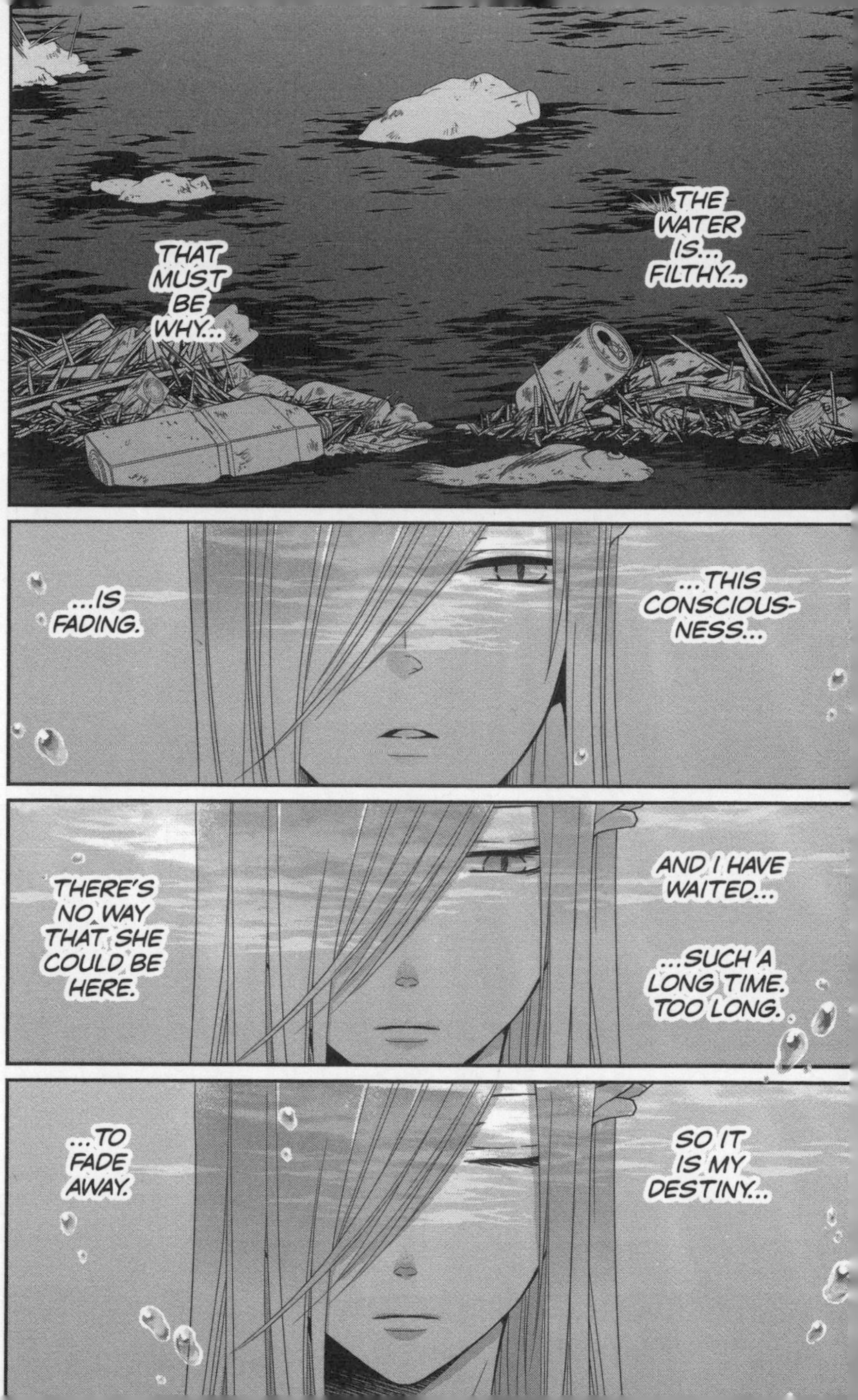
THE WATER IS... FILTHY...
THAT MUST BE WHY...
...THIS CONSCIOUS-NESS...
...IS FADING.
AND I HAVE WAITED...
...SUCH A LONG TIME. TOO LONG.
THERE'S NO WAY THAT SHE COULD BE HERE.
SO IT IS MY DESTINY...
...TO FADE AWAY.

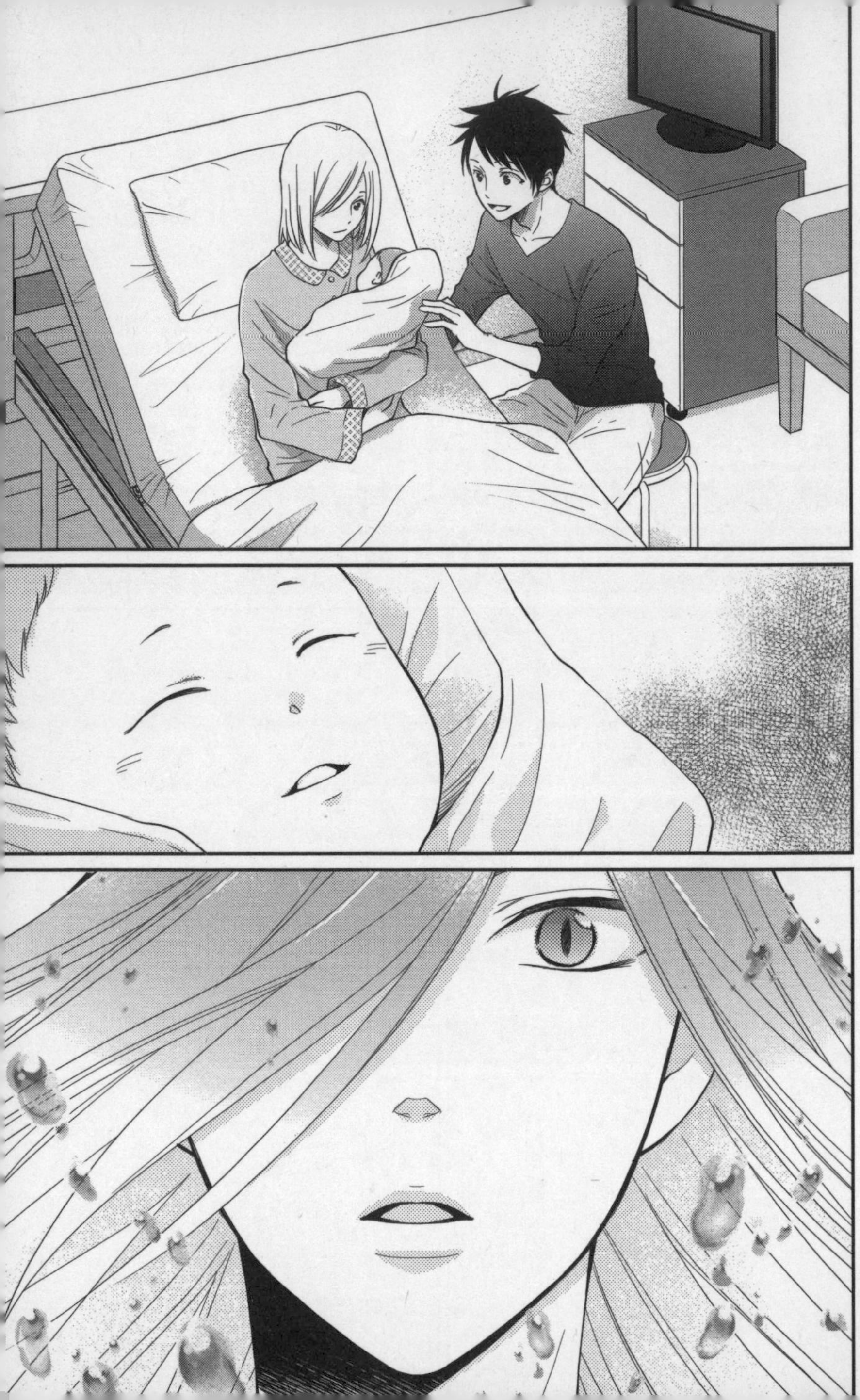

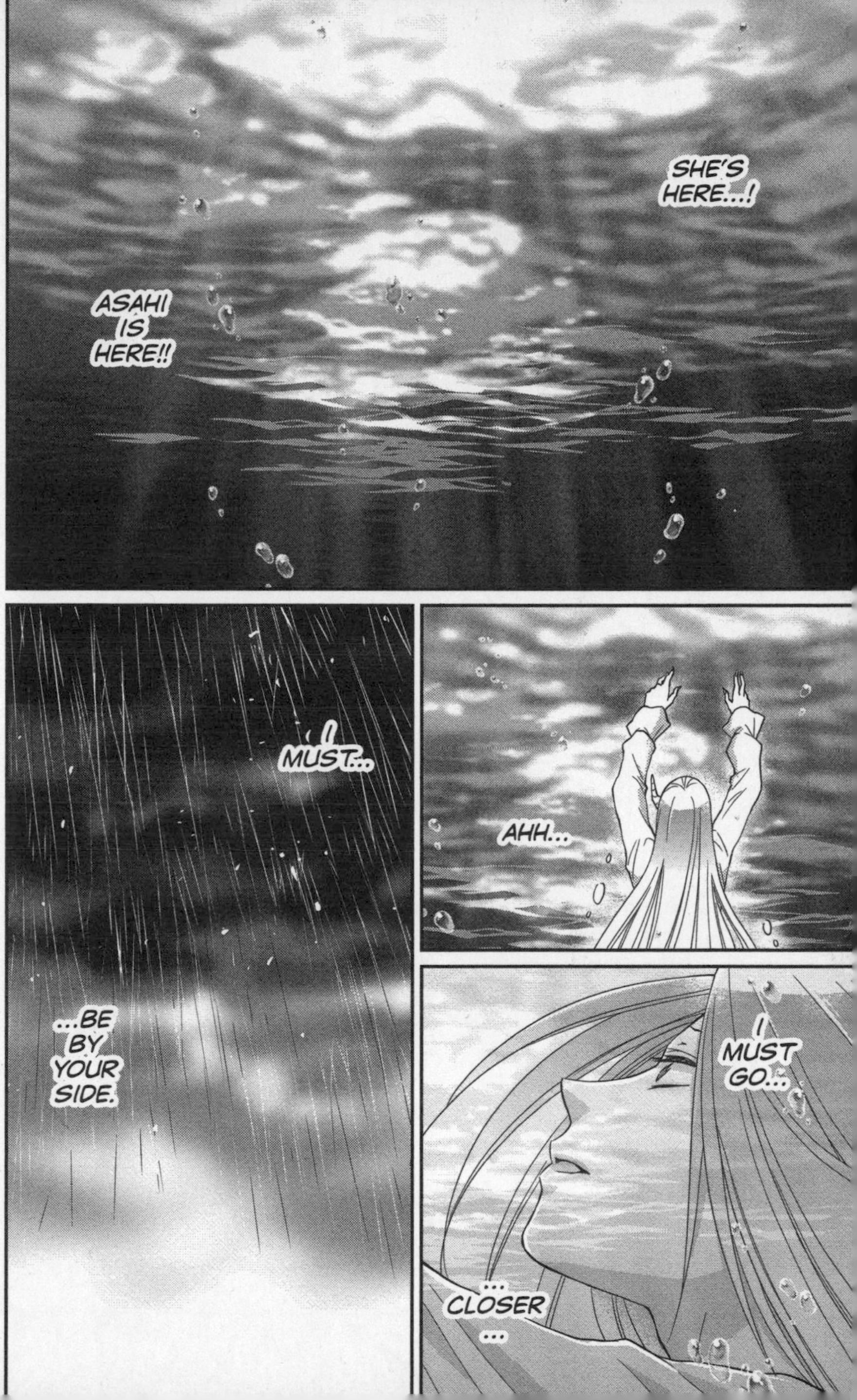
SHE'S HERE...!
ASAHI IS HERE!!
AHH...
I MUST GO...
...CLOSER...
I MUST...
...BE BY YOUR SIDE.

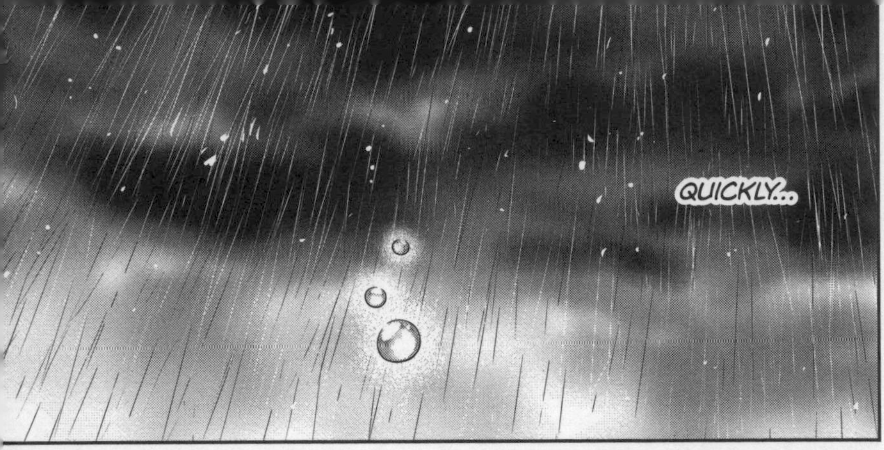
QUICKLY...
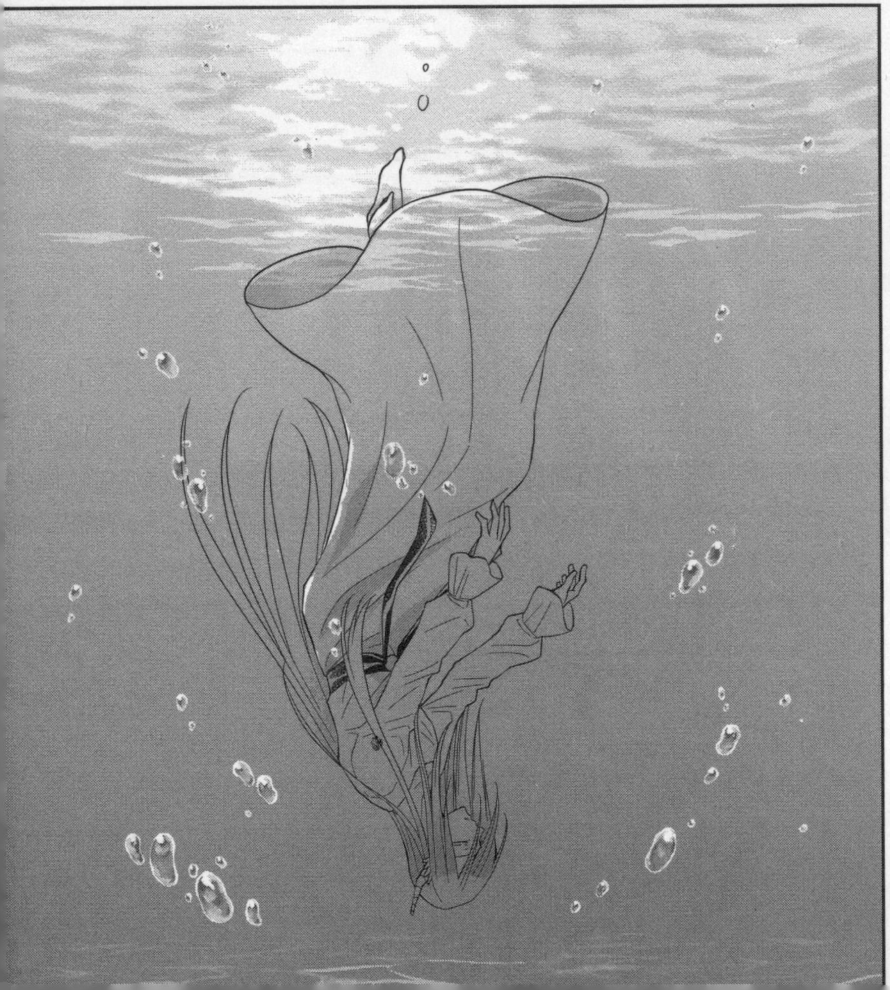

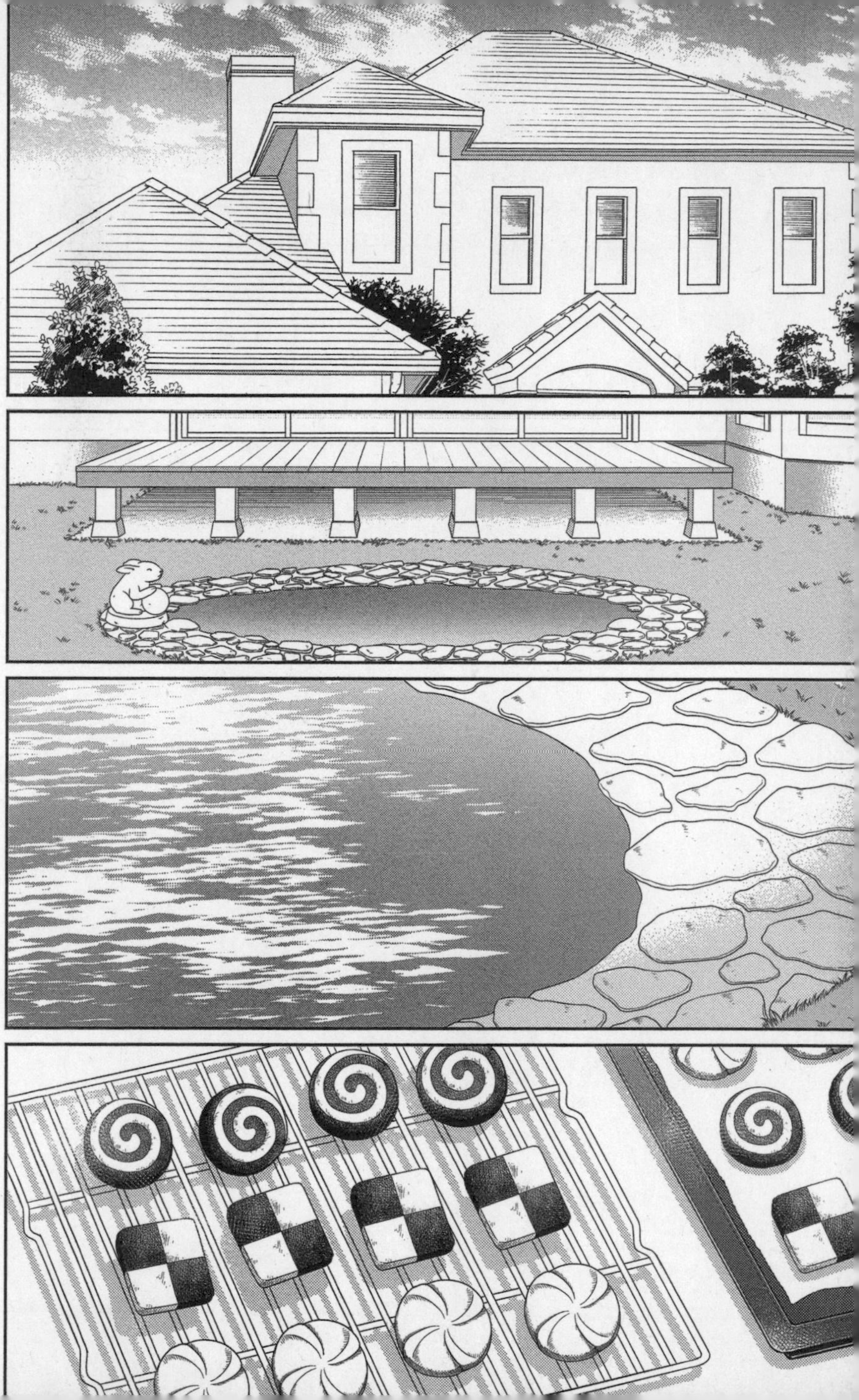

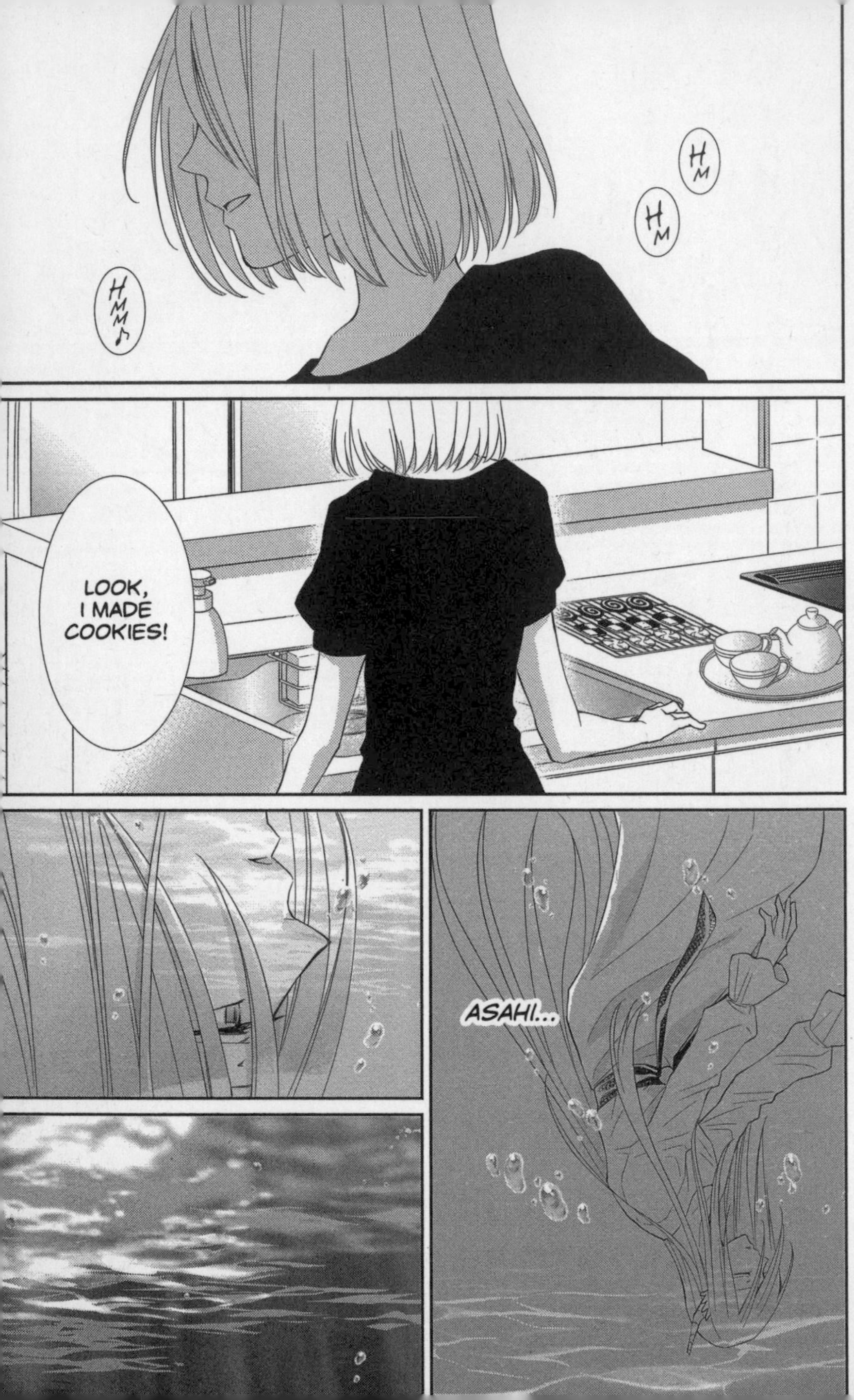
HM
HM
HMM♪
LOOK, I MADE COOKIES!
ASAHI...

HEY! COME LOOK AT THIS!

WHAT IS IT, DAD?

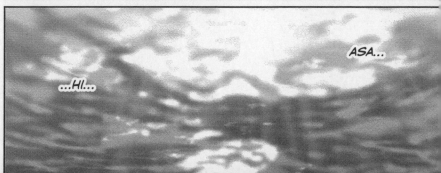

ASA...

...HI...

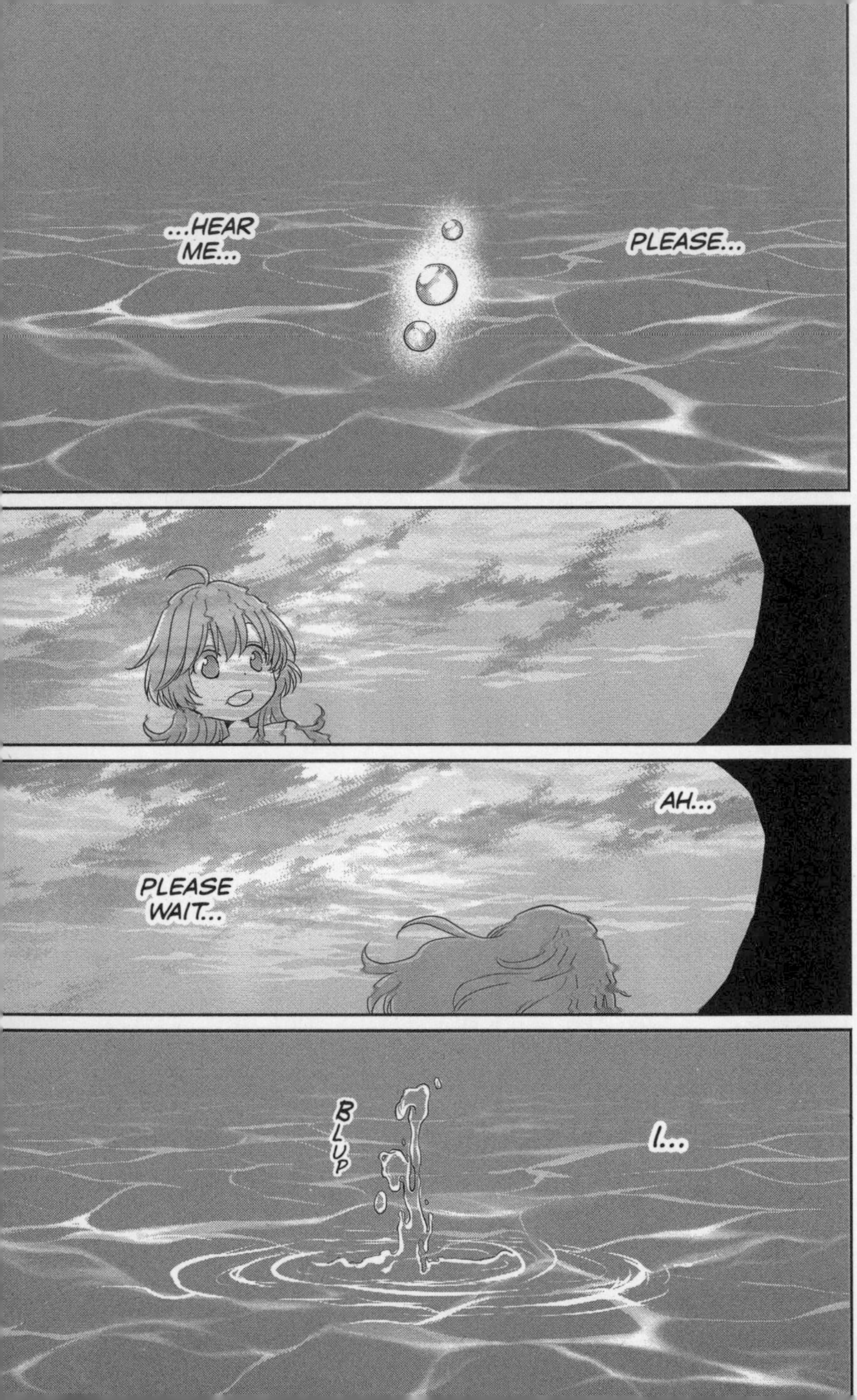
PLEASE...
...HEAR ME...
AH...
PLEASE WAIT...
I...
BLUP

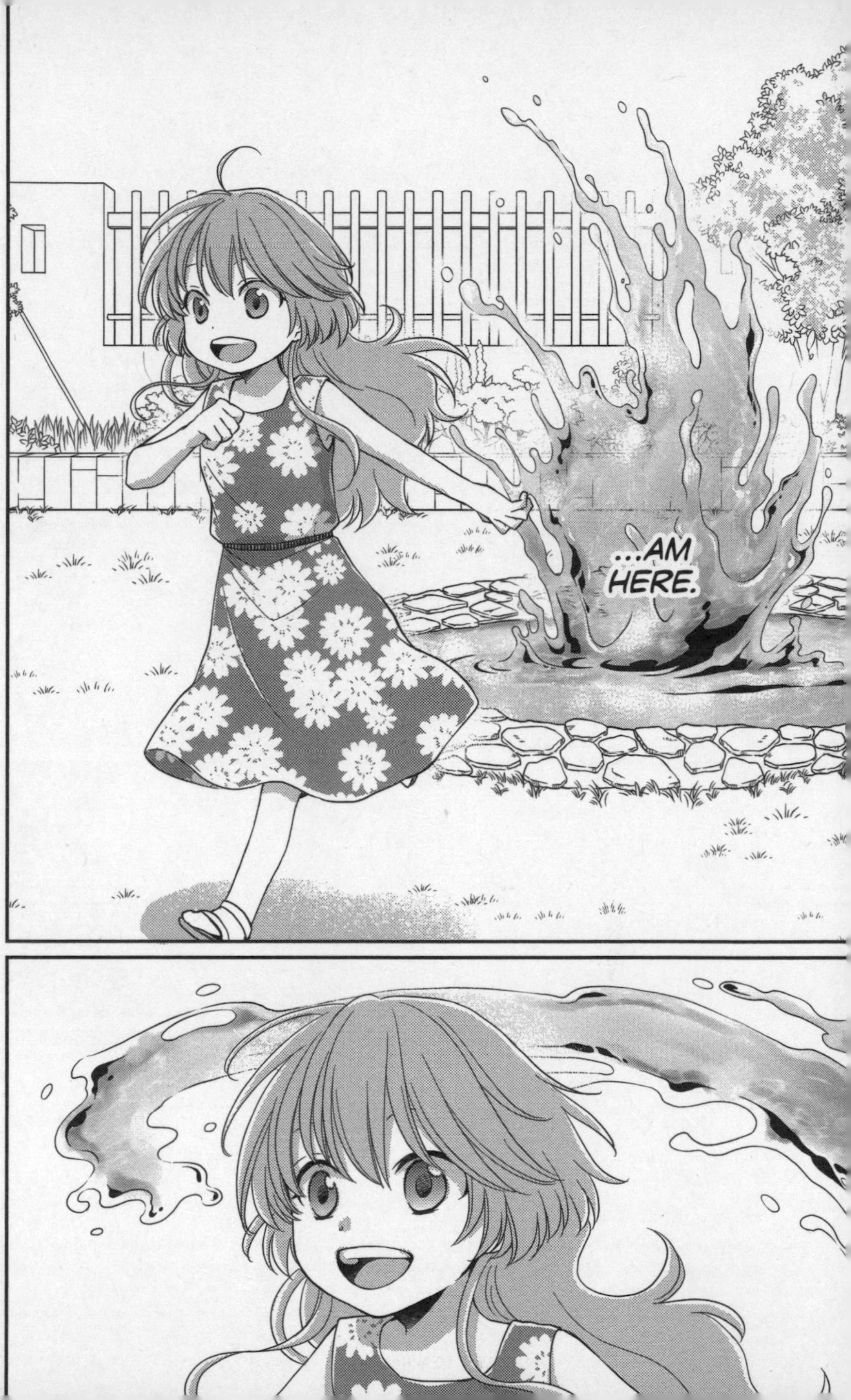
...AM
HERE.

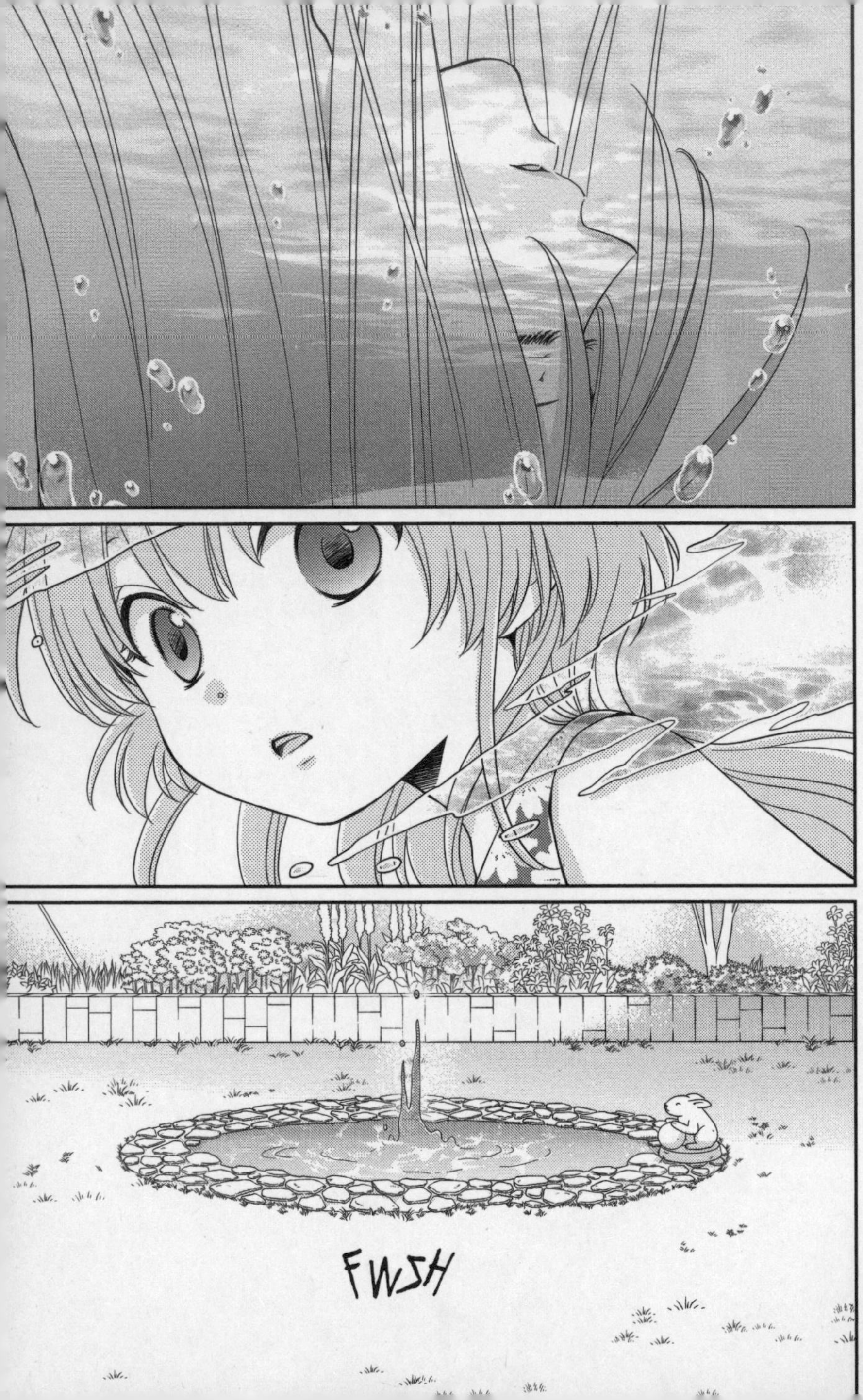
FWSH

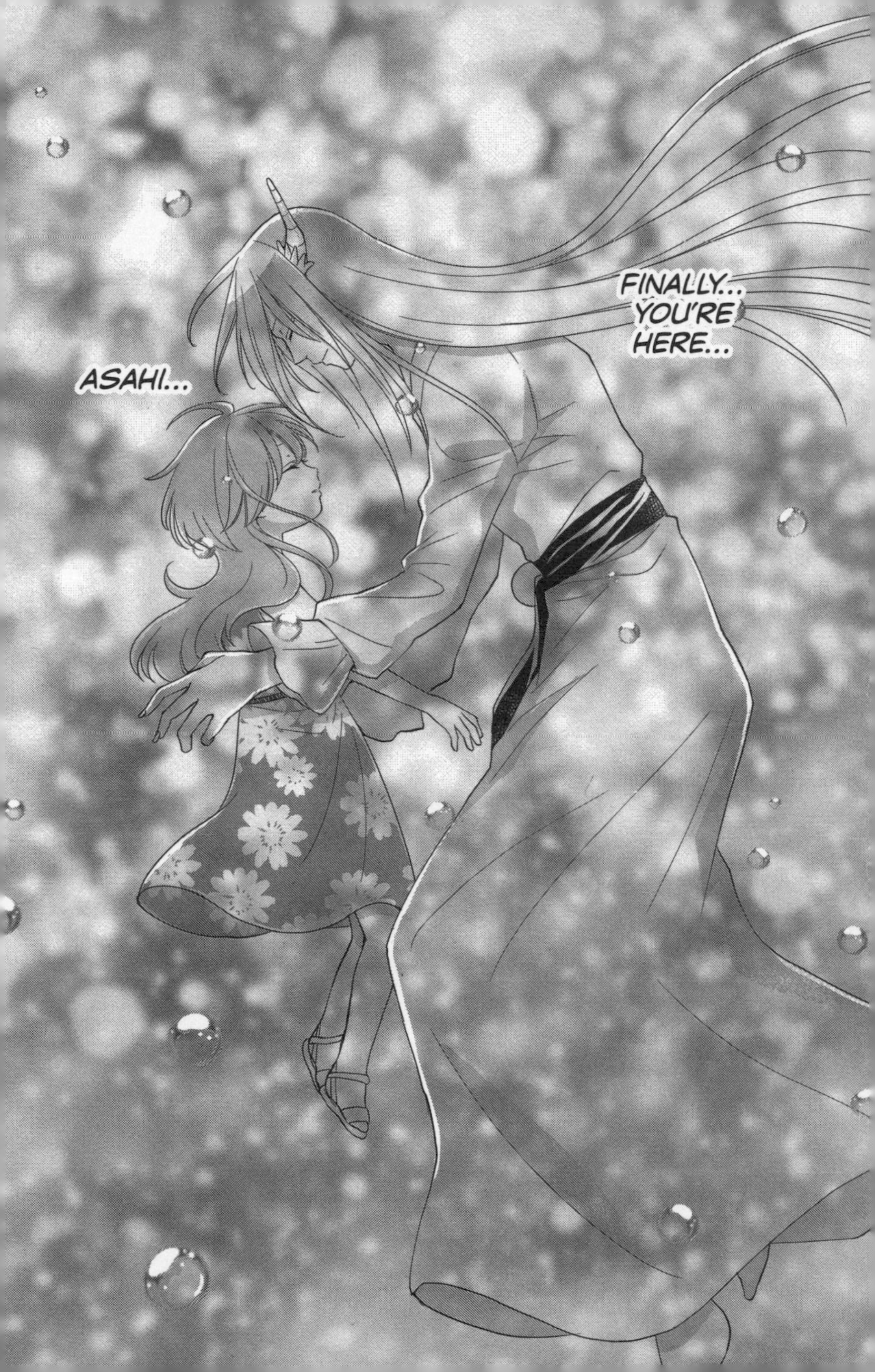
FINALLY... YOU'RE HERE...
ASAHI...

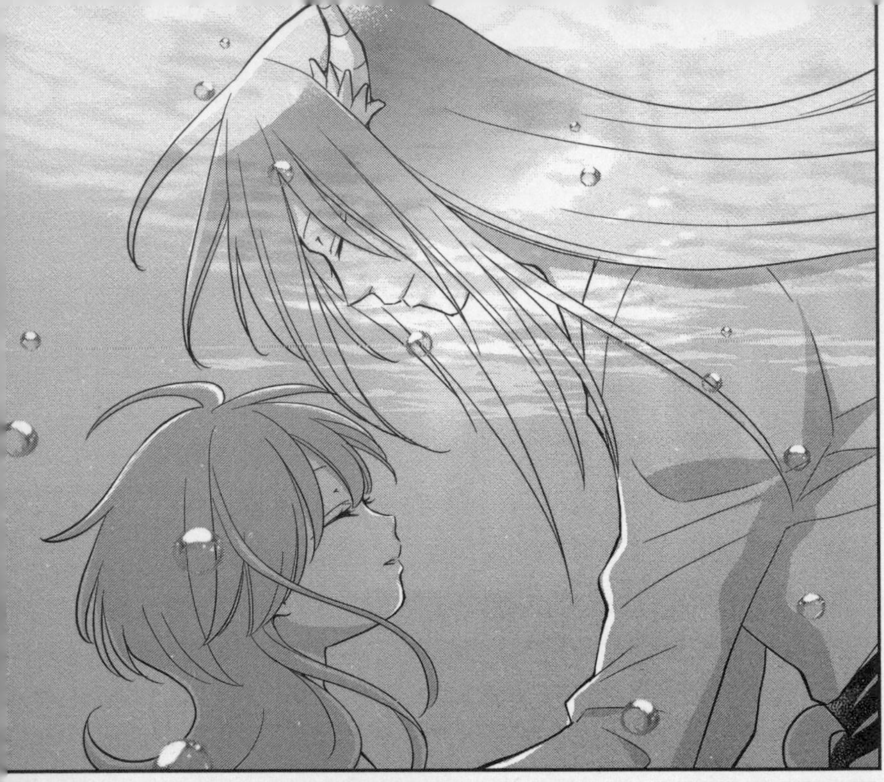
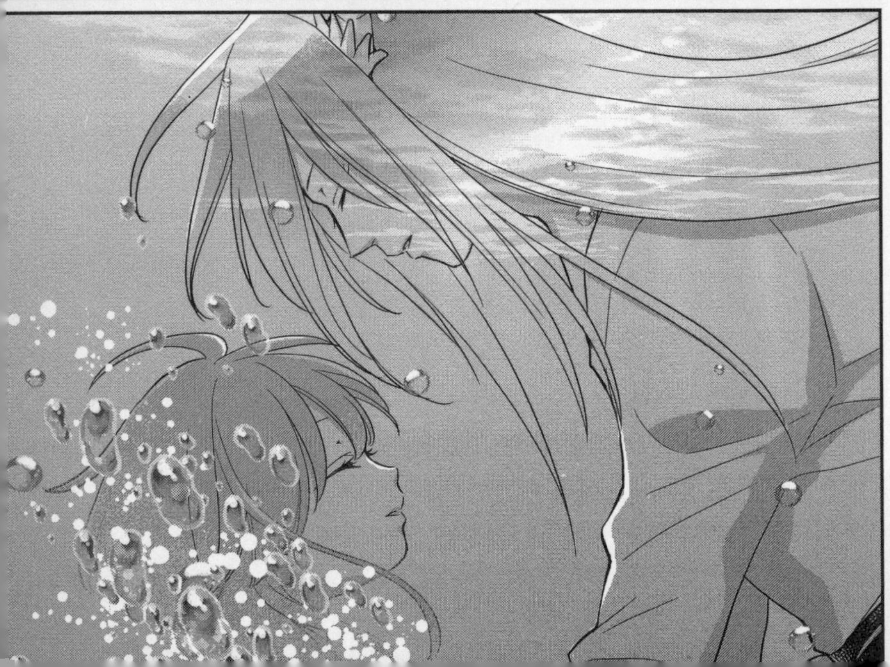

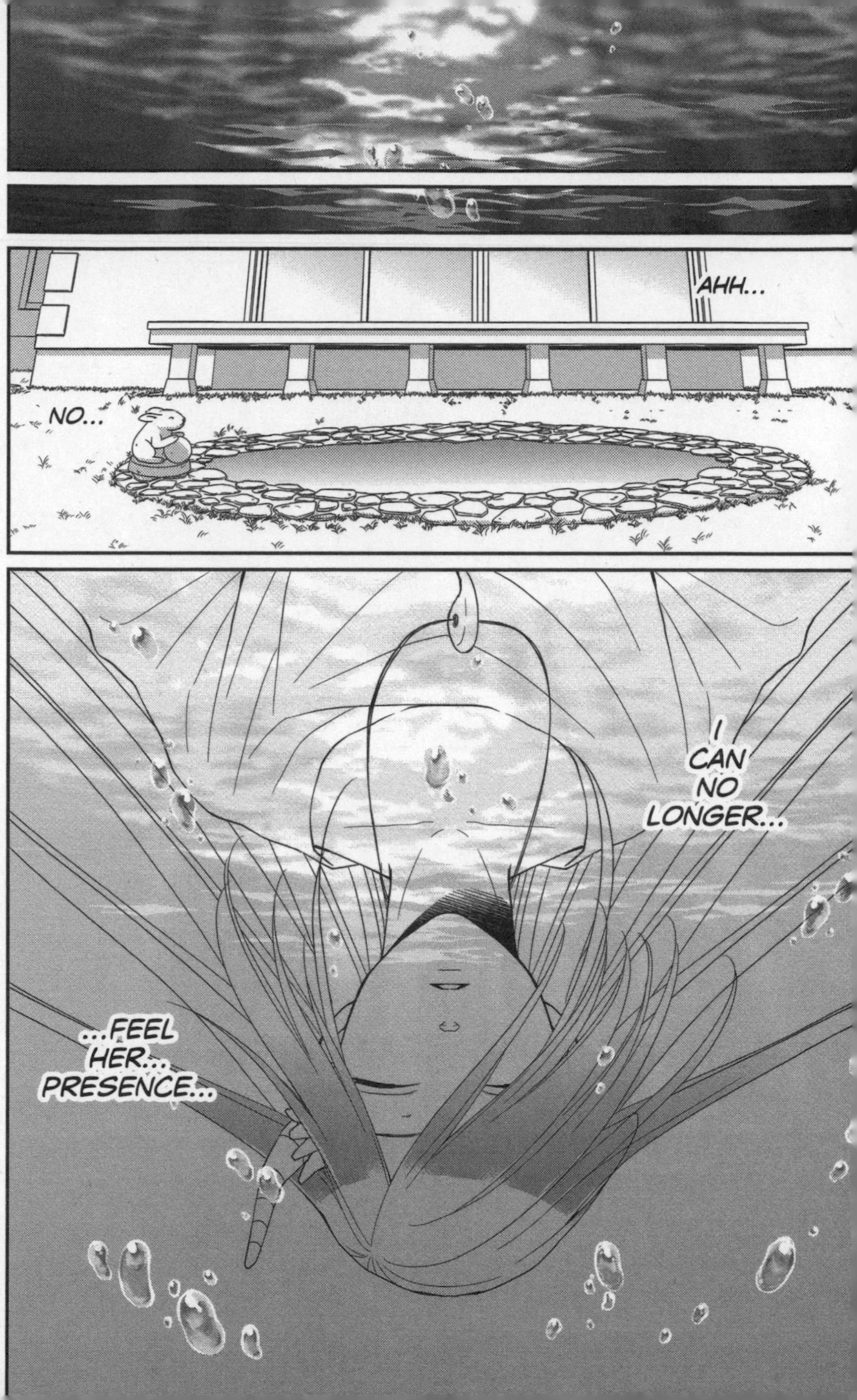
AHH...
NO...
I CAN NO LONGER...
...FEEL HER... PRESENCE...

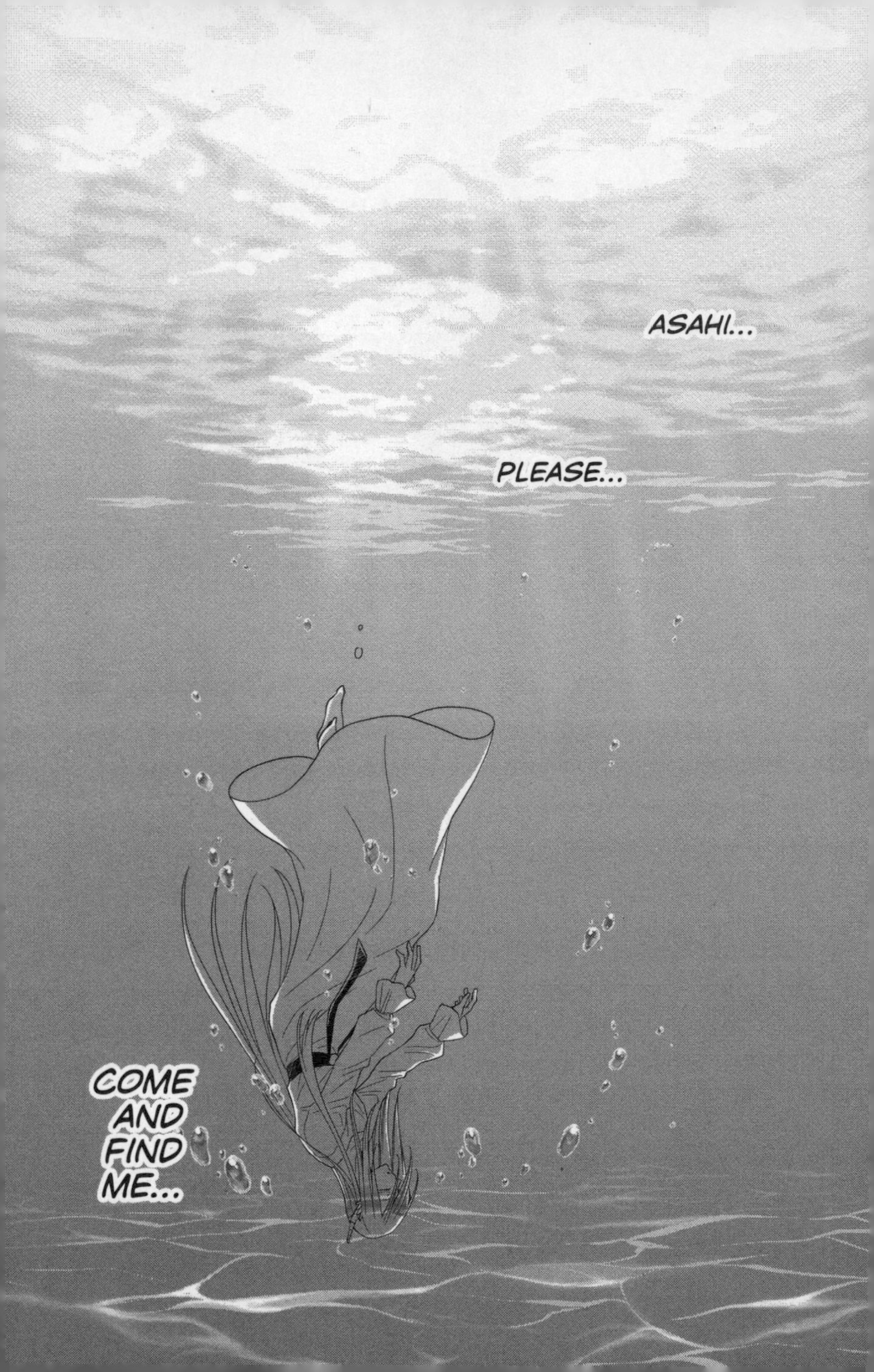
ASAHI...
PLEASE...
COME AND FIND ME...

THE CHARACTER WHO WAS THE MOST FUN TO
DRAW WAS DEFINITELY THE WATER DRAGON GOD.
I HONESTLY FEEL LIKE I HAVEN'T GOTTEN
MY FILL OF DRAWING HIM YET.

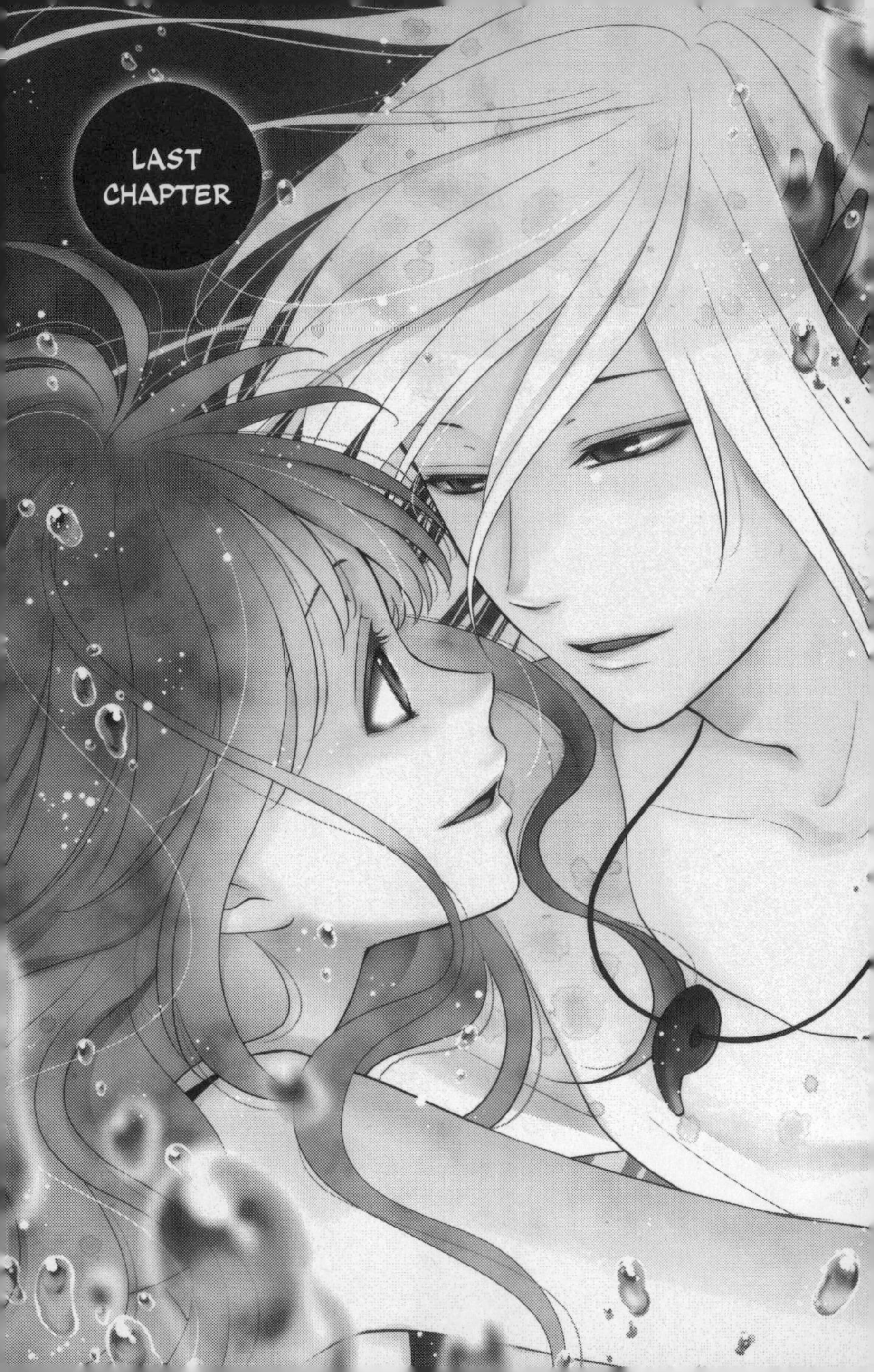
LAST CHAPTER

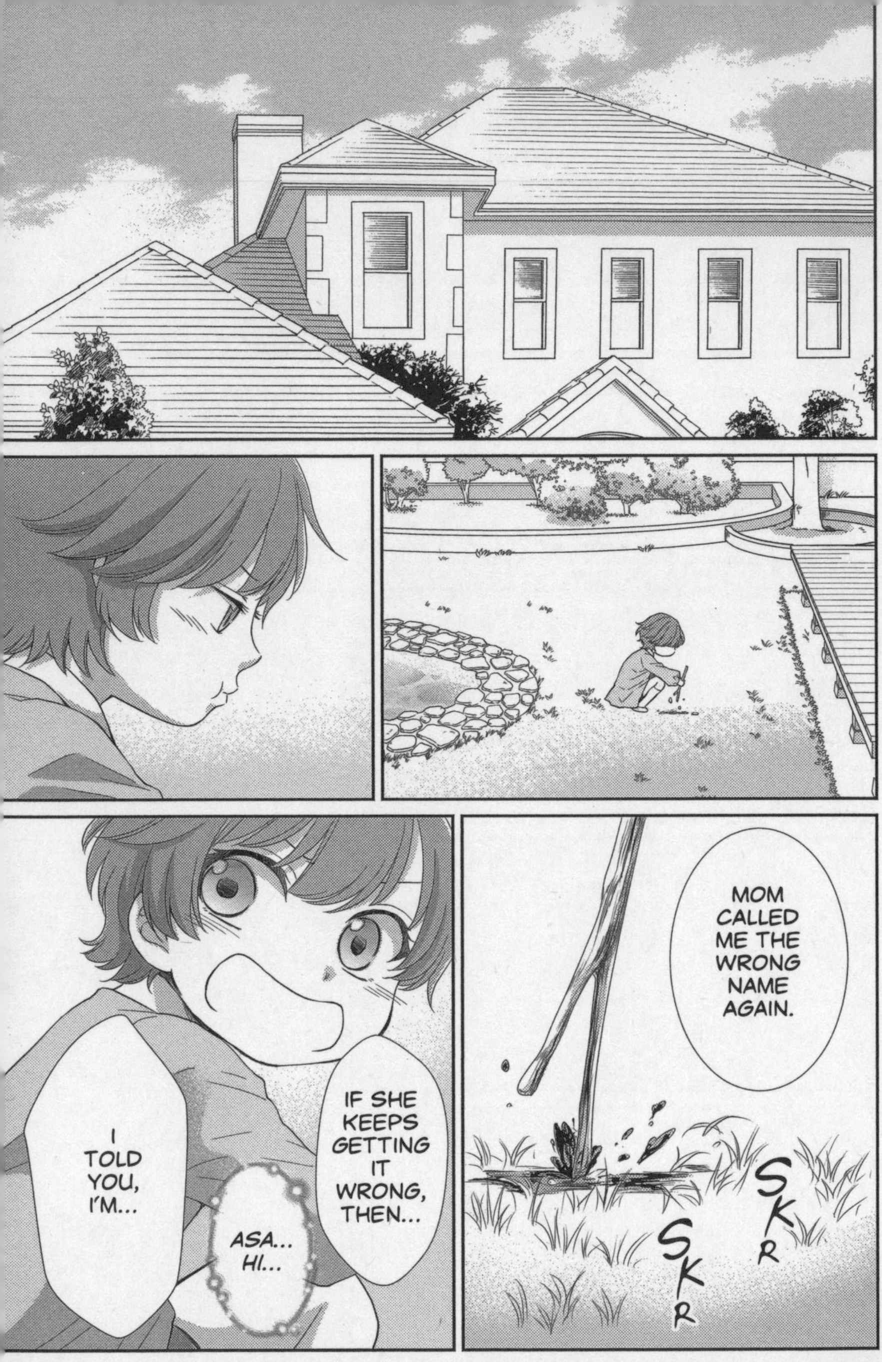
MOM CALLED ME THE WRONG NAME AGAIN.
SKR
SKR
IF SHE KEEPS GETTING IT WRONG, THEN...
I TOLD YOU, I'M...
ASA... HI...

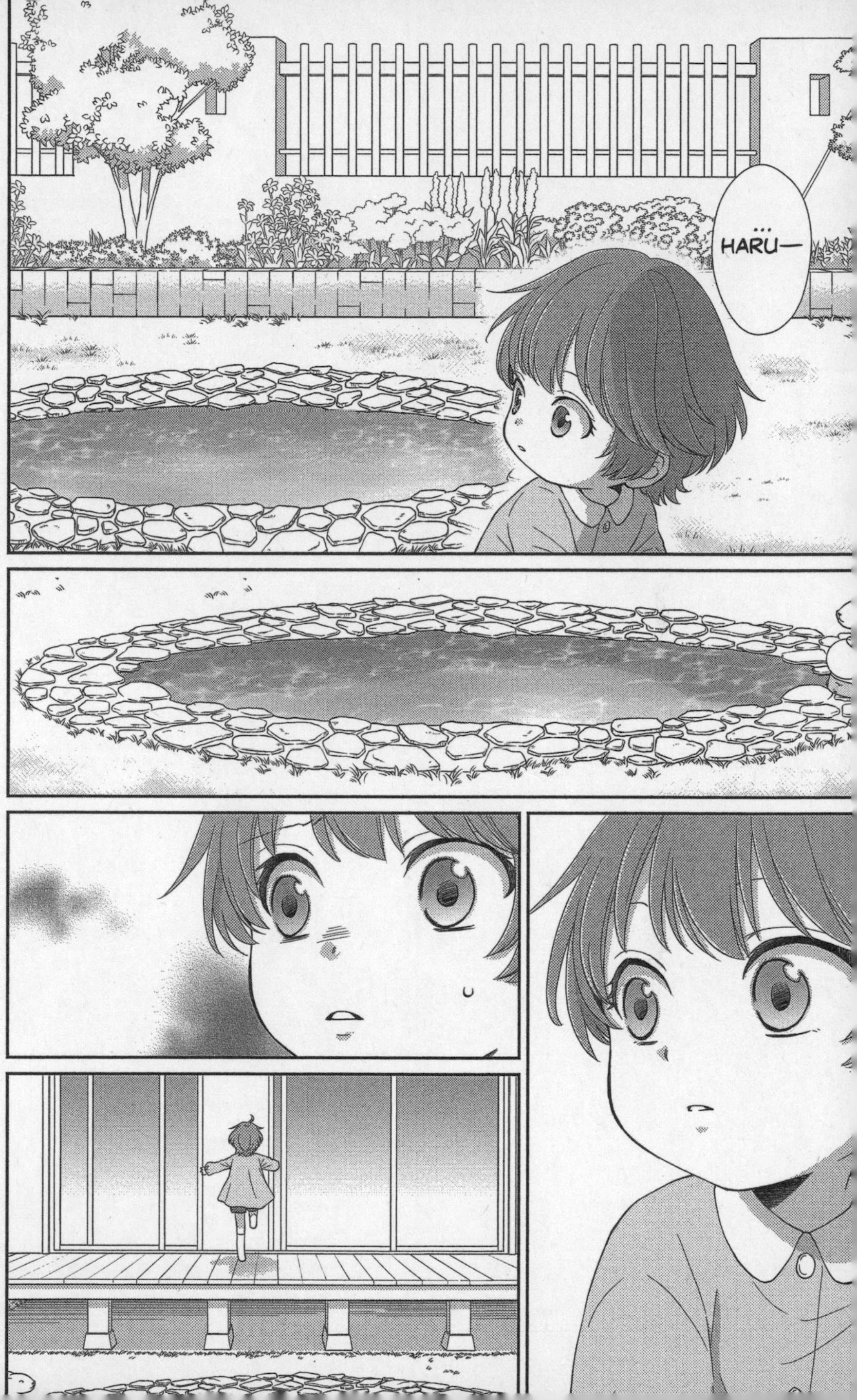
...
HARU—

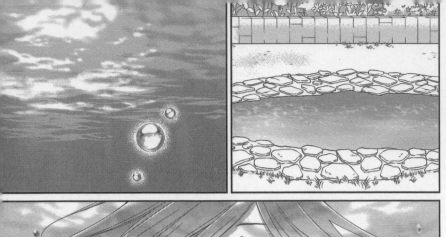

ASAHI...

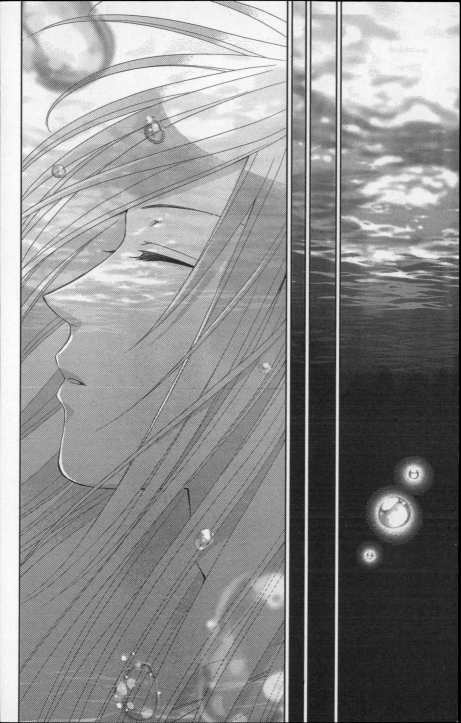

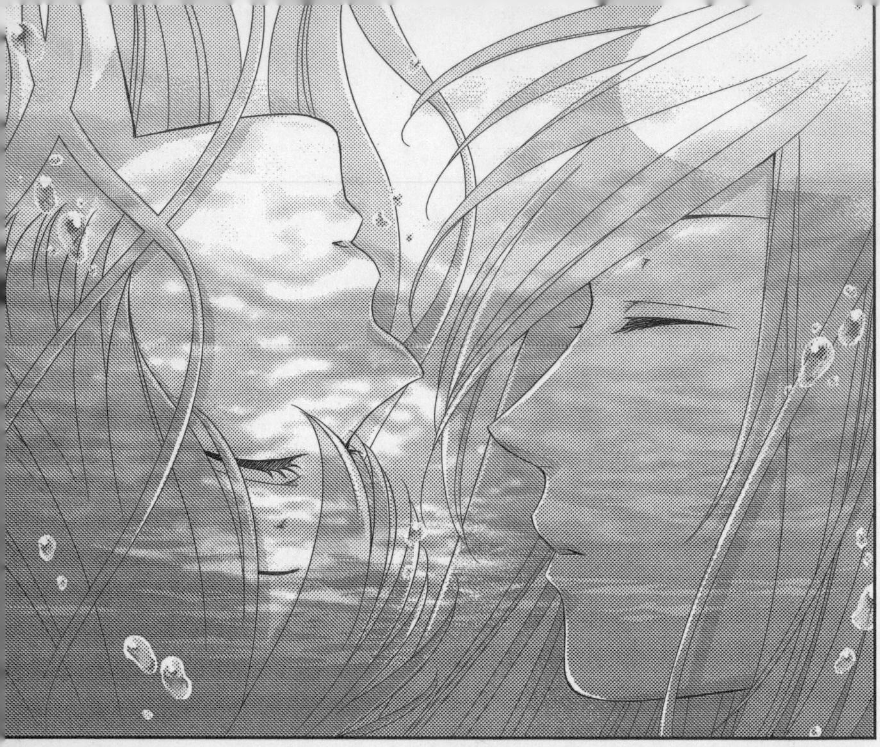
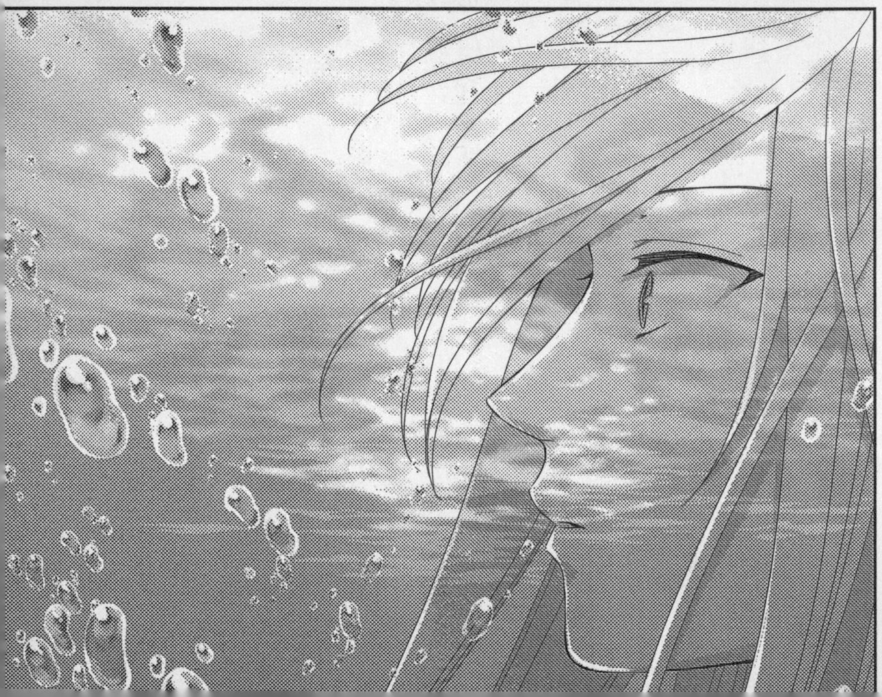

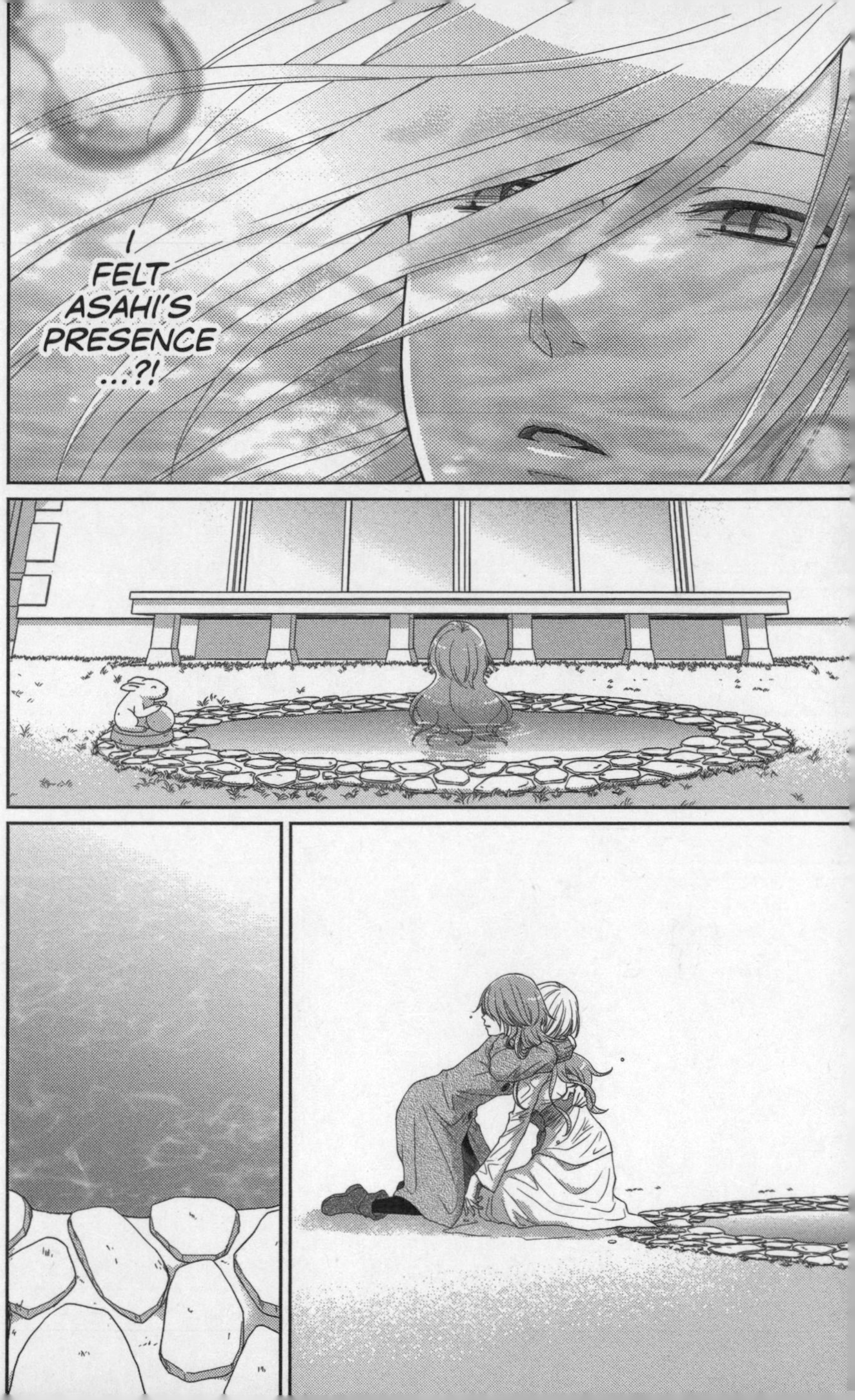
I FELT ASAHI'S PRESENCE ...?!

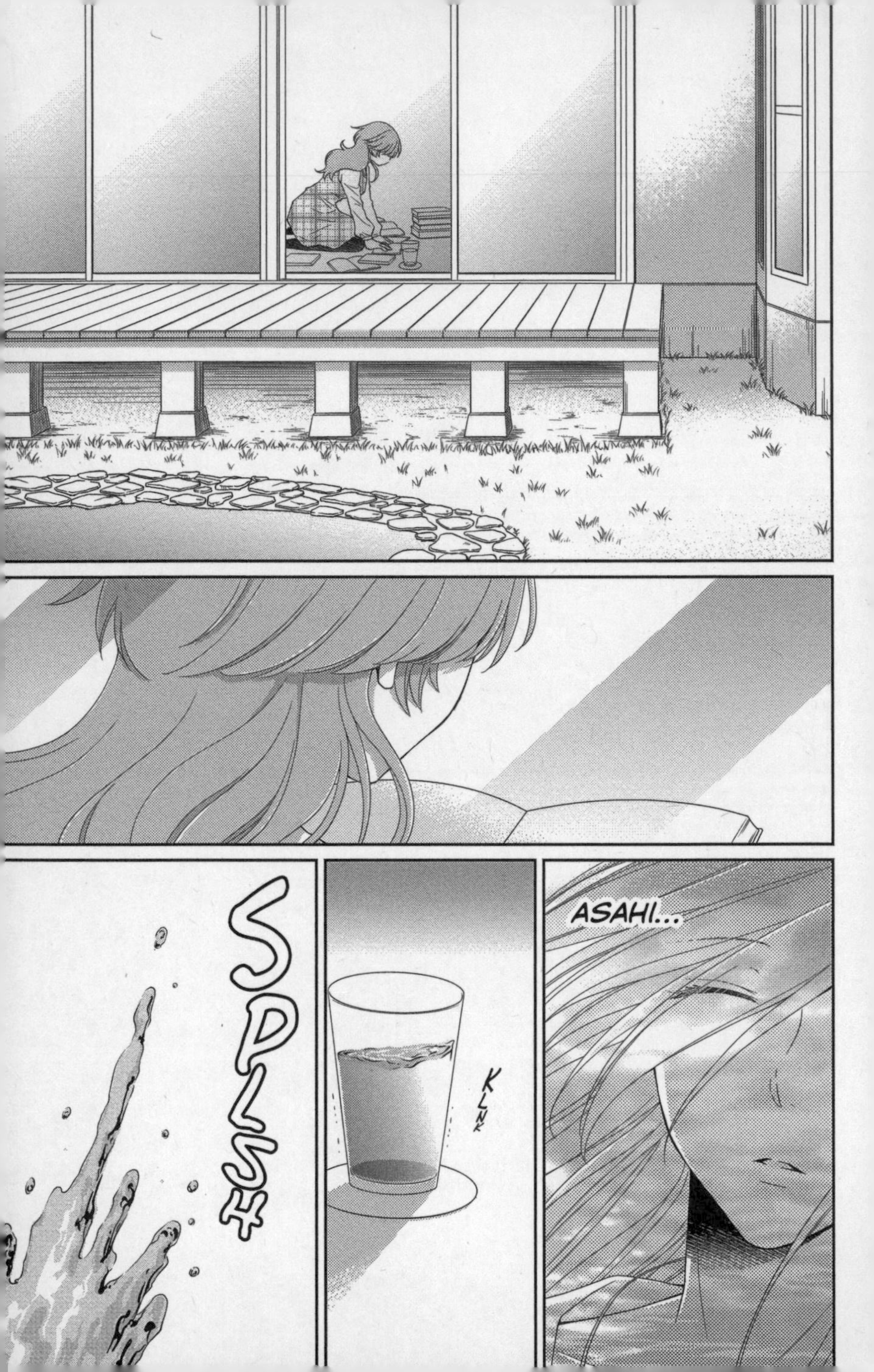
ASAHI...
KLNK
SPLSH

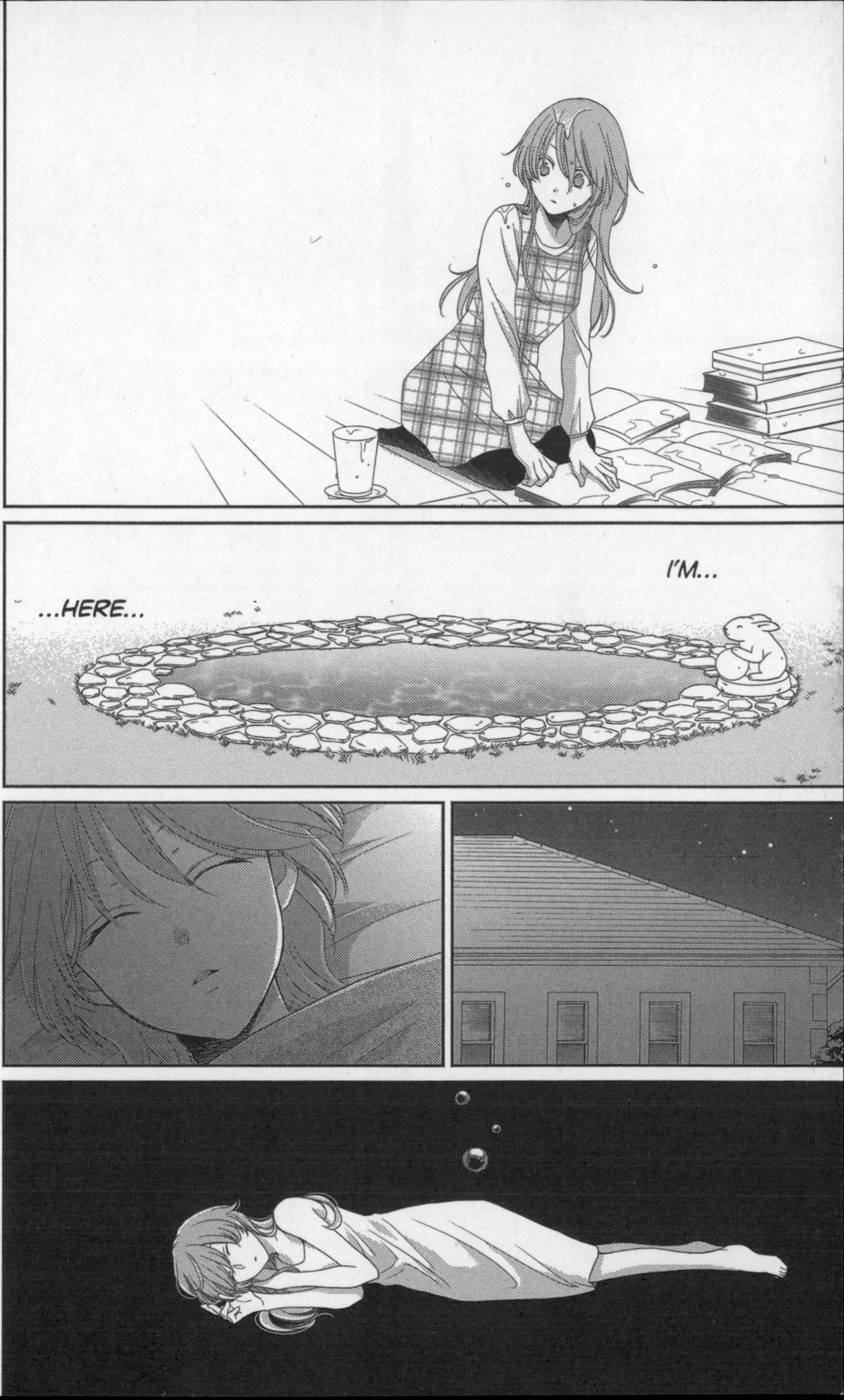
I'M...
...HERE...

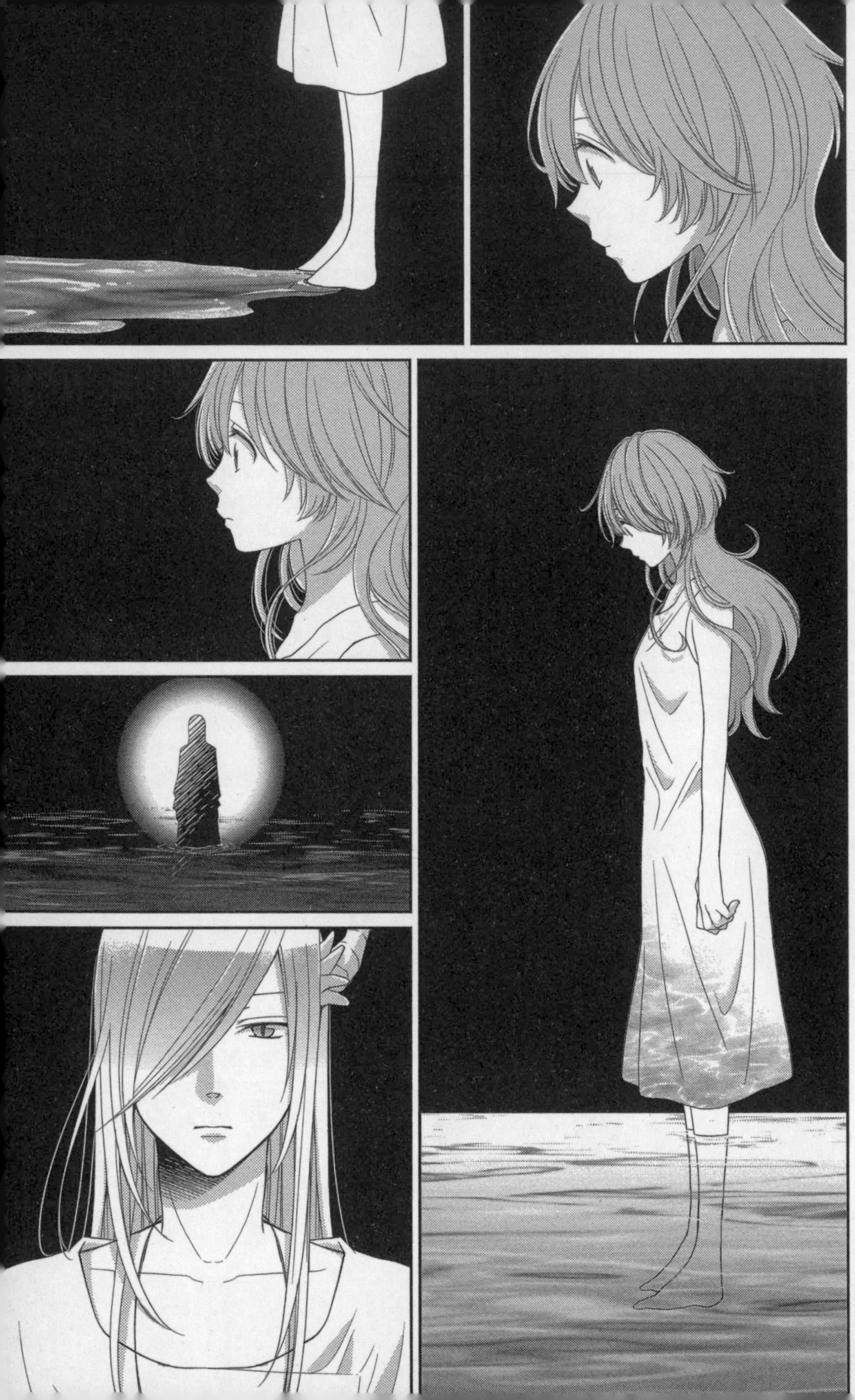

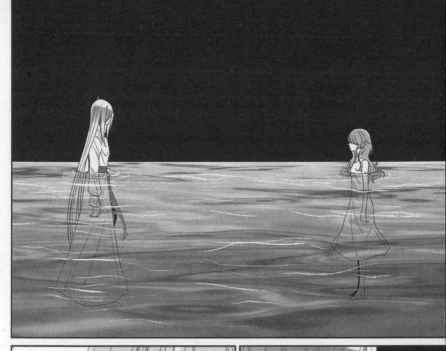

THIS
IS...

...A
DREAM...

AH...

MY
VOICE
WILL
NOT
REACH
HER...

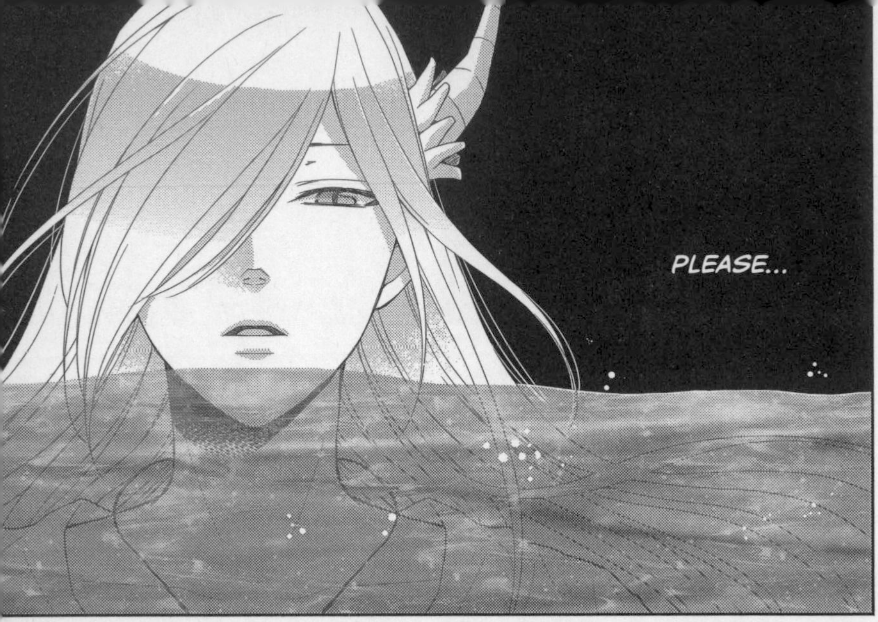
PLEASE...
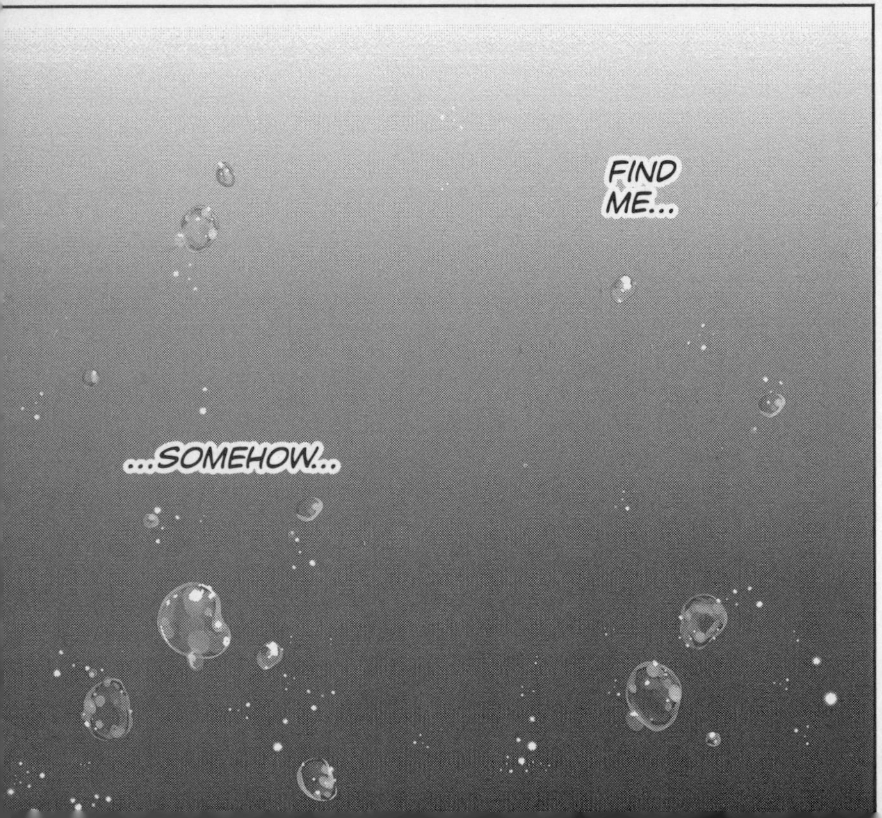
FIND ME...
...SOMEHOW...

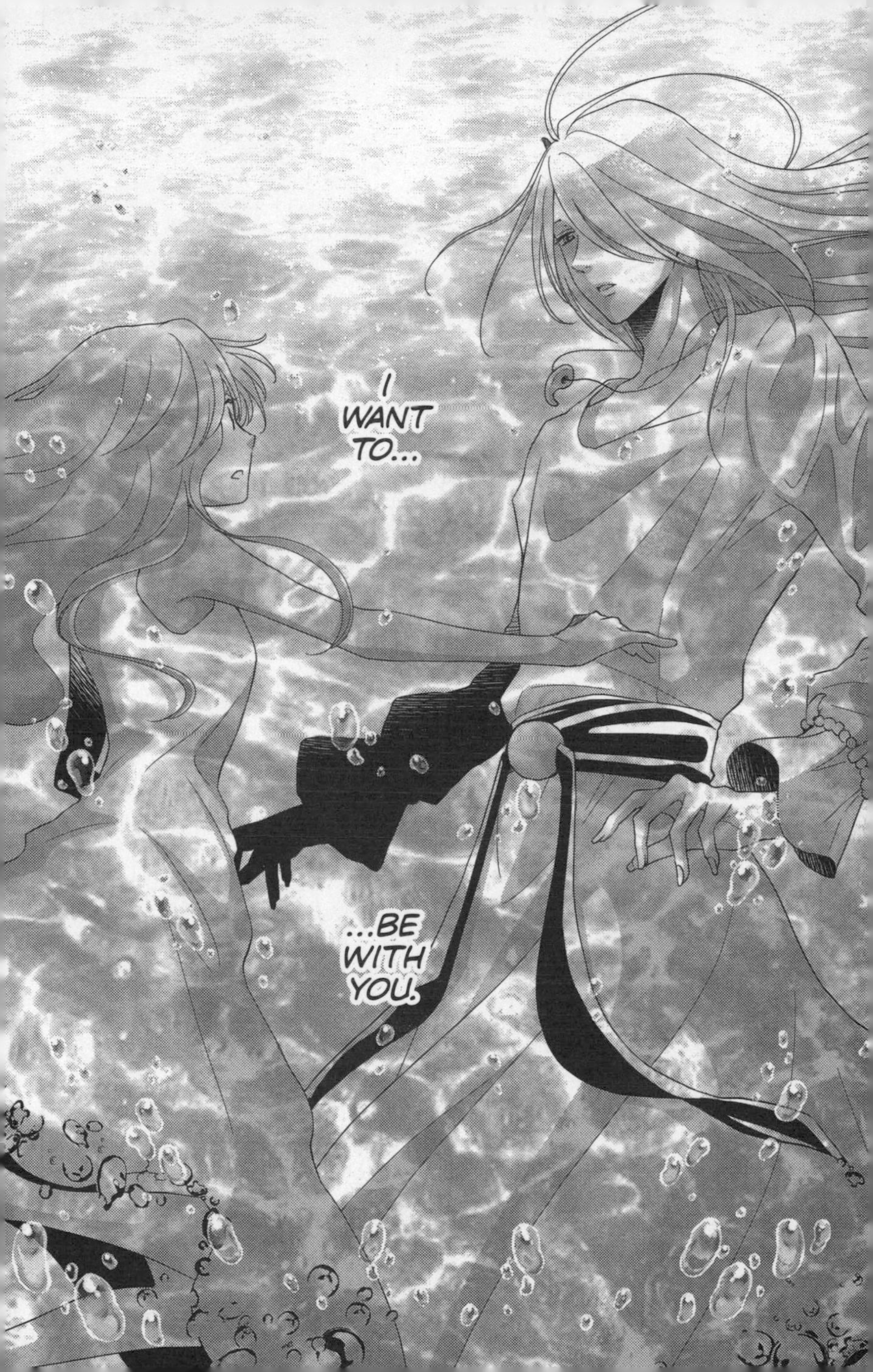
I WANT TO...
...BE WITH YOU.

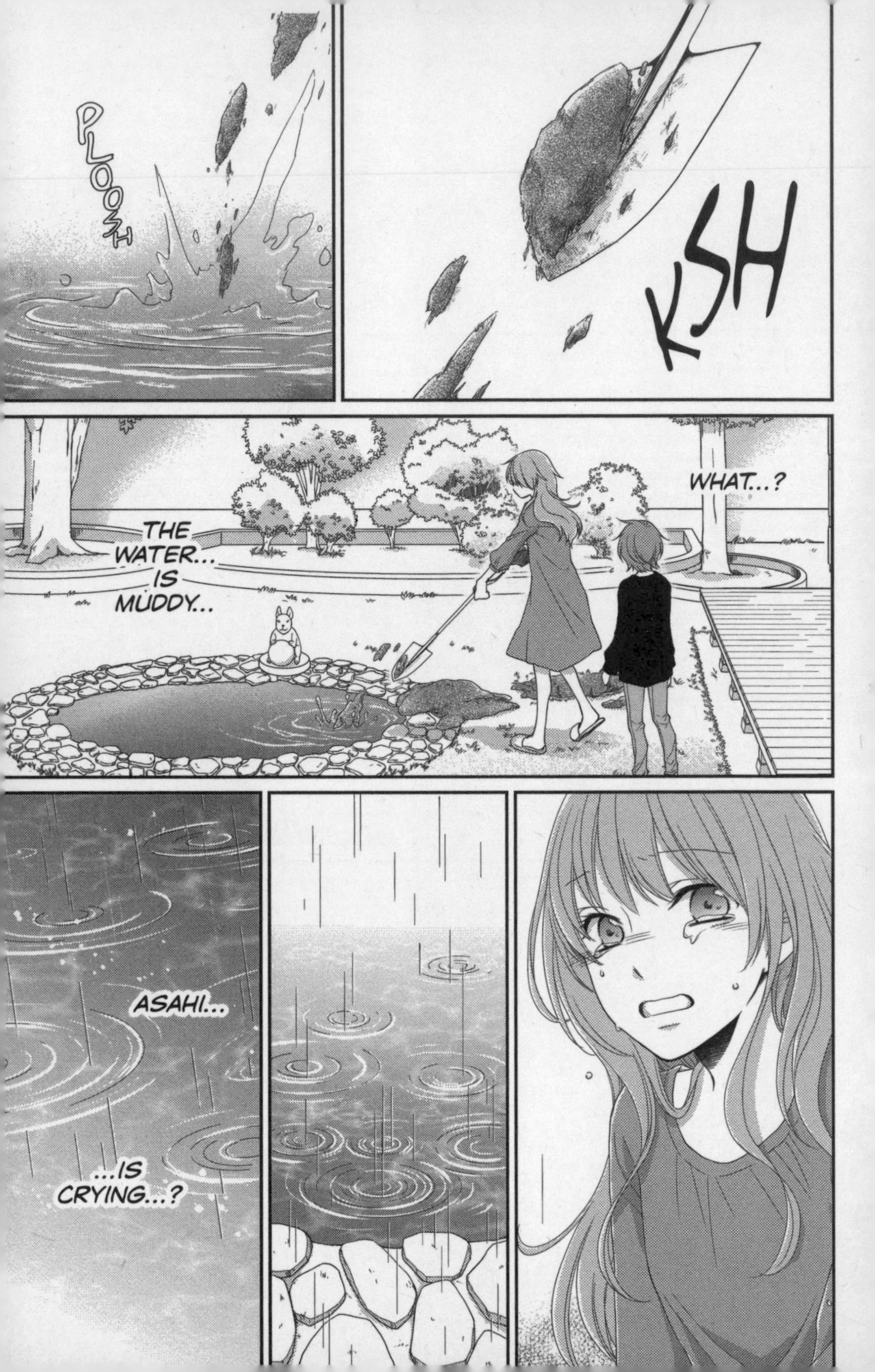
KSH
PLOOMH
WHAT...?
THE WATER... IS MUDDY...
ASAHI...
...IS CRYING...?

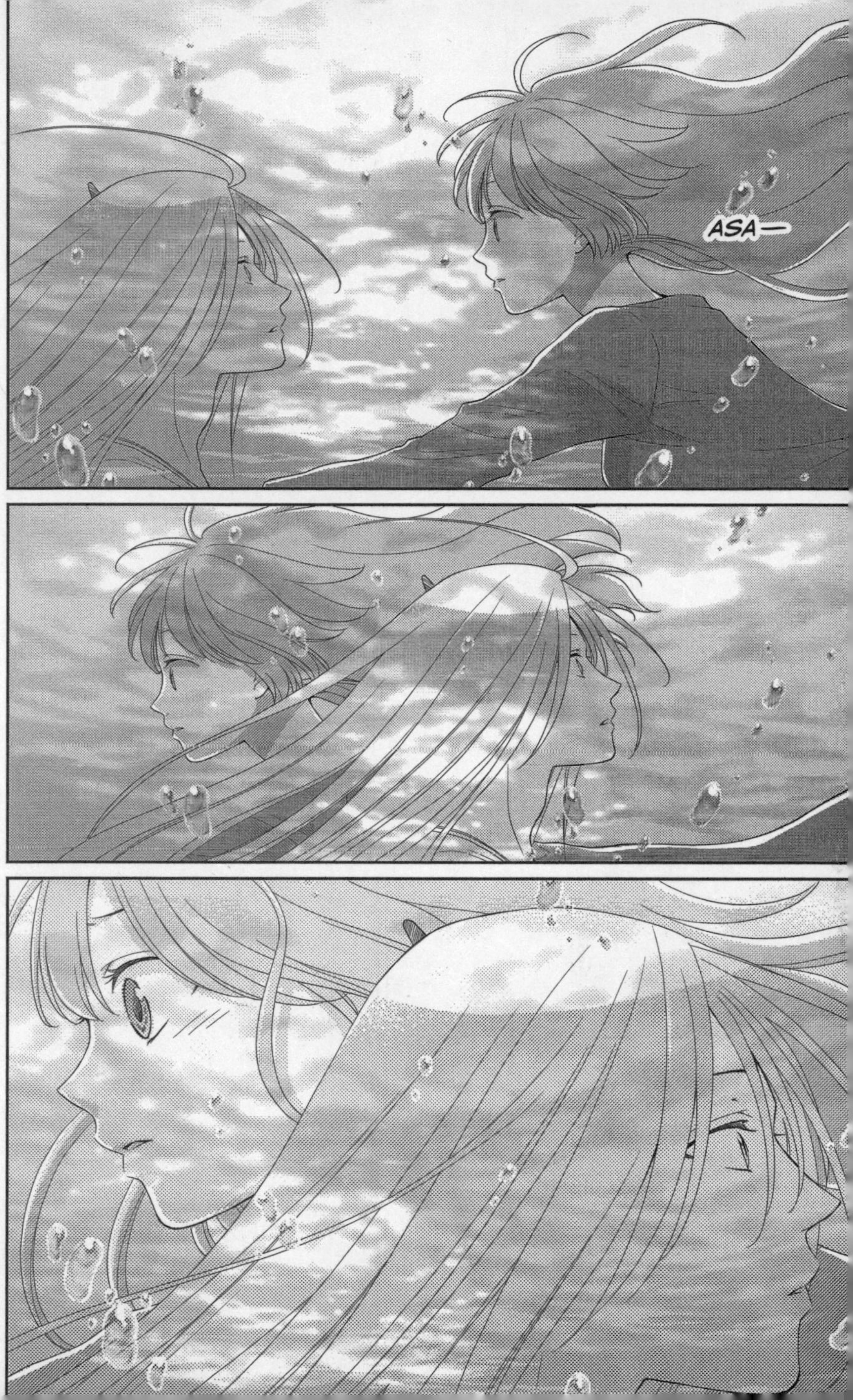
ASA—

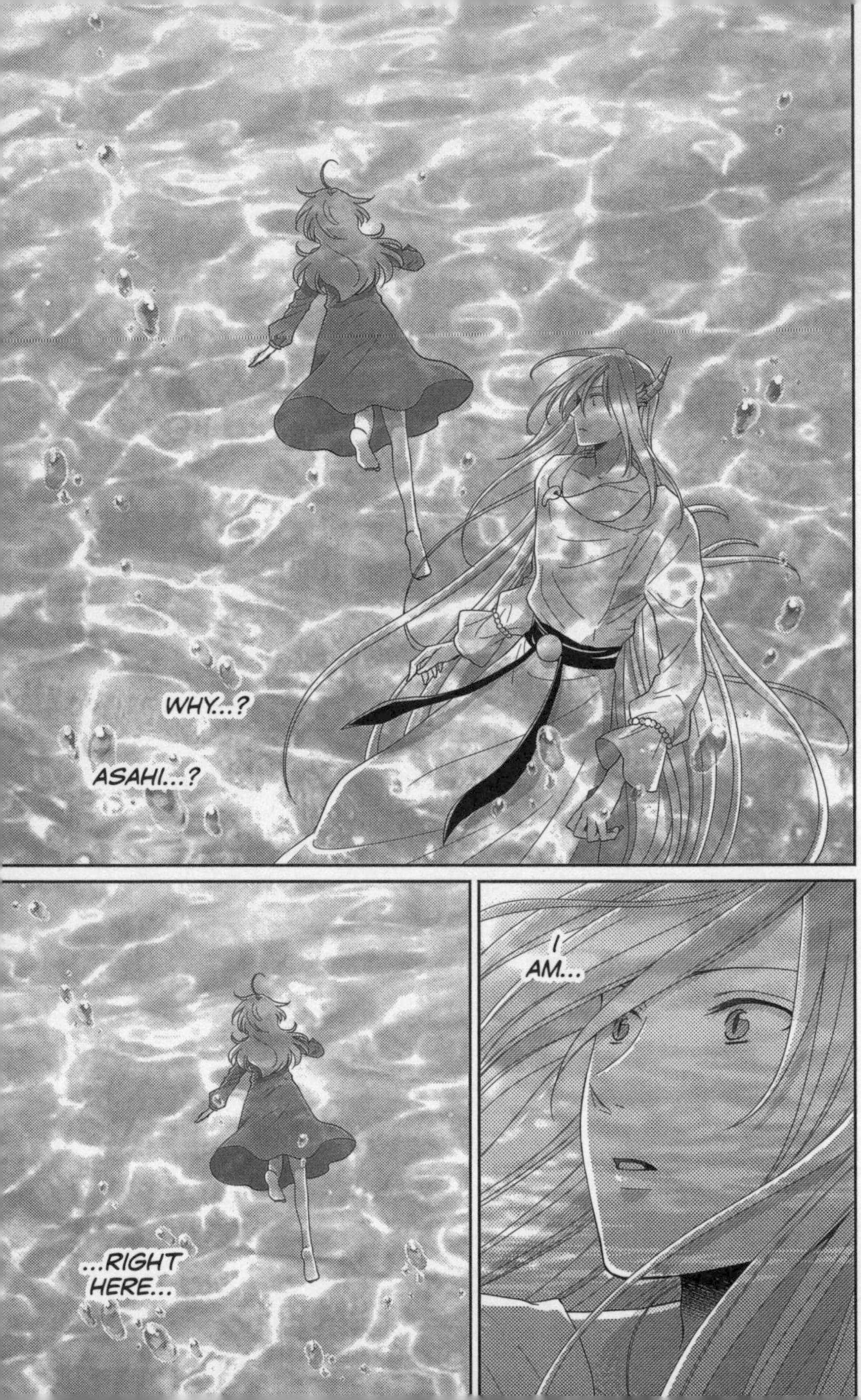
WHY...?
ASAHI...?
I AM...
...RIGHT HERE...

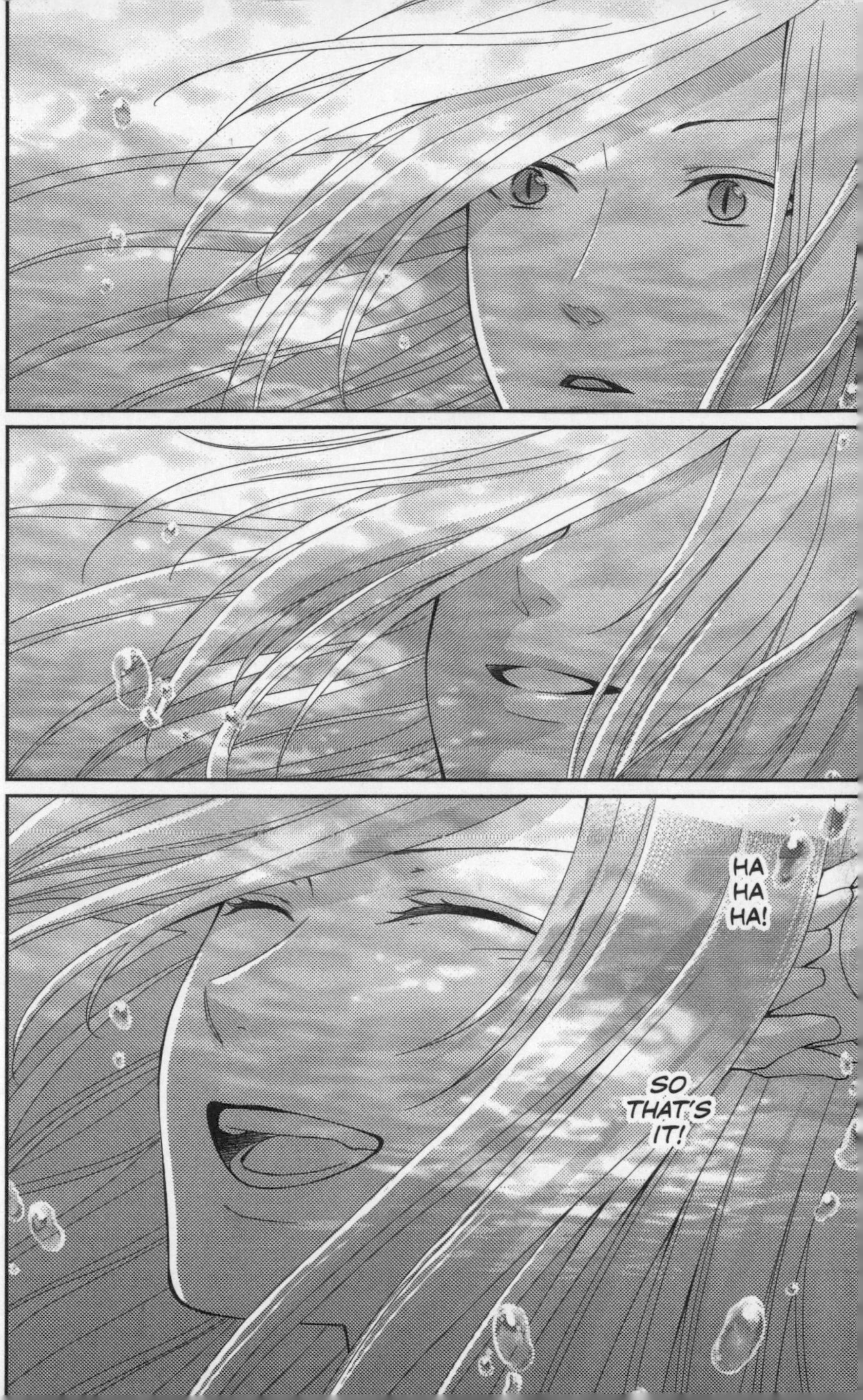
HA HA HA!
SO THAT'S IT!

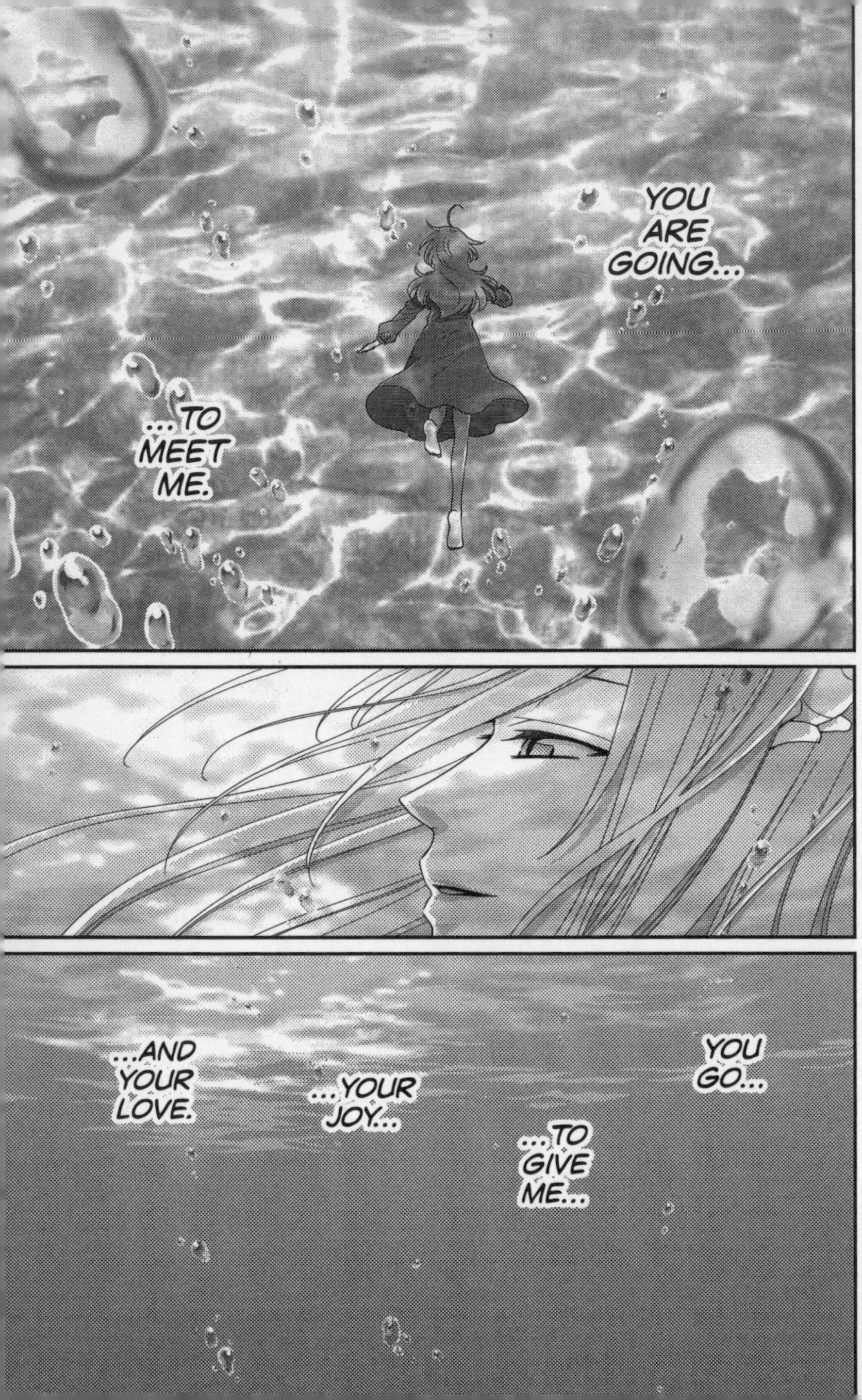
YOU ARE GOING...
...TO MEET ME.
YOU GO...
...TO GIVE ME...
...YOUR JOY...
...AND YOUR LOVE.

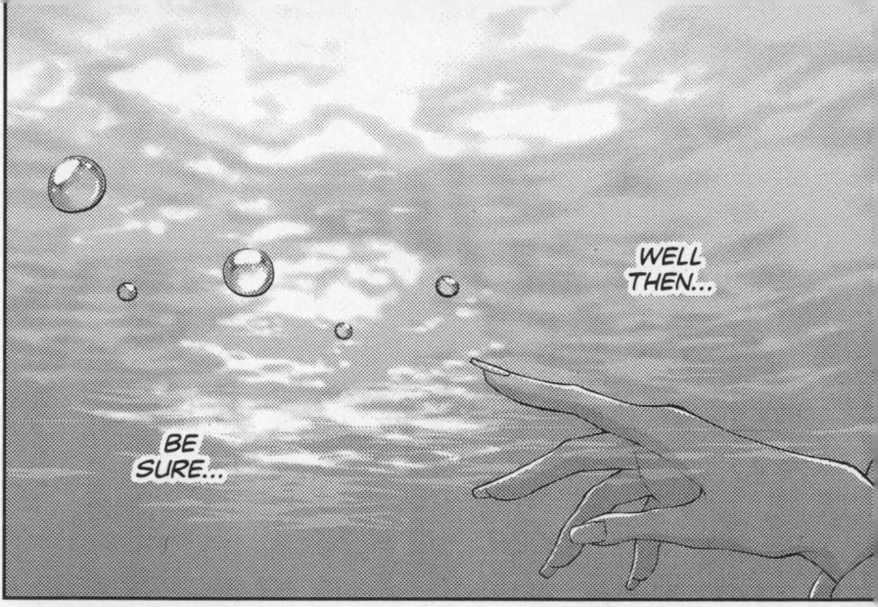
WELL THEN...
BE SURE...
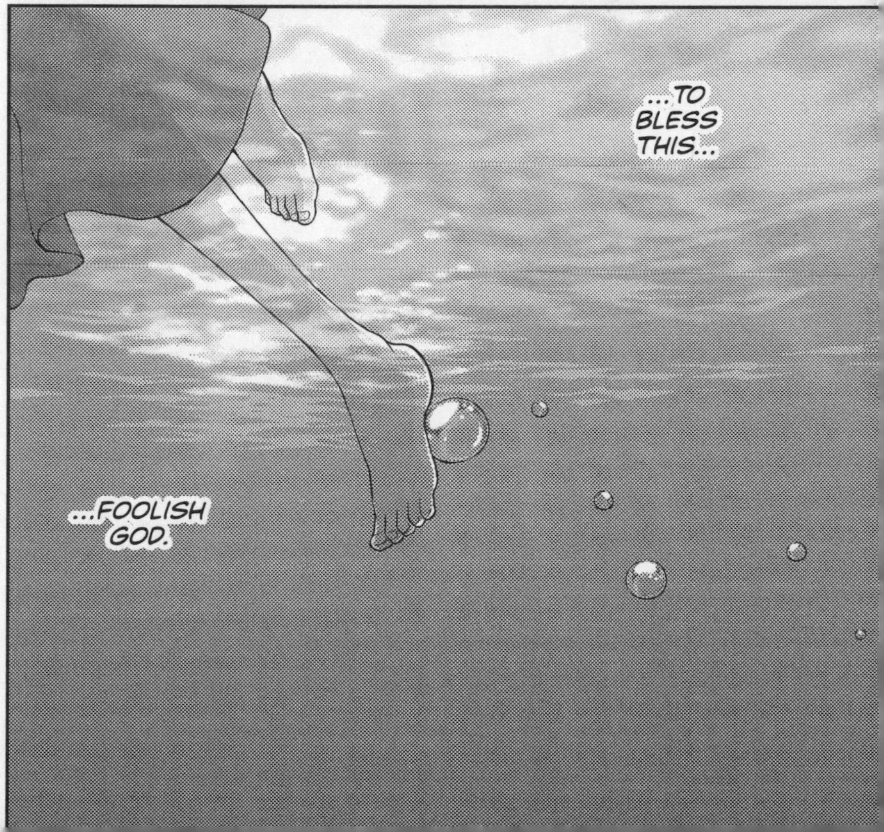
...TO BLESS THIS...
...FOOLISH GOD.

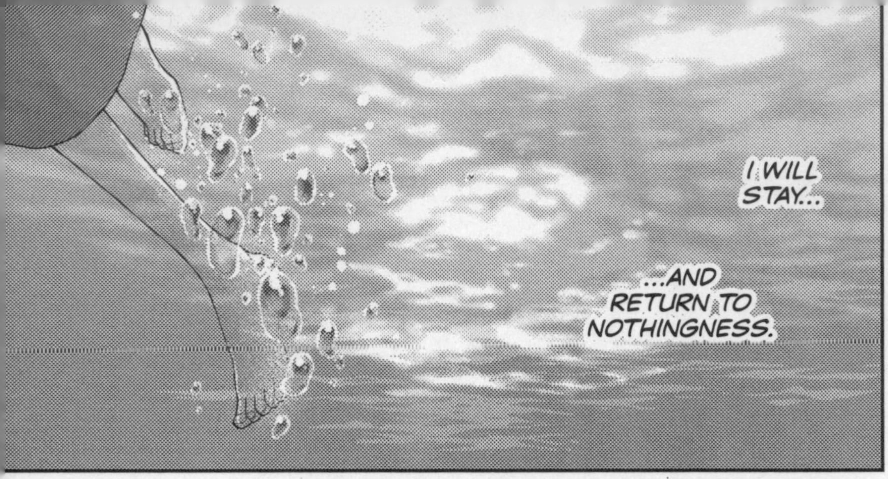
I WILL STAY...
...AND RETURN TO NOTHINGNESS.
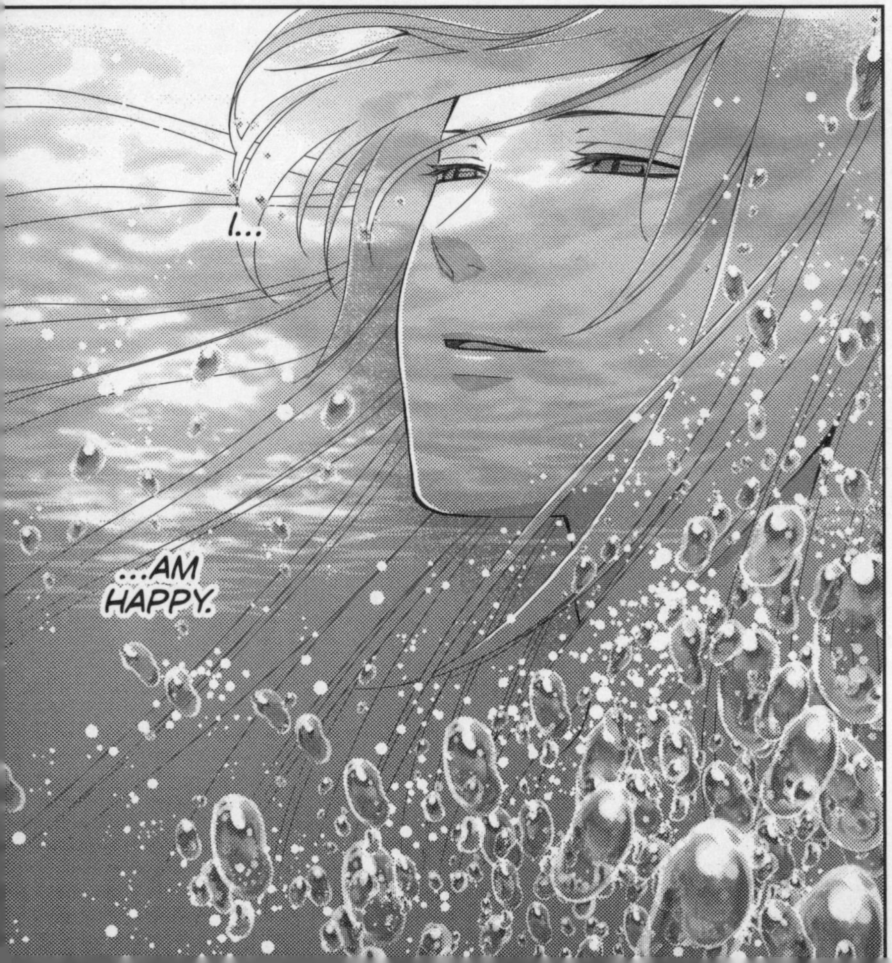
I...
...AM HAPPY.

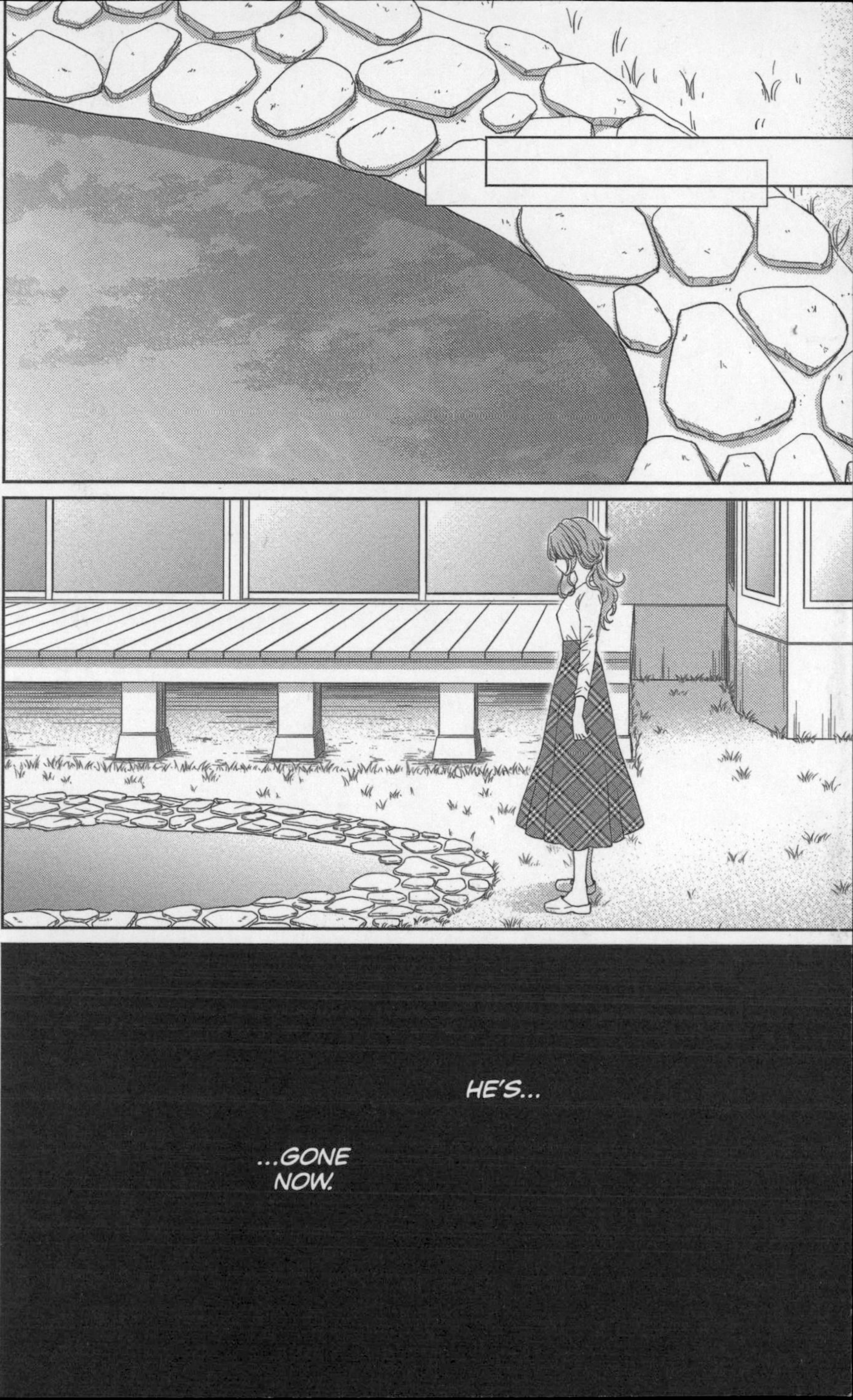
HE'S...
...GONE NOW.

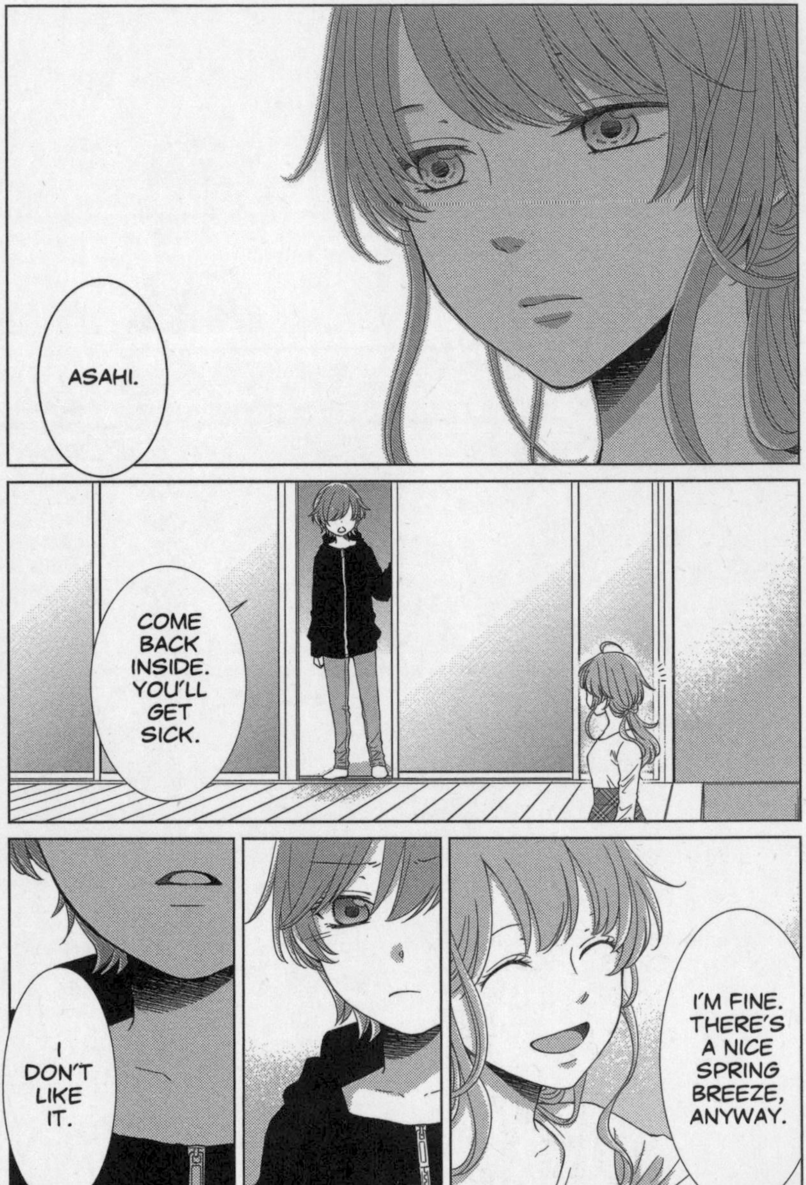
ASAHI.
COME BACK INSIDE. YOU'LL GET SICK.
I'M FINE. THERE'S A NICE SPRING BREEZE, ANYWAY.
I DON'T LIKE IT.

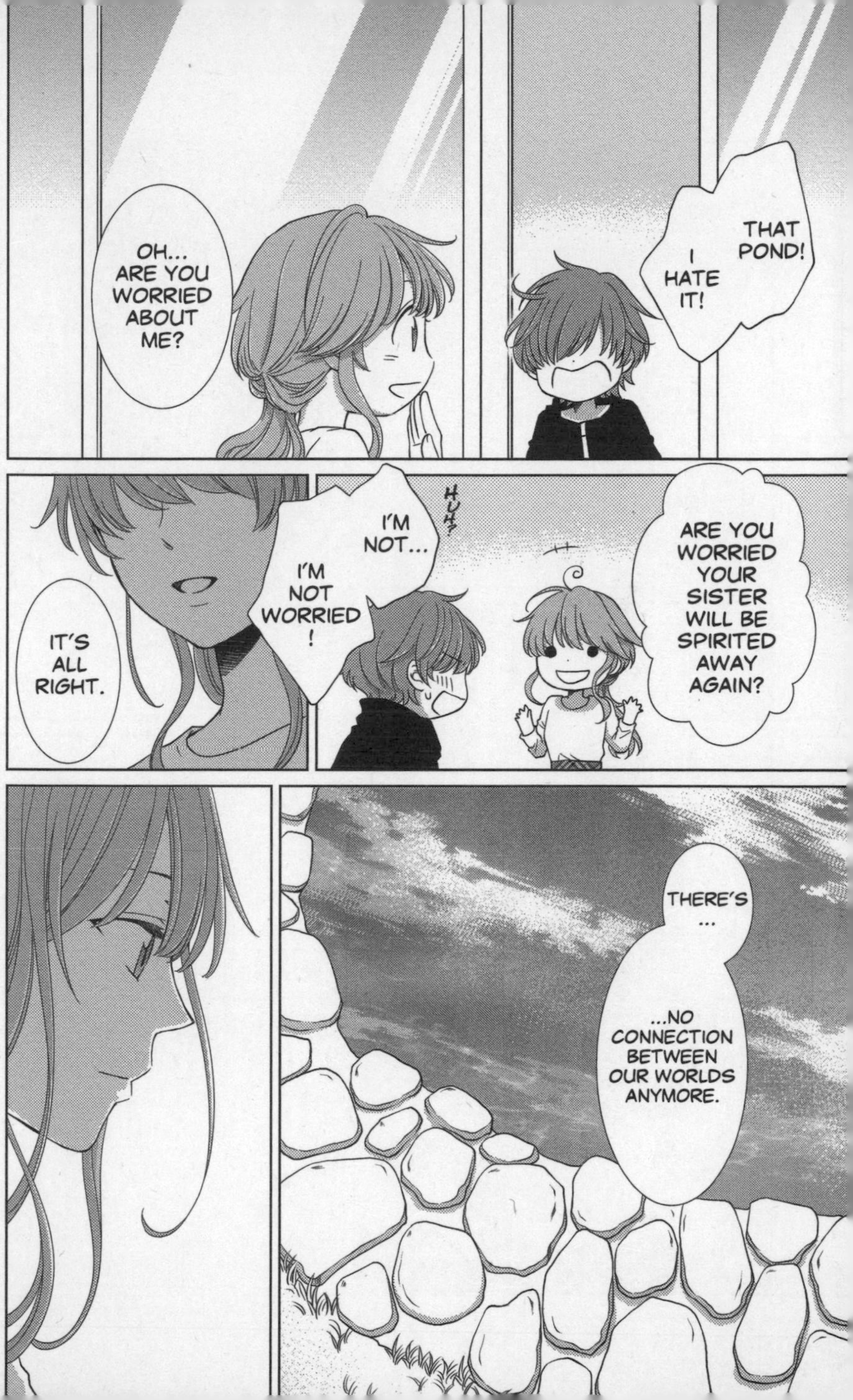
THAT POND! I HATE IT!
OH... ARE YOU WORRIED ABOUT ME?
ARE YOU WORRIED YOUR SISTER WILL BE SPIRITED AWAY AGAIN?
HUH?
I'M NOT...
I'M NOT WORRIED!
IT'S ALL RIGHT.
THERE'S...
...NO CONNECTION BETWEEN OUR WORLDS ANYMORE.

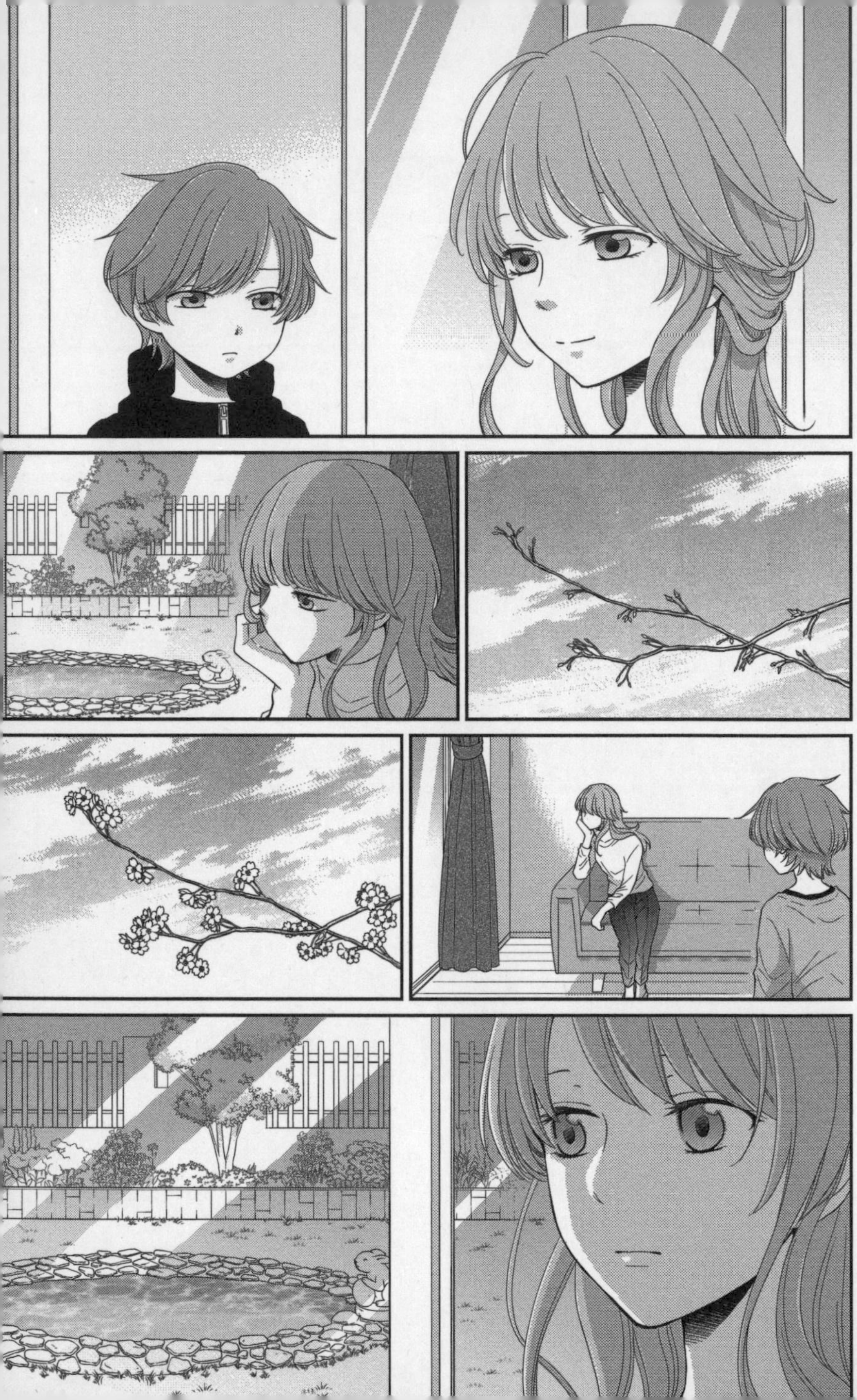

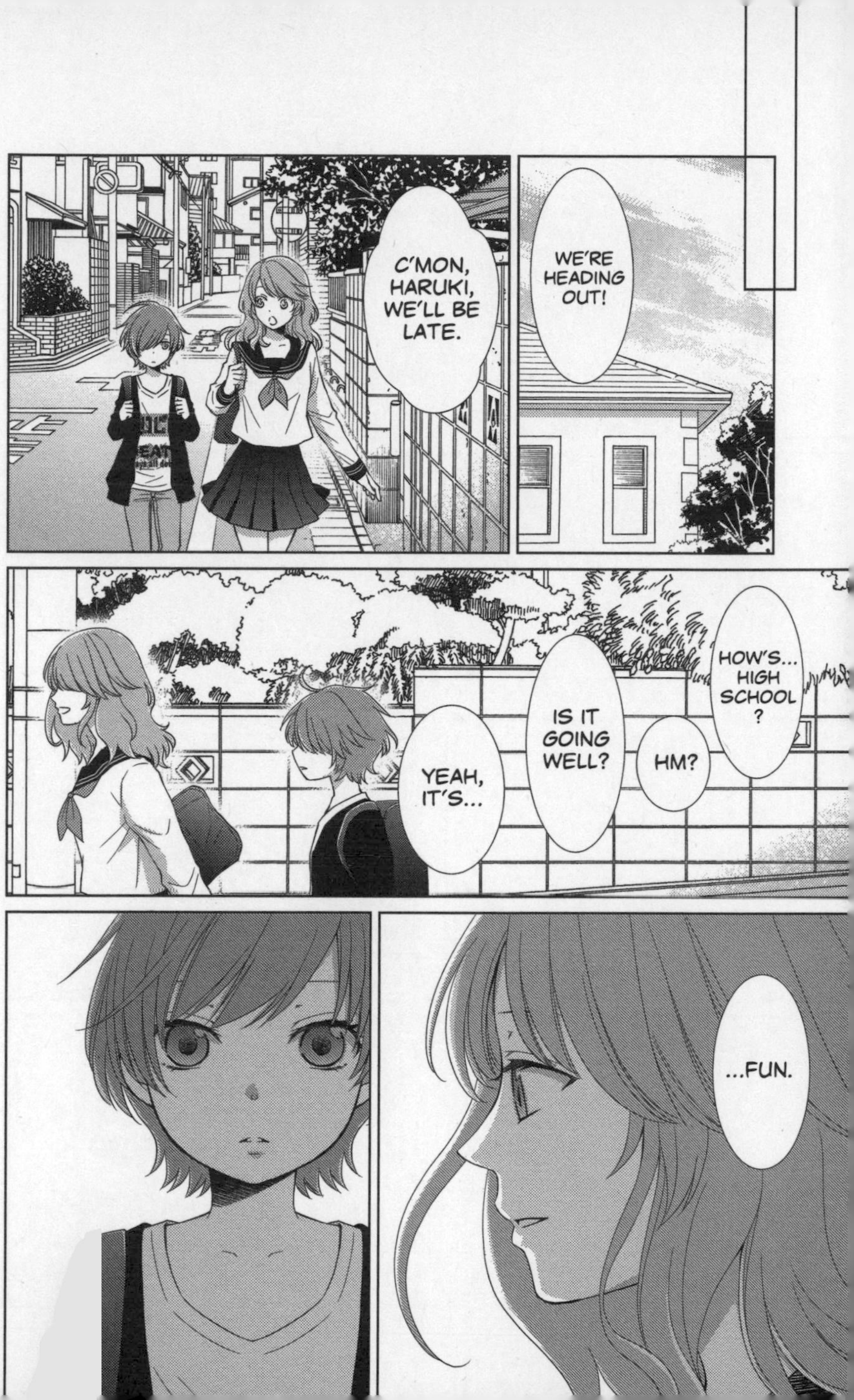
WE'RE HEADING OUT!
C'MON, HARUKI, WE'LL BE LATE.
HOW'S... HIGH SCHOOL?
HM?
IS IT GOING WELL?
YEAH, IT'S...
...FUN.

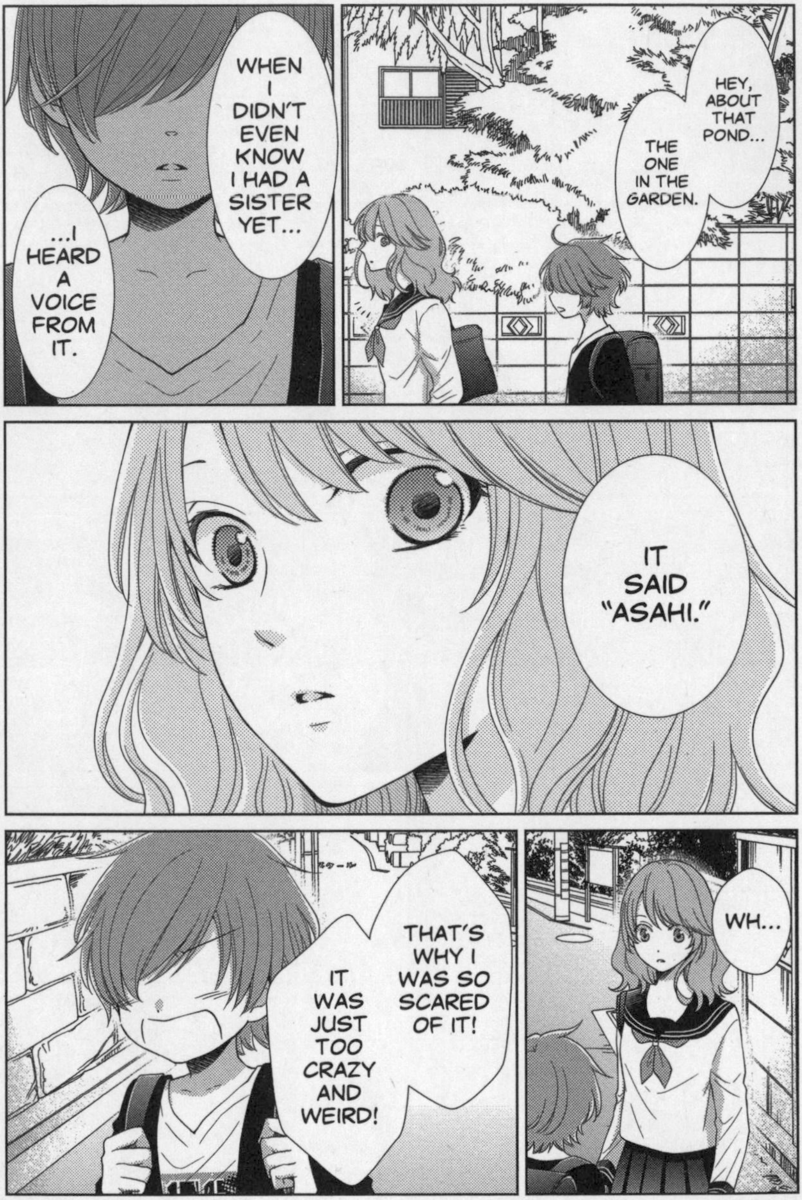
HEY, ABOUT THAT POND...
THE ONE IN THE GARDEN.
WHEN I DIDN'T EVEN KNOW I HAD A SISTER YET...
...I HEARD A VOICE FROM IT.
IT SAID "ASAHI."
WH...
THAT'S WHY I WAS SO SCARED OF IT!
IT WAS JUST TOO CRAZY AND WEIRD!

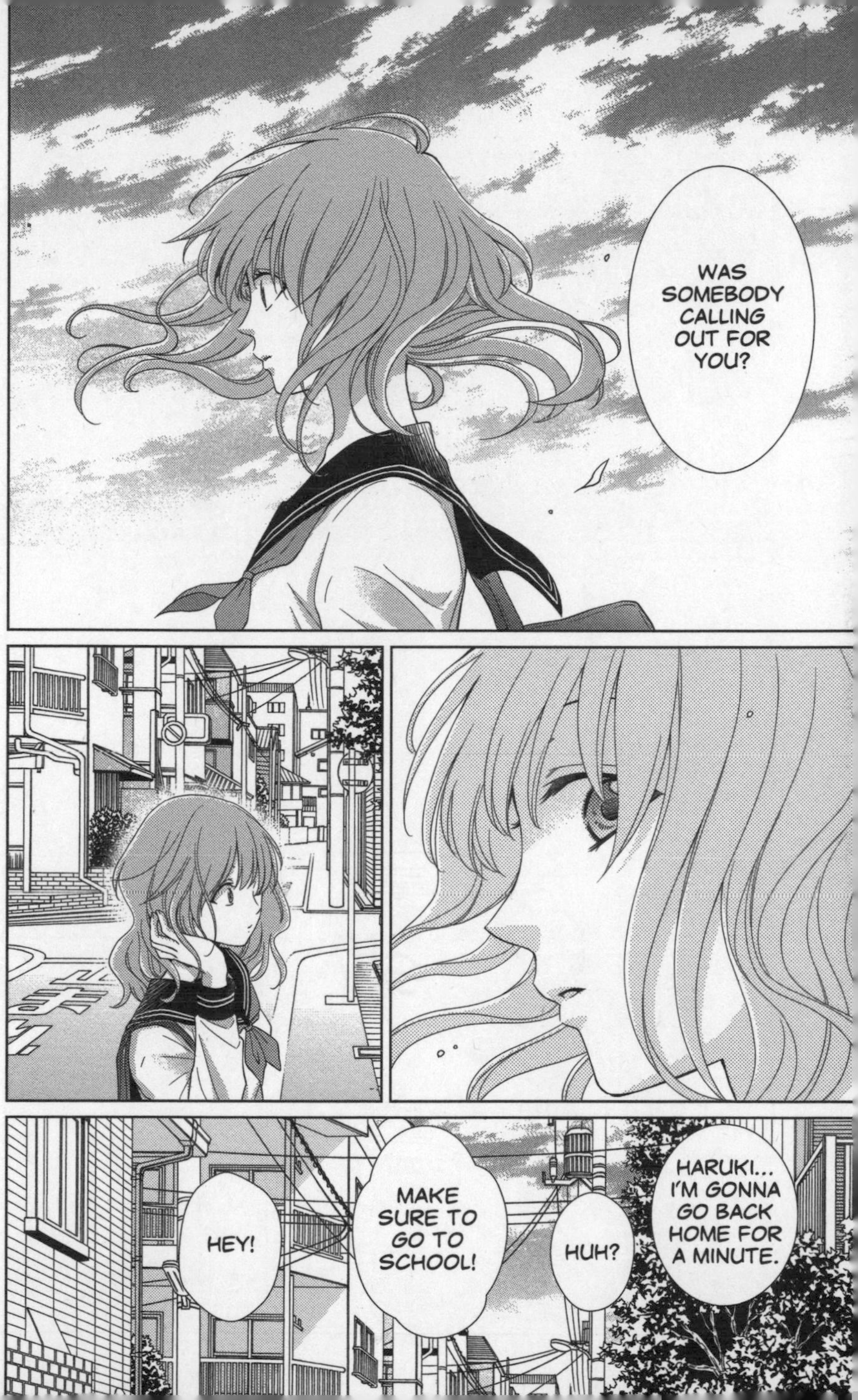
WAS SOMEBODY CALLING OUT FOR YOU?
HARUKI... I'M GONNA GO BACK HOME FOR A MINUTE.
HUH?
MAKE SURE TO GO TO SCHOOL!
HEY!

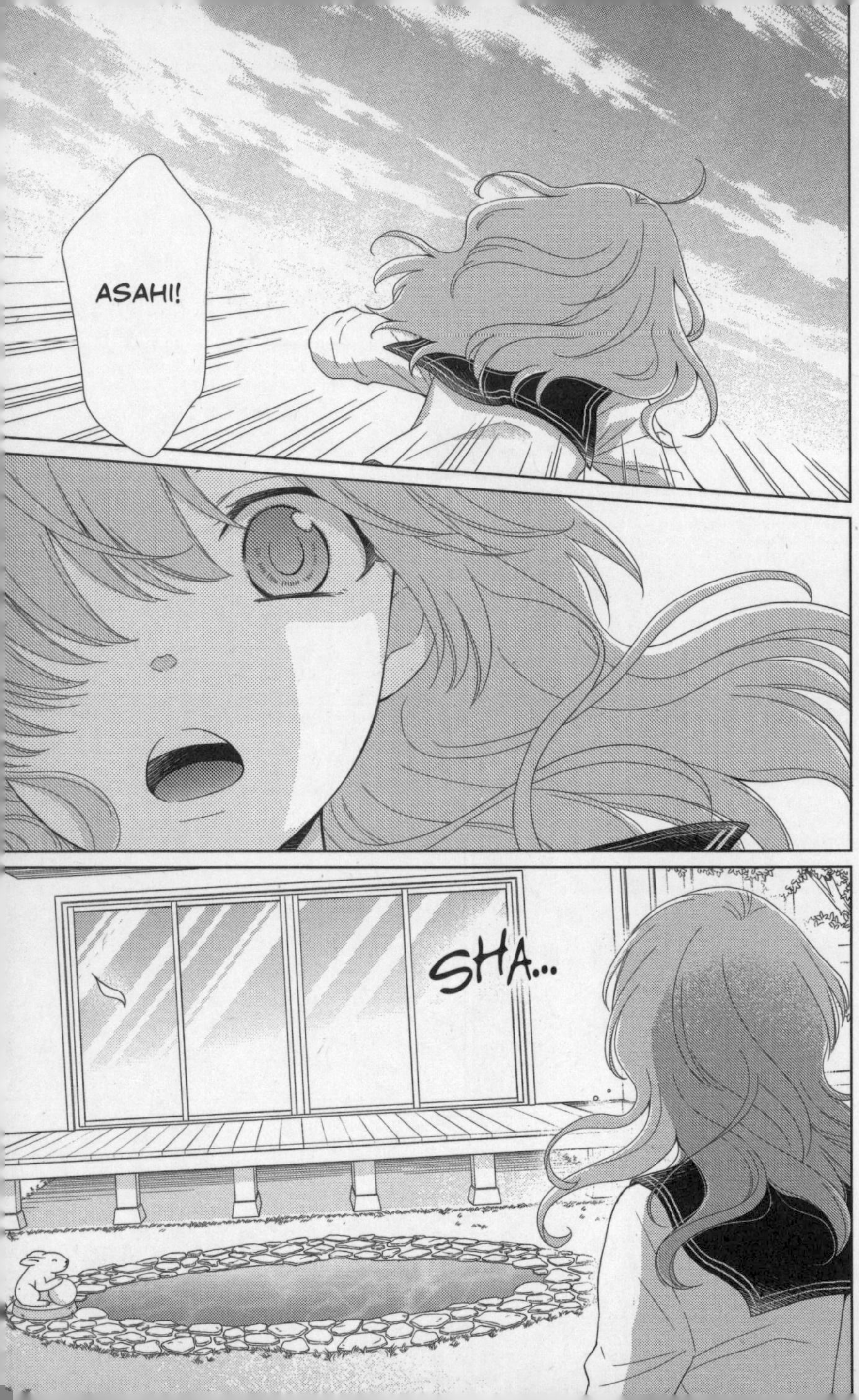
ASAHI!
SHA...

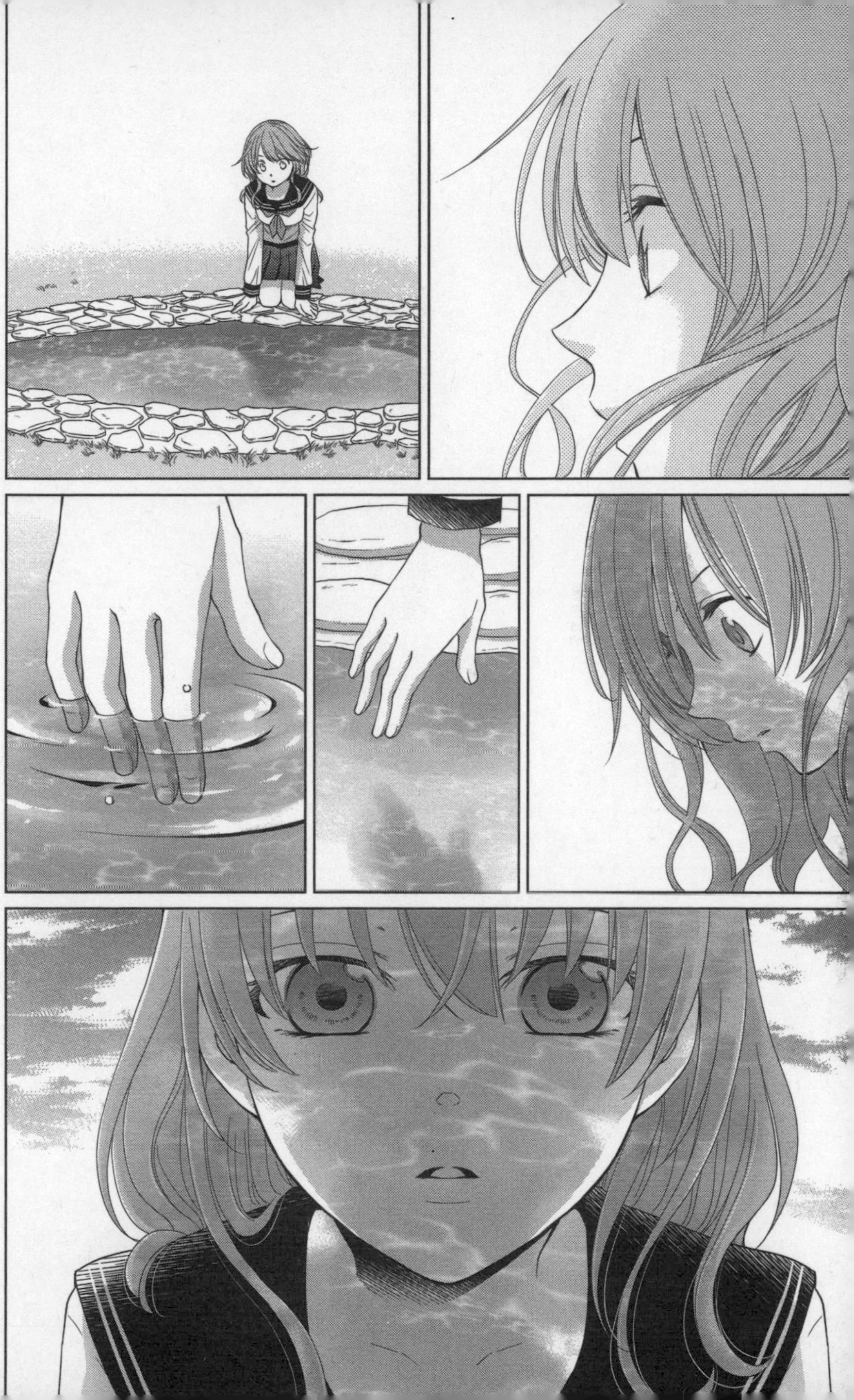

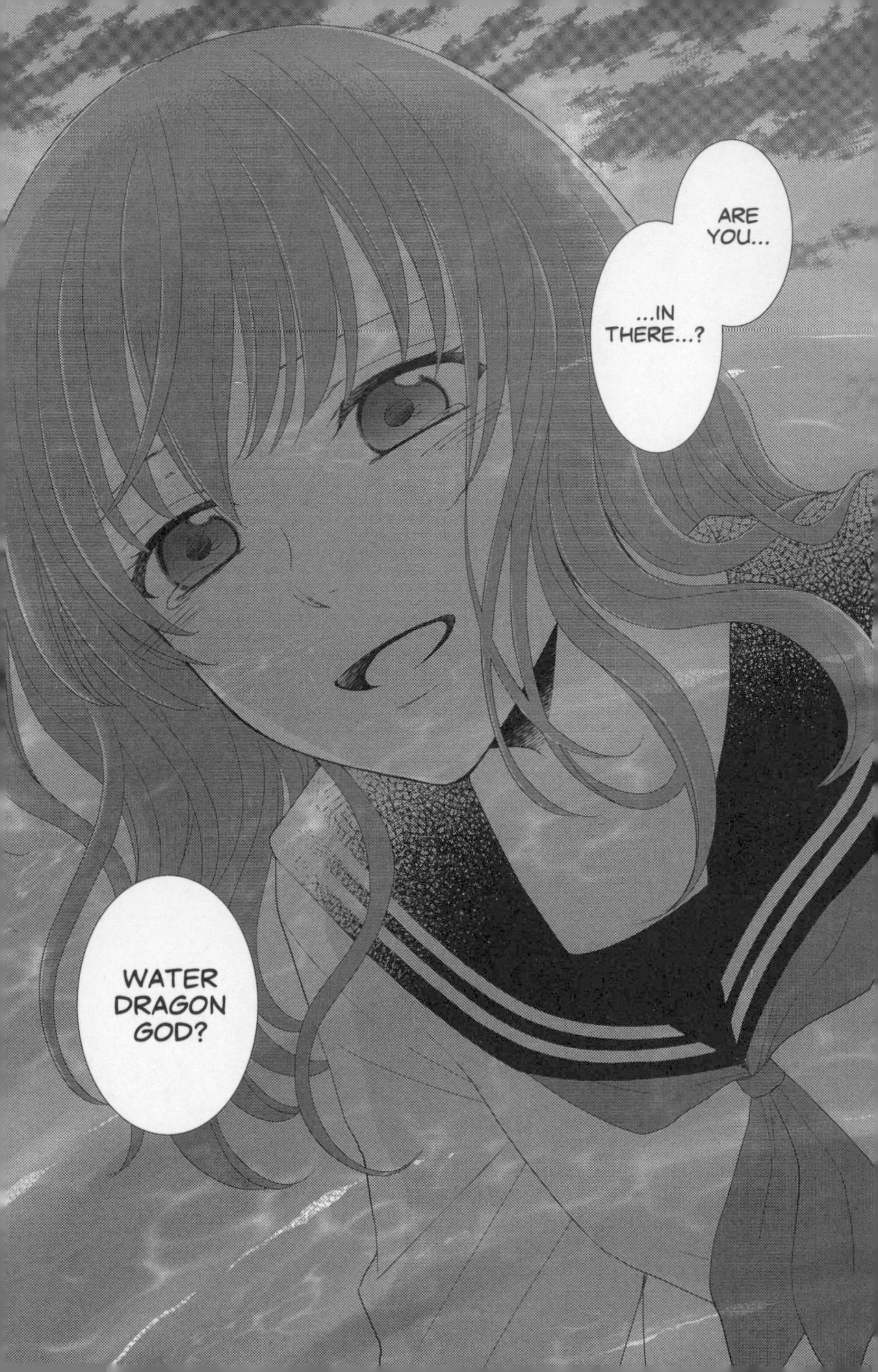
ARE YOU...
...IN THERE...?
WATER DRAGON GOD?

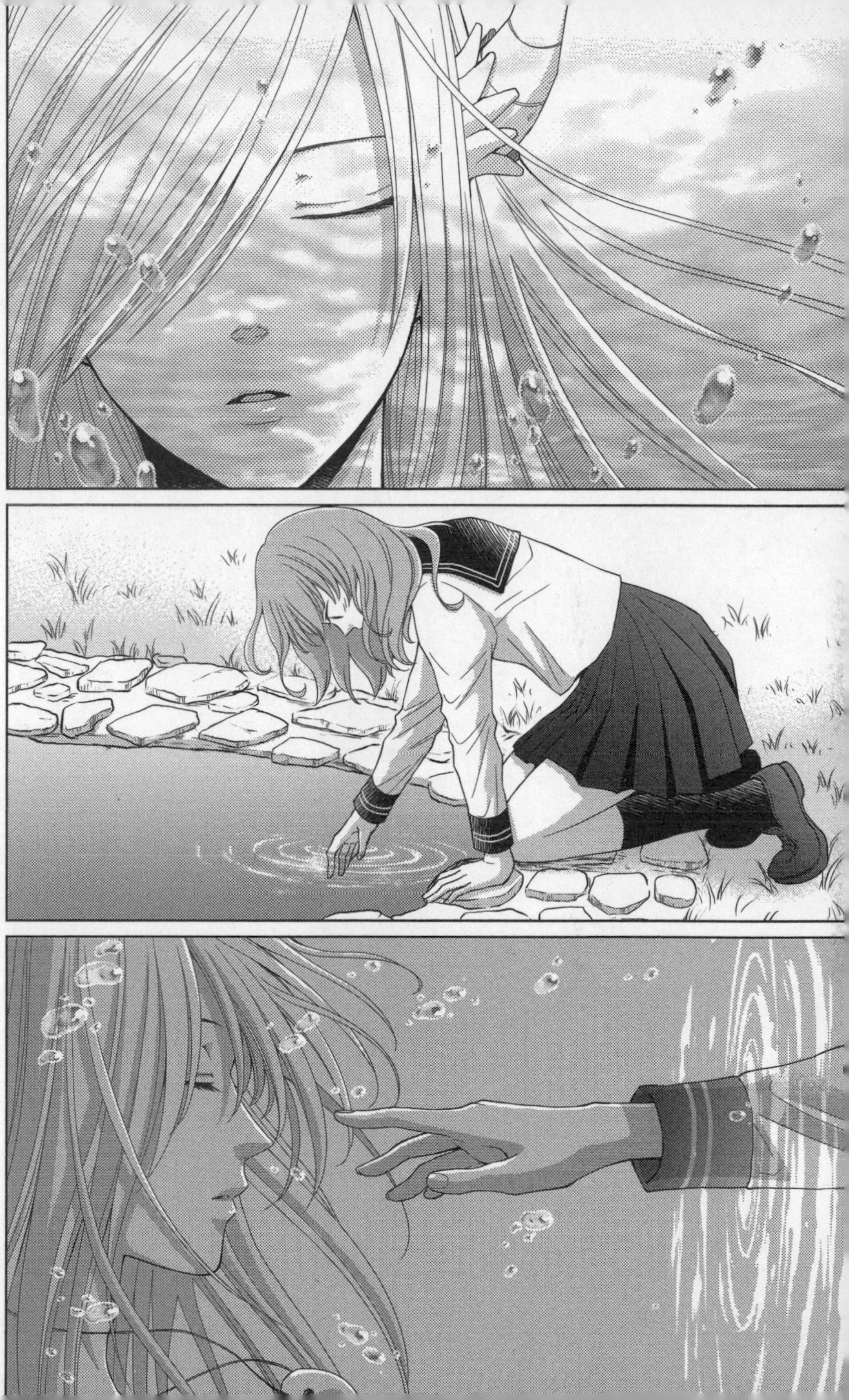

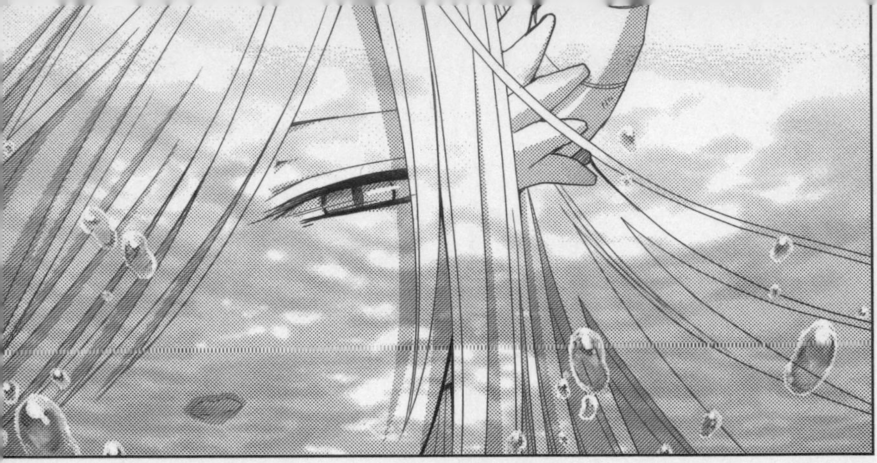
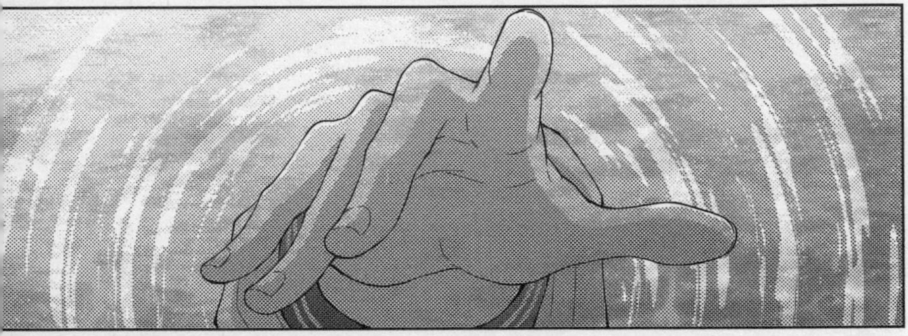
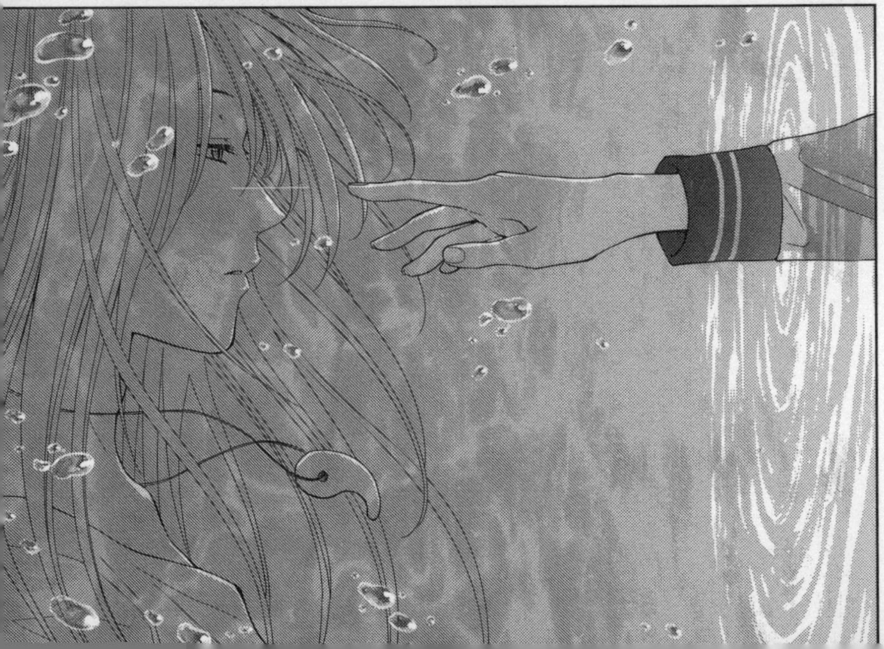

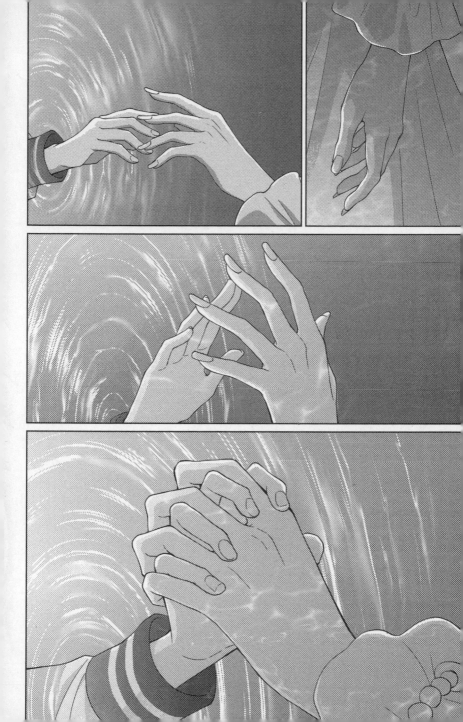

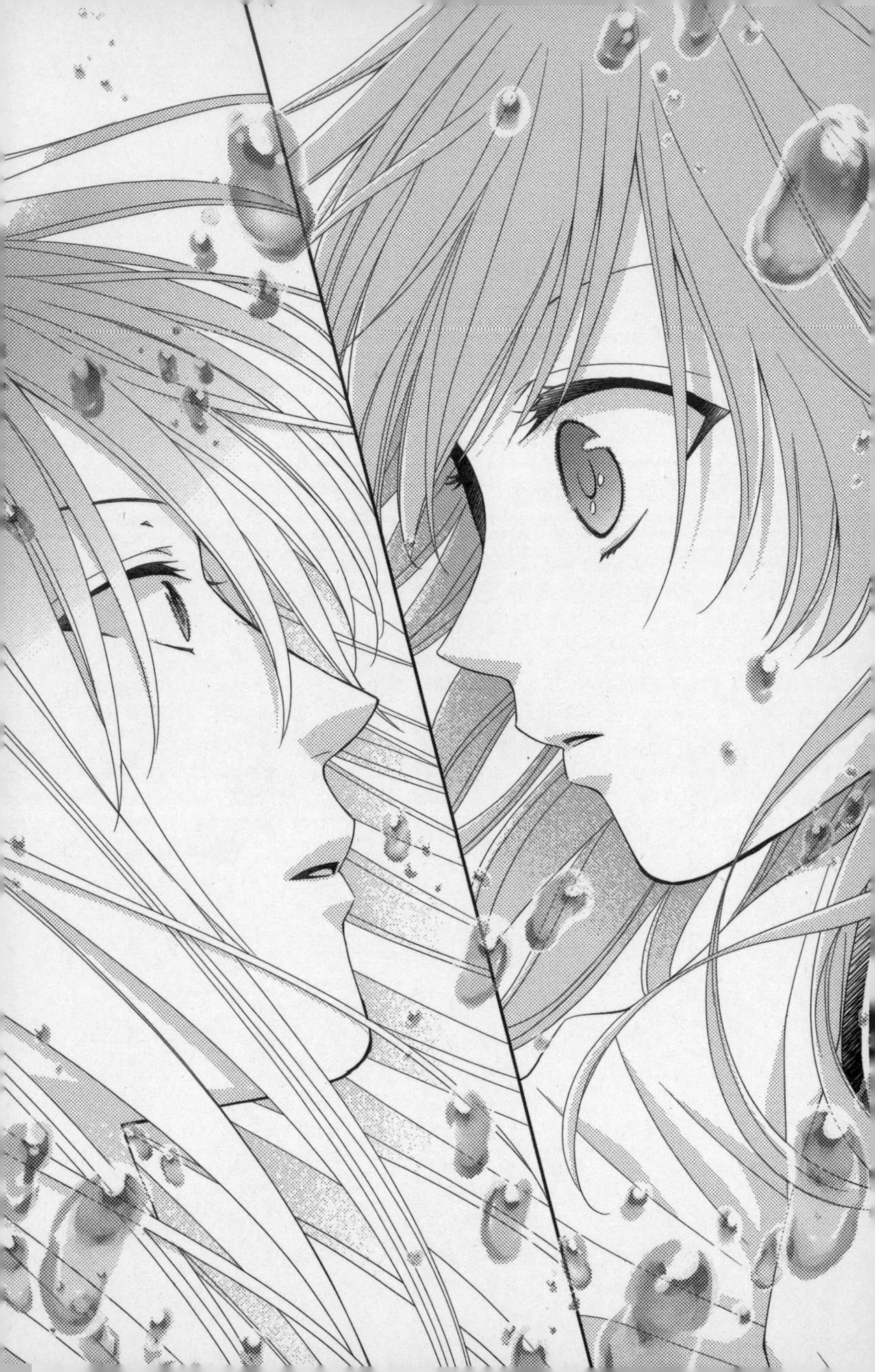

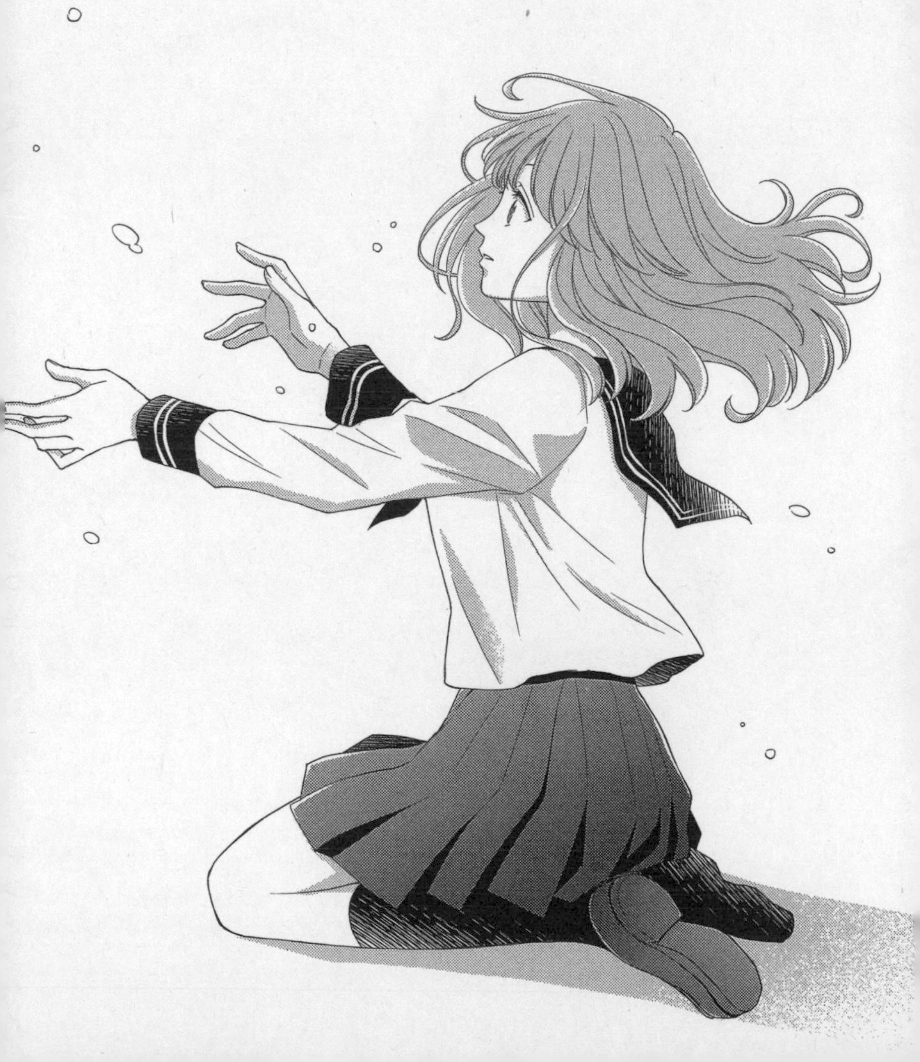

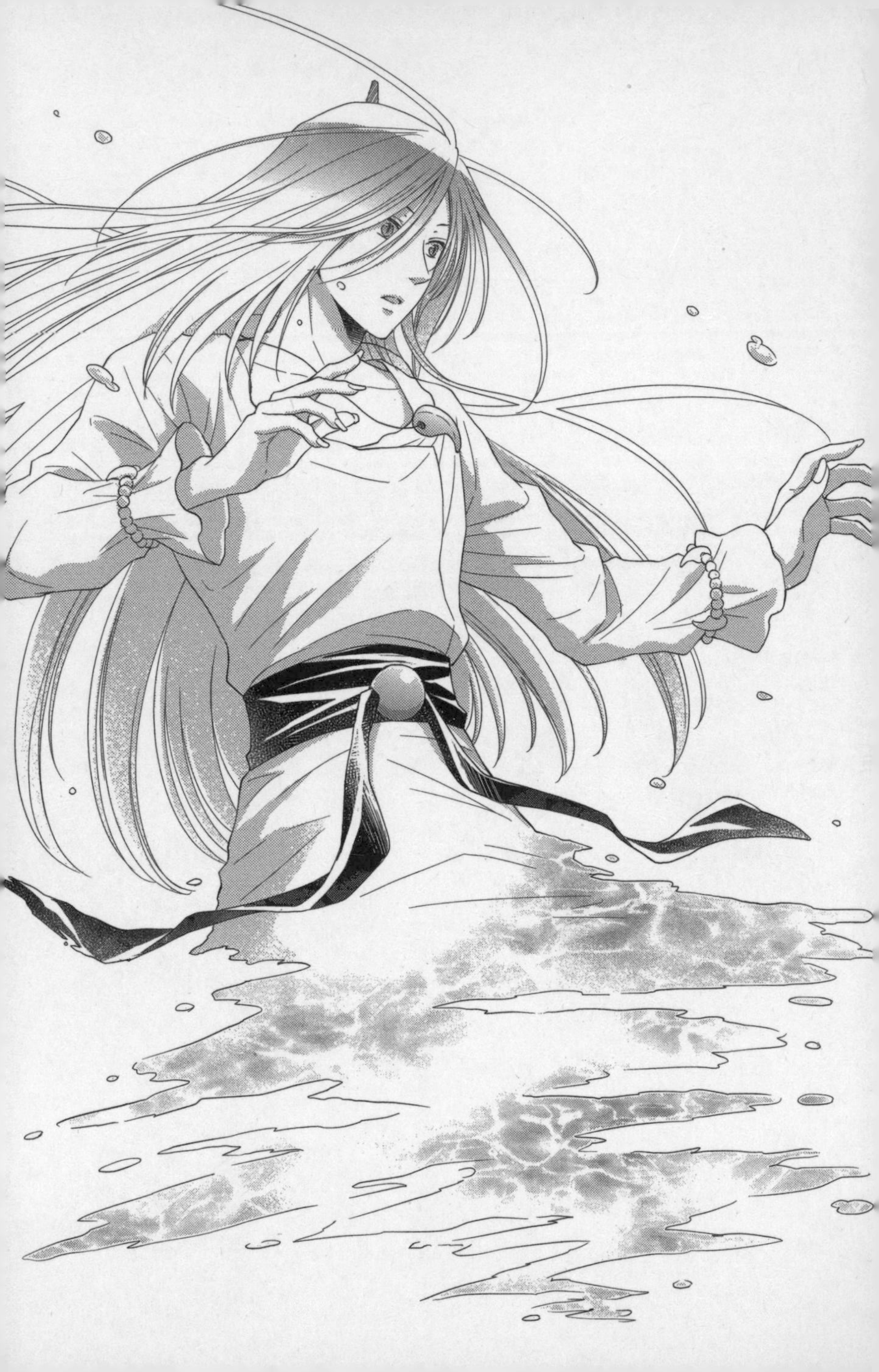

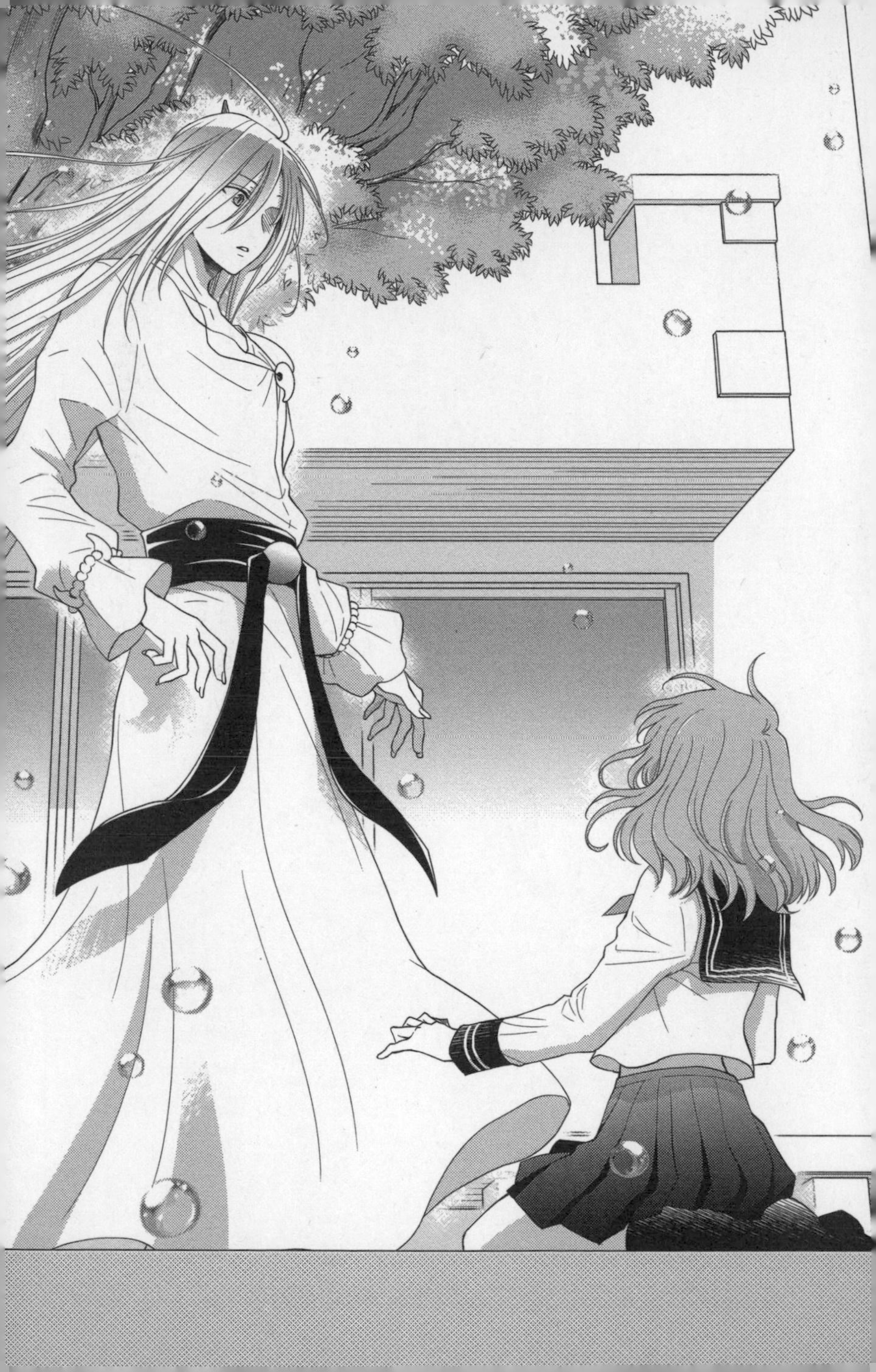

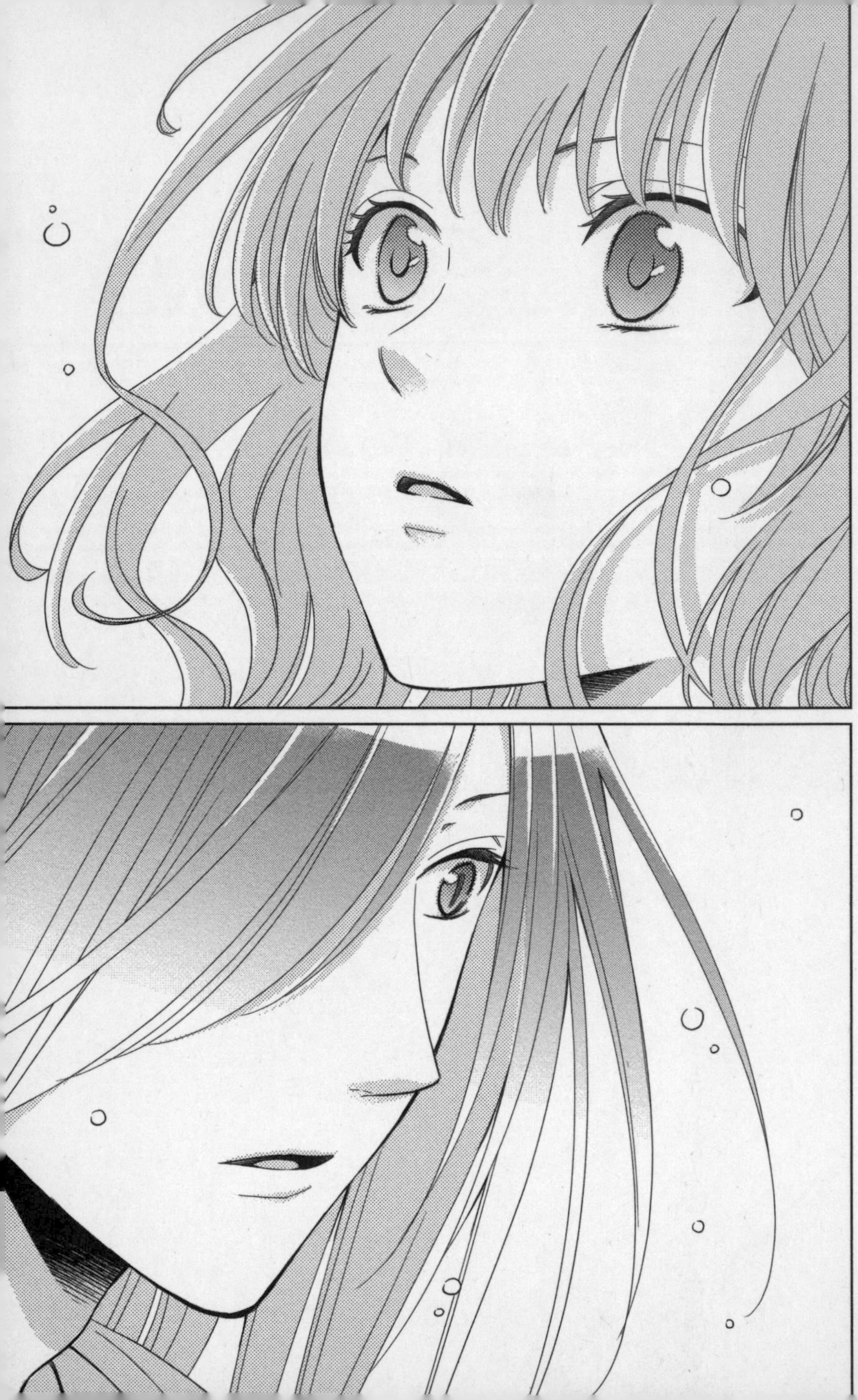

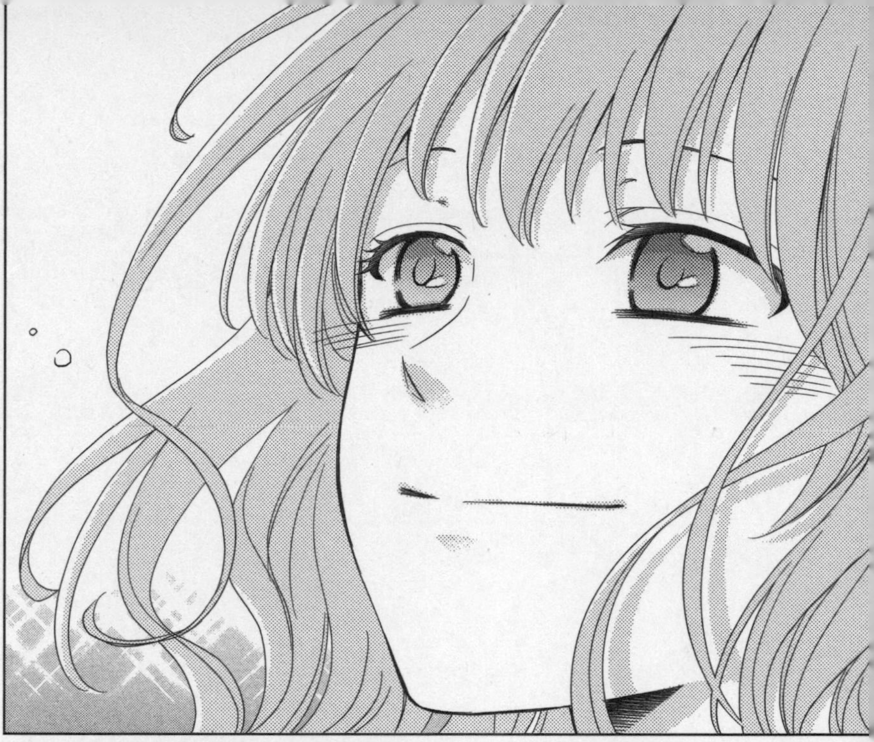
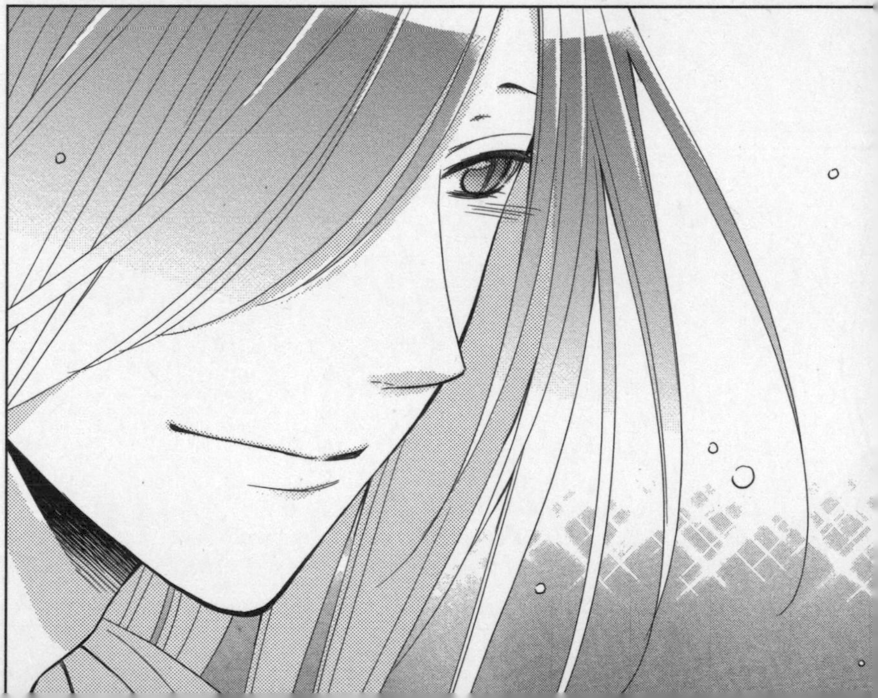

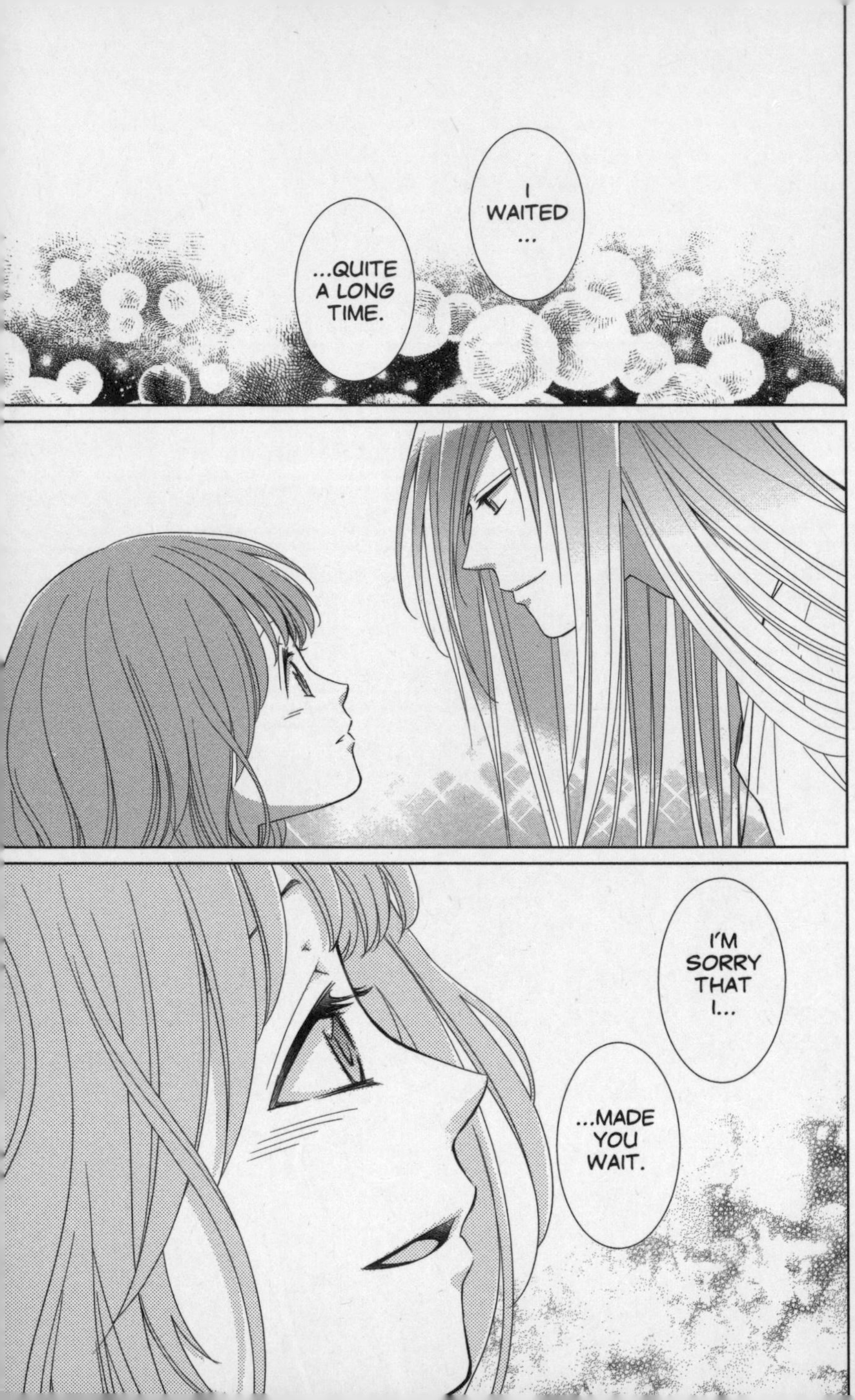
I WAITED ...
...QUITE A LONG TIME.
I'M SORRY THAT I...
...MADE YOU WAIT.

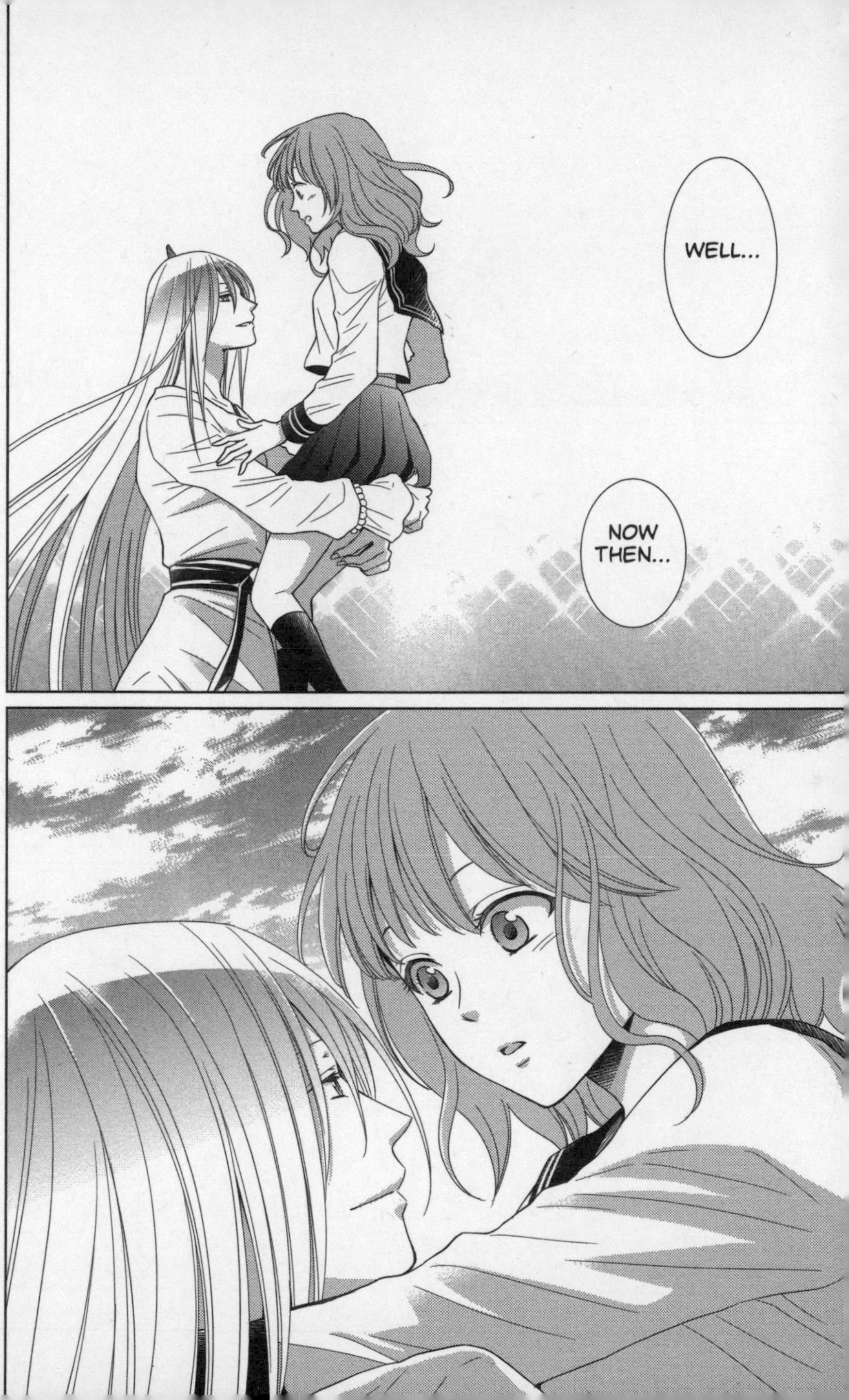
WELL...
NOW THEN...

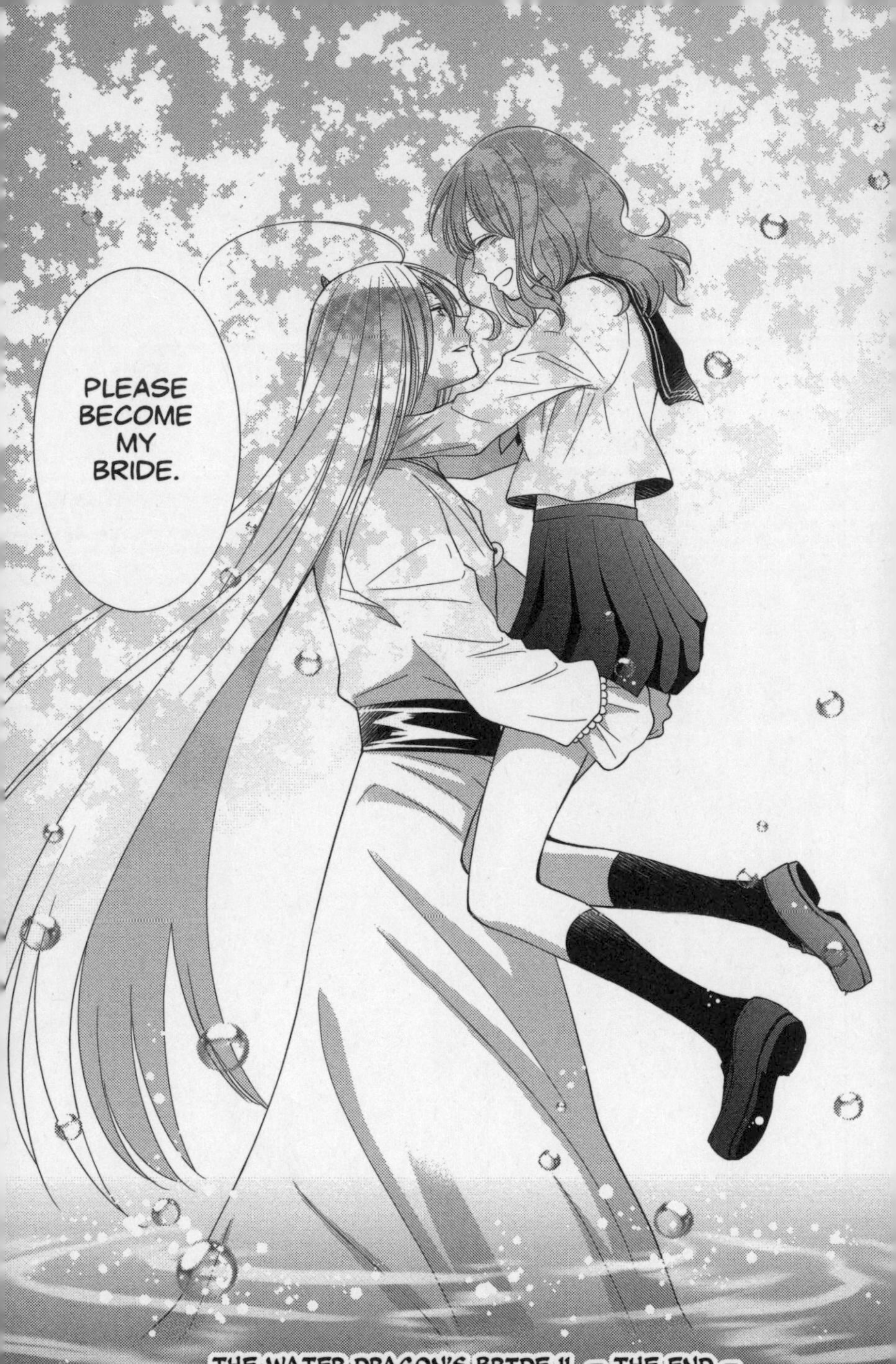
PLEASE BECOME MY BRIDE.

THE WATER DRAGON'S BRIDE 11 —THE END—

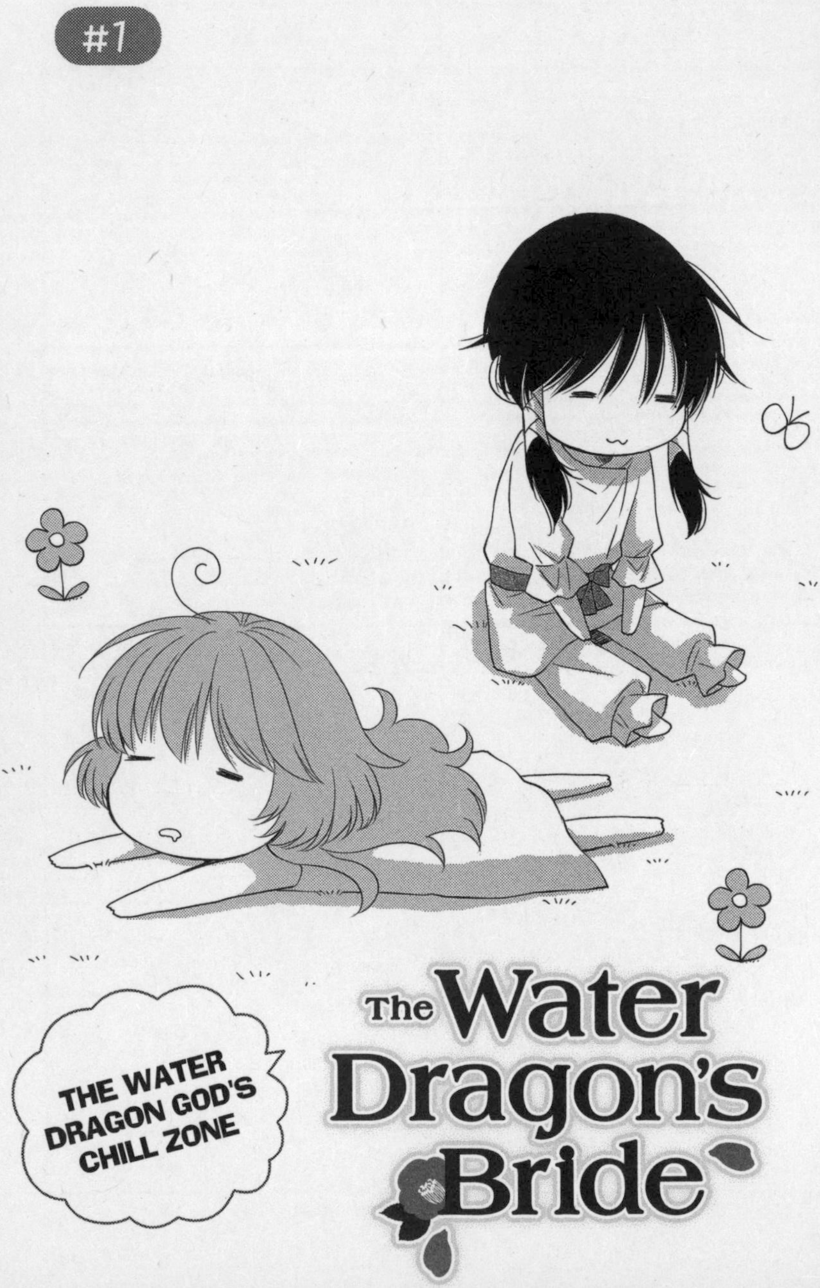
#1
THE WATER DRAGON GOD'S CHILL ZONE
The Water Dragon's Bride

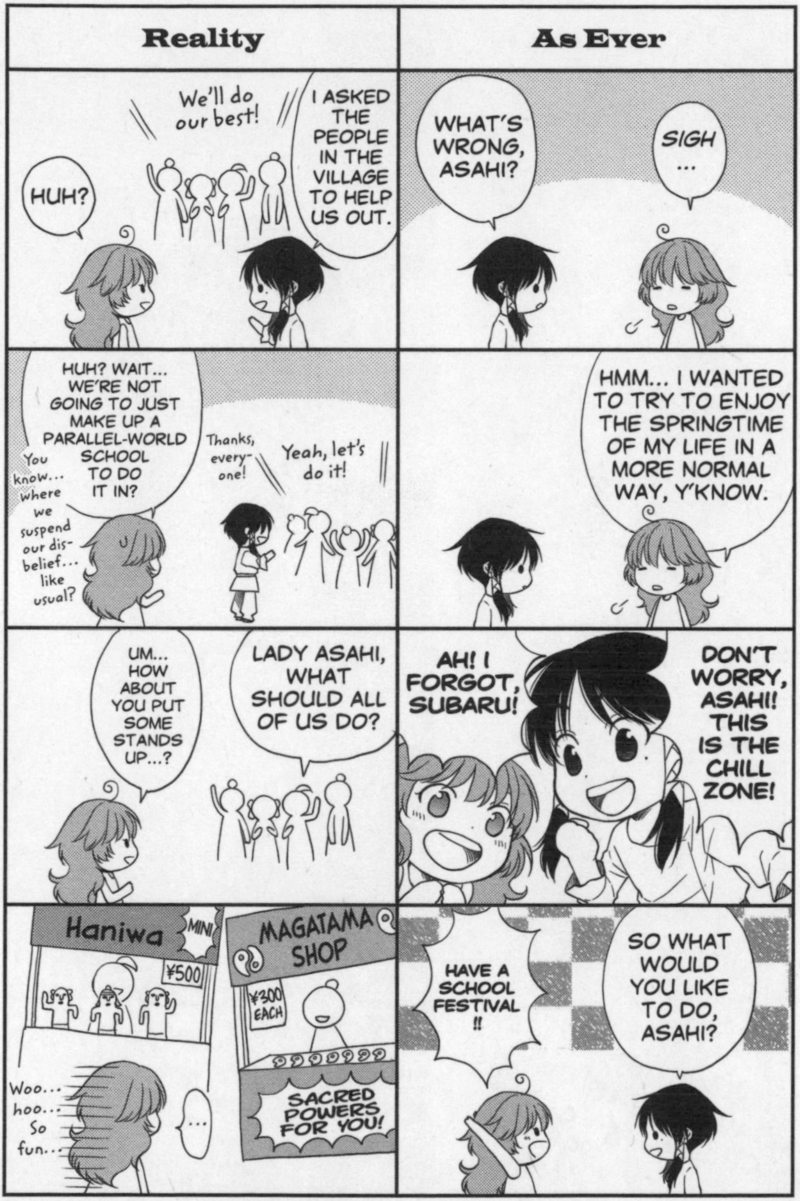
As Ever
SIGH ...
WHAT'S WRONG, ASAHI?
HMM... I WANTED TO TRY TO ENJOY THE SPRINGTIME OF MY LIFE IN A MORE NORMAL WAY, Y'KNOW.
DON'T WORRY, ASAHI! THIS IS THE CHILL ZONE!
AH! I FORGOT, SUBARU!
SO WHAT WOULD YOU LIKE TO DO, ASAHI?
HAVE A SCHOOL FESTIVAL !!
Reality
I ASKED THE PEOPLE IN THE VILLAGE TO HELP US OUT.
We'll do our best!
HUH?
Yeah, let's do it!
Thanks, every-one!
HUH? WAIT... WE'RE NOT GOING TO JUST MAKE UP A PARALLEL-WORLD SCHOOL TO DO IT IN?
You know... where we suspend our dis-belief... like usual?
LADY ASAHI, WHAT SHOULD ALL OF US DO?
UM... HOW ABOUT YOU PUT SOME STANDS UP...?
MAGATAMA SHOP
¥300 EACH
SACRED POWERS FOR YOU!
Haniwa
MINI
¥500
...
Woo... hoo... So fun...

*THIS COMIC HAS NOTHING TO DO WITH THE ACTUAL STORY.

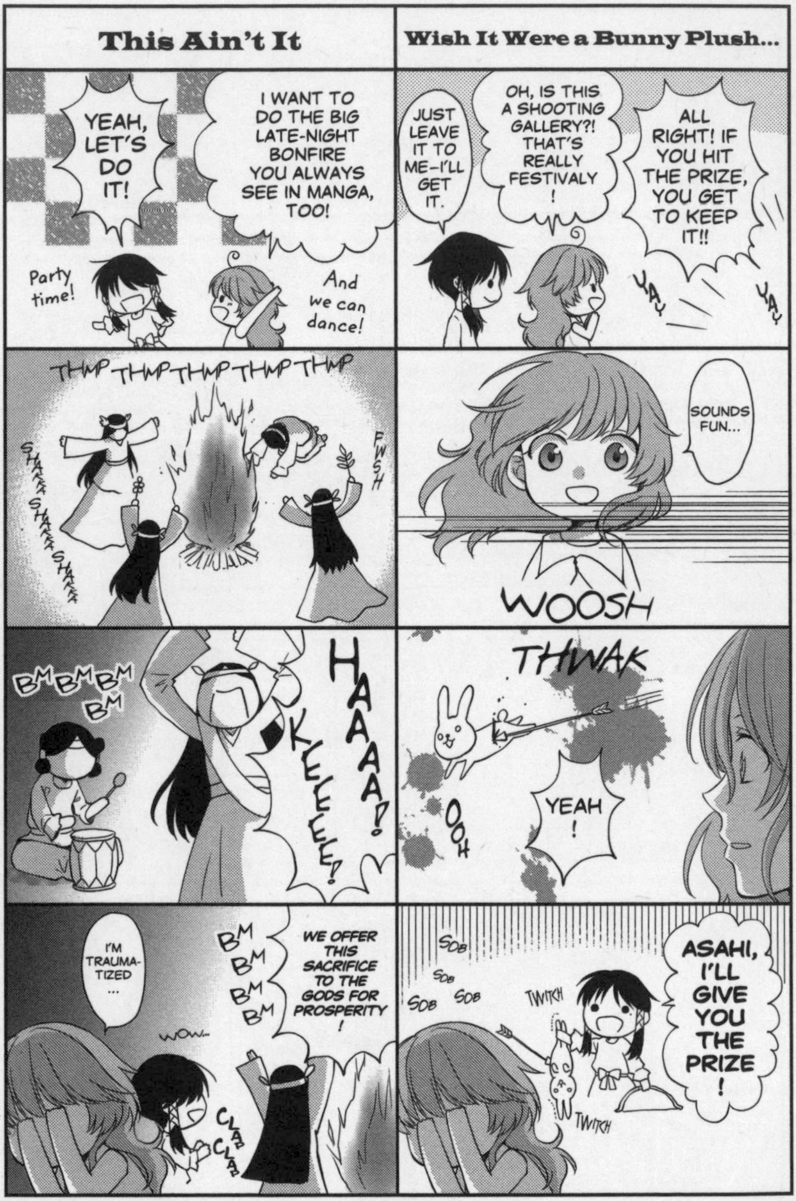
Wish It Were a Bunny Plush...
ALL RIGHT! IF YOU HIT THE PRIZE, YOU GET TO KEEP IT!!
YAY
YAY
OH, IS THIS A SHOOTING GALLERY?! THAT'S REALLY FESTIVALY!
JUST LEAVE IT TO ME—I'LL GET IT.
SOUNDS FUN...
WOOSH
THWAK
YEAH!
OOH
ASAHI, I'LL GIVE YOU THE PRIZE!
SOB
SOB
SOB
SOB
TWITCH
TWITCH
This Ain't It
I WANT TO DO THE BIG LATE-NIGHT BONFIRE YOU ALWAYS SEE IN MANGA, TOO!
YEAH, LET'S DO IT!
And we can dance!
Party time!
THMP THMP THMP THMP THMP
FWSH
SHAKKA SHAKKA SHAKKA SHAKKA
HAAAAA!
KEEEEE!
BM BM BM BM
WE OFFER THIS SACRIFICE TO THE GODS FOR PROSPERITY!
BM BM BM BM
I'M TRAUMATIZED...
WOW...
CLAP CLAP

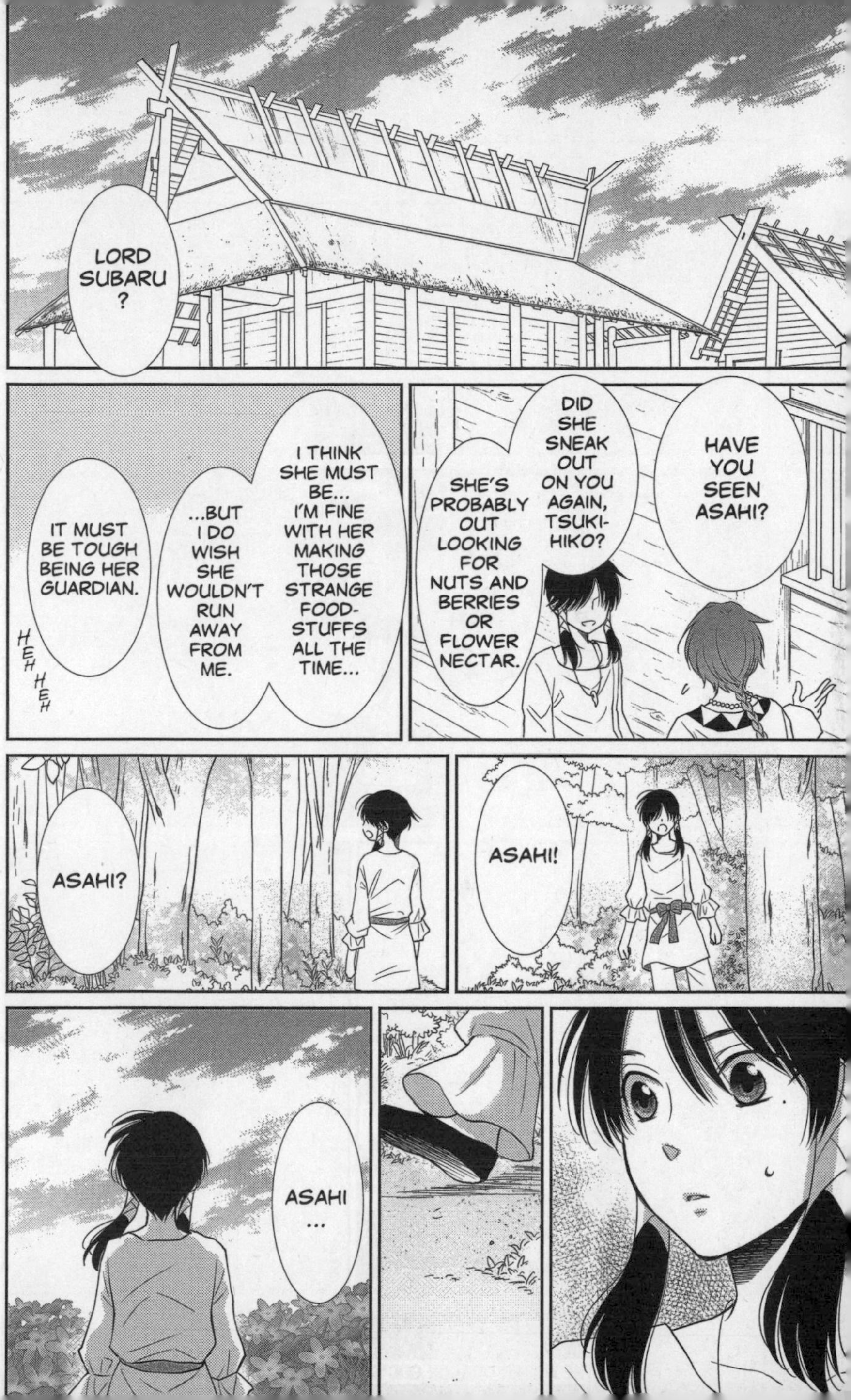
LORD SUBARU?
HAVE YOU SEEN ASAHI?
DID SHE SNEAK OUT ON YOU AGAIN, TSUKI-HIKO?
SHE'S PROBABLY OUT LOOKING FOR NUTS AND BERRIES OR FLOWER NECTAR.
I THINK SHE MUST BE... I'M FINE WITH HER MAKING THOSE STRANGE FOOD-STUFFS ALL THE TIME...
...BUT I DO WISH SHE WOULDN'T RUN AWAY FROM ME.
IT MUST BE TOUGH BEING HER GUARDIAN.
HEH HEH HEH
ASAHI!
ASAHI?
ASAHI...

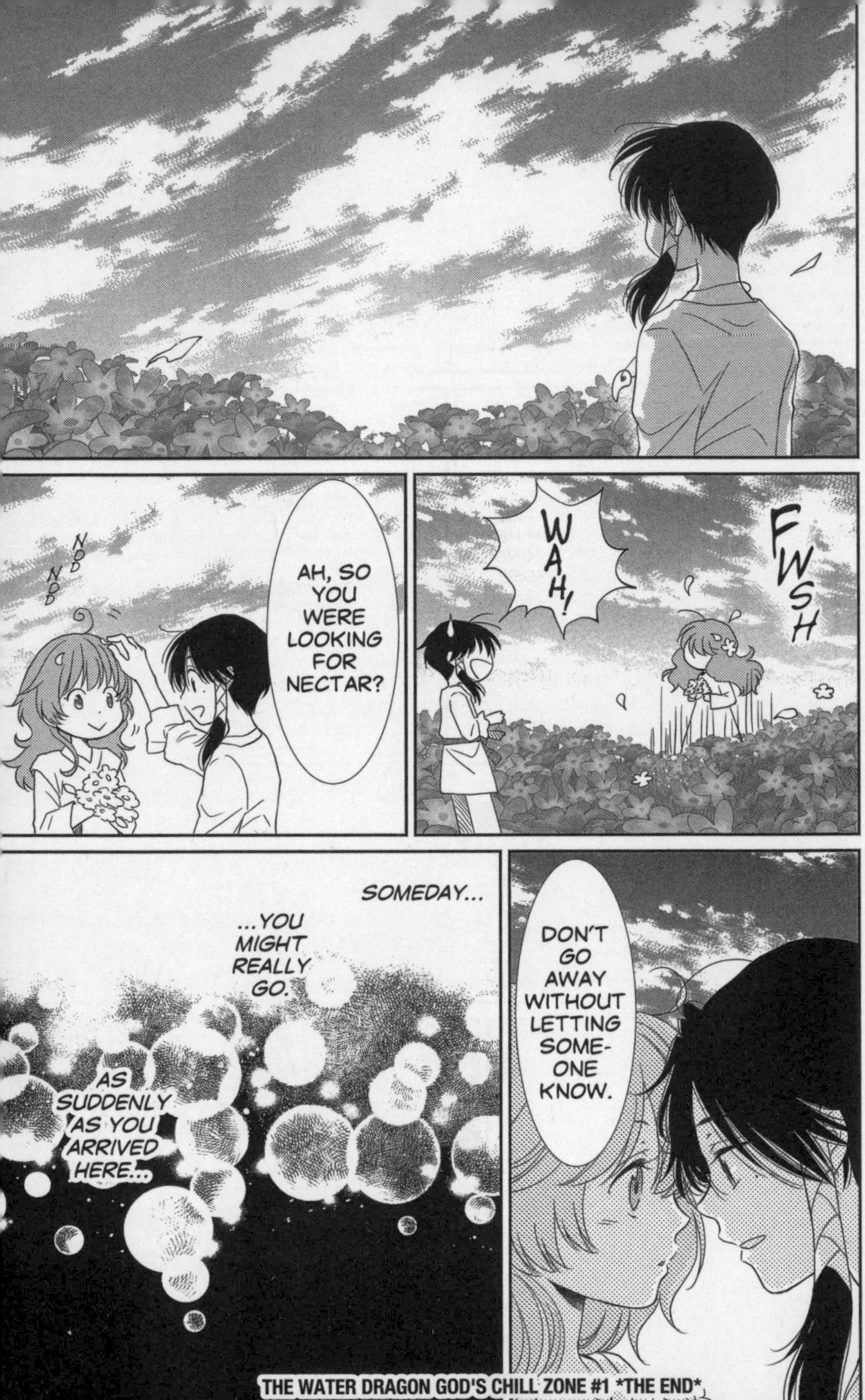
WAH!
FWSH
NOD NOD
AH, SO YOU WERE LOOKING FOR NECTAR?
DON'T GO AWAY WITHOUT LETTING SOME-ONE KNOW.
SOMEDAY...
AS SUDDENLY AS YOU ARRIVED HERE...
...YOU MIGHT REALLY GO.
THE WATER DRAGON GOD'S CHILL ZONE #1 *THE END*

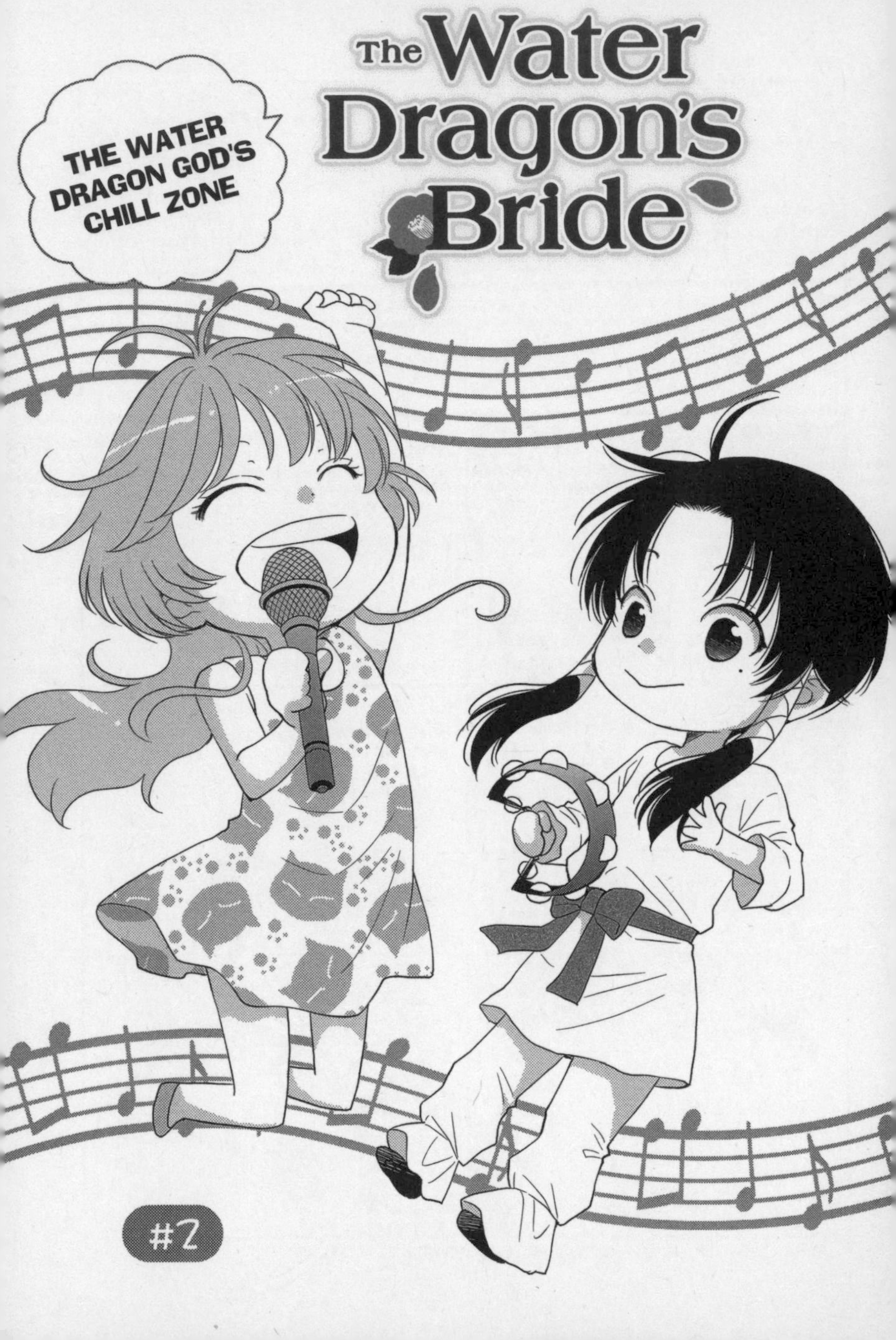
The Water Dragon's Bride
THE WATER DRAGON GOD'S CHILL ZONE
#2

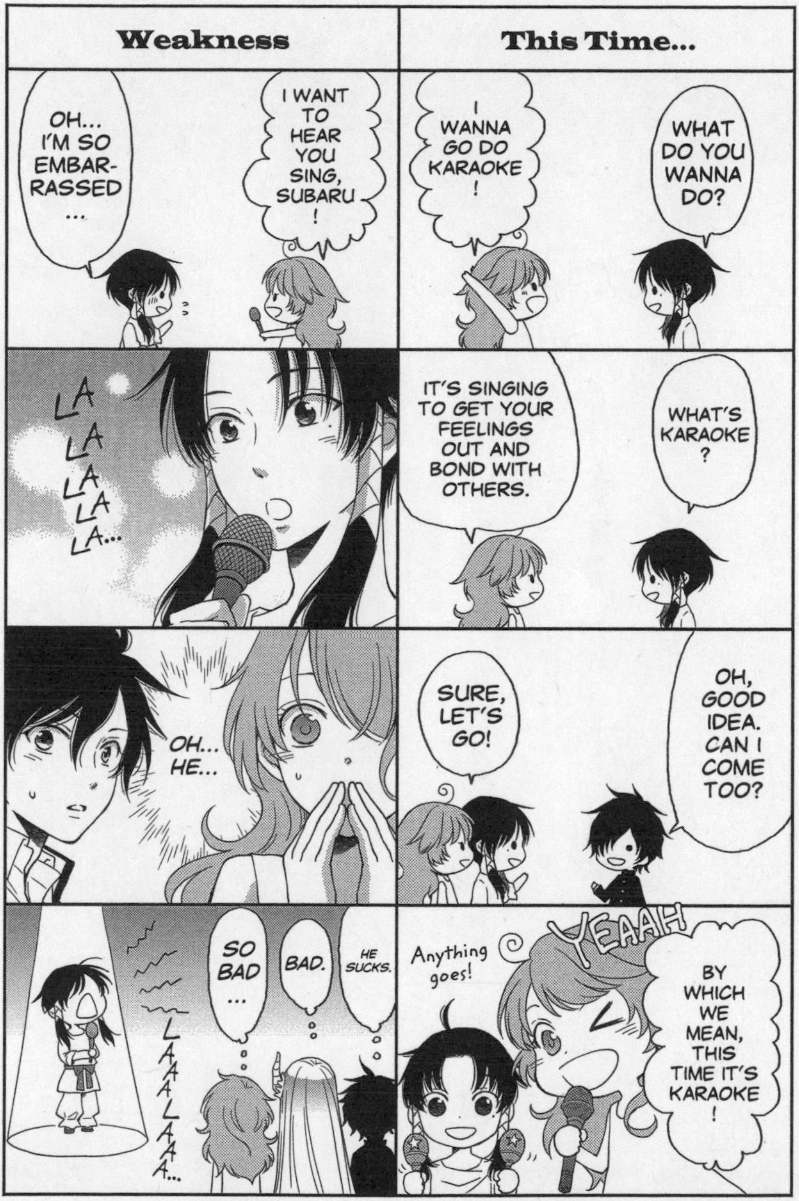
This Time...
WHAT DO YOU WANNA DO?
I WANNA GO DO KARAOKE!
WHAT'S KARAOKE?
IT'S SINGING TO GET YOUR FEELINGS OUT AND BOND WITH OTHERS.
OH, GOOD IDEA. CAN I COME TOO?
SURE, LET'S GO!
YEAAAH
BY WHICH WE MEAN, THIS TIME IT'S KARAOKE!
Anything goes!
Weakness
I WANT TO HEAR YOU SING, SUBARU!
OH... I'M SO EMBARRASSED...
LA LA LA LA LA LA...
OH... HE...
HE SUCKS.
BAD.
SO BAD...
LAAAALAAAA...

*THIS COMIC HAS NOTHING TO DO WITH THE ACTUAL STORY.

The Important Part Is to Have Fun, Though

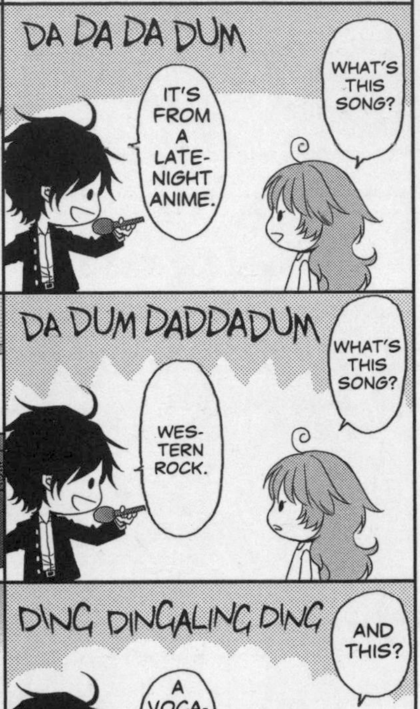
DA DA DA DUM
WHAT'S THIS SONG?
IT'S FROM A LATE-NIGHT ANIME.
DA DUM DADDADUM
WHAT'S THIS SONG?
WESTERN ROCK.
DING DINGALING DING
AND THIS?
A VOCALOID SONG.
THIS IS WHY, KUROSE. THIS IS WHY.
Also, the way you hold the mike is annoying.
PAT
HUH?

He Needs Training

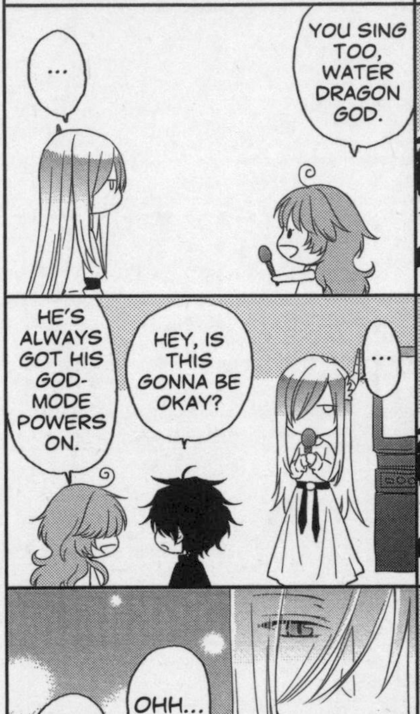
YOU SING TOO, WATER DRAGON GOD.
...
...
HEY, IS THIS GONNA BE OKAY?
HE'S ALWAYS GOT HIS GOD-MODE POWERS ON.
OHH...
THIS IS...
GOD-ALOID...
HE'S PERFECTLY ON BEAT AND ON TEMPO...
...but it still sounds so robotic...

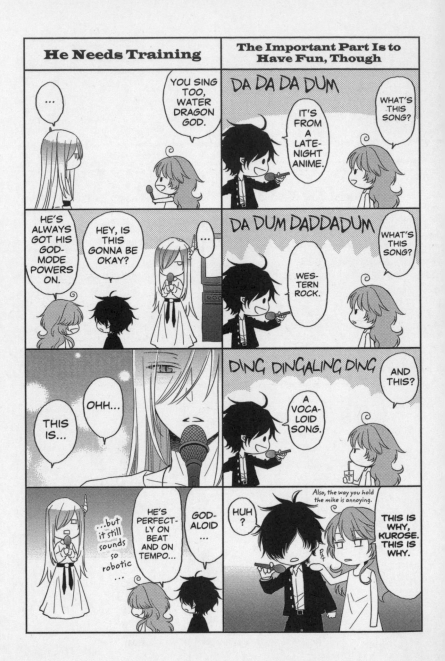

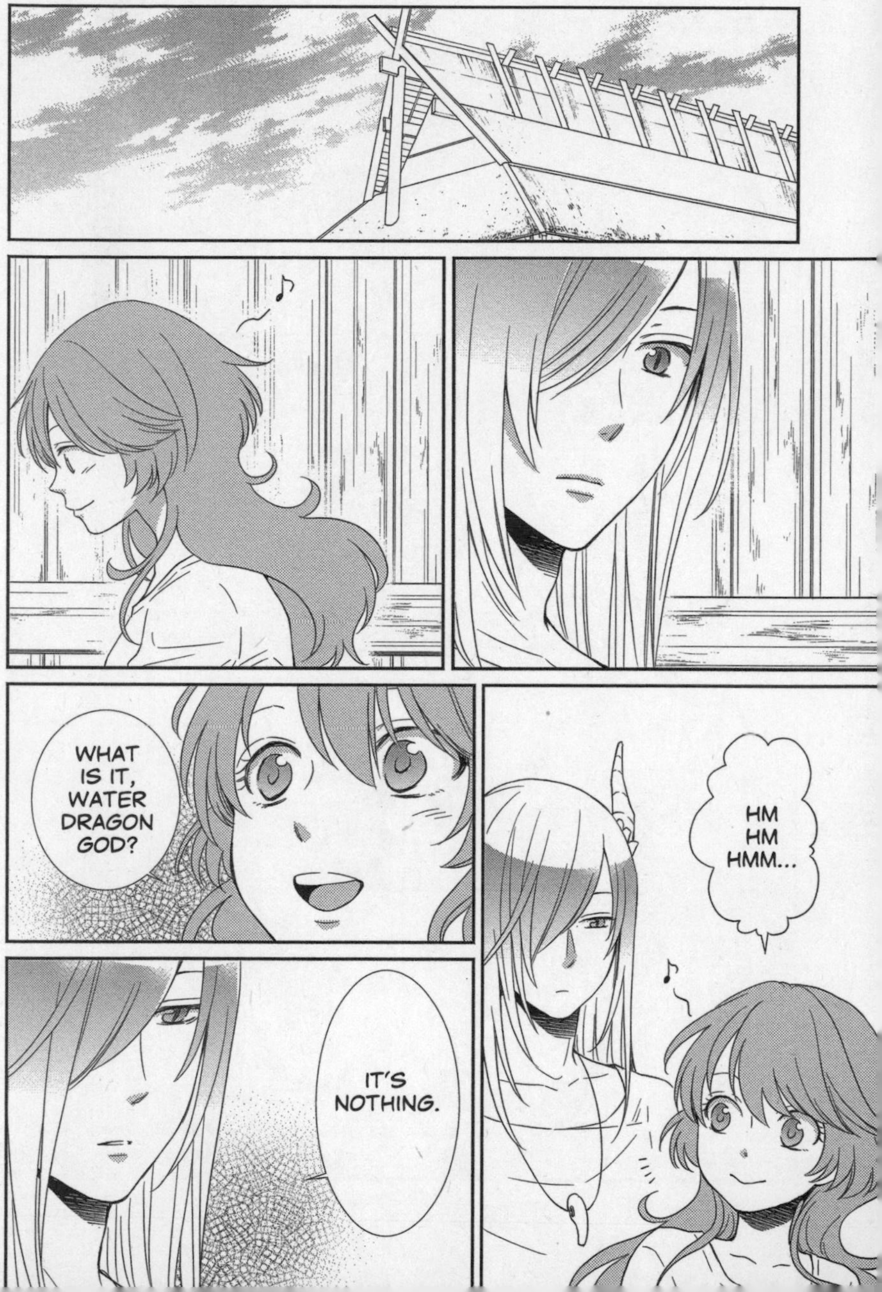
HM HM HMM...
WHAT IS IT, WATER DRAGON GOD?
IT'S NOTHING.

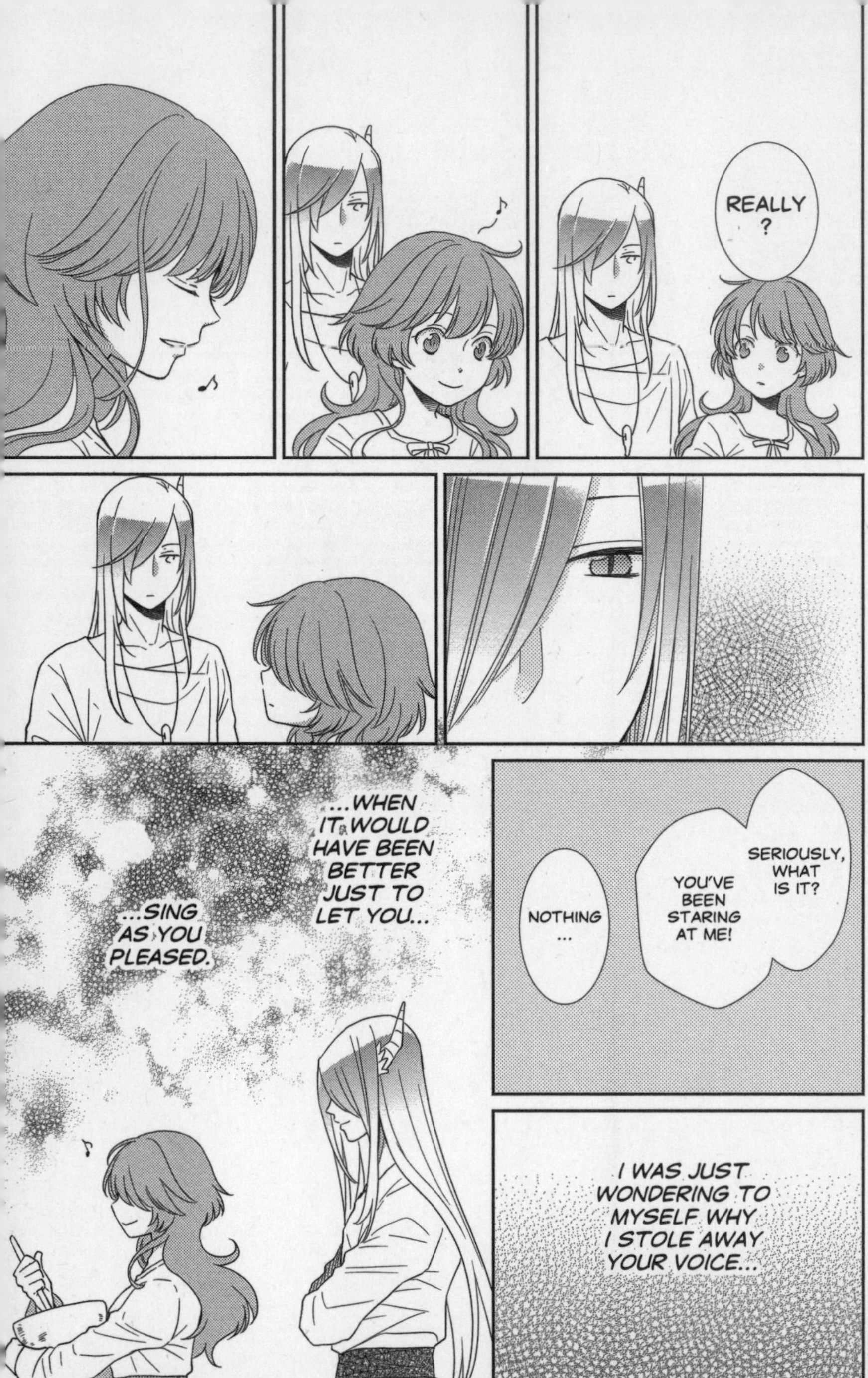
REALLY ?
SERIOUSLY, WHAT IS IT?
YOU'VE BEEN STARING AT ME!
NOTHING ...
I WAS JUST WONDERING TO MYSELF WHY I STOLE AWAY YOUR VOICE...
...WHEN IT WOULD HAVE BEEN BETTER JUST TO LET YOU...
...SING AS YOU PLEASED.
THE WATER DRAGON GOD'S CHILL ZONE #2 *THE END*

TO EVERYONE WHO READ THIS STORY...
TO THE ASSISTANTS WHO HELPED ME...
TO MY ESTEEMED EDITOR, WHO
SUPPORTED ME WHEN I WAS THIS
CLOSE TO DEADLINE EVERY TIME...

TO EVERYONE WHO FELL IN LOVE WITH
THE WATER DRAGON GOD'S WORLD...

I HAVE SO MANY PEOPLE WHO I NEED
TO EXPRESS MY GRATITUDE TO!

THANK YOU SO MUCH FOR READING ALONG!

Rei Toma

PLEASE TELL ME WHAT YOU THINK!

REI TOMA
C/O THE WATER DRAGON'S BRIDE EDITOR
VIZ MEDIA
P.O. BOX 77010
SAN FRANCISCO, CA 94107

I REALLY WANTED TO DRAW MORE OF THIS COMIC... IS THAT
REDUNDANT TO SAY? I MEAN, I WOULD LOVE TO DRAW A BIT
MORE. MAYBE A SEQUEL? OR AN EXTRA VOLUME? I PLAN TO DRAW
SOMETHING ELSE, THOUGH. IT MIGHT END UP HAVING A LESS
SERIOUS ATMOSPHERE, SO PLEASE LOOK FORWARD TO IT.

THE WATER
DRAGON GOD'S
CHILL ZONE

The Water Dragon's Bride

#3

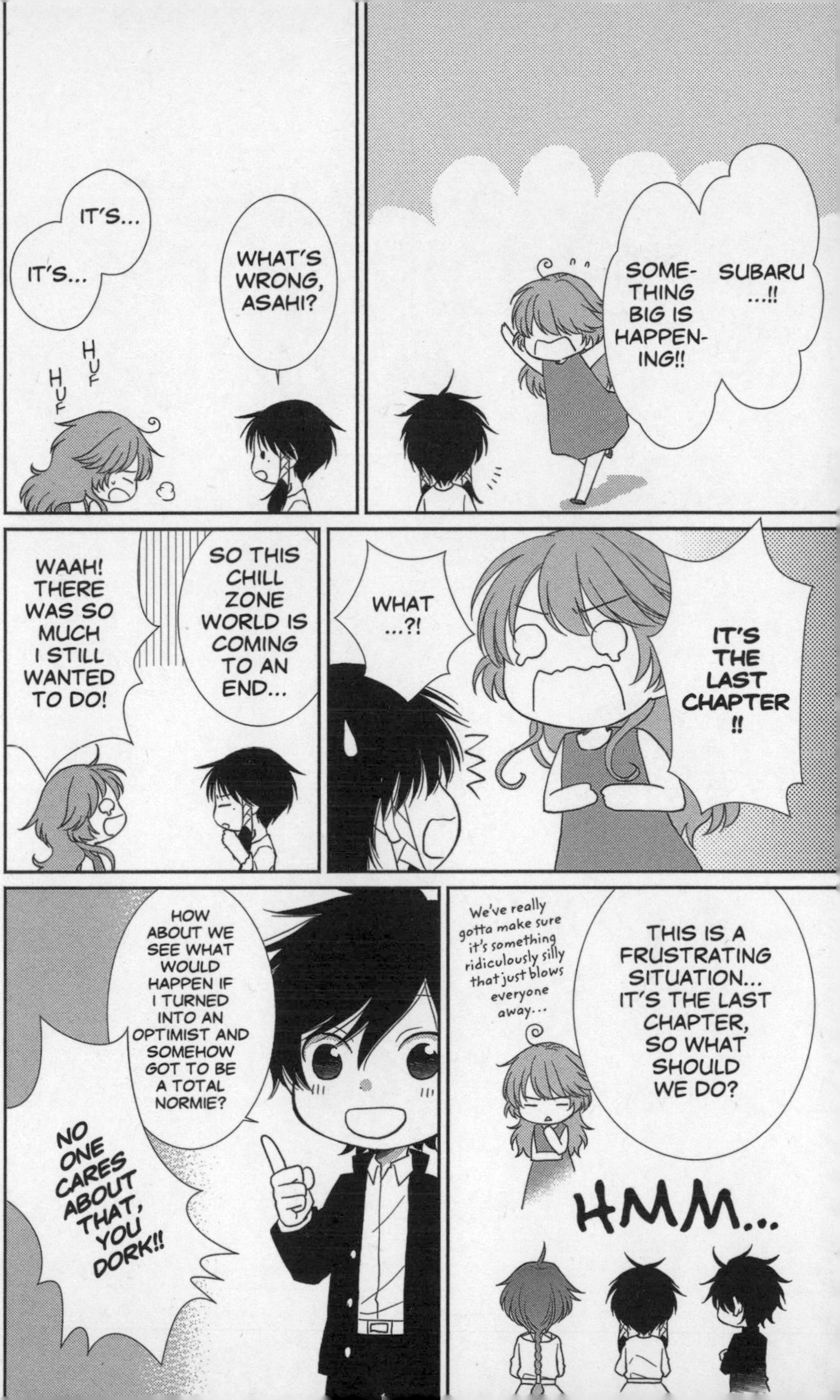
SUBARU ...!!
SOME-THING BIG IS HAPPEN-ING!!
WHAT'S WRONG, ASAHI?
IT'S... IT'S...
HUF HUF
IT'S THE LAST CHAPTER !!
WHAT ...?!
SO THIS CHILL ZONE WORLD IS COMING TO AN END...
WAAH! THERE WAS SO MUCH I STILL WANTED TO DO!
THIS IS A FRUSTRATING SITUATION... IT'S THE LAST CHAPTER, SO WHAT SHOULD WE DO?
We've really gotta make sure it's something ridiculously silly that just blows everyone away...
HMM...
HOW ABOUT WE SEE WHAT WOULD HAPPEN IF I TURNED INTO AN OPTIMIST AND SOMEHOW GOT TO BE A TOTAL NORMIE?
NO ONE CARES ABOUT THAT, YOU DORK!!

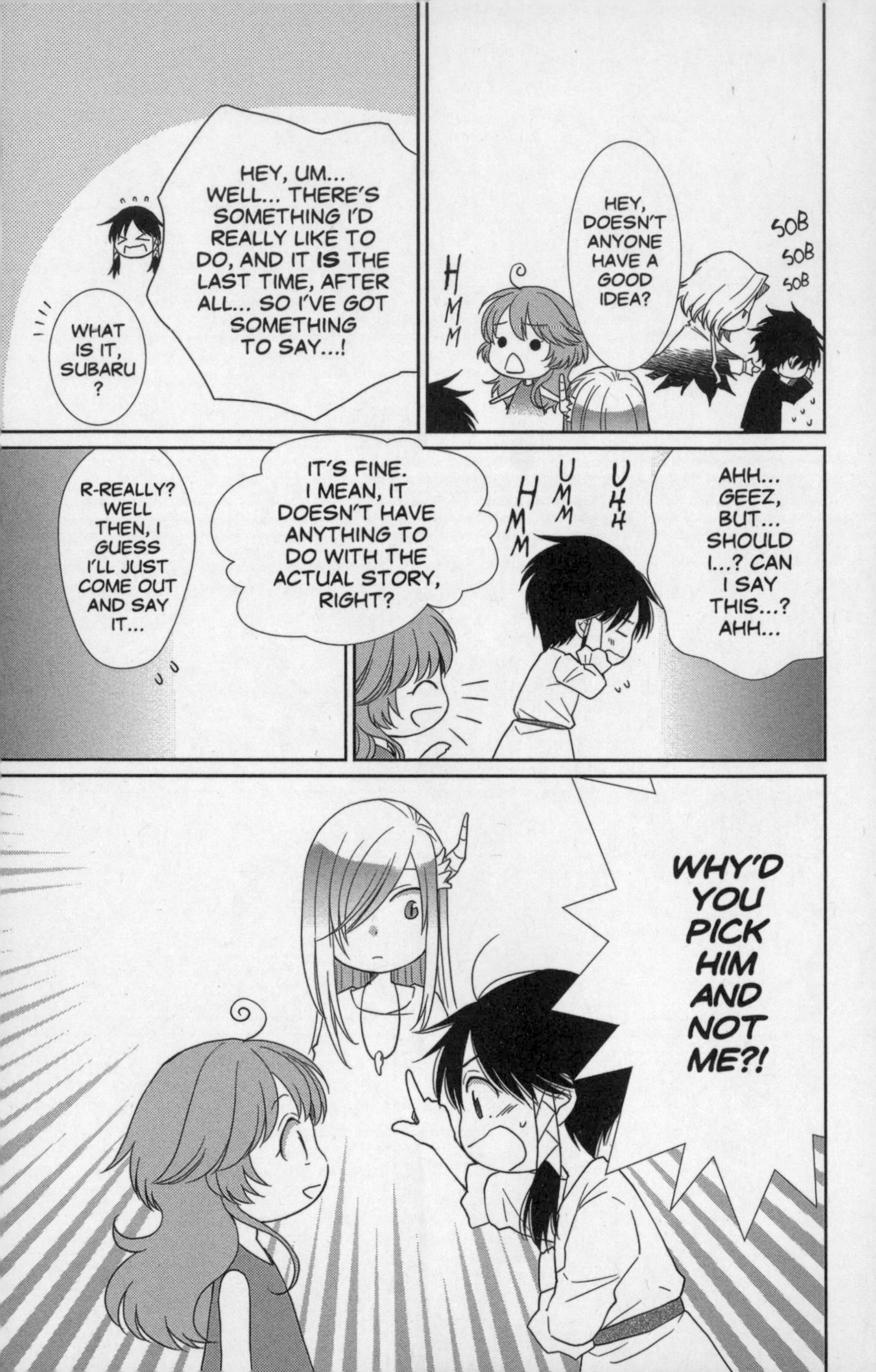

HEY, DOESN'T ANYONE HAVE A GOOD IDEA?
SOB SOB SOB
HMM
HEY, UM... WELL... THERE'S SOMETHING I'D REALLY LIKE TO DO, AND IT **IS** THE LAST TIME, AFTER ALL... SO I'VE GOT SOMETHING TO SAY...!
WHAT IS IT, SUBARU?
AHH... GEEZ, BUT... SHOULD I...? CAN I SAY THIS...? AHH...
UHH
UMM
HMM
IT'S FINE. I MEAN, IT DOESN'T HAVE ANYTHING TO DO WITH THE ACTUAL STORY, RIGHT?
R-REALLY? WELL THEN, I GUESS I'LL JUST COME OUT AND SAY IT...
WHY'D YOU PICK HIM AND NOT ME?!

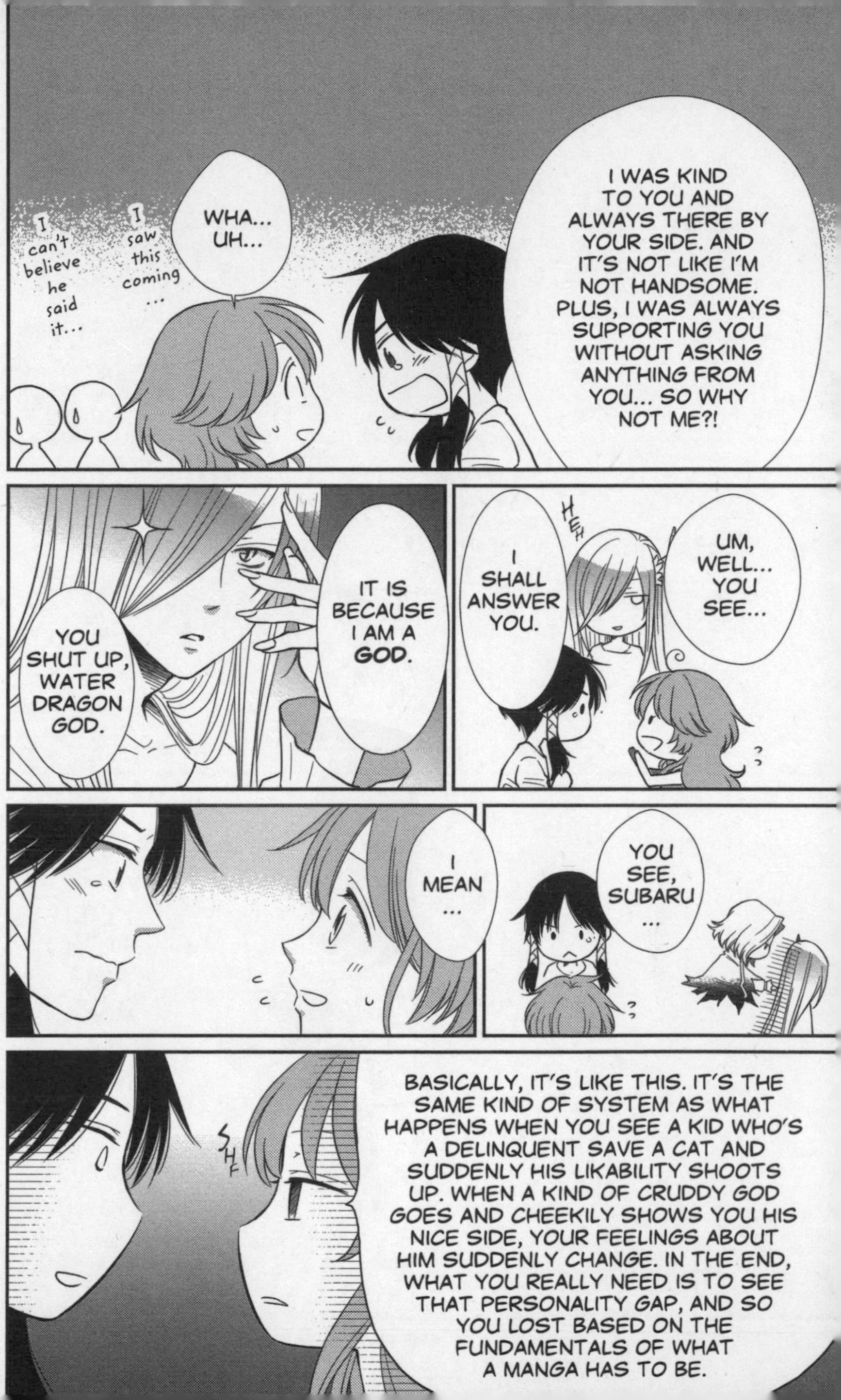
I WAS KIND TO YOU AND ALWAYS THERE BY YOUR SIDE. AND IT'S NOT LIKE I'M NOT HANDSOME. PLUS, I WAS ALWAYS SUPPORTING YOU WITHOUT ASKING ANYTHING FROM YOU... SO WHY NOT ME?!
WHA... UH...
I saw this coming...
I can't believe he said it...
UM, WELL... YOU SEE...
HEH
I SHALL ANSWER YOU.
IT IS BECAUSE I AM A GOD.
YOU SHUT UP, WATER DRAGON GOD.
YOU SEE, SUBARU...
I MEAN...
SHF
BASICALLY, IT'S LIKE THIS. IT'S THE SAME KIND OF SYSTEM AS WHAT HAPPENS WHEN YOU SEE A KID WHO'S A DELINQUENT SAVE A CAT AND SUDDENLY HIS LIKABILITY SHOOTS UP. WHEN A KIND OF CRUDDY GOD GOES AND CHEEKILY SHOWS YOU HIS NICE SIDE, YOUR FEELINGS ABOUT HIM SUDDENLY CHANGE. IN THE END, WHAT YOU REALLY NEED IS TO SEE THAT PERSONALITY GAP, AND SO YOU LOST BASED ON THE FUNDAMENTALS OF WHAT A MANGA HAS TO BE.

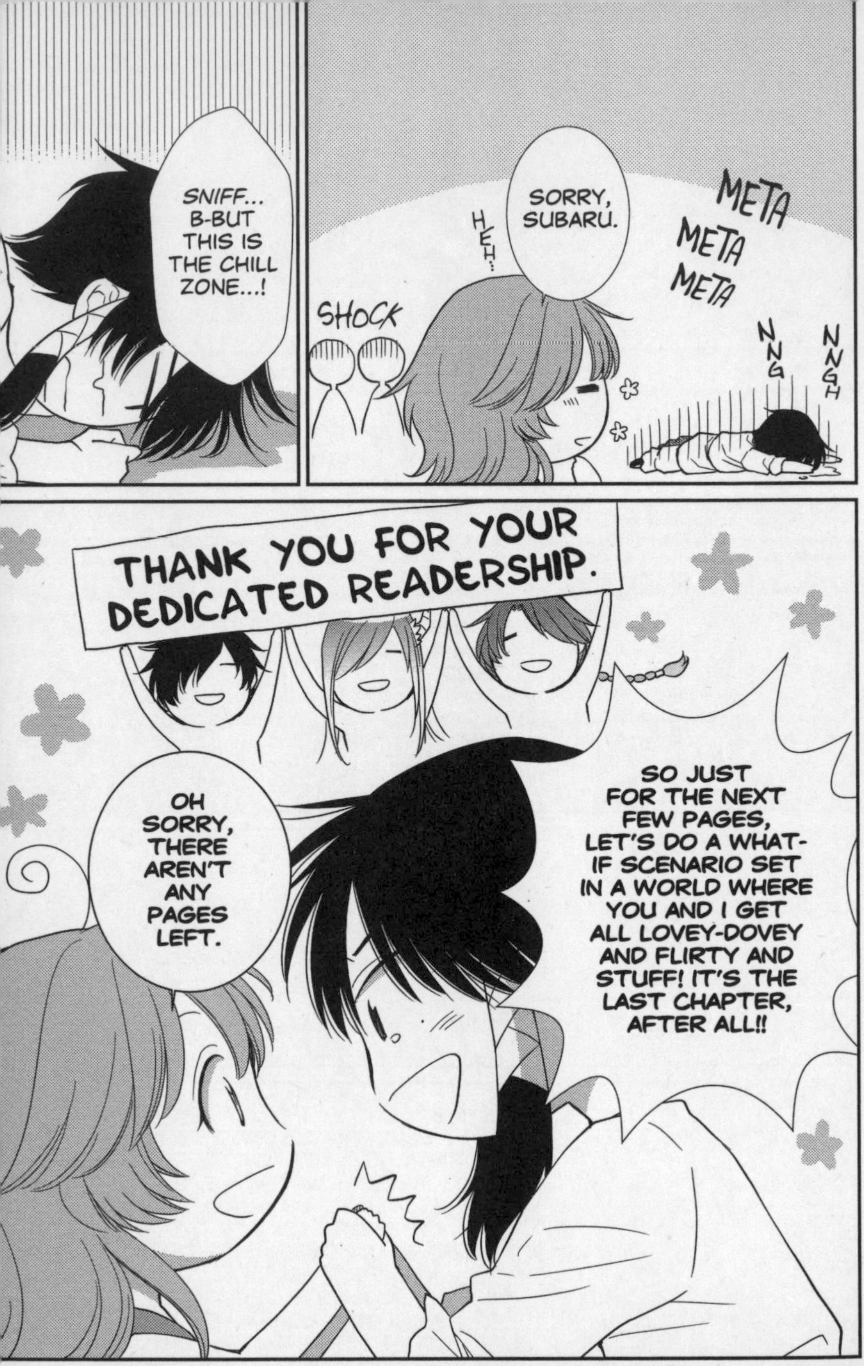
SORRY, SUBARU.
HEH...
META META META
NNG NNGH
SHOCK
SNIFF... B-BUT THIS IS THE CHILL ZONE...!
THANK YOU FOR YOUR DEDICATED READERSHIP.
SO JUST FOR THE NEXT FEW PAGES, LET'S DO A WHAT-IF SCENARIO SET IN A WORLD WHERE YOU AND I GET ALL LOVEY-DOVEY AND FLIRTY AND STUFF! IT'S THE LAST CHAPTER, AFTER ALL!!
OH SORRY, THERE AREN'T ANY PAGES LEFT.

THE END

THE WATER DRAGON GOD'S CHILL ZONE #3 *THE END*

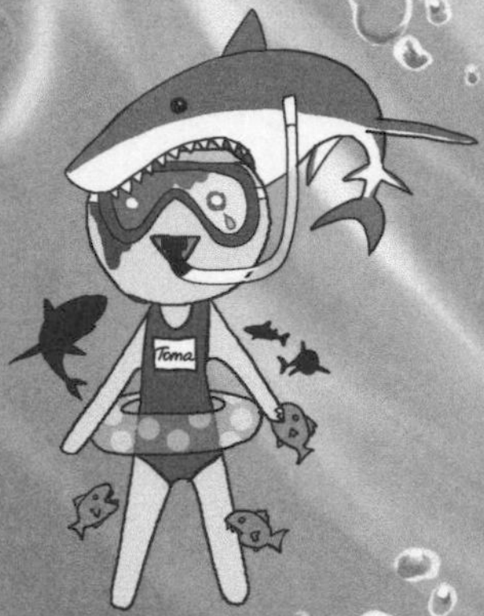
Toma

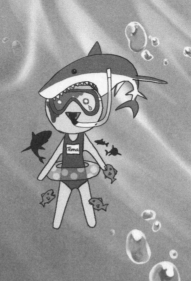

This is the last volume.
Thank you very much!
– REI TOMA

Rei Toma has been drawing since childhood, and she created her first complete manga for a graduation project in design school. When she drew the short story manga "Help Me, Dentist," it attracted a publisher's attention and she made her debut right away. After she found success as a manga artist, acclaim in other art fields started to follow as she did illustrations for novels and video game character designs. She is also the creator of *Dawn of the Arcana*, available in North America from VIZ Media.

The Water Dragon's Bride
VOL. 11
Shojo Beat Edition

Story and Art by
Rei Toma

SUIJIN NO HANAYOME Vol.11
by Rei TOMA
© 2015 Rei TOMA
All rights reserved.
Original Japanese edition published by SHOGAKUKAN.
English translation rights in the United States of America,
Canada, the United Kingdom, Ireland, Australia and New
Zealand arranged with SHOGAKUKAN.

ORIGINAL COVER DESIGN/Hibiki CHIKADA (fireworks.vc)

English Translation & Adaptation **Abby Lehrke**
Touch-Up Art & Lettering **Monaliza de Asis**
Design **Alice Lewis**
Editor **Amy Yu**

Printed in the U.S.A.

Published by VIZ Media, LLC
P.O. Box 77010
San Francisco, CA 94107

10 9 8 7 6 5 4 3 2 1
First printing, November 2019

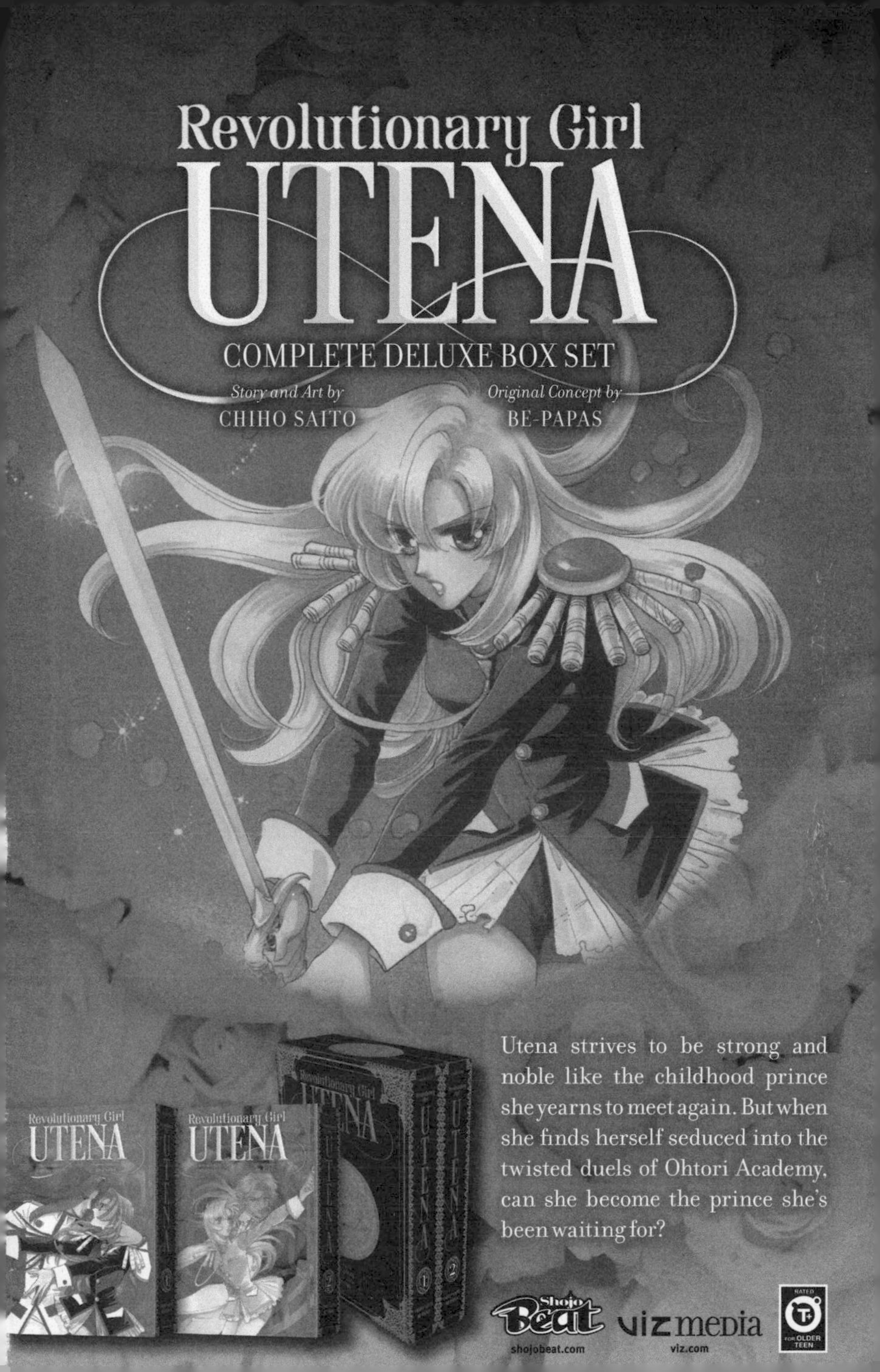
Revolutionary Girl
UTENA
COMPLETE DELUXE BOX SET
Story and Art by
CHIHO SAITO
Original Concept by
BE-PAPAS
Utena strives to be strong and noble like the childhood prince she yearns to meet again. But when she finds herself seduced into the twisted duels of Ohtori Academy, can she become the prince she's been waiting for?
Shojo Beat
shojobeat.com
viz media
viz.com
RATED
T+
FOR OLDER TEEN

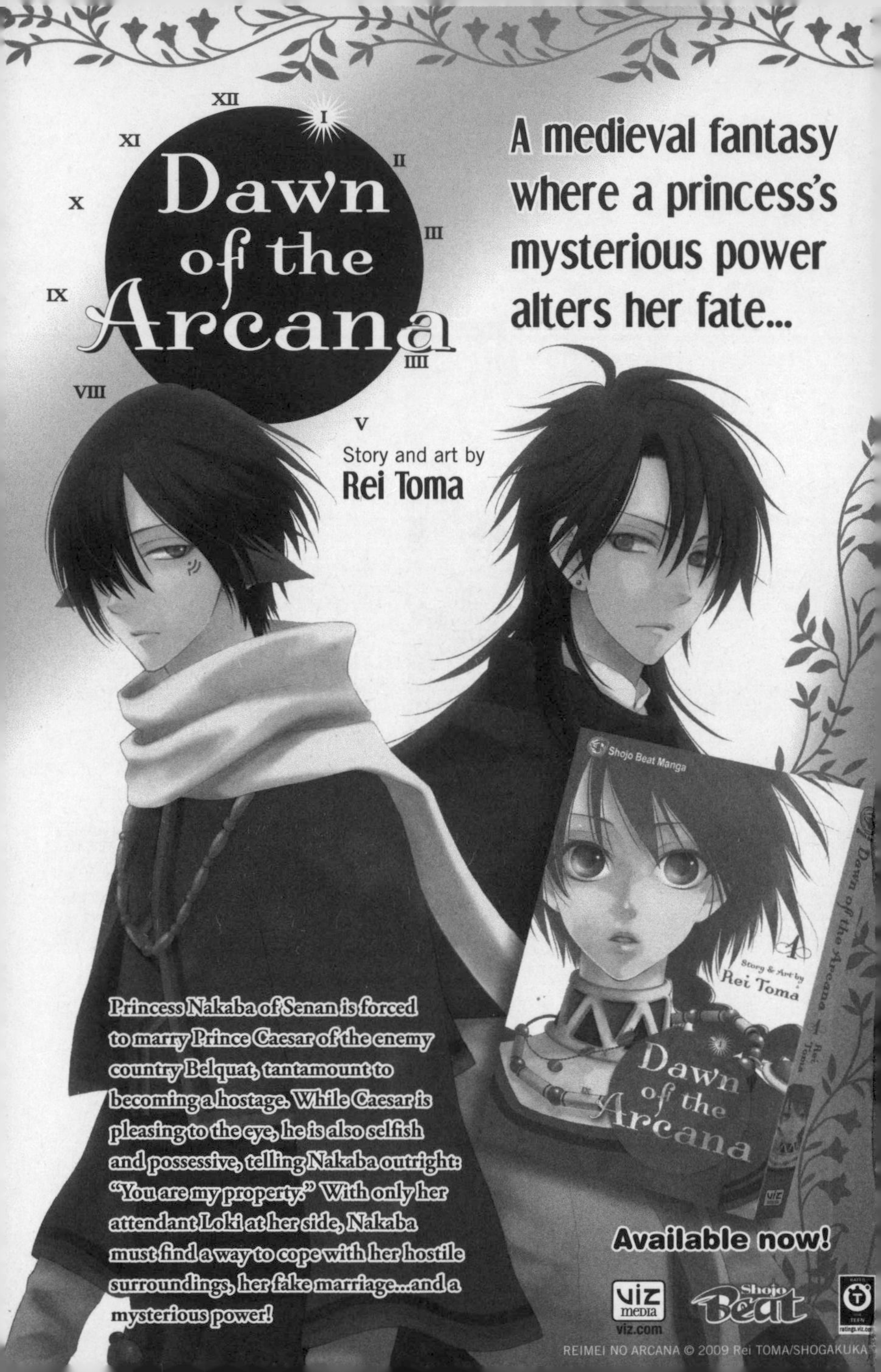
Dawn of the Arcana
XII
I
II
III
IIII
V
VIII
IX
X
XI
A medieval fantasy where a princess's mysterious power alters her fate...
Story and art by
Rei Toma
Shojo Beat Manga
Story & Art by Rei Toma
1
Princess Nakaba of Senan is forced to marry Prince Caesar of the enemy country Belquat, tantamount to becoming a hostage. While Caesar is pleasing to the eye, he is also selfish and possessive, telling Nakaba outright: "You are my property." With only her attendant Loki at her side, Nakaba must find a way to cope with her hostile surroundings, her fake marriage...and a mysterious power!
Available now!
VIZ media
viz.com
Shojo Beat
REIMEI NO ARCANA © 2009 Rei TOMA/SHOGAKUKAN

QQ sweeper

Story & Art by
Kyousuke Motomi

By the creator of *Dengeki Daisy* and *Beast Master*!

One day, Kyutaro Horikita, the tall, dark and handsome cleaning expert of Kurokado High, comes across a sleeping maiden named Fumi Nishioka at school... Unfortunately, their meeting is anything but a fairy-tale encounter! It turns out Kyutaro is a "Sweeper" who cleans away negative energy from people's hearts—and Fumi is about to become his apprentice!

QQ sweeper

1

Story & Art by KYOUSUKE MOTOMI

Queen's Quality

Story & Art by
Kyousuke Motomi

Fumi Nishioka lives with Kyutaro Horikita
and his family of "Sweepers," people who
specialize in cleaning the minds of those
overcome by negative energy and harmful
spirits. Fumi has always displayed mysterious
abilities, but will those powers be used for
evil when she begins to truly awaken
as a Queen?

You may be reading the wrong way!

In keeping with the original Japanese comic format, this book reads from right to left—so action, sound effects and word balloons are completely reversed. This preserves the orientation of the original artwork—plus, it's fun!

Check out the diagram shown here to get the hang of things, and then turn to the other side of the book to get started!

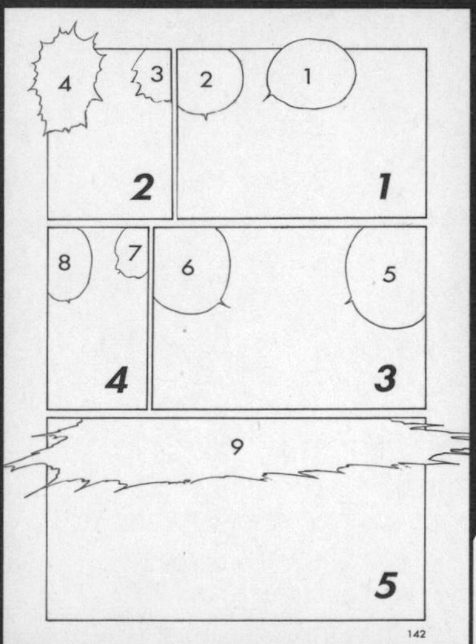
1
2
3
4
1
2
5
6
7
8
3
4
9
5
142

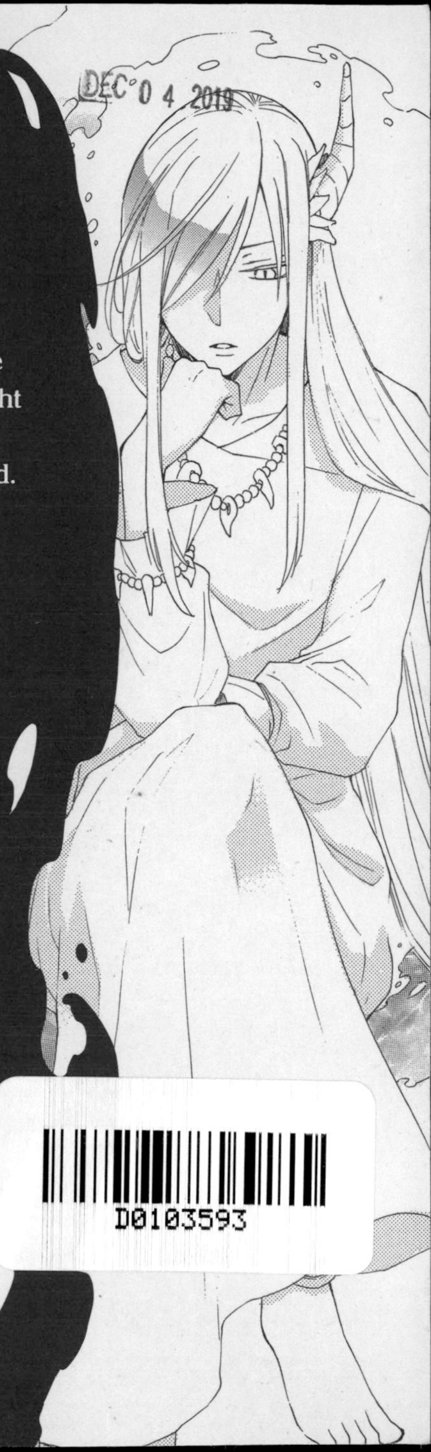